# Democratizing Legal Services

# Democratizing Legal Services

## *Obstacles and Opportunities*

Laura Snyder

LEXINGTON BOOKS
Lanham • Boulder • New York • London

Published by Lexington Books
An imprint of The Rowman & Littlefield Publishing Group, Inc.
4501 Forbes Boulevard, Suite 200, Lanham, Maryland 20706
www.rowman.com

Unit A, Whitacre Mews, 26-34 Stannary Street, London SE11 4AB



British Library Cataloguing in Publication Information Available

**Library of Congress Cataloging-in-Publication Data**

Names: Snyder, Laura.
Title: Democratizing legal services : obstacles and opportunities / Laura Snyder.
Description: Lanham [Md.] : Lexington Books, [2017] | Includes bibliographical references and index.
Identifiers: LCCN 2016029369 (print) | LCCN 2016029933 (ebook) (print) | LCCN 2016029934 (ebook) | ISBN 9781498529792 (cloth : alk. paper) | ISBN 9781498529808 (electronic)
Subjects: LCSH: Legal services. | Legal assistance to the poor. | Practice of law. | Lawyers.
Classification: LCC K133 .S63 2017 (print) | LCC K133 (ebook) | DDC 347—dc23 LC record available at https://lccn.loc.gov/2016029369

∞™ The paper used in this publication meets the minimum requirements of American National Standard for Information Sciences Permanence of Paper for Printed Library Materials, ANSI/NISO Z39.48-1992.

Printed in the United States of America

# Contents


Preface ix

Acknowledgments xiii

Introduction xv

Manner of Regulation Today xxi

Why Changing the Regulatory Framework is Difficult xxv

The Approach of this Book xxvi

Notes xxvii

**Part I: The Opposition to Alternative Structures** **1**

**1** Alternative Structures Will Undermine Professionalism and Ethics 3

Stories 8

Notes 8

**2** There Is No Way to Regulate Alternative Structures 11

Stories 17

Notes 17

**3** The Adoption of Alternative Structures Will Jeopardize Self-Regulation of the Profession 19

Stories 31

Notes 32

**4** There is No Demonstrated Need, Demand, or Problem 37

Notes 41

**5** New Delivery Models Can Be Developed Without Changing Rule 5.4 43

Stories 46

Notes 47

**6** The Payment of Salary Is Adequate Compensation for Nonlawyers 49
Stories 55
Notes 56
**7** No One in Their Right Mind Would Want to Invest in a Law Firm 59
Stories 61
Notes 61
**8** Alternative Structures Will Lead to a Consolidated Market Controlled by Large Firms 63
Stories 71
Notes 72
**9** Alternative Structures Cannot Help Those Who Cannot Pay for Legal Services 75
Stories 82
Notes 83
**10** Alternative Structures Will Make Things Harder for Un- and Underemployed Lawyers 85
Stories 88
Notes 88
**11** The Burden of Proof Has Not Been Met 89
Stories 93
Notes 93

**Part II: The Opportunities Offered by Alternative Structures 95**

**12** Opportunities for Legal Aid 97
Stories 104
Notes 105
**13** Opportunities for Downstream Markets and the Economy as a Whole 107
Stories 122
Notes 122
**14** Opportunities for Lawyers 127
Stories 134
Notes 135
**15** Opportunities for In-House Legal Departments in the Private and Public Sectors 139
Stories 141
Note 142
**16** Opportunities for an Improved Regulatory Approach 143
Stories 155
Notes 156

**17** Opportunities for Failure 161
Hacking Ashton 161
ILH Group Ltd. 162
Quindell Legal Services and Slater and Gordon 162
Notes 164

**Part III: Access to Justice** **167**
Notes 167

**18** Unacknowledged Complexity 169
Motivations for the Regulatory Changes in England and Wales and Australia 169
What is Access to Justice? 170
How Can Access to Justice Be Measured? 171
What Evidence is There? 172
Stories 175
Notes 175

**19** Access to Justice Comes in All Shapes and Sizes, Sometimes Obvious and Sometimes Not 177
Notes 184

**20** Unmet Need as Human Rights Crisis 185
Notes 194

**Part IV: The (Non) Regulation of Legal Services and the World Stage** **197**

**21** Abdication of Regulatory Power 199
One Example on a State Level 199
Two Examples on a National Level 205
Notes 206

**22** International Obligations and Commitments 209
"Ensure Equal Access to Justice For All" 210
"Effective, Accountable and Transparent Institutions at All Levels" 211
Notes 214

**23** Endless Objections and Calls for Evidence and the Lawyer Monopoly on Legal Services (Or, Having Your Cake and Eating It, Too) 217
Notes 225

**24** Good Governance Requires . . . Actual Governance 227
Notes 229

**Part V: Stories** **231**

**25** Letting the Old Lady Scream 233
Using Business and IT Processes to Increase Efficiency and Reduce Costs 233
Business Outsourcing 234
Adopting a Corporate Structure to Foster Growth 236
Holistic Services 237
Dispersed Law Firms 239
Turning Employees into Owners 241
Opposites Attract? Law, Charity, and Free Legal Services 242
Law School: Alternative Structure as an Educational Program and Center for Research and Experimentation 244
In-House Legal as Source of Revenue 246
Is It or Isn't It an Alternative Structure? 248
What Is It Like for a Lawyer To Be Employed By An Alternative Structure? 250
Perspective of an Investor 252
Alternative Voices: For Consumers, For Citizens, an Industry Observer 254
Experience from Washington, DC 256
Canada's Almost Alternative Structures 257
Voices of Modern Regulation 259
The Story Behind the Stories 260
Notes 262

Appendix 263

Bibliography 269

Index 293

About the Author 307

# Preface

This book can trace its beginnings to three events:

1. *London, June 2013*: In a course taught by Lisa Webley and John Flood at the University of Westminster, I listened in utter disbelief—even shock—as they explained to me how, in England and Wales, nonlawyers could own and run law firms, and how legal services could be combined with nonlegal services and offered from the same structure. While of course before the class I'd seen in the legal press references to the new rules, I considered myself too busy to pay much attention. Plus, it was beyond the realm of my imagination that a few rule changes in England and Wales could have any kind of significant meaning or impact elsewhere. In sum, until I entered Lisa's and John's classroom, I saw no reason to care.

Lisa and John obviously changed that. Although I didn't make it easy for them. I have memories of constantly challenging them during those four days: "Really?" "Are you sure?" "But that couldn't possibly work." "But what about . . . ?" "No way!" All the time my jaw to the floor, incredulous at the new legal world they painted for me. Finally, in the moment when I finally believed them, seemingly all the possibilities of that new legal world flashed before my eyes. Whereas before I had only seen limitations in how legal services could be delivered, now those limitations disappeared and were replaced by seemingly infinite possibilities for how legal services could be delivered in ways that were new, different, better. . . . If in my life I have ever had an epiphany moment, that was it.

After that, I couldn't learn enough about this new legal world. I read as much as I could, and I made several trips from my home in France back to London in order to attend more classes, notably those designed as continuing legal education classes for solicitors on the practical aspects of functioning in this new world (COLPs and COFAs, material breaches, insurance, outcomes-focused regulation, qualified to supervise, . . .). There wasn't anything related to this new world that I wasn't interested in learning more about, and there wasn't much I wouldn't do to get my hands on the information. I didn't ask myself what I would do with the information, I just knew that I wanted it.

2. *Big Island, Hawaii, November 2013*: In the meantime, Ron Baker, the author of *Implementing Value Pricing: A Radical Business Model for Professional Firms*, among other books, had graciously invited me to join the biennial conference of his Verasage Institute, to be held at the obviously undesirable location of the Big Island of Hawaii. How could I not go? But I needed to make a contribution to the group of accountants and lawyers gathered there, all focused on how to provide professional services better—what could I offer? Talking about what I had learned about England and Wales seemed like the obvious response.

After I made my presentation, I returned to my seat next to John Chisholm, the managing director of John Chisholm Consulting in Melbourne, Australia and a senior fellow of the Verasage Institute. As soon as I sat down, he said to me, "What are you going to do with that?" It was a good question, and in hearing it I realized that I could—and should—do something with it. But what?

3. *New York City, February 2014*: A few months later, I attended the Reinvent Law conference in New York City. At a reception after the event, I found myself speaking with Allen Pusey, the editor and publisher of the *ABA Journal*. At some point our conversation turned to the regulatory changes in England and Wales. Allen expressed an interest in publishing an article about them in the *ABA Journal*, and a light went on for me. Was this the response to John's question? I suggested to Allen that I might be able to help.

In the weeks that followed, I wrote a few pages to give Allen an idea of how I might approach the article. He flung the pages back at me (not literally but it was the impression his email gave me), telling me, essentially, that I wrote too much like a lawyer and not enough like a journalist. It clearly wasn't meant as a compliment, but given that I was a lawyer and not a journalist, and had no aspirations to become one, I struggled to feel insulted.

Allen told me that I needed to talk to people, that I needed to get their stories—that I needed to provide the perspectives of real people using new business structures, and the perspectives of those who regulate them. For better or for worse, I considered his words to be a challenge. So, I talked. I talked to many people.

When I started, I expected that a conversation would last about 20 to 30 minutes and that, if I was lucky, it might result in one or two good quotes. But that is not what happened. As I spoke with different people—people who had founded alternative structures, people who were managing them, people who were employed by them, and people who regulated them—I found that they had fascinating and highly compelling stories to tell. The conversations lasted not 20 or 30 minutes, but easily as long as an hour, and often more. Sometimes we couldn't finish in the time allotted, so we scheduled second calls in order to finish.

When it came time to write, how could I edit these stories down to "one or two good quotes"? The stories were the new legal world that Lisa and John had painted for me. And the stories were more than that—they took that canvas—still theoretical and abstract—and transformed it into something very real and concrete. These stories needed to be told, and they needed to be told in much more than one or two good quotes.

The end result was 43 pages of material. A portion of this was eventually published in the *ABA Journal*—a January 2015 article entitled "Does the UK Know Something We Don't About Alternative Business Structures?"

But the *ABA Journal* couldn't use most of the 43 pages. What could I do with it? It was an awkward length—too long for a magazine or journal article, but too short for a book. The only thing that was clear to me was that I couldn't sit on the stories I had collected. They were too compelling to not be shared with a large audience.

The response seemed to be to make the material even longer—to make it the right length for a book.

In thinking about a book, my strong preference was to focus exclusively on the stories. More specifically, my preference was to conduct additional interviews in order to gain additional stories, and then to publish them as a collection. The stories would be left to stand for themselves, accompanied by limited to no commentary.

There were two reasons why this was my strong preference. To begin, many people had already written many things about alternative structures. It was difficult for me to understand what commentary I could write that would make a valuable or unique contribution. Any attempt to do so, and this was the second reason, would be a huge undertaking. Alternative structures are by no means a neutral subject, and anything of value to be published about them would surely be subject to much more than the standard levels of scrutiny and critique. Whatever I wrote would have to be very, very good, as it would have to withstand what would surely be repeated attacks.

However, as resistant as I was to writing commentary to accompany the stories, I understood that it had to be done. I understood that in the absence of a context, the full value of the stories would be difficult to recognize for many, if not for most.

So I wrote. And wrote and wrote. The end result—context to the stories—is in your hands.

# Acknowledgments

This book is entirely my own, and, especially, any errors are entirely my own. Of course, this book would have been impossible without the assistance and support of many people:

Those who spent time with me on the phone or Skype exploring some of the issues addressed in this book: Malcolm Mercer, Susan Fortney, Laurel Terry, Noel Semple, Jim Moliterno, Mitch Kowalski, Colin Lachance, and Malcolm Heins. Each in your own way shed light on a great many things.

Those who reviewed and commented on draft manuscripts (in whole or in part): Thomas Morgan, Tom Gordon, Jim Moliterno, John Chisholm, Laurel Terry, Jimmy Lopez, and the anonymous peer reviewers. Because of your invaluable suggestions, this is a much, much better book.

Those who held my hand (figuratively speaking): Mark Haney and Lisa Webley. When my confidence escaped me, you knew exactly where to find it.

Those I interviewed: You are what make this book unique. I can't thank each of you enough for your openness as well as for your understanding and patience through what turned out to be a very long process.

Finally, Neil Rose and his team merit particular acknowledgement. I can't imagine writing this book without the Legal Futures website.

# Introduction

In the United States, legal services are traditionally viewed as something provided by individual lawyers. A lawyer may work alone, as a "sole practitioner," or a lawyer may join with others, in a law firm or in an in-house corporate or governmental legal department. Either way, the traditional perspective is that legal services are provided by individuals, and not by just any individuals, but by special ones who have a specific education and qualifications.

But is this traditional perspective a truly accurate one? Do lawyers really act alone? Are the best—the most useful—legal services provided by lawyers (and only lawyers) working as individuals?

The legal affairs of most people and companies span multiple states if not countries as well as multiple areas of law. It is beyond the intellectual capacity of any single individual lawyer, however gifted, to master the sheer volume of knowledge and process that would be required for that individual, acting alone, to be all things to any one client, or, in many cases, to even be anything to one client.

And legal matters are rarely strictly legal matters that can be addressed in isolation of other, nonlegal matters. To the contrary, legal matters arise in their own specific contexts and, in order to be addressed effectively, need to be addressed in that specific context: a business matter, a financial matter, an environmental matter, a health matter, a family matter. . . . It is beyond the capacity of any single individual lawyer, however gifted, to master the full context in which any legal matter may arise.

It is for these reasons that, in reality, most lawyers work not individually but in teams. Obviously, they work in teams with other lawyers, so that they may complement each other's legal skills and expertise. Perhaps less obviously, they also work in teams with persons who are not lawyers but who have expertise in other areas—medicine, science, social work, economics, finance, accounting, IT, business, marketing, and even law (paralegals) . . . in order to address a client's needs in a holistic manner. Finally, and perhaps not obviously at all, lawyers also work with technology—not simply word processing and email, but software for document generation, electronic discovery, predictive coding and technology-assisted review, analysis by rules-based expert systems, blockchain.

In sum, as the world has evolved and grown more complex, so have the practice of law and the provision of legal services.[1]

However, the regulations that govern legal services in the United States have not evolved in a comparable manner, and they do not take account of such complexity.

There are multiple ways in which this is the case. Most notably the regulatory framework continues:

1. To restrict the services that lawyers may provide across state borders.
2. To restrict who may provide legal services—they may be provided only by lawyers.
3. To regulate lawyers only as individuals—the organizations within which lawyers work are regulated only in an indirect manner, through lawyers as individuals.
4. To restrict who may own and who may manage the organizations that provide legal services—they may be owned and managed only by lawyers.
5. To prohibit organizations that provide legal services from providing any other kind of good or service—that is, to prohibit multidisciplinary practices.[2]

Why does it matter that the regulatory framework has not evolved? Because even if it has been possible for legal services to evolve, and to evolve significantly, continued evolution is necessary. But as long as the current regulatory framework remains in place, this evolution cannot occur.[3]

What kind of evolution is needed?

Evolution is needed in the way that legal services are accessed (or, more accurately, not accessed): In the United States today, many people and businesses struggle to obtain legal services. They struggle in a number of ways: They don't realize that their issue is a legal one,[4] they don't know who can help them, they don't know who they can trust to help them, they don't know where to go to find help, they look for help but can't find anyone willing to help them, they are afraid of what it will cost, they simply don't want to take the time and trouble to figure it all out. And even if they manage to secure legal services, their problems do not end—they have to contend with arcane and complex court procedures, they receive poor customer service from their lawyer, they question if the work could have been done more efficiently and, as a result, more cheaply, they don't understand the information they are given, they are not able to judge the quality of the services they receive, they receive bills they do not understand, for amounts they never anticipated.[5]

Evolution is needed in the way that legal services are produced: While the ways that lawyers work have changed in many respects, in certain respects it has changed very little. A primary example is the use, by most lawyers, of the service model termed "professional consultancy"[6] or "solution shop."[7] Under this model, lawyers do not sell products or "precut solutions."[8] Instead, they solve problems by spending time working on the problems, under the assumption that the problem requires a solution tailored especially for the specific client. For lawyers to solve additional problems, they spend more time. The scalability of this model is limited—more problems can be solved only by adding more lawyers, who need to spend more time. As a result, the number of clients that can be served using this model is limited.

Finally, evolution is needed in the way that legal services are priced. This problem has multiple facets. One facet results from the professional consultancy model—under the model, when lawyers solve additional problems, there is little or no reduction in marginal costs. Additional work incurs additional marginal costs, such that increased volume cannot result in lower prices. A second facet is that under the professional consultancy model, pricing is driven by the number of hours that lawyers bill—work accomplished in some other manner, such as by nonlawyer staff or by automated processes, is not billed. This incentivizes the delegation of as much work as possible to lawyers, and discourages the development of processes that would relieve lawyers of lower-level and routine tasks in order to have them carried out in a less expensive or less labor intensive manner. Finally, the traditional way of pricing legal services is based upon billable hours, or time spent. This is true even for many fixed price arrangements that many law firms offer, in that the fixed fees are based upon an estimation of the number of hours required to do the work. Most other industries have developed more or less sophisticated means to price their goods and services in a manner that is mostly or wholly independent of the time required to produce the good or service—lawyers, for the most part, struggle immensely to do this.[9]

Theoretically, law firm partnerships could instigate at least some of this needed evolution. The reality is, however, quite different. The reasons for this can be debated: Is it because many law firm partnerships cling tightly to the solution shop model as a matter of culture? Is it because law firm partnerships are sheltered from competition from other forms of service models, and so have little incentive to develop new service models? Is it because, for reasons of nature or nurture, lawyers are particularly adverse to risk? Whatever the reason(s), and regardless of the theory, the reality is that it would be a mistake to rely upon evolution of any significant scale to be instigated by traditional law firm partnerships.

Without the needed evolution, legal services are placed out of reach for a large portion of the US population. This population obviously includes people who are so poor that they cannot afford to pay anything for legal services, because even though government-funded legal aid and private pro bono services do exist, they are able to meet only a small fraction of the needs of this market. Less obviously but no less importantly, the population shut out of legal services also includes the middle class, as well as many start-ups and small businesses. Generally speaking, they are able to pay some amount. But that does not mean that they are able to pay any amount—much less sign up to pay an unknown amount. And this entire population—the poor, the middle class, start-ups, small businesses—all of them suffer from the same problems described above: difficulty knowing where to find legal services, and not knowing who to trust or how to judge quality.

While these problems are not the only cause of the problem of access to justice in the United States, they constitute, in themselves, an often impregnable barrier. And the access to justice problem in the United States is not a small one. To the contrary, it would be difficult to overstate its enormity. The extent of the unmet legal need in the United States is so high, some consider it a human rights crisis, with the result that the United States is in breach of its obligations under a number of human rights treaties, which require the United States, for example, to provide effective remedies to rights violations, to provide for procedural fairness, and to protect against discrimination and provide equal protection under the law. As regards the question of affordable and accessible civil justice, the World Justice Project *Rule of Law Index 2015* ranks the United States 65th out of a total of 102 countries (behind Russia, Ukraine, and Kyrgyzstan), and out of the regional group of North America and Western Europe, it ranks the United States last (behind Romania and Bulgaria).[10]

A catalog of all the causes of the access to justice problem in the United States would be lengthy and complex. Addressing the causes in full will require multiple, complex solutions. There is not any one or even any two changes that could be made that would have the effect of addressing all the causes and ending the problem, or even of ending the problem for most people. What is required is a multitude of solutions to address the multitude of causes.

We could take the position that this is simply the reality of legal services, and there is nothing that can be done to change it. We could throw up our hands in frustration, not knowing where to start to make a change, and as a result, start nowhere.

Or, we could start somewhere.

An obvious place to start is with the regulatory framework. We can move away from the current regulatory framework that centers nearly exclusively on lawyers, in favor of a framework that instead focuses on legal services.[11]

While the benefits of this fundamental change are numerous, this book will focus on one of them: that such a regulatory change will allow for a greater variety of legal service providers to enter the market, and especially a greater variety of organizations. It will do this firstly by facilitating the regulation of organizations (or entities) alongside individuals (lawyers and nonlawyers). And then, in doing so, it will enable the restrictions on who may own and who may manage legal service providers as well as the restrictions on multidisciplinary practices to be lifted.

The reason for this focus is twofold: (i) because lifting such restrictions in order to allow for these different kinds of organizations is today a highly controversial topic—arguably the most controversial of the consequences that would result from changing the regulatory framework, and (ii) because it is the restrictions on these different kinds of organizations that serve the most to limit evolution in legal services.

Why do these restrictions serve to limit evolution in legal services? For multiple reasons:

1. They favor the partnership structure over the corporate structure. While a partnership structure surely does work for some legal service providers, it does not work for all of them: (i) by conditioning ownership on employment with the firm, it forces the partnership to make investment decisions on a short-term basis only, and (ii) it obliges the partners, and the partners alone, to assume full responsibility for the risks of the firm—risks cannot be shared with outside, more diversified investors (private or public). This limits the risks that the partnership is willing to assume.[12]
2. They limit the capital available to legal service providers. Under the regulations, because only a lawyer can be an owner of a legal service provider, only lawyers can make capital contributions. Third parties, such as venture capital funds or other passive investors (again, private or public), may not. While lawyers are not restricted by regulation regarding the amount of capital they can contribute, in reality they are: For most lawyers, the firm is a source of income, not opportunity for investment. As a result, not only do lawyers seek to limit their capital contributions, but also most firms retain only enough profits to cover immediate operating expenses, and pay out the rest to the partners each year. This limits the ability of a law firm to make capital-intensive investments.[13]
3. They limit the expertise available to legal service providers. A legal service provider needs people proficient in law, for sure. But it also

needs people proficient in other areas, and notably in IT, business management, marketing, finance, accounting, pricing, and human resources. It is possible for a lawyer to develop proficiency in one and even perhaps in two of these areas, but not in all of them. People proficient in these areas can be and are hired as employees—indeed many firms today employ persons specialized in these areas.[14] But those persons cannot hold executive management positions and they may not hold shares. These limitations handicap legal service providers: (i) in recruiting and retaining employees, as the best ones can opt instead for other types of businesses where their career progression and ability to share in profits are not stymied by regulation, and (ii) in fully motivating the employees they do retain, since those employees cannot and never will have a stake in the business.

4. They make it more complicated for clients to have their needs addressed in a holistic manner. As noted above, most legal matters do not arise and cannot be addressed in isolation from other, nonlegal matters. In the absence of a multidisciplinary practice, clients have to identify multiple service providers and coordinate their services. Multidisciplinary practices can provide a one-stop shop for clients and make it easier to have their needs met in their totality.[15]
5. They limit the way that legal services can be provided at no or very low cost.[16] Under current regulations, there are very few options for funding pro bono legal services—the only choices are either through government (taxpayer) funding, interest on lawyer trust accounts, or private donations, or through the donation of time by members of the bar. These methods are neither sustainable nor scalable.
6. They stifle the motivation for persons who are not lawyers to take ideas for better ways to deliver legal services and turn them into viable businesses. They understand that the permitted range of activities for such businesses is small, and that even within that limited range, there is significant risk that such businesses will be challenged as the "unauthorized practice of law" and will lose value if not simply be forced to close.[17]

What difference would it make if people who are not lawyers could share in the ownership of legal service providers? What difference would it make if legal services could be offered together with other (nonlegal) goods and services? In other words, what if "alternative structures" (alternative to law firm partnerships) were permitted?

Here are the differences that it would make:

1. It would enable the development of: (i) business and technological processes to reduce the marginal cost as well as the time required to

provide a service, (ii) large-scale branding and marketing to reduce the search costs for clients, and (iii) reliable methods to price legal services on a fixed price basis, independent of time spent. With these developments, a greater number of persons would be able to access a greater variety of legal services, under more acceptable conditions, with more confidence, and at more predictable prices. But these developments require a number of elements: a corporate structure, access to capital for long-term investment, the ability and willingness to take significant business risks, and advanced expertise in business management, technology, marketing, finance, human resources, and pricing. Under the current regulations, these elements are out of reach to law firms.[18]

2. It would enable lawyers to join forces with other service providers, such as accountants, financial planners, doctors, psychologists, scientists, social workers, economists, and lobbyists, in order to provide holistic services that address a client's entire problem rather than only the legal aspects. Under current regulations, services cannot be combined in this manner.[19]
3. It would enable the development of more sustainable and scalable means to provide pro bono (free) legal services—means that do not rely upon state or private donations of time or money. For example, it would enable a charitable, philanthropic, or educational organization to own and operate a legal services provider that would provide legal services for free. The legal services provider could be funded by private donations, or, in a more sustainable manner, it could be funded from the profits of a sister company that offered legal services on a paid basis. Under current regulations, this kind of arrangement is impossible.

So, you may ask, why not just change the regulatory framework and, as one consequence of doing so, permit alternative structures? Because it is not easy to do.

## MANNER OF REGULATION TODAY

The current manner of regulation in the United States is highly complex. To begin, most regulation is on a state rather than national level. That's 50 different regulatory systems, plus the District of Columbia. Ostensibly, it is the supreme court of most states that holds regulatory power (in many states by sharing it with the state's bar association), but there are examples of state legislatures attempting to assert their own authority to regulate, at least with respect to certain issues. Finally, and most importantly for our purposes here, is the role of the American Bar Association (ABA).

The ABA is a voluntary, national association of lawyers and law students. It counts about 400,000 members out of the total of 1.2 million lawyers in the United States. It is governed by a body called the House of Delegates—most of its 560 members are selected or, in a few cases elected, by state and local bar associations.

The ABA is a private (nongovernmental) organization that, officially, does not have any regulatory authority at all. However, in practice the ABA's regulatory power is immense, or, as two Canadian commentators describe it, "hegemonic."[20] It is the ABA that developed the Model Rules of Professional Conduct, a set of rules that, as the ABA explains on its website,[21] has its origins in large part from an 1836 list of "Fifty Resolutions" in a book entitled "A Course of Legal Study." The most current form of the rules, under its current name, was adopted by the ABA House of Delegates in 1983. While officially the Model Rules are only the recommendations of an unelected private organization, the reality is that 49 states as well as the District of Columbia and the US Virgin Islands have adopted the Model Rules, if not in their entirety then in very large part.

It is the ABA Model Rules that today form in large part the basis for the regulatory framework governing lawyers across those jurisdictions. As specifically regards the restrictions on nonlawyer ownership of law firms and on multidisciplinary practices, they are found principally in Model Rule 5.4. (California has not adopted the ABA Model Rules in the manner that the other states have. However, the California rules have the effect of prohibiting nonlawyer ownership and multidisciplinary practices in the same manner as Model Rule 5.4).[22]

From time to time, the ABA House of Delegates adopts amendments to the Model Rules. Those amendments are, in most cases, subsequently reviewed by each state's bar association(s), and then proposed to the state's supreme court for adoption. While there is no legal provision that prevents a state supreme court from adopting rules that do not conform to the ABA's Model Rules, in reality this seldom occurs, and the greater the opposition of the ABA and/or the state bar association(s) to the amendment in question, the less likely it is to occur. This fact was recently underscored by Stephen Younger, an attorney who chaired a 2012 review of Model Rule 5.4 by the New York State Bar Association (a review that recommended to the ABA that the rule not be changed): "Most chief judges who are responsible for the ethics rules in our states don't want to get too far ahead of the bar."[23]

In 1983 and again from 1999 to 2000, the ABA considered revising Model Rule 5.4 in order to allow for nonlawyer ownership and multidisciplinary practices in some form, but in each case the House of Delegates declined to make any changes.[24] The position that the House of Delegates took in July 2000 was particularly strong, stating:

> The sharing of legal fees with nonlawyers and the ownership and control of the practice of law by nonlawyers are inconsistent with the core values of the legal profession.
>
> The law governing lawyers, that prohibits lawyers from sharing legal fees with nonlawyers and from directly or indirectly transferring to nonlawyers ownership or control over entities practicing law, should not be revised.[25]

The question was put on the table again in 2010, when the president of the ABA established the Commission on Ethics 20/20 "to perform a thorough review of the [Model Rules] and the US system of lawyer regulation in the context of advances in technology and global legal practice developments,"[26] with a view toward making recommendations to the House of Delegates for amendments to the Model Rules. The commission, composed of 17 lawyers, deliberated over a period of three years. Their work included a review of Model Rule 5.4, and in particular whether it should be revised in order to allow for alternative structures. In 2012, the commission decided to not recommend to the House of Delegates any changes to Model Rule 5.4 because the case for such changes "had not been made."[27]

In August 2014, the ABA appointed a new commission, the Commission on the Future of Legal Services. The commission had a much broader mandate than that of the Ethics 20/20 Commission, although it was not so broad as to encompass the entire regulatory framework as a whole. The mandate of the new commission was to seek input from the public and the legal profession to learn their vision for more efficient and effective ways to deliver legal services, to analyze and synthesize the insights gained, and, on that basis, to "propose new approaches that are not constrained by traditional models for delivering legal services and are rooted in the essential values of protecting the public, enhancing diversity and inclusion, and pursuing justice for all."[28]

In November 2015, the commission submitted a proposed Resolution and Report on Regulatory Objectives for consideration by the House of Delegates during its midyear meeting in February 2016. The proposal contained a list of ten regulatory objectives, as well as an explanation that "each state's highest court" not only be guided by the objectives when assessing the court's "existing regulatory framework," but also with respect to "any other regulations they may choose to develop concerning nontraditional legal service providers."[29]

While this proposal might have been considered a breakthrough, the House of Delegates adopted it in February 2016 with a significant caveat: "that nothing contained in this Resolution abrogates in any manner existing ABA policy prohibiting non lawyer ownership of law firms or the core values adopted by the House of Delegates . . . on July 11, 2000."[30] Interestingly, and seemingly in defiance of this caveat, in late March and early April 2016 the commission issued two "Issues Papers" calling for comments, one with respect to the regulation of as-yet "unregulated legal service providers,"[31] and the other with respect to alternative structures.[32] At the time this book went to press, it was too early to know the outcome of these papers.

If the United States does change its regulatory framework in order to regulate legal services instead of only lawyers, and thereby, as one consequence, permit alternative structures, it will not be the first country to do so. It will not be the second either, and, unless it acts quickly, it is even unlikely to be the third. The Australian state of New South Wales was the first to make these changes—it modified its rules gradually, between 1990 and 2001. Since 2001, under a framework that evolved to regulate legal services rather than lawyers, legal practices in NSW have been permitted to incorporate, to create multidisciplinary practices, to share fees with nonlawyers, and even to publicly list on the Australian Securities Exchange. The other states and territories of Australia followed the lead of NSW in the years soon thereafter. Today about one-third of Australia's legal service providers are "incorporated legal practices" (ILPs).[33]

The second place to make these changes was a part of the UK. The principal instigator of the changes was a 2004 report entitled "Review of the Regulatory Framework for Legal Services in England and Wales."[34] The report was commissioned by the government of Tony Blair and issued by David Clementi, a former governor of the Bank of England. Referred to as the "Clementi Report," it led to the 2007 Legal Services Act, which radically overhauled the regulatory framework in England and Wales (the other two countries of the UK, Northern Ireland and Scotland, were not covered by the Act). An important part of the changes was to grant to regulators the authority to regulate not just lawyers but also entities that provide legal services. In doing so, England and Wales now permit nonlawyers to own and manage legal service providers, subject to a fitness test, and also permit multidisciplinary practices. The relevant provisions of the Act entered into effect in 2011, and at the time this book went to press approximately 745[35] "alternative business structures" (ABSs) were authorized to operate.[36]

The third place that is on the path to make these changes is Canada.[37] In August 2014, the Canadian Bar Association's "Futures Initiative" issued a report[38] strongly endorsing changes to Canadian regulations (the Canadian Bar Association represents, but does not regulate, lawyers on a national level). Nova Scotia has already implemented a certain number of changes in a move toward entity regulation,[39] and Manitoba is in the process of doing so, together with the other "Prairie provinces" of Alberta and Saskatchewan.[40] Ontario, after a false start, may be following in their path,[41] as well as British Columbia.[42]

Moving from north to south of the US border, Mexico has always permitted alternative structures. In contrast to Australia and England and Wales, this is due not to any intentional regulatory design, but to the fact that, as a general manner, legal services are only lightly regulated in Mexico. The few regulations that are in place address neither nonlawyer ownership nor multidisciplinary practices. Because neither is expressly prohibited, each is permitted.

## WHY CHANGING THE REGULATORY FRAMEWORK IS DIFFICULT

It is possible to change the regulatory framework in the United States and, as one consequence, permit alternative structures, but it is extremely difficult. This is for several reasons.

To begin, many lawyers and lawyer organizations are strongly opposed to alternative structures. They offer a number of arguments in this regard—those arguments are examined in part I of this book.

Next, the changes needed are not simple ones. Lawyers are regulated on a state-by-state basis, resulting in a lengthy and complicated process to make any changes for the entire country, even straightforward ones. And changing an entire regulatory framework is highly complex. It is not just Model Rule 5.4, but all the rules that will need to be reviewed in order to enlarge the regulatory framework from lawyers to legal services. The review will need to include a revision of the unauthorized practice of law rules in order to reduce restrictions not only on who may provide legal services, but also on the provision of legal services across state lines. It will need to address the situation of structures that operate in more than one state, if any one or more of those states do not also change their regulatory framework, and notably if they do not change them to allow for alternative structures. In sum, an extensive re-working of a number of regulations will be required.

Finally, it is not at all clear whose responsibility it is, or, at least, whose responsibility it should be, to decide upon and implement the changes. Should it be the ABA, an unelected, private organization with no political accountability and a history of resistance to change?[43] Should it be each of the state supreme courts, who would be required, on a state-by-state basis, to step widely outside their comfort zones given their traditional reliance upon the decisions of the ABA? Should it be a combination of the ABA and the state supreme courts, working together via the Conference of Chief Justices—again, not a process that, to date, has generated significant change? Should it be each of the state legislatures, who may be seen as defying state constitutions (which, in many states, allocate the regulation of attorney conduct to the state's supreme court), on the grounds that they are regulating not attorney conduct but legal services and corporate structures more generally? Or, should it be the executive or the legislative branches of the federal government of the United States, who would then override a 200-plus-year tradition of the regulation of the legal profession on the state level, on the grounds that it is regulating not attorney conduct but restrictions on competition, economic policy, and the protection of human rights?[44]

No, it will not be easy at all.

## THE APPROACH OF THIS BOOK

This book is divided in five parts. The first four parts address the topic of alternative structures in a conventional manner: The first part examines the variety of objections that are made to alternative structures. The second part explores the opportunities that they offer. The third part delves in-depth into the issue of access to justice. And, finally, the fourth part places the question of alternative structures in its larger context of how and by whom legal services are regulated.

A famous quote attributed to Mark Twain runs along the lines of "Don't say the old lady screamed. Bring her on and let her scream." In part V, the old lady is brought on and allowed to scream. She does this in the form of stories and experiences told firsthand by people who have created, are managing, are employees of, and/or have invested in alternative structures, as well as with persons who regulate them. (And, in one case, by a person who has closely studied alternative structures that existed in the United States a century ago). The stories offer unique, direct perspectives on the variety of issues that are raised in the first four parts of the book. The stories move the discussion of alternative structures from the realm of the theoretical, the general, and the academic and place it firmly in the realm of the concrete, the specific, and the entirely real. In fact, part V contains a sampling of 16 out of 58 firsthand stories. The remaining stories are available online at this link: www.notjustforlawyers.com.

All of the stories, whether in part V or posted online, speak (or, using Twain's terminology, scream) indirectly to the variety of topics that are raised in the chapters of the book. Many also speak directly, in more or less detail. To the extent this is the case, there appears at the end of the relevant chapter references to the related stories that appear in part V or online. In this manner, the book provides a direct link from theoretical, general, and academic discussions to concrete, specific, and very real examples. With the stories, alternative structures come alive.

*Note About Terminology*: A variety of terms are used to refer to organizations that are owned and/or managed by one or more nonlawyers and/or that are multidisciplinary practices (in other words, to refer to legal service providers that are not the traditional structures of either sole practitioner or law firm partnership). In Australia as well as in England and Wales, where there exist formal regulatory frameworks for such organizations, the terminology is fixed and easy to identify: In Australia they are referred to as "incorporated legal practices" or "ILPs" (as well as "multidisciplinary partnerships," or "MDPs," and the recently coined "unincorporated legal practices," or "ULPs"). In England and Wales, they are referred to in common speech as "alternative business structures" or "ABSs," and in the formal legal texts as "licensed bodies." In the Canadian provinces, which are moving toward formal regulatory frameworks for such organizations but have not yet established them, the English/Welsh reference of "alternative business structures" or "ABSs" is often used, but by no means is it the only one used. Others include "new business models," "new business structures," "alternative business models," and "liberalized structures." In the United States, "alternative business structures" and "ABSs" are also often used, but so are expressions like "alternative law practice structures" (an expression occasionally used by the ABA Commission on Ethics 20/20) and "alternative law firm structures."

In this book, I have chosen to use the term "alternative structures" as a general, all-purpose term of reference. I have done this for these reasons:

- In order to reserve the terms ILP and ABS for reference to the Australian and the English/Welsh entities specifically.
- In order to distance the general concept of these kinds of organizations from the specifically Australian and the specifically English/Welsh manifestations of them (manifestations which, as compared to each other, have significant differences). In doing so, I seek to underline that while in the United States we can and should be informed by Australian ILPs and English/Welsh ABSs in creating our own versions of them, there is no need that we identically copy their terminology, much less create identical copies of the structures themselves. In other words, Australian ILPs and English/Welsh ABSs are only two of the many possible manifestations of these kinds of organizations—the term "alternative structures" is used to encompass all possible manifestations.
- Perhaps most importantly, because the term "business" is too limiting, and, for that reason, misleading. These structures are about much more than "business": They are about new ways of developing and delivering legal services.

## NOTES

1. A pioneer on this topic is Ted Schneyer, for example, "Professional Discipline for Law Firms," *Cornell Law Review* 77 (1991): 1–46, http://scholarship.law.cornell.edu/cgi/viewcontent.cgi?article=3509&context=clr. Further, Thomas D. Morgan has published extensively in

this regard. See, for example, Thomas D. Morgan, "Comments of Professor Thomas D. Morgan on the Discussion Paper on Alternative Law Practice Structures," January 30, 2012, http://www.americanbar.org/content/dam/aba/administrative/ethics_2020/ethics_20_20_comments/morgan_alpsdiscussiondraft.authcheckdam.pdf; Thomas D. Morgan, "The Rise of Institutional Law Practice," *Hofstra Law Review* 40 (2012) 1005–26, http://scholarlycommons.law.hofstra.edu/cgi/viewcontent.cgi?article=2682&context=hlr; Thomas D. Morgan, "The Shift to Institutional Law Practice," in *The Relevant Lawyer: Reimagining the Future of the Legal Profession*, ed. Paul A. Haskins (Chicago: ABA Publishing, 2015), 143–55.

2. See, for example, Gillian K. Hadfield and Deborah L. Rhode, "How to Regulate Legal Services to Promote Access, Innovation, and the Quality of Lawyering," *Hastings Law Journal* forthcoming; USC CLASS Research Papers Series No. CLASS16–6; USC Law Legal Studies Paper No. 16–7 (2016), 5, http://ssrn.com/abstract=2733382.

3. The OECD recently stated: "[C]urrent regulatory frameworks are the most important barrier to innovation in the legal services market, as well as to the benefits it brings." Organisation for Economic Co-operation and Development, "Protecting and Promoting Competition in Response to 'Disruptive' Innovations in Legal Services: Issues Paper by the Secretariat," March 9, 2016, 13, http://www.oecd.org/officialdocuments/publicdisplaydocumentpdf/?cote=DAF/COMP/WP2(2016)1&docLanguage=En.

4. See, for example, ABA Standing Committee on the Delivery of Legal Services, "Issues on the Future of Legal Services," December 2, 2014, http://www.americanbar.org/content/dam/aba/images/office_president/delivery_of_legal_services.pdf. See also Rebecca Sandefur, "Accessing Justice in the Contemporary USA: Findings from the Community Needs and Services Study," August 8, 2014, http://ssrn.com/abstract=2478040.

5. For a general discussion of the reasons people don't seek out counsel and the difficulties they face when they do so, see, for example, Noel Semple, *Legal Services Regulation at the Crossroads: Justitia's Legions* (Cheltenham, UK: Edward Elgar Publishing, 2015), 133–82.

6. See, for example, Malcolm Mercer, "So Many Lawyers, So Many Unmet Legal Needs," *Law Practice Magazine*, July/August 2015, 44–47, http://www.lawpracticemagazine.com/lawpracticemagazine/july_august_2015#pg46; and Malcolm Mercer, "Utopia, Dystopia and Alternative Business Structures," *Slaw*, November 11, 2013, http://www.slaw.ca/2013/11/11/utopia-dystopia-and-alternative-business-structures/.

7. Ray Worthy Campbell, "Rethinking Regulation and Innovation in the US Legal Services Market," *New York University Journal of Law and Business* 9 (2012): 1–70, 24–25, http://www.nyujlb.org/wp-content/uploads/nyb_9-1-1_scissored.7-76.pdf. Campbell drew this term from the works of Clayton Christensen; see, for example, Clayton Christensen and Mark Johnson, "What Are Business Models, and How Are They Built?" 2010, http://www.thefgi.net/wp-content/uploads/2010/09/What-is-a-Business-Model.pdf.

8. Campbell, "Rethinking Regulation," 25.

9. See, for example, Mike Ayotte, "How Fixed Fees Are Going to Change BigLaw Forever," *The Last Honest Lawyer*, August 28, 2013, http://lasthonestlawyer.org/2013/08/28/how-fixed-fees-are-going-to-change-biglaw-forever/.

10. The World Justice Project, *Rule of Law Index 2015*, 2015, http://worldjusticeproject.org/sites/default/files/roli_2015_0.pdf. This ranking is derived from the data (xls) that is available for download from the World Justice Project website.

11. Certainly this author is not the first or the only to advocate for an enlargement of the regulatory sphere to include legal services rather than just lawyers. See, for example, Andrew M. Perlman, "Towards the Law of Legal Services," *Cardozo Law Review* 37 (2015): 49–112, http://ssrn.com/abstract=2561014. Perlman, however, deliberately turns attention away from alternative structures (as well as, without expressly mentioning them, the general concepts of entity regulation and compliance-based / proactive regulation) in favor of a focus on the provision of legal services by individuals (rather than entities) who are not lawyers and by existing legal service providers, notably "consumer facing automated document assembly companies." Ibid., 55, 89–112. While there is nothing inherently objectionable in Perlman's proposals, his proposals do not address most of the fundamental limitations on the provision of legal services that alternative structures address (access to capital, access to nonlegal expertise, the ability to offer holistic services by combining legal and nonlegal services, . . .). At any rate, in

certain states, notably Washington State (discussed in part IV) and New York nonlawyers (individuals) already provide precisely delineated legal services, and a significant number of "consumer facing automated document assembly companies" and other nonregulated legal service providers already exist and offer their services throughout the country. In proposing that these kinds of already existing providers (but no other kind) finally be brought under a regulatory regime, Perlman substantiates Moliterno's observation that the profession does "nothing more than modify existing lawyer regulation in ways that have been dictated by changes from outside the profession." James E. Moliterno, *The American Legal Profession in Crisis: Resistance and Responses to Change* (New York: Oxford University Press, 2013), 17.

12. For a general discussion of risk in the context of law firms, see Edward M. Iacobucci and Michael J. Trebilcock, "An Economic Analysis of Alternative Business Structures for the Practice of Law," paper presented at the Law Society of Upper Canada's symposium for the Alternative Business Structures, October 4, 2013, http://www.lsuc.on.ca/uploadedFiles/ABS-report-Iacobucci-Trebilcock-september-2014.pdf.

13. See, for example, Dan Katz, video "Innovation in the Legal Services Industry—The Future is Already Here, It is Just *Not* Evenly Distributed," posted October 2, 2013, http://computationallegalstudies.com/2013/10/innovation-in-the-legal-services-industry-the-future-is-already-here-it-is-just-not-evenly-distributed-via-reinvent-law-channel/. See also Gillian Hadfield, "Legal Barriers to Innovation: The Growing Economic Cost of Professional Control Over Corporate Legal Markets," *Stanford Law Review* 60 (2008): 101–46, http://ssrn.com/abstract=1104902.

14. For a general discussion on the value to law firms of persons with expertise in areas other than law, see John Sterling, "Non-Lawyers: A Critical Success Factor for the Law Firm of the Future," Sterling Strategies, December 5, 2013, http://sterlingstrat.com/non-lawyers-a-critical-success-factor-for-the-law-firm-of-the-future.html; see also Frank H. Stephen, *Lawyers, Markets and Regulation* (Cheltenham, UK: Edward Elgar, 2013), 128–131.

15. See, for example, Michael Kelly, "Ethical Issues Associated with Multidisciplinary Practices in Texas," *Saint Mary's Law Journal* 41 (2010): 750–52, http://www.stmaryslawjournal.org/pdfs/kelly.pdf.

16. On the opportunities that "deregulation" of the legal services market would offer in relation to the "justice gap," see, for example, Clifford Winston, Robert W. Crandall and Vikram Maheshri, *First Thing We Do, Let's Deregulate All the Lawyers* (Washington D.C: R.R. Donnelley, 2011), 91–93.

17. See, for example, Mary Juetten, "Technology and the Unauthorized Practice of Law," *Law Technology Today*, June 12, 2015, http://www.lawtechnologytoday.org/2015/06/technology-and-the-unauthorized-practice-of-law/; see also Campbell, "Rethinking Regulation," 35–39.

18. A number of persons have written on this topic, perhaps most notably Gillian Hadfield. See, for example: Gillian K. Hadfield, "The Cost of Law: Promoting Access to Justice through the (Un)Corporate Practice of Law," *International Review of Law and Economics* 38 (2014) 43–63, http://ssrn.com/abstract=2333990; Gillian K. Hadfield and Jamie Heine, "Life in the Law-Thick World: The Legal Resource Landscape for Ordinary Americans," USC CLASS Research Papers Series No. CLASS15-2; USC Law Legal Studies Paper No. 15–2, January 9, 2015, http://dx.doi.org/10.2139/ssrn.2547664; Hadfield, "Legal Barriers to Innovation," 101–146. See also, for example, Renee Newman Knake, "Democratizing the Delivery of Legal Services," *Ohio State Law Journal* 73 (2012): 1–46, http://dx.doi.org/10.2139/ssrn.1800258; and Edward S. Adams and John H. Matheson, "Law Firms on the Big Board?: A Proposal for Nonlawyer Investment in Law Firms," *California Law Review* 86 (1998): 1–40, http://scholarship.law.umn.edu/cgi/viewcontent.cgi?article=1100&context=faculty_articles.

19. See, for example, John S. Dzienkowski and Robert J. Peroni, "Multidisciplinary Practice and the American Legal Profession: A Market Approach to Regulating the Delivery of Legal Services in the Twenty-First Century," *Fordham Law Review* 69 (2000): 83–207, http://ssrn.com/abstract=2277718; and David A. Hoffman and Richard N. Wolman, "Multidisciplinary Practice: Three-Dimensional Client Service," *Massachusetts Psychological Association Quarterly*, Summer 2004, http://www.bostonlawcollaborative.com/blc/60-BLC/version/default/part/AttachmentData/data/2005-07-mass-psych-multi-practice.pdf?branch=main&lan

guage=default.

20. Richard Devlin and Ora Morison, "Access to Justice and the Ethics and Politics of Alternative Business Structures," *Canadian Bar Review* 91 (2012): 526, http://ssrn.com/abstract=2437035.

21. American Bar Association. "Model Rules of Professional Conduct: Preface," accessed August 27, 2015, http://www.americanbar.org/groups/professional_responsibility/publications/model_rules_of_professional_conduct/model_rules_of_professional_conduct_preface.html.

22. Rules 1–310 and 1–320 of the California Rules of Professional Conduct: http://rules.calbar.ca.gov/Rules/RulesofProfessionalConduct/CurrentRules/Rule1310.aspx and http://rules.calbar.ca.gov/Rules/RulesofProfessionalConduct/CurrentRules/Rule1320.aspx.

23. Lance Duroni, "US Law Firms Still Flirting with Going Public," *Law 360*, July 15, 2015, http://www.law360.com/articles/671281/us-law-firms-still-flirting-with-going-public.

24. Devlin and Morison humorously liken the different attempts to change Model Rule 5.4 to a series of zombie movies. Devlin and Morison, "Access to Justice," 527–37.

25. Florencio Ramirez, "The Debate Continues," *GPSolo*, Vol. 18 No. 1, January/February 2001, http://www.americanbar.org/content/newsletter/publications/gp_solo_magazine_home/gp_solo_magazine_index/2001_jan_feb_ramirez.html.

26. "Message from the Co-Chairs: Message from Commission on Ethics 20/20 Co-Chairs Jamie S. Gorelick and Michael Traynor," American Bar Association, accessed August 20, 2015, http://www.americanbar.org/groups/professional_responsibility/aba_commission_on_ethics_20_20/about_us/message_from_the_co_chairs.html.

27. ABA Commission on Ethics 20/20, "ABA Commission on Ethics 20/20 Will Not Propose Changes to ABA Policy Prohibiting Nonlawyer Ownership of Law Firms," April 16, 2012, http://www.americanbar.org/content/dam/aba/administrative/ethics_2020/20120416_news_release_re_nonlawyer_ownership_law_firms.authcheckdam.pdf.

28. "Commission on the Future of Legal Services: Background," American Bar Association, accessed August 20, 2015, http://www.americanbar.org/groups/centers_commissions/commission-on-the-future-of-legal-services.html.

29. Commission on the Future of Legal Services, et. al., "Report to the House of Delegates," November, 2015, 1, http://www.americanbar.org/content/dam/aba/images/office_president/final_regulatory_objectives_resolution_november_2015.pdf.

30. Resolution 105, American Bar Association, February, 2016, http://www.americanbar.org/content/dam/aba/images/abanews/2016mymres/105.pdf. See also Richard Zorza, "Good News from the ABA—Regulatory Objectives Adopted," Richard Zorza's Access to Justice Blog, February 9, 2016, http://accesstojustice.net/; Susan Beck, "Divided ABA Adopts Resolution on Nonlawyer Legal Services," *The American Lawyer*, February 8, 2016, http://www.americanlawyer.com/id=1202749202171/Divided-ABA-Adopts-Resolution-on-Nonlawyer-Legal-Services?mcode=0&curindex=0&curpage=ALL.

31. ABA Commission on the Future of Legal Services, "For Comment: Issues Paper Concerning Unregulated LSP Entities," March 31, 2016, http://www.americanbar.org/content/dam/aba/images/office_president/final_unregulated_lsp_entities_issues_paper.pdf.

32. ABA Commission on the Future of Legal Services, "For Comment: Issues Paper Regarding Alternative Business Structures," April 8, 2016, http://www.americanbar.org/content/dam/aba/images/office_president/alternative_business_issues_paper.pdf.

33. See, generally, Devlin and Morison, "Access to Justice," 499–508.

34. Sir David Clementi, "Report of the Review of the Regulatory Framework for Legal Services in England and Wales," December, 2004, accessed August 20, 2015, http://webarchive.nationalarchives.gov.uk/+/http://www.legal-services-review.org.uk/content/report/index.htm ("Clementi Report").

35. At the time this book went to press, four "front-line" regulators in England and Wales had the authority to grant ABS licenses. The Legal Services Act requires that each such regulator maintain a registry of the ABSs that it has licensed. Those registries may be consulted online at these links (all accessed July 15, 2016): Solicitors Regulation Authority (SRA): http://www.sra.org.uk/solicitors/firm-based-authorisation/abs/abs-search.page; Council for Licensed Conveyancers (CLC): http://www.conveyancer.org.uk/CLC-Consumers/ABS-Register.aspx; Institute of Chartered Accountants in England and Wales (ICAEW) (licensed for probate

work): http : //www.icaew.com/~/media/corporate/files/technical/legal%20and %20regulatory/probate %20and%20abs/probate%20register.ashx. At the time this book went to press, the SRA had authorized approximately 525 ABSs, the CLC approximately 50, and the ICAEW approximately 150. The fourth front-line regulator, the Intellectual Property Regulation Board (IPReg), had just begun the licensing process, and at that point 20 out of an expected total of 45 firms had been licensed. See IPReg, "Firms Requiring to Transition to Licensed Bodies Pursuant to the Legal Services Act 2007," November 16, 2015, http://ipreg.org.uk/wp-content/files/2015/03/IPReg-Transitioning-Firms-as-at-16-November-2015.pdf. Finally, at the time this book went to press, the Bar Standards Board, which regulates barristers, had submitted an application for comparable authority; that application was pending.

36. See, generally, Devlin and Morison, "Access to Justice," 508–25.

37. For a pan-Canadian summary see, for example, "Regulation Reform: A Cross-Canada Checkup," Nova Scotia Barristers' Society, accessed May 20, 2016, http://nsbs.org/regulation-reform-cross-canada-checkup. See also Mitch Kowalski, "Entity Regulation Comes to Canada," *Financial Post*, February 23, 2016, http://business.financialpost.com/legal-post/mitch-kowalski-entity-regulation-comes-to-canada.

38. CBA Legal Futures Initiative, "Futures: Transforming the Delivery of Legal Services in Canada," August, 2014, http://www.cba.org/CBAMediaLibrary/cba_na/PDFs/CBA%20Legal%20Futures%20PDFS/Futures-Final-eng.pdf.

39. "Legal Services Regulation," Nova Scotia Barristers' Society, accessed May 16, 2016, http://nsbs.org/legal-services-regulation.

40. "Innovating Regulation: A Collaboration of the Prairie Law Societies," November, 2015, http://www.lawsociety.sk.ca/media/127107/INNOVATINGREGULATION.pdf; "Innovating Regulation," Law Societies of Alberta, Manitoba and Saskatchewan, accessed May 16, 2016, http://www.lawsocietylistens.ca/.

41. Law Society of Upper Canada Compliance-Based Entity Regulation Task Force, "Report to Convocation," December 4, 2015, https://www.lsuc.on.ca/uploadedFiles/For_the_Public/About_the_Law_Society/Convocation_Decisions/2015/convocation%20december%202015%20compliance.pdf; "Compliance-Based Entity Regulation," The Law Society of Upper Canada, accessed February 1, 2016, https://www.lsuc.on.ca/better-practices/.

42. "Law Firm Regulation Consultation, Phase Two," The Law Society of British Columbia, January 28, 2016, https://www.lawsociety.bc.ca/newsroom/highlights.cfm#c4191. See also Law Firm Regulation Task Force, "Law Firm Regulation Consultation Brief," October 26, 2015, https://www.lawsociety.bc.ca/docs/newsroom/highlights/FirmRegulation-brief.pdf; and The Law Society of British Columbia, "Law Firm Regulation Consultation: FAQs," n.d., https://www.lawsociety.bc.ca/docs/newsroom/highlights/FirmRegulation-FAQ.pdf.

43. On the ABA's history of resistance to change, see Moliterno, *The American Legal Profession in Crisis*.

44. For a general discussion on the lack of clarity over the authority of bodies other than supreme courts to regulate the legal profession and legal services more generally, see Hadfield, "Legal Barriers to Innovation," 108–13. For a discussion of the control that the legal profession in general, and the ABA in particular, has with respect to the regulation of legal services in the United States, see Gillian Hadfield, "Innovating to Improve Access: Changing the Way Courts Regulate Legal Markets," *Daedalus* 143 (2014) 3, 10–11, http://ssrn.com/abstract=2419308. For a discussion of the significant limitations of judicial regulation and an analysis of the advantages and disadvantages of regulation by the legislature, see Benjamin H. Barton, "An Institutional Analysis of Lawyer Regulation: Who Should Control Lawyer Regulation—Courts, Legislatures, or the Market?" *Georgia Law Review* 37 (2003): 1167–1250.

*Part I*

# The Opposition to Alternative Structures

A number of lawyers, speaking individually or on behalf of organizations such as law firms and state and local bar associations, have expressed opposition to alternative structures, and, in many cases, very strong opposition. Part I examines their arguments.

## *Chapter One*

# Alternative Structures Will Undermine Professionalism and Ethics

Many persons have argued that permitting nonlawyers to own shares in or to manage a law firm, or allowing a lawyer to partner with a nonlawyer in a multidisciplinary practice, will lead to the loss of professionalism. "Law is a profession, not a business,"[1] which is "an entirely different set of values,"[2] and in permitting alternative structures, law will become a business. Other variations of this argumentation include:

- Alternative structures will undermine the attorney-client relationship by placing into question confidentiality and attorney-client privilege.[3]
- Alternative structures will undermine lawyer independence and professional judgment because lawyers will prioritize the interests of their shareholders and their nonlawyer managers and partners over the interests of clients.[4]
- Alternative structures will prioritize profits above service.[5]
- Alternative structures will lead to unethical practices because nonlawyers are not bound by lawyers' ethical rules.[6]

A number of responses have been offered to these arguments. They can be summarized as follows:

1. A debate as to whether law is, or should be, a profession or a business is nonsensical at best and hypocritical at worst. Everyone, including lawyers, needs to make a profit in order to stay in business, and the firms that appear on *The American Lawyer*'s annual listing of the top grossing law firms have clearly made profitability a priority. From this

perspective, the suggestion that alternative structures will prioritize profits over service is disingenuous.

2. There is nothing inherent about being a lawyer or about not being a lawyer that makes a person more or less ethical, or more or less able to understand and follow ethical rules. It is repugnant to suggest that companies cannot act ethically, for the simple reason that they are companies and have shareholders. Many companies operate in an ethical manner—the mere fact that they are companies does not pose any greater or lesser challenge for them to act ethically, or make them any more or less likely to act ethically. At the same time, there are a number of examples to demonstrate that lawyers can and do act unethically.
3. The protection of the attorney-client relationship and the respect of ethical rules and lawyer independence are important values that must be respected and protected. But the persons who argue that alternative structures will undermine these values offer no proof of their arguments, no empirical research—they simply imagine a multitude of scenarios, more or less plausible, in which it could happen, and then assert that it necessarily will happen.

It is certainly true that an alternative structure, and anyone associated with one (shareholder, manager, employee), can act unethically and/or pressure someone else associated with the structure to act unethically. In fact, there are many, and perhaps an infinite number of ways that an alternative structure and the people associated with it could act unethically, and an infinite number of reasons why they could be motivated to do so. A multitude of possible scenarios have been proposed, including: (i) an insurance company that offers legal services in personal injury that lobbies the government for regulations to reduce personal injury payouts by insurance companies,[7] (ii) a company that offers criminal defense legal services and also operates prisons,[8] and (iii) Walmart, one of the country's largest and most controversial employers, offering employment law service to its customers, as employees.[9]

By the same token, it is equally true that an alternative structure, as well as those associated with it, might be enabled as well as motivated to act ethically in an exemplary manner. For example, a firm could bring in executives who are expert in business processes, who could institute for the firm processes to ensure a high standard of compliance. Another example is a large company whose value is in its brand—knowing that the mere appearance or suspicion of unethical behavior could wipe out the value of the brand, the company could be highly motivated to operate in ways that would place it beyond reproach. A third example is a listed company—listed companies are vulnerable to short sellers, and a listed company that provides legal services is arguably especially vulnerable to short sellers with respect to ethical matters. For that reason, a listed company that provides legal services arguably has every motivation to be scrupulously ethical. And if they are not, the public will soon be made aware and the company's stock will suffer for it—short sellers will make sure of it.

At any rate, how are lawyers different? Aren't there also many, and perhaps an infinite number of ways that lawyers can act unethically? Aren't there many, and perhaps an infinite number of reasons why a lawyer or a law firm can be motivated to act unethically? The records of the various state disciplinary authorities evidence that some lawyers do act unethically—sometimes in predictable ways and with predictable motivations, and sometimes in less predictable ways and with less predictable motivations.

We do not use the possibility of unethical behavior, predictable or not, as a reason to keep all lawyers out of the market—because they might act unethically, or because they might have or might one day develop motivations to act unethically. Instead, we have put in place a system to regulate the ethical conduct of lawyers. The system we have put in place in the United States is a set of rules that delineates proper and improper conduct, and we have vested power in certain institutions to enforce those rules, including the power to bar from the market those lawyers who demonstrate by their actions that they cannot be trusted to act ethically.

The examples of England and Wales and of Australia demonstrate that, in adopting a new regulatory framework that governs legal services rather than simply lawyers, it is possible to put in place a system to govern the ethical conduct of all legal service providers, including alternative structures and those associated with them. While the systems that those two countries have implemented vary in their complexity, they share these two pertinent elements:

1. Entity-based regulation and appointment of at least one responsible lawyer: Both Australia and England and Wales have moved to entity-based regulation. In this manner, they have moved from regulating lawyers, exclusively, to also regulating legal services, more generally. In addition, their rules require the designation of at least one person to bear responsibility for the ethical compliance of the entity. More specifically:

In New South Wales and Victoria (Australia), each "principal" of a structure that provides legal services (regardless of the type of structure, and notably regardless of whether it is an ILP or not) is responsible for the firm's compliance with professional conduct and other rules. As regards ILPs, "principals" are each of the lawyers of the ILP who are "validly appointed" directors. As regards other types of structures, and notably partnerships, "principals" are each of the partners of the firm. A principal bears responsibility if the principal "knowingly authorized or permitted" the act (or omission), or if the principal "was in or ought reasonably to have been in a position to influence" the relevant conduct of the ILP.[10]

In Queensland and the other states of Australia, responsibility for the compliance of an ILP is placed upon the shoulders of a "Legal Practitioner Director" (LPD), a person that the ILP itself designates and who must be a lawyer. The LPD is responsible for ensuring that the firm has appropriate management systems in place that enable the firm to provide legal services in accordance with the applicable ethical rules. And, in the event of an violation by the firm and/or by any employee of the firm, the LPD as well as the firm itself can be held responsible[11]: Not only can the LPD lose his/her practicing certificate (that is, be disbarred), but the entire ILP can be liquidated.[12]

In England and Wales, all firms (ABS or not) are required to appoint a Compliance Officer for Legal Practice (COLP), as well as a Compliance Officer for Finance and Administration (COFA). Every firm must at all times have a designated COLP as well as COFA. The COLP is responsible for ensuring that the firm has in place the systems and controls needed to comply with the applicable ethical and professional standards. The COFA is responsible for ensuring that the firm complies with the Solicitors Regulation Authority's (SRA, the largest "front-line" legal regulator in England and Wales) accounting rules. These persons bear principal responsibility for the firm's compliance and they are obliged to report to the SRA material noncompliance. In the event the SRA suspects dishonesty or failure to comply with the Code of Conduct or accounting rules, the SRA can suspend the COLP's practicing certificate and can revoke the firm's authorization, effectively forcing it to wind up.[13]

2. Adoption of proactive, management-based regulation (Australia) / outcomes-focused regulation (England and Wales): Both Australia and England and Wales have moved away from proscriptive, rules-based regulation (the kind in place in the United States) in favor of what has been termed in Australia as "proactive, management based regulation"[14] (PMBR) and in England and Wales as "outcomes-focused regulation" (OFR) (and, as discussed in chapter 2, what Canada is calling "compliance-based regulation"). With this change, rather than being obliged to conform to a specific set of proscriptive rules, firms are required to deliver specific outcomes regarding the management and the ethical compliance of the firm. An example is England and Wales's Outcome 3.4: "[Y]ou do not act if there is [a conflict with your own interests] or a significant risk of [a conflict with your own interests]."[15] Each firm is responsible for designing and implementing its own systems and processes necessary to achieve those outcomes, under the rationale that the systems and processes appropriate for one firm are not the same that are appropriate for another. With such a system, there is no need to devise rules that try to anticipate every possible kind of ethical violation, and no need for a regulator to prove that any such specific rule was violated. Instead, a regulator simply needs to inquire as to why a firm did not act with integrity or why a specific outcome was not achieved.

Alternative structures have existed in Australia since 2001, and in England and Wales since 2012. There is nothing in the public record in either country indicating that they have had an adverse effect on professionalism or ethics. There is no evidence that ethical rules have been violated for reasons connected to the status of a firm as an ILP or ABS. As Steve Mark, the former Legal Services Commissioner for New South Wales and one of the persons principally responsible for the development of PMBR in Australia has observed: "The legal ethics sky has not fallen . . . chicken little has survived!"[16]

In fact, in Australia, research has demonstrated that the number of complaints received in relation to ILPs are two-thirds lower than the number of complaints received in relation to traditional firms.[17] In this manner, some have argued, Australia's proactive regulatory framework curbs unethical behavior in a way that a reactive regulatory framework cannot,[18] justifying Mark's description of the framework as an "ethical infrastructure."[19]

In England and Wales, some firms, ABS or not, have adjusted more easily to the new regulatory framework than others. This has notably been the case with respect to the role of the COLP, with some firms, both ABS and not, reporting that they have had trouble identifying, and according to their COLPs, asserting the right level of authority.[20] Regardless of these struggles to adjust, the data shows that from 2011 to 2013, Legal Disciplinary Practices (LDPs, a precursor structure to ABSs) were the subject of the smallest number of complaints, as a ratio to turnover. The data also shows that while the rate of complaints against ABSs is not lower than those against traditional firms: (i) the complaints are not connected to the ABS status of the firm, and (ii) ABSs, together with LDPs, have better complaint resolution ratios (that is, they address complaints more efficiently and effectively).[21]

In its December 2014 Consumer Impact Report, the Legal Services Consumer Panel observed:

> [T]he dire predictions about a collapse in ethics and reduction in access to justice as a result of ABS have not materialised. There have been no major disciplinary failings by ABS firms or unusual levels of complaints in the Legal Ombudsman's published data. Our Tracker Survey isn't able to segment between ABS and non ABS firms, but does show that overall consumer confidence in the quality of work and professionalism of lawyers has held steady since 2011. The data indicates that service satisfaction reduces as the size of the law firm used increases, but this is a function of size rather than ownership structure.[22]

The Legal Ombudsman, mentioned in the quote above, is an independent body that offers an avenue for the resolution of complaints against regulated legal service providers (individuals as well as entities) in England and Wales. Indeed, the reports issued by the Legal Ombudsman are highly telling: Each year since 2012, the number of complaints filed with the Ombudsman has fallen by between 5 percent and 8 percent as compared to the previous year.[23]

## STORIES

### (PART V OR ONLINE)

*John Ray, Senior Consultant, Law Firm Consulting Group* (online): Ray argues it is the fact that lawyers do not have access to adequate capital that adversely affects their professional judgment. It limits the cases they are willing to take on, and it limits the extent to which they are willing to prosecute the cases that they do take on.

*Paddy Oliver, Managing Director and Founder, Lexcel Consulting* (online): Oliver argues that outside investment and greater public scrutiny will result in better managed law firms that act ethically from both a legal and business perspective.

*John Briton, Former Legal Services Commissioner, Queensland* (online): Briton acknowledges that lawyers can be influenced by a number of different people, including nonlawyer shareholders. However, he argues that this is not a reason to exclude them, it is merely a reason to manage the risk.

*Darrel Pink, Executive Director, Nova Scotia Barristers' Society* (online): Pink explains that alternative structures can be discussed in Nova Scotia only after first addressing the regulation of entities in addition to the regulation of individuals.

*Kristin Dangerfield, CEO, The Law Society of Manitoba* (online): Dangerfield explains that entity regulation will permit Manitoba to move toward permitting lawyers to partner with nonlawyers and allowing law firms to accept capitalization from other sources.

## NOTES

1. Charles Ruffin, Comment Submitted to ABA Commission on Ethics 20/20, February 10, 2012, http://www.americanbar.org/content/dam/aba/administrative/ethics_2020/ethics_20_20_comments/ruffin_alpsdiscussiondraft.authcheckdam.pdf; Forrest A. Norman, "Alternative Business Structures – Comment," April 26, 2016, http://www.americanbar.org/content/dam/aba/images/office_president/forrest_a_norman_abs.pdf.

2. John E. Thies, "President's Page: The Battle against Non-Lawyer Involvement in Legal Practice," *Illinois Bar Journal* 101 (2013): 8, http://www.isba.org/ibj/2013/01/thebattleagainstnonlawyerinvolvemen.

3. State Bar of Texas, Letter to Katy Englehart, May 5, 2016, http://www.americanbar.org/content/dam/aba/images/office_president/state_bar_of_texas_abs.pdf.

4. Paul Bennet, "Comment on Alternative Business Structures," April 25, 2016, http://www.americanbar.org/content/dam/aba/images/office_president/paul_w_bennett_abs.pdf; Jess

C. Rickman, "ABS Survey—Rejection of the Proposal," April 27, 2016, http://www.americanbar.org/content/dam/aba/images/office_president/jess_c_rickman_abs.pdf.

5. International Association of Defense Counsel, "ABA Commission on the Future of Legal Services – Alternative Business Structures," May 3, 2016, 1, http://www.americanbar.org/content/dam/aba/images/office_president/international_association_of_defense_counsel_abs.pdf; William W. Clifton, Jr., "ABA Commission on the Fuiture [sic] of Legal Services Report," April 28, 2016, http://www.americanbar.org/content/dam/aba/images/office_president/william_w_clifton_jr_abs.pdf.

6. Thomas W. Seiler, "Non Lawyer Ownership of Law Firms," April 29, 2016, http://www.americanbar.org/content/dam/aba/images/office_president/thomas_w_seiler_abs.pdf; J. Michael Weston, "ABA Commission on the Future of Legal Services – Alternative Business Structures," April 27, 2016, http://www.americanbar.org/content/dam/aba/images/office_president/lederer_weston_craig_abs.pdf.

7. Nick Robinson, "When Lawyers Don't Get All the Profits: Non-Lawyer Ownership of Legal Services, Access, and Professionalism," *Georgetown Journal of Legal Ethics* 29 (2016), HLS Program on the Legal Profession Research Paper No. 2014–20, 43, http://ssrn.com/abstract=2487878.

8. Ibid., 14.

9. Ibid., 43–44.

10. Legal Profession Uniform Law (New South Wales), 2014, Section 35(1), http://www5.austlii.edu.au/au/legis/nsw/consol_act/lpul333/s35.html.

11. See, for example, Queensland Legal Services Commission, "Obligations of LPDs," last modified November 11, 2013, https://www.lsc.qld.gov.au/compliance/incorporated-legal-practices/obligations-of-legal-practitioner-directors.

12. For a more detailed description of the regulatory framework that Queensland adopted from New South Wales, see Steve Mark, "The Future Is Here: Globalisation and the Regulation of the Legal Profession—Views from an Australian Regulator," May 27, 2009, http://www.americanbar.org/content/dam/aba/migrated/cpr/regulation/steve_paper.authcheckdam.pdf.

13. With respect to England and Wales, see Hadfield and Rhode, "How to Regulate Legal Services," 20–32.

14. Ted Schneyer is credited with coining the phrase "proactive, management-based regulation. See, for example, Schneyer, "The Case for Proactive Management-Based Self-Regulation to Improve Professional Self-Regulation for US Lawyers," *Hofstra Law Review* 42 (2013): 233–265. http://www.hofstralawreview.org/wp-content/uploads/2014/02/BB.7.Schneyer.final2_.pdf.

15. SRA Code of Conduct 2011, accessed May 20, 2016, http://www.sra.org.uk/solicitors/handbook/code/content.page.

16. Mark, "The Future Is Here," 3.

17. Christine Parker, Tahlia Ruth Gordon, and Steve A. Mark, "Regulating Law Firm Ethics Management: An Empirical Assessment of the Regulation of Incorporated Legal Practices in NSW," *Journal of Law and Society* 37 (2010): 466–500, http://dx.doi.org/10.2139/ssrn.1527315.

18. Andrew Grech and Tahlia Gordon, "Modern Law Firm Management: Should Non-Lawyer Ownership Be Endorsed and Encouraged?" Working Paper, April 2015, 8, http://www.law.georgetown.edu/academics/centers-institutes/legal-profession/upload/Grech-Gordon-Non-Lawyer-Ownership-Paper-Final.pdf.

19. Mark, "The Future Is Here," 3. Mark credits Schneyer as well as Elizabeth Chambliss and David B. Wilkins for the development of the term "ethical infrastructure": Ted Schneyer, "A Tale of Four Systems: Reflections on How Law Influences the 'Ethical Infrastructure' of Law Firms," *South Texas Law Review* 39 (1998): 245–277; Elizabeth Chambliss and David B. Wilkins, "A New Framework for Law Firm Discipline," *Georgetown Journal of Legal Ethics* 16 (2002): 336–341, http://heinonline.org/HOL/LandingPage?handle=hein.journals/geojlege16anddiv=18andid=andpage=.

20. Nick Hilborne, "COLPs Failing to Report Problems to SRA, Groundbreaking Study Finds," *Legal Futures*, March 3, 2016, http://www.legalfutures.co.uk/latest-news/colps-failing-to-report-problems-to-sra-groundbreaking-study-finds.

21. Legal Services Board, "Evaluation: Changes in Competition in Different Legal Markets—An Empirical Analysis," October, 2013, 6–7, https://research.legalservicesboard.org.uk/wp-content/media/Changes-in-competition-in-market-segments-REPORT.pdf.

22. Legal Services Consumer Panel, "Consumer Impact Report 2014," December 5, 2014, 15, http://www.legalservicesconsumerpanel.org.uk/publications/research_and_reports/documents/Consumer%20Impact%20Report%203.pdf (hereinafter "UK 2014 Consumer Impact Report").

23. For each year ending in March, the number of complaints was 22,350 (2012), 20,500 (2013), 19,450 (2014), and 18,185 (2015).The drop in complaints for the year ended March 2015 as compared to the year ended March 2012 was 18.62 percent. Legal Ombudsman, "Annual Report and Accounts for the Year Ending 31 March 2015," January 28, 2016, 12, http://www.legalombudsman.org.uk/wp-content/uploads/2014/09/Annual-Report-2014-15.pdf. See also Neil Rose, "Complaints About Lawyers Fall to Lowest Level Yet," *Legal Futures*, January 29, 2016, http://www.legalfutures.co.uk/latest-news/complaints-about-lawyers-fall-to-lowest-level-yet.

## *Chapter Two*

# There Is No Way to Regulate Alternative Structures

Some have argued against allowing alternative structures on the grounds that there is no way to regulate them, or, at least, that there is no way to adequately regulate them.[1] Examples of these arguments include:

- "Nonlawyers are not officers of the court. Nor do they have an ethical obligation to advance the client's interests. . . . [N]on-lawyers are not members of a bar subject to the same consequences for failure to uphold [the Rules of Professional Conduct]. Whatever else is true, nonlawyers cannot be disbarred."[2]
- "It would not be adequate . . . to simply create new rules in the hope of protecting the public against the types of conflicts of interest that are inevitable in an ABS environment. This will require significantly increased resources and infrastructure . . . to regulate such matters."[3]
- "Where will [the bar] get the resources to monitor the conduct of perhaps thousands of 'new partners' that are not dues-paying members of [the bar]?"[4]
- "[T]he Australian and English adaptations of ABS are predicated on the existence in those jurisdictions of a regulator that has authority to audit the performance of each ABS, and that is adequately staffed and funded to do so. This is not realistic in the US because we have no national regulator and no ready source of funds to finance such an ambitious effort."[5]

These arguments are correct in that it will not be sufficient to simply modify Model Rule 5.4 to end its prohibition on fee sharing. Much more will be required. As discussed in chapter 1, two types of changes will be needed in particular: the adoption of entity regulation as well as the adoption of proactive, management-based regulation.

In the United States today, regulation occurs largely—nearly exclusively—at the level of the individual lawyer. As discussed in greater detail in part II, the current regulations do place limited supervisory responsibilities upon certain law firm partners, but these responsibilities pale in comparison to the responsibilities that, as discussed in chapter 1, the regulations of Queensland place upon the LPD and the regulations of England and Wales place upon the COLP and COFA. In these jurisdictions, entity regulation does not replace the regulation of individual lawyers or weaken their professional responsibilities on an individual basis. Instead, it adds an additional layer of regulation in order to account both for the fact that most lawyers today practice in structures rather than individually, and that these structures have enormous influence on the way that lawyers work.

Further, in the United States today, regulation is largely, if not exclusively, proscriptive and rules-based rather than proactive and management-based. As discussed in chapter 1, a proactive, management-based system eliminates the need to devise rules that try to anticipate every possible kind of ethical violation, as well as the need for a regulator to prove that any such specific rule was violated. Instead, a regulator simply needs to inquire as to why a firm did not act with integrity or why a specific outcome was not achieved.

In all likelihood, the work involved to make these changes to the regulatory infrastructure will be extensive, especially if considered on a national level of 50 states. But the fact that extensive preliminary work is necessary is not a reason to do nothing or to change nothing. It simply means that there is work to be done. Further, while the work can lead to a lifting of the ban on alternative structures, it will not necessarily have to do so. And if it ultimately does not, the effort will by no means be lost. To the contrary (and as discussed in detail in part II), the preliminary work, standing alone, offers great value in the form of a significantly improved regulatory infrastructure. Several provinces in Canada have recognized the high value of this preliminary work, and, accordingly, they have made significant progress on their respective paths to implementation.

The first of those provinces is Nova Scotia. In 2013, this province's regulatory body, the Nova Scotia Barristers' Society, embarked on a multi-year program to shift to "a new model of regulating legal services, in a manner that is risk-focused, proactive, principled and proportionate."[6] In Nova Scotia, existing legislation already grants to the Society a certain level of authority to regulate entities.[7] Today, the Society is using that authority as a building block in the implementation of a 19-point Policy Framework that includes:

- The adoption of six regulatory objectives (the objectives include "protect those who use legal services," "promote the rule of law and the public interest in the justice system," "promote access to legal services and the justice system," and "establish required standards for professional responsibility and competence").[8]
- A focus on the anticipated risks associated with each area of regulated activity and, in assessing risk, the Society "will always give priority to the protection of the public."
- The regulation of the delivery of legal services by lawyers as well as by legal entities, "which include lawyers, law firms, law corporations, law departments and other similar entities."
- Regulation that requires "each law firm and legal entity" to designate an individual who will be responsible for the entity's compliance with its regulatory requirements, and to ensure that all persons associated with the entity who deliver or assist in the delivery of legal services comply with the applicable code of conduct.
- Regulation that will require "each law firm and legal entity" (i) to establish and maintain a management system that promotes competent and ethical legal practice, and (ii) to undertake to self-assess and report to the Society on its management system.
- Amendments to the applicable code of conduct "to eliminate barriers to fee sharing with nonlawyers."[9]

The Society is in the process of consulting with members of the legal profession and other stakeholders to develop and propose to the Nova Scotia legislature the legislative amendments that will be needed in order for the Society to be able to fully implement the Policy Framework.

Conspicuously absent from the Policy Framework is any reference to "alternative business structure" or the use of any comparable expression. This absence is not an oversight: It reflects an understanding on the part of the Society that the Policy Framework is the preliminary work that is necessary in order to allow alternative structures to function. At the same time, however, the Policy Framework is an end in itself. In the words of the Society, once implemented, the Policy Framework will result in a new model of regulation that "is designed to be more responsive to a diverse and profoundly changing environment, to enhance the quality of legal services, to encourage ethical legal practice, to foster innovation in legal services, and to increase access to justice."[10]

The second of the Canadian provinces that has made significant progress is Manitoba. In spring 2015, the Law Society of Manitoba (LSM) recommended to the government of Manitoba that the Legal Profession Act be amended, notably: (i) to grant to the LSM the power to regulate law firms in addition to individual lawyers, and (ii) to define law firm broadly enough to include any entity that provides legal services, regardless of whether or not it is owned or managed, in whole or in part, by nonlawyers.[11]

In May 2015, the government of Manitoba complied with the LSM's recommendation, proposing to the Manitoba Legislative Assembly Bill 19,[12] which, in part:

- Expands the definition of "law firm" to include, in addition to traditional structures such as a sole proprietorship and a partnership, also "a law corporation or any other joint arrangement or legal entity that provides legal services."[13]
- Grants to the LSM the power "to permit and regulate" not only law firms, but also "different types of arrangements to provide legal services, including arrangements between lawyers and between lawyers and nonlawyers."[14]

The Manitoba legislature responded to this proposal very quickly, enacting Bill 19 in November 2015.[15] The LSM is now engaging in a consulting process in order to propose specific changes to the rules of conduct in implementation of the new legislation.[16]

At the same time that the LSM is working within Manitoba, it is also working in collaboration with other Canadian provinces, and, most notably, the other "Prairie provinces" of Saskatchewan and Alberta. To this end, the law societies of the three provinces together issued a discussion paper describing a joint approach to the three "components" of "entity regulation, compliance-based regulation and ABS." The paper explains that for the three law societies, the three components are "intimately connected." More specifically, the paper states:

> The work of the Prairie provinces began with a focus on alternative business structures (ABS). Looking at what was happening around the world, and at the actual changes in the way legal services are delivered led to the conclusion that limitations we as regulators currently impose on lawyers are likely outdated. In particular, given the pressures lawyers face to run their practices as businesses, regulatory restrictions around fee sharing, referral fees, and other limitations may no longer be appropriate. Further, a move towards allowing ABS has the potential to open the door to innovations, which may assist in addressing unmet legal needs.
>
> These factors, and others, led the Prairie law societies to an initial focus on ABS. However, as discussions evolved, it became clear that it was largely impractical to look at ABS alone. How would we regulate an ABS? What are the appropriate tools? In order to create opportunities for ABSs, we could regulate not only individual lawyers but also their organizations as a whole. In other words, we would have to regulate entities.
>
> Further, as we began to investigate the possibility of entity regulation, it became clear that while paving the way for ABS was one motivation, even

> more important were the proactive regulatory possibilities that entity regulation presented. We know that most lawyers organize themselves into firms. In practice, it is the infrastructure of the firm that dictates how ethical issues such as conflicts are managed. The opportunity to influence everything from the way files are managed to the culture of the profession also resides at the firm level. If law societies were able to ensure that the appropriate infrastructures exist within a firm to avoid complaints, this would truly be a proactive and preventative approach to protecting the public. This took us back to the beginning and the recognition that three components—entity regulation, compliance-based regulation and ABS—are all intimately connected.
>
> In brief, entity regulation would represent a move from largely regulating only individual lawyers to also regulating the organizations in which they work. A possible mechanism for entity regulation is compliance-based regulation, which would set out a series of objectives and require lawyers and their organizations to demonstrate how they are meeting those objectives within their organizations. Finally, ABSs would be a type of entity regulated through a compliance-based regime. There are many possible forms of ABS but they might include provisions for nonlawyer investment in law firms, multi-disciplinary practices or a variety of other arrangements.[17]

In contrast to the Nova Scotia Barristers' Society, the Prairie Law Societies have not shied away from an open discussion, as well as an open consideration, of alternative structures. However, like the Nova Scotia Barristers' Society, the Prairie Law Societies also see the implementation of entity regulation together with the implementation of proactive, management-based regulation as necessary in order to lay the foundation for the regulation of alternative structures in their provinces. In other words, they see entity regulation together with proactive, management-based regulation as the way to be able both to update and improve their regulatory frameworks, as well as to regulate alternative structures.

Finally, two other Canadian provinces are following in the footsteps of Nova Scotia and the Prairie provinces: In 2015 the law societies of Ontario (Upper Canada) and British Columbia appointed task forces mandated to explore compliance-based entity (or, in the case of British Columbia, law firm) regulation. Each was completing its respective consultation process at the time this book went to press.[18]

At least two states in the United States appear to be following the examples of these Canadian provinces, albeit in highly tentative manners. The first of those states is Colorado: In late 2015, the Office of Attorney Regulation Counsel of the Colorado Supreme Court formally announced that "Colorado is studying an approach to attorney regulation that is centered on prevention, not solely discipline" that, if enacted, "would be the first of its kind in this country."[19] Calling it the "Colorado Proactive Management Based Regulation (PMBR) program," the Office of Attorney Regulation Counsel described PMBR as:

> [providing] lawyers with resources to develop their own management systems and processes to ensure ethical conduct (an ethical infrastructure) in their firm. Importantly, PMBR generally allows law firms, including sole practitioners, to develop their own processes and management systems using self-assessment tools.[20]

The Office of Attorney Regulation Counsel described the advantages of PMBR as follows:

> First, PMBR encourages the regulator to devote resources to (1) improving the management and culture of law firms and (2) prevent client and public harm, rather than focusing on individual conduct and discipline after-the-fact. Putting more emphasis on PMBR encourages those who control a law practice to develop management training, supervision and quality control systems. Second, PMBR improves the relationship between the regulator and the regulated because the regulator focuses on helping to improve the practice as a whole and reduce complaints while shifting the regulatory focus away from discipline alone.[21]

Further, the Office of Attorney Regulation Counsel argues that PMBR will not cost more money:

> In those jurisdictions that have adopted PMBR programs, complaints against lawyers for misconduct have dropped considerably. Thus, the cost of developing and maintaining a PMBR program is offset by savings from fewer disciplinary actions against lawyers in the jurisdiction. Research by Professor Susan Saab Fortney, of Hofstra University in New York, in conjunction with the regulatory authority in New South Wales, revealed that lawyers who completed the self-assessment process ended up revising their firm systems, policies and procedures, or adopting new ones, and thereby strengthened their firm management through such self-assessment.[22]

The second US state that appears to be following the examples of the Canadian provinces is Illinois: At a presentation in Chicago in April 2016, Jim Grogan, deputy administrator and chief counsel of the Illinois Attorney Registration and Disciplinary Commission (ARDC), explained his understanding of PMBR and stated that the ARDC had been "talking about" it for about one year. More specifically, he explained that the ARDC is developing an online self-assessment process by which lawyers answer questions about their practices intended to "get them thinking" about ethical policies and procedures. The questions will address topics such as confidentiality and client communications, and also, perhaps, diversity.[23]

In comparison to the Canadian provinces (let alone to England and Wales and Australia), the work being done in Colorado and Illinois could be described as "baby steps." Nothing in the Colorado Office of Attorney Regulation Counsel's announcement mentions alternative structures, and it appears that nothing in Grogan's presentation did either. Nevertheless, if successful, these will be the first steps to lay a regulatory groundwork for them.

## STORIES

(PART V OR ONLINE)

*John Briton, Former Legal Services Commissioner, Queensland* (online): Briton describes the manner by which Queensland regulates ILPs, including by both entity regulation and PMBR. In doing so, Briton establishes that alternative structures can, in fact, be regulated.

*Darrel Pink, Executive Director, Nova Scotia Barristers' Society* (online): Pink explains that for Nova Scotia, the way to regulate alternative structures is to first put in place entity regulation and PMBR.

*Kristin Dangerfield, CEO, The Law Society of Manitoba* (online): Echoing Pink, Dangerfield explains that the way to regulate alternative structures in Manitoba is via entity regulation.

## NOTES

1. See, for example, DRI—The Voice of the Defense Bar, "Issues Paper Regarding Alternative Business Structures," May 4, 2016, 4, http://www.americanbar.org/content/dam/aba/images/office_president/dri_the_voice_of_the_defense_bar_abs.pdf; Matthew Walko, "Comment on ABA's Issues Paper Regarding Alternative Business Structures dated April 8, 2016," April 25, 2016, http://www.americanbar.org/content/dam/aba/images/office_president/matthew_walko_abs.pdf; Bill Wagner, "For Comment: Issues Paper Regarding Alternative Business Structures (ABS)," April 27, 2016, http://www.americanbar.org/content/dam/aba/images/office_president/bill_wagner_abs.pdf.

2. Mark Chandler et al., "Comments of Nine General Counsel on the ABA Commission on Ethics 20/20's Discussion Paper on Alternative Law Practice Structures," February 29, 2012, 4, http://www.americanbar.org/content/dam/aba/administrative/ethics_2020/ethics_20_20_comments/ninegeneralcounselcomments_alpschoiceoflawinitialdraftproposal.authcheckdam.pdf.

3. Ontario Trial Lawyers Association, "Submission on Alternative Business Structures," December 15, 2014, 2, http://www.lsuc.on.ca/uploadedFiles/Ontario%20Trial%20Lawyers%20Association.pdf.

4. Larry D. Murrell, "Ethics 20/20 Non-lawyer Ownership of Law Firms," March 2, 2012, http://www.americanbar.org/content/dam/aba/administrative/ethics_2020/ethics_20_20_comments/murrell_alpsdiscussiondraft.authcheckdam.pdf.

5. New York State Bar Association, "New York State Bar Association's Comments on the ABA Commission on the Future of Legal Services' Issues Papers on Legal Checkups, Unregulated LSP Entities and Alternative Business Structures," April 28, 2016, 6, http://www.americanbar.org/content/dam/aba/images/office_president/new_york_state_bar_association_abs.pdf.

6. "Legal Services Regulation," Nova Scotia Barristers' Society, accessed May 16, 2016, http://nsbs.org/legal-services-regulation.

7. Legal Profession Act. 2004, c. 28, as amended by S.N.S. 2010, c 56, accessed December 3, 2015, http://nsbs.org/sites/default/files/cms/menu-pdf/legalprofessionact.pdf.

8. For a detailed discussion on the topic of regulatory objectives, see Laurel S. Terry, Steve Mark, and Tahlia Gordon, "Adopting Regulatory Objectives for the Legal Profession," *Fordham Law Review* 80 (2012): 2685–760, http://ssrn.com/abstract=2085003.

9. Nova Scotia Barristers' Society, "Legal Services Regulation: The Policy Framework," accessed May 21, 2016, http://nsbs.org/legal-services-regulation-policy-framework.

10. "Legal Services Regulation," accessed December 3, 2015, http://nsbs.org/legal-services-regulation.

11. Karen Clearwater, "President's Report: The Map Followed . . . ," *The Law Society of Manitoba Communiqué 2.0*, May, 2015, 1, http://www.lawsociety.mb.ca/publications/communique/May%202015.pdf.

12. 40th Legislature of Manitoba, Government Bill 19, "The Legal Profession Amendment Act," 2015, http://web2.gov.mb.ca/bills/40-4/pdf/b019.pdf.

13. Ibid., 1.

14. Ibid., 4.

15. "Fourth Session, Fortieth Legislature," The Legislative Assembly of Manitoba, accessed December 3, 2015, https://web2.gov.mb.ca/bills/40-4/index.php.

16. See "Innovating Regulation: Collaboration on the Prairies," The Law Society of Manitoba, accessed February 1, 2016, http://www.lawsociety.mb.ca/news/innovating-regulation-collaboration-on-the-prairies.

17. "Innovating Regulation: A Collaboration of the Prairie Law Societies," 2.

18. With respect to Ontario, see Law Society of Upper Canada, "Compliance-Based Entity Regulation," accessed March 4, 2016, https://www.lsuc.on.ca/better-practices/; with respect to British Columbia, see Law Society of British Columbia, "Law Firm Regulation – Consultation," accessed March 4, 2016, https://www.lawsociety.bc.ca/page.cfm?cid=4195&t=Law-firm-regulation.

19. Jim Coyle, "A New Model of Attorney Regulation?" Colorado Supreme Court, Fall 2015, http://www.coloradosupremecourt.us/newsletters/fall2015/a%20new%20model%20of%20regulation.htm.

20. Ibid.

21. Ibid.

22. Ibid., referencing Susan Saab Fortney, "Promoting Public Protection through an 'Attorney Integrity' System: Lessons from the Australian Experience with Proactive Regulation of Lawyers," *The Professional Lawyer* 23 (2015): 1–12, http://www.americanbar.org/content/dam/aba/publications/professional_lawyer/volume_23_number_1/ABA_PLN_v023n01_001_promoting_public_protection_through_an_attorney_integrity_system_lessons_from_the_australian_experience_with_proactive_regulation_of_lawyers.authcheckdam.pdf; and Susan Saab Fortney, "The Role of Ethics Audits in Improving Management Systems and Practices: An Empirical Examination of Management-Based Regulation of Law Firms," *St. Mary's Journal on Legal Malpractice and Ethics* 4 (2015): 112–49, http://ssrn.com/abstract=2660358.

23. Jayne Reardon, "Where Is Our Legal Profession Heading? (Part Two)," 2Civility, April 21, 2016, http://www.2civility.org/where-is-our-legal-profession-heading-part-two/.

*Chapter Three*

# The Adoption of Alternative Structures Will Jeopardize Self-Regulation of the Profession

Many have argued that allowing for alternative structures will jeopardize the self-regulation of the profession: "[T]here is a very real concern that legislatures or nonjudicial entities might claim a right to regulate this new form of practice."[1] Going further, many argue that the Australian and the English and Welsh experiences suggest that "allowing nonlawyers control over law firms—even if only in small measure—will pave the way for a fundamental reworking of the profession."[2] For this reason, some have argued, the door to nonlawyer ownership should not be opened "even a crack."[3]

In a number of countries, and notably in England and Wales and Australia, the legislature plays a significant if not principal role in the regulation of legal services. Indeed, the changes in those two countries that brought in new regulatory frameworks were the direct result of parliamentary acts. And, in England and Wales the reforms go even further: They decisively ended self-regulation of the legal profession by providing that neither the chair of the Legal Services Board (LSB, the oversight regulator in England and Wales), nor the majority of the governing board of the LSB may be lawyers.[4]

In the United States, the legal profession is often described as being self-regulated. However, the extent to which that is, in fact, the case has been a subject of dispute among academics and legal commentators.[5] Those that see a self-regulated profession point to the facts that:

- State supreme courts, who have the authority to adopt rules of professional conduct and the responsibility to enforce discipline, are made up of lawyers.[6]

- Most state supreme courts adopt the Model Rules of Professional Conduct promulgated and amended from time to time by the ABA with limited and, in many cases, no modifications. In this manner, the ABA, a voluntary association of practicing lawyers, plays a key role in the regulation of the legal profession. (Further, to the extent the rules are adopted with modifications, those modifications are generated by the state and local bar associations and other groups of practicing attorneys rather than by the state supreme courts themselves).
- State supreme courts have delegated disciplinary enforcement to bodies that are also made up of lawyers. And, most notably, in 21 states the state supreme courts have delegated disciplinary authority to a state bar association whose members are practicing lawyers and that exercises both representative and regulatory functions.[7]

On the other hand, those that do not see a self-regulated profession point to the facts that:

- While the members of state supreme courts are lawyers, they are not practicing attorneys. They have the authority to make decisions in a manner that is independent of national and state bar associations. While state supreme courts (usually after consultation with the ABA via the Conference of Chief Justices and with state and local bar associations) often adopt the ABA's Model Rules and while they often delegate disciplinary authority to a state bar association, there is no legal requirement that they do either, and they may at any time stop doing so.
- Other bodies have exercised authority over the legal profession. Examples include the US Supreme Court (such as by striking down bans on attorney advertising), federal regulatory authorities (such as the FTC and the SEC), and Congress (most notably with Sarbanes-Oxley).

It is not the purpose of this book to debate, much less resolve, the question of whether or not the legal profession in the United States is self-regulated. It is the purpose of this book to explore a new regulatory framework and the obstacles to adoption of alternative structures. From that perspective, setting aside the semantics of whether the legal profession in the United States is self-regulated, changing the regulatory framework with the consequences of permitting alternative structures will necessitate significant changes in the way that lawyers are regulated.

It is certainly possible that the ABA's House of Delegates might vote to adopt an entirely new regulatory framework, but it is highly unlikely. The ABA is the largest voluntary and representative organization of lawyers in the United States. Its members are not elected and the organization has no political accountability. Most of the members of it decision-making body, the

House of Delegates, are either selected or, in a few cases, elected, by state and local bar associations, and it is to those state and local bar associations that they are answerable.[8]

Today, the ABA combines both a representative function as well as a de facto regulatory one:

The ABA describes its mission as "tireless work" toward four goals, the very first two of which are to "serve our members" and "improve our profession."[9] Indeed, various groups of the ABA work extensively as representatives of the profession. A notable example is the ABA's Governmental Affairs Office—which lobbies in Washington, DC, to convey to national lawmakers "the Association's concerns and views on matters of importance to the legal profession,"[10] and to advocate for ABA policies as they are adopted by the ABA's "policy making body,"[11] the House of Delegates.

Alongside this significant representative role, the ABA plays a regulatory role, most notably its adoption and periodic review by the House of Delegates of the Model Rules of Professional Conduct: the rules serve as the model for the ethical rules adopted by nearly every state of the United States (all except California). In many cases, after consultation first with the ABA via the Conference of Chief Justices, and then with their respective state and local bar associations, the state supreme courts adopt the Model Rules with limited (and oftentimes no) modifications. This deference by the state supreme courts to the ABA House of Delegates gives the ABA a de facto regulatory role (not to mention the additional deference to state and local bar associations).[12] In other words, the ABA plays a regulatory role not because of any legal authority that it holds—it holds none—but because of the deference the ABA receives from those who do hold legal authority.

In her 2014 article "Globalization and the ABA Commission On Ethics 20/20: Reflections On Missed Opportunities and the Road Not Taken," Laurel Terry examines the work of this ABA commission that was charged with performing a "thorough" review of the Model Rules (including, but not limited to, Model Rule 5.4), as well as a review of the "US system of lawyer regulation in the context of advances in technology and global legal practice development."[13] In her examination, she describes the role of the ABA as a "quasi-regulator."[14] More particularly, she states that the ABA "wears two very different 'hats,'" one when it is acting as a trade group or a representative body of the legal profession, and the other, its "quasi-regulator" hat, when the ABA "endeavors to put aside member self-interest, and provide fair and balanced recommendations to regulators, knowing that the state courts that are the true lawyer regulators rely heavily on recommendations from the 'quasi-regulator' ABA."[15] When the ABA is wearing its "quasi-regulator" hat, Terry argues:

> I do not believe that anyone would seriously argue that when drafting Model Rules, it would be appropriate for the ABA to wear its "trade group" hat and promote the interests of its member lawyers over the interests of clients, the courts, or the public. In short, I believe that in light of the historic deference that has been given to Model Rules by regulators, when the ABA prepares model rules, it should not be acting with its "trade representative" hat on, nor should it try to advance the self-interest of its members. It should instead try to stand in the shoes of the regulators and develop well-balanced rules that properly take into account all of the competing interests. [16]

Assuming that Terry is right that no one would "seriously argue" that it would be appropriate (and it is not clear that she is right), it does not mean that it does not occur. More so, it does not mean that it did not occur with respect to the Ethics 20/20 Commission, and notably on the topic of alternative structures. To begin, when the commission called for comments on the topic, nearly all of the comments it received were from lawyers, speaking either individually as lawyers or on behalf of a group of lawyers, such as a committee of the ABA, a local bar association, a law firm, and, in one case, a group of general counsel of nine large corporations. [17] There is no indication that the commission made a serious effort (or, indeed, any effort at all) to obtain input from experts with respect to other "competing interests," such as those of economic policy, human rights, competition, consumer affairs... [18] Without obtaining that input, it is difficult to understand how the commission could take those interests into account in a meaningful way. Further, much of the input the commission did receive from the lawyers, again, speaking either individually or on behalf of a group, demonstrates a very strong if not exclusive focus on the perceived interests of lawyers. Here are some examples:

- "[T]his seems like nothing more than an effort by multinational law firms to maximize their profit making ability with little regard for how the rule change will impact the profession as a whole. We should not lose sight of the reality that 50 percent of the profession practices in a small firm or solo setting. Imagine how "nonlawyer" ownership will work on Main Street, USA." [19]
- "The [New Jersey State Bar Association] is greatly distrustful of any encroachment on attorneys' accountability and independent professional judgment, fearful of the temptation to appease nonattorney ownership interests, and concerned about the potential for confusion on the part of those dealing with the firm's principals." [20]
- "The Working Group has . . . gathered absolutely no evidence that nonlawyer ownership in firms even in the limited fashion proposed is desired by any material percentage of United States lawyers." [21]
- "Law is a profession, not a business. Thus, I am opposed to nonlawyer ownership." [22]

- "The proposals that have been offered for consideration have been given great public distribution resulting in the public perception that the profession is interested in allowing nonlawyers to invest in and own law firms. The commission should clearly state now that the profession is not for sale to the highest bidder. It can do nothing less than this."[23]

After receiving these comments and others like them, the Ethics 20/20 Commission rejected alternative structures. The only grounds the commission gave for its decision was that it had "considered the pros and cons" and "concluded that the case had not been made."[24] In his 2015 article "Towards the Law of Legal Services," Andrew Perlman, who acted as the chief reporter of the commission and thus had a front-row seat to the commission's activities, states:

> History offers a useful guide as to why the ABA House of Delegates was highly likely to reject any changes proposed by the Commission in this area. Since the Model Rules were adopted more than thirty years ago, the House of Delegates has repeatedly indicated its strong opposition to the idea of ABSs.[25]

Perlman explains that for the ABA House of Delegates, and for the Ethics 20/20 Commission in particular, the entire proposal of alternative structures was a "nonstarter" and that any proposal to allow them "would likely have failed."[26] He offered several reasons for this, including the "lack of empirical support for the idea that ABSs would benefit the public."[27] However, and much more persuasive than that, he explains, was the "significant political effort" on the part of state bar associations to oppose them,[28] and especially because "some members of the House of Delegates were opposed to change as a matter of principle," even if there had been evidence that change "would benefit the public without attendant harm."[29]

At the time this book went to press, the consultancy process of the ABA Commission on the Future of Legal Services on the topic of alternative structures (indeed, on any topic) gave little indication that it would be different from that of the Ethics 20/20 Commission. Like the Ethics 20/20 Commission, nearly all of the comments it received were from lawyers, speaking either individually as lawyers or on behalf of a group of lawyers, notably bar associations. Further, there is no indication that the Commission on the Future of Legal Services made a serious effort (or, indeed, any effort at all) to obtain input from experts with respect to the other "competing interests" that Terry admonished should be taken into account. Finally, the input that the Commission on the Future of Legal Services received from the lawyers went much further than simply demonstrating a focus on the perceived interests of lawyers: Many of the submissions rejected outright the idea that the interests of anyone else had equal value, if, indeed, any value at all. Here are some examples:

- "The ABA is in the midst of a membership crisis . . . which is creating a severe financial strain . . . which will inevitably dictate cuts in service to our members which will cause us to continue to bleed members. I do not think that this particular proposal helps us in that regard. . . . While the stated goals might be laudable, I think the ABA continues to push dues paying members away with the executive decisions we make and the policies we adopt. Goal 1 of the Association is service to our members."[30]
- "It appears that ABA is choosing to disregard a core principle of its mission statement: serving as the national representative of the legal profession. The ABA's very existence is founded on representing a profession, not corporate sponsors. The ABA should not even consider serving as the agent for venture capitalists and nonlawyers that are seeking to profit from the public at any cost."[31]
- "Goal 1 of the ABA's mission to service our members cannot be ignored or marginalized. [The commission's Issues Paper regarding alternative business structures] seems to stray from the core of ABA Goal 1 and risks further alienation of our membership."[32]
- "For the ABA to even consider allowing nonlawyer ownership of law firms causes me and many of my colleagues' [sic] great concern. I am absolutely against such an alternative business structure as proposed. I have been a long-time member of the ABA. I am strongly considering not renewing my membership."[33]
- "Please do not put the House of Delegates through another bruising battle. It will only result in the American Bar Association enduring yet another decline in membership as our profession views the ABA as having lost its way, losing the respect it once had when giants like Robert MacCrate[34] defended our eternal values and principles and lawyers proudly displayed their ABA membership certificate on their office walls."[35]
- "I am absolutely astounded that something this significant could be proposed by the ABA without a careful market survey of its constituents. . . . The ABA is losing touch with its constituents. The current political climate clearly demonstrates the voters' total dissatisfaction with leadership which has disconnected from constituents. . . . This type of proposal leads me to believe that the ABA may be losing touch with its core values, its mission and the needs of its constituents—the lawyers in the profession."[36]
- "I urge the ABA to stand tall for the profession and the future of the profession. Reject any attempt to allow nonlawyers [to] own some or all of a law firm."[37]

- "The American Bar Association is an organization which should promote and preserve the professional essence of what it means to be a lawyer. I trust it will live true to its mission and reject the ABS proposal."[38]
- "As a bar organization, how about proposing ideas that will help lawyers—not nonlawyers?"[39]

The comments below merit particular attention, because they were submitted by persons who identified themselves as members of the House of Delegates:

- "[T]he ABA is losing membership and money. From a purely self-preservation perspective, we are more likely to have members drop from adopting and seemingly promoting these ABS recommendations than gain constituents. You are making it harder for me to entice lawyers into joining the ABA than to disavow it. Lawyers want to be part of a professional association that lobbies for them, not against them."[40]
- "Goal 1 of the ABA is to serve its members and such changes would not."[41]

The comments above strongly rebuke the commission simply for having raised the issue of alternative structures. These comments demonstrate that many associated with the ABA (including at least two members of the House of Delegates) either are not familiar with or have chosen to disregard—if not reject—Terry's admonition that "when the ABA prepares model rules, it should not be acting with its 'trade representative' hat on, nor should it try to advance the self-interest of its members."[42]

A dual representative and regulatory role in the same body is something to which David Clementi, in England and Wales, strongly objected. In the Clementi Report he wrote:

> It is difficult to understand how one body can effectively both regulate a profession and also represent and lobby for its interests without prejudice to either its regulatory or representative functions. There is a conflict of interest between the two roles which should be tackled. In a regulatory body the public interest should have primacy. Issues such as changes in practice rules should be examined, not against the wishes of the membership, but against the test of public interest. . . .[43]
>
> It is particularly difficult for professional bodies who combine both regulatory and representative roles to deal with competition issues. Regulatory bodies should be expected to encourage open competition, subject to maintaining quality standards; representative bodies have a legitimate right to fight their corner, warning that the public may suffer if the market is opened too widely. This is a difficult set of conflicting issues for one body to balance. . . .[44]
>
> [With respect to the Law Society,] changes to practices rules have been held back by the difficulty of getting it though its large representative Council.

> [With respect to the Bar Council,] there is little evidence that the Bar has been a force for innovation in customs and practice.[45]

Is the ABA—and, in particular, its House of Delegates—the right organization to determine what is in the public interest? What is appropriate for open competition? Does the ABA—a private organization that is accountable only to state and local bar associations—have the objectivity, the expertise, and the resources to make these determinations, in the absence of effective oversight of any governmental body that has political accountability to the public at large? Further, state and local bar associations and other groups of practicing attorneys who do not have political accountability also play pivotal roles in the process—are they the right persons and do they have the necessary objectivity, expertise, and resources to make decisions of this kind—which have profound repercussions not just for all lawyers but also for the public and for the country as a whole? At least two persons would respond "no" to these questions.[46]

The first person who would respond "no" is James Moliterno. In his book *The American Legal Profession in Crisis: Resistance and Responses to Change*, Moliterno does not directly pose the question of whether or not the legal profession is self-regulated. On the other hand, in asking who speaks for the legal profession, he makes the observation that:

> Actions of courts and legislatures in their supervision of the legal profession continue to be a useful source of information about the views of the legal profession. Many such actions are taken at the behest of the profession itself and are adopted by lawyer-dominated institutions.[47]

In his book, Moliterno examines in-depth a number of "crises" that the legal profession faced in the twentieth and early twenty-first centuries, such as the immigration rush of the early twentieth century, the communist infiltration, the civil rights movement, Watergate, and globalization and technology. In examining how the legal profession, and, in particular, the ABA, reacted to each crises, Moliterno makes this finding:

> Calm in the face of crisis is an attractive trait. . . . [T]he profession's reaction to crisis varied by the nature of the crisis but always served maintenance of the professional status quo. When outsiders threatened to invade the bar's homogeneity, the profession reacted harshly and often without much reflection. . . . By contrast, when social, economic or technological change was occurring around the profession, the profession's calm became intractability and myopia. . . . In either event, the profession sought the status quo and resisted 'innovation and change that was being demanded,' even when change was inevitable or desirable.[48]

As a result of this finding, Moliterno posits this thesis:

> [T]he profession too often looks inward to diagnose and solve its crises. Doing so has caused the profession to be a late-arriving member of society during times of change. Doing so has caused the profession too often to fail in what could have been a leadership role in society. Rather, the profession has too often seen itself as a last bastion of a prior time, clinging too tightly to its past and failing to grow in step with world developments. This is not to say that the profession should dismiss its core attributes at the first sign of societal change; it is to say that a perceptive growing with change would be preferable to consistent, persistent resistance to change. We credit the greatest lawyers with being able to anticipate and predict the course of the law's change and the readiness of society for such change. The legal profession has been a poor lawyer by this measure. The legal profession, as an institution, most often stays blind to change that is happening all around it.[49]

The second person who would respond "no" is Toby Brown. As a participant on a panel on the future of the legal profession for the National Conference of Bar Presidents, which discussed, in part, Washington State's new Limited License Legal Technicians (LLLTs, discussed further in part IV), he reported his experience as follows:

> [The panel began with a presentation of LLLT]. The audience focused in on the details of the LLLT program, trying to poke holes in it. This audience was made up of Bar Presidents and Executive Directors. These people are well positioned to drive change across the profession. But instead of talking about how they could adopt similar changes in an accelerated fashion, they were looking for ways to kill it.
>
> I sat there as long as I could listening to this. Finally I could take it no longer and interjected. I "suggested" that a failure to drive disruptions would lead to others moving in and taking over the legal market. . . .
>
> After the presentation a number of attendees from state bars sat down to chat with me about all of this. A universal theme was that whatever they might do to disrupt the market and drive innovation will be met with strong resistance by the bar membership. As I see it, bar associations have little to gain by pushing on this issue, even though they have a lot to lose by doing nothing. Their members will not abide any efforts short of turning the clock back. I gave numerous suggestions for how a bar might drive change to the group. All were met with exacerbation and a recognition that any efforts will be met with broad and strong resistance.
>
> For a long time I have held out hope that the legal profession would step up and address the needs of the market: for both lawyers and clients. After this experience, I have come to the hard conclusion: *That is not going to happen.* As smart as lawyers are, their training and experience have made them a reactive and dogmatic group. In their minds, the way they have been doing it is the only way to keep doing it. Anything else is a threat to the profession and their practice specifically.[50]

The ABA (which, again, is answerable only to state and local bar associations) has the power to ban alternative structures only because the governmental bodies that have or could assert the power to end the ban choose not to act.

As unlikely as it is to happen, what if the ABA did try to put in place a new regulatory framework—one that governed not only lawyers but also other actors: entities as well as individuals who are not lawyers? If they did so, it is likely that someone would object. After all, what could justify the ABA—again, a private, unelected organization of lawyers—exercising any kind of regulatory power over persons who are not lawyers? That being said, it is not entirely clear who could act in the ABA's place, nor how they could do so.

In the United States, legal services, or, at least, the legal profession, are regulated at the state level. While there are many similarities among the states in this regard, there are also many differences that make it difficult to generalize, let alone clearly identify the authorities with the power to act. One important difference is the fact that while 18 states have a voluntary bar association, the other 32 (plus the District of Columbia) have unified (or integrated) bars.[51] The difference is this: In states with a voluntary bar association, the *de jure* regulatory authority (that is, the authority accorded by law) lies with a governmental entity, in most cases the state's supreme court or another governmental authority to whom the court has delegated authority. Regardless, that entity does not represent the interests of the members of the bar. Instead, that function is filled by one or more separate, nongovernmental associations of lawyers, and for the lawyers of that state, membership in any such association in voluntary.

In contrast, in states with a unified (or integrated) bar, lawyers are required to be members of the state bar organization, and this organization combines both regulatory and representative functions. To add to the complexity, there are significant differences in the manner by which authority is allocated between the supreme courts of these states and their unified bars: in some states the authority is held by the supreme court who delegates it to the unified bar (and who, theoretically, could withdraw that delegation at any time), in some states the unified bar holds its authority by virtue of a legislative act, and, in one state, California, the unified bar is recognized in the state's constitution.

In the 18 states that have a voluntary bar association,[52] the most obvious bodies that could assert power to change the regulatory framework, and thereby end abdication to the ABA, are the state supreme courts. In those eighteen states, the authority of state supreme courts to adopt rules that are different from the ABA's Model Rules is clear. It is the state supreme courts that, to date, have chosen to take a mostly passive role. A number of reasons have been suggested for this choice: because judges believe that the formulation of the rules is best left to the ABA, because the development of abstract rules is something judges are not comfortable doing (they are comfortable responding to concrete cases), because the state supreme courts do not have the resources to conduct legislative-like research and hearings.

As regards the thirty-two states (as well as the District of Columbia) that have unified (integrated) bars, the situation is less clear. In some of these states, the supreme court retains responsibility for rule-making, with the bar organization responsible for enforcement. But in other states with a unified bar, it is the bar organization that not only enforces the rules, but also formulates them, subject, at most, to the approval of the state's supreme court. In these states, it is not at all clear that the state supreme court has any real power to adopt rules with which the bar does not agree. In the end, whatever the explanation may be, the fact that state supreme courts do not play an active role in the formulation of the rules is an important reason behind the de facto regulatory power of the ABA.[53]

Outside of the ABA and state supreme courts, there are, at least in theory, other bodies that could also assert authority to put in place a new regulatory framework. These include: (i) state executive and/or legislative branches, on the grounds that they are regulating not attorney conduct but consumer services and corporate structures, (ii) federal agencies, such as the FTC, on the grounds that they are regulating not attorney conduct but restrictions on competition, and (iii) the executive and/or the legislative branches of the federal government, on the grounds that they are regulating not attorney conduct but trade and commerce, economic policy, and the protection of human rights.[54] Of course, unlike state supreme courts, if any of these bodies did attempt to assert their authority in this manner, it would not go unchallenged: The bar, and notably the ABA, has on a number of occasions formally challenged the right of any governmental body, other than state supreme courts, to attempt to regulate lawyers in any manner.

In spite of the challenges, some potential actors—particularly the FTC[55]—may feel emboldened by the February 2015 decision of the US Supreme Court in *North Carolina Board of Dental Examiners v. FTC*. In this case, the North Carolina dental board, consisting mostly of practicing dentists, took certain actions to keep nondentists from offering teeth-whitening services in North Carolina. The FTC sued the dental board under federal antitrust laws, claiming anticompetitive conduct. However, the issue before the US Supreme Court was not if the actions of the dental board were anticompetitive. Instead, the issue was whether the dental board was acting under a doctrine that would give it, as a "state actor," immunity from claims of anticompetitive conduct in violation of federal antitrust law. The dental board claimed that is was a state actor and thus was eligible for such immunity, on the grounds that an act of the North Carolina legislature appointed the dental board as the "agency of the State for the regulation of the practice of dentistry."[56] The Court, however, disagreed, stating that "active market participants cannot be allowed to regulate their own markets free from antitrust accountability"[57] and that "prohibitions against anticompetitive self-regulation by active market participants are an axiom of federal antitrust policy."[58] Additionally, the Supreme Court stated, "The question is not whether the challenged conduct is efficient, well-functioning, or wise. . . . [t]he question is whether the State's review mechanisms provide 'realistic assurance' that a [private party]'s anticompetitive conduct 'promotes state policy, rather than merely the party's individual interests.'"[59] While this case involved the dental rather than the legal profession, the decision of the court is highly pertinent for the legal profession. It places anticompetitive actions by any group of "active market participants"—such as bar associations—under intensified scrutiny.[60]

Challenging the regulatory power of the ABA should not be confused with advocating for the loss of independence of the legal profession. Again, the ABA's regulatory power is only *de facto*—the ABA has regulatory power only because the state supreme courts decline, for the most part, to exercise their *de jure* regulatory powers (that is, the powers accorded to them by law), and notably because they decline to take a more active role in the formulation of the rules that govern the legal profession. At the same time, a principal justification offered for vesting *de jure* regulatory authority in state supreme courts is in order to maintain the legal profession's independence from the government. Seen from this context, it is difficult to understand how state supreme courts asserting a more active role not only in rule formulation but also in creating a new regulatory framework would result in the loss of independence of the legal profession, or of legal services providers more generally.

Further, the example of England and Wales shows that it is possible to establish regulatory bodies and procedures that permit the legal service providers to remain independent—not only of the representative interests of the legal profession and of the government but also of the courts, all while maintaining political accountability. With respect to solicitors, England and Wales has done this in two steps:

- By removing the regulatory function of the Law Society and placing it into a newly created Solicitors Regulation Authority (SRA), leaving the Law Society as a purely representative body (or nearly so[61]).
- By placing both the SRA and the Law Society, as well as other regulators of legal services, under the authority of a newly created regulatory oversight body, the Legal Services Board (LSB), whose members consist of a chairman, appointed by the Lord Chancellor, and between seven and ten "ordinary" members (the majority of which must be nonlawyers), ap-

pointed by the Lord Chancellor in consultation with the Lord Chief Justice.[62]

Under this structure, the LSB has political accountability—to the Parliament, via the Lord Chancellor, and under the "sponsorship" of the Ministry of Justice—yet the LSB remains independent of the state (that is, free of political influence or pressure by the government in power).

Self-regulation of the legal profession and independence of the legal profession from the state are not synonymous terms—there is no reason why challenging the power of the ABA to regulate legal services will necessarily result in ending the independence of the legal profession from the state (that is, in leaving the legal profession vulnerable to political influence or pressure by the government). The work of creating a new regulatory framework for legal services can and should include a review of the existing regulatory bodies to ensure that they operate independently of both the profession and the state. England and Wales provides just one example of how that can be done.

## STORIES

### (PART V OR ONLINE)

*John Ray, Senior Consultant, Law Firm Consulting Group* (online): Ray explains that, with respect to Model Rule 5.4, the decision makers of the ABA have a conflict of interest because the large corporations that the decision makers, as lawyers, represent have a vested interest in opposing alternative structures.

*Sir David Clementi* (Part V): Clementi rejects self-regulation of the legal profession on the grounds that regulation is a public service. For that reason, and like the regulation of all other service providers, it should be carried out in the interest of the public and be independent of representation of the profession.

*John Briton, Former Legal Services Commissioner, Queensland* (online): Briton argues that a membership body will always find it difficult if not impossible to take regulatory action that its members perceive to be a threat to their livelihoods, no matter how great the benefit to the public may be.

*Darrel Pink, Executive Director, Nova Scotia Barristers' Society* (online): Pink argues that a lesson from England and Wales and from Australia is that it's not about self-regulation, but about independent and professional regulation.

# NOTES

1. Chandler et al., "Comments of Nine General Counsel," 6. See also: DRI—The Voice of the Defense Bar, 5; Texas Association of Defense Counsel et al, "Comment and Opposition by Texas Association of Defense Counsel, Texas Trial Lawyers Association, and Texas Chapters of the American Board of Trial Advocates on Alternate Business Structures," May 4, 2016, 1, http://www.americanbar.org/content/dam/aba/images/office_president/texas_association_of_defense_counsel_abs.pdf.

2. Ibid., 5.

3. Ibid., 2.

4. "Framework Document: Agreement between the Ministry of Justice and the Legal Services Board," June, 2011, 8, http://www.legalservicesboard.org.uk/about_us/lsb_framework_document/pdf/moj_framework_agreement_june_2011.pdf.

5. On this topic generally, see Fred C. Zacharias, "The Myth of Self-Regulation," *Minnesota Law Review* 93 (2009): 1147–90, http://www.minnesotalawreview.org/wp-content/uploads/2012/01/Zacharias_MLR.pdf.

6. See, for example, Benjamin H. Barton, "Do Judges Systematically Favor the Interests of the Legal Profession?" University of Tennessee Legal Studies Research Paper No. 1, 2007, 8–9, http://ssrn.com/abstract=976478.

7. Judith L. Maute, "Global Continental Shifts in a New Governance Paradigm in Lawyer Regulation and Consumer Protection: Riding the Wave," in *Alternative Perspectives on Lawyers and Legal Ethics: Reimagining the Profession*, ed. Francesca Bartlett, Reid Mortensen, and Kieran Tranter (London: Routledge, 2011), 30.

8. Andrew Perlman describes the state bar associations as "important constituencies" for the House of Delegates. Perlman, "Towards the Law," 78.

9. "ABA Mission and Goals," American Bar Association, accessed August 21, 2015, http://www.americanbar.org/about_the_aba/aba-mission-goals.html.

10. "Governmental Affairs Office," American Bar Association, accessed August 21, 2015, http://www.americanbar.org/groups/departments_offices/government_affairs_office.html.

11. "ABA House of Delegates," American Bar Association, accessed August 21, 2015, http://www.americanbar.org/groups/leadership/house_of_delegates.html.

12. Schneyer has described the "professional conduct systems for lawyers" in the United States as "professional self-regulation," notably due to the magnitude of the role played by the ABA. See Schneyer, "The Case for Proactive Management-Based Self-Regulation."

13. Laurel S. Terry, "Globalization and the ABA Commission on Ethics 20/20: Reflections on Missed Opportunities and the Road Not Taken," *Hofstra Law Review* 43 (2014): 95, http://www.hofstralawreview.org/wp-content/uploads/2015/01/BB.3.Terry_.final2_.pdf

14. Ibid., 117.

15. Ibid.

16. Ibid., 117–18.

17. A list of and links to the submissions are available at the ABA website: "Alternative Law Practice Structures Comments Chart—Last Updated 8/28/2012," http://www.americanbar.org/content/dam/aba/administrative/ethics_2020/alps_working_group_comments_chart.authcheckdam.pdf. Certainly some of the comments attempt to address other interests (in particular, Responsive Law attempts to address the interests of consumers of legal services), but the fact remains that nearly all of the comments were submitted by lawyers.

18. This failure accords with Devlin and Morison's reflection that the governance of legal services in the United States is a "monologue rather than a dialogue" overwhelmingly dominated by the ABA. Devlin and Morison, "Access to Justice," 527.

19. Murrell, "Ethics 20/20 Non-lawyer Ownership of Law Firms."

20. New Jersey State Bar Association, Comment Submitted to ABA Commission on Ethics 20/20, January 31, 2012, 1, http://www.americanbar.org/content/dam/aba/administrative/ethics_2020/ethics_20_20_comments/njstatebarassociation_alpsdiscussiondraft.authcheckdam.pdf.

21. Douglas R. Richmond, "Discussion Paper on Alternative Law Practice Structures," January 6, 2012, 1, http://www.americanbar.org/content/dam/aba/administrative/ethics_2020

/ethics_20_20_comments/richmond_alpsdiscussiondraft.authcheckdam.pdf.

22. Ruffin, Comment Submitted to ABA Commission on Ethics 20/20.

23. Richard L. Thies, Letter to the ABA Commission on Ethics 20/20, February 23, 2012, 4, http://www.americanbar.org/content/dam/aba/administrative/ethics_2020/ethics_20_20_comments/thies_alpsdiscussiondraft.authcheckdam.pdf.

24. ABA Commission on Ethics 20/20, "ABA Commission on Ethics 20/20 Will Not Propose Changes."

25. Perlman, "Towards the Law," 75.

26. Ibid.

27. Ibid., 78.

28. Ibid.

29. Ibid., 79. With these words alone, Perlman proves Terry wrong: By failing to condemn this attitude by those members of the House of Delegates, Perlman implies that it can be appropriate for the ABA to wear its "trade group" hat when the ABA prepares Model Rules. Indeed, Perlman's account is as interesting for what it says as it is for what it does not say. At no point does Perlman question either: (i) the process the ABA followed (for example, that no significant input was sought or received from persons outside the legal profession (such as experts in economic policy, competition, human rights, consumer affairs, . . .) nor (ii) the legitimacy of the ABA's regulatory power in this regard.

30. Forum on the Entertainment and Sports Law Industries, "ABA Commission on the Future of Legal Services—Issues Paper on Alternative Business Structures/Comments Requested," May 3, 2016, http://www.americanbar.org/content/dam/aba/images/office_president/entertainment_and_sports_abs.pdf.

31. Middlesex County Bar Association, "Issues Paper Regarding Alternative Business Structures," May 6, 2016, 3, http://www.americanbar.org/content/dam/aba/images/office_president/middlesex_county_bar_association_abs.pdf.

32. Tort Trial and Insurance Practice Section, "ABA Commission on the Future of Legal Services / Issue Paper Regarding Alternative Business Structures," May 6, 2016, 1, http://www.americanbar.org/content/dam/aba/images/office_president/tips_abs.pdf.

33. Leonard R. Grossman, "Alternative Business Structure Proposal of the ABA," May 2, 2016, http://www.americanbar.org/content/dam/aba/images/office_president/leonard_r_grossman_abs.pdf.

34. Robert MacCrate, a former President of the ABA, is credited as the driving force behind the resolution that the ABA House of Delegates adopted in 2000 stating: "The sharing of legal fees with nonlawyers and the ownership and control of the practice of law by nonlawyers are inconsistent with the core values of the legal profession. The law governing lawyers, that prohibits lawyers from sharing legal fees with nonlawyers and from directly or indirectly transferring to nonlawyers ownership or control over entities practicing law, should not be revised." See John Gibeaut, "'It's a Done Deal': House of Delegates Vote Crushes Chances for MDP," *ABA Journal* 9 (2000): 92–93, http://www.jstor.org/stable/27841689; Paul D. Paton, "Multidisciplinary Practice Redux: Globalization, Core Values, and Reviving the MDP Debate in America," *Fordham Law Review* 78 (2010): 2209, http://ir.lawnet.fordham.edu/cgi/viewcontent.cgi?article=4527andcontext=flr.

35. Lawrence J. Fox, "What Would Bob MacCrate Think?", 2016, http://www.americanbar.org/content/dam/aba/images/office_president/lawrence_j_fox_abs.pdf.

36. Henry Mills Gallivan, "ABA Proposal in Alternative Business Structures," April 28, 2016, http://www.americanbar.org/content/dam/aba/images/office_president/henry_mills_gallivan_abs.pdf.

37. Benjamin H. Hill, III, "Non-Lawyer Ownership of Law Firms," April 25, 2016, http://www.americanbar.org/content/dam/aba/images/office_president/benjamin_j_hill_abs.pdf.

38. James T. Murphy, "Comment: Issues Paper Regarding Alternative Business Stuctures [sic]," April 26, 2016, http://www.americanbar.org/content/dam/aba/images/office_president/james_t_murphy_abs.pdf.

39. Christopher G. Betke, "Proposal for ABS," April 28, 2016, http://www.americanbar.org/content/dam/aba/images/office_president/christopher_g_betke_abs.pdf.

40. Laura Bellegie Sharp, "Comments Regarding the Alternative Business Solutions Issues Paper," April 28, 2016, 2, http://www.americanbar.org/content/dam/aba/images/office_president/laura_sharp_abs.pdf. Sharp further wrote:

> My Austin Bar Association, who I represent in the HOD, has strongly and repeatedly indicated that I oppose all measures to allow any nonlawyer participation in law firms. Pursuant to those directives, and while they permit me to represent them in the HOD, I will fight any measure to dilute the practice of law that would allow in any way nonattorneys to participate as owners of firms. . . . However, even if they did not, I as an individual member of the ABA and legal profession strongly object to the repeated attacks by what most of us see as a subsection of the ABA who have members that are promoting ideas that only benefit the few…How will small town attorneys and small law firms compete? They will not be able to, they will find something else to do. Law schools will have even further declining enrollment because only LaWmart and the largest law firms will be hiring. The brightest students will not apply to law schools because the LaWmart pay will be too low to ever pay their student loans. We might as well just go ahead and "kill all the lawyers" rather than subject them to a lingering death by attrition. Ibid., 1–2.

41. Paula Hudson Holderman, "Commentary on the Report from the ABA's Commission on the Future of Legal Services," April 27, 2016, http://www.americanbar.org/content/dam/aba/images/office_president/paula_hudson_holderman_abs.pdf.
42. Terry, "Globalization and the ABA Commission on Ethics 20/20," 95.
43. Clementi Report, 27–28.
44. Ibid., 29.
45. Ibid., 29–30.
46. At least one group would also respond no: the OECD. In a 2016 Issues Paper, it wrote:

> [L]egal professional self-regulators may be unable, or ill-suited, to identify accommodations that permit innovative entrants to serve consumers…there is the possibility that incumbents engage in anticompetitive behaviour to prevent innovative new entrants from accessing their markets. There is a risk that legal professional organisations may act to maintain the traditional market structure and business model of the legal services industry in a manner that exceeds their regulatory mandate. Organisation for Economic Co-operation and Development, "Protecting and Promoting Competition," 2, 12.

47. Moliterno, *The American Legal Profession in Crisis,* 13.
48. Ibid., 3.
49. Ibid., 4.
50. Toby Brown, "The Legal Profession is Doomed," *3 Geeks and a Law Blog*, February 10, 2015, http://www.geeklawblog.com/2015/02/the-profession-is-doomed.html?utm_content=buffera11a0andutm_medium=socialandutm_source=twitter.comandutm_campaign=buffer.
51. Maute, "Global Continental Shifts," 30. But also see Barton, "Do Judges Systematically Favor," 10, stating that there are unified bars in 36 states plus the District of Columbia.
52. Those states are Arkansas, Colorado, Delaware, Illinois, Indiana, Iowa, Maine, Kansas, Massachusetts, Minnesota, New Hampshire, New Jersey, New York, Ohio, Pennsylvania, Rhode Island, Tennessee, and Vermont.
53. See, for example, Benjamin H. Barton, "The Lawyer's Monopoly—What Goes and What Stays," *Fordham Law Review* 82 (2014): 3080–81, http://ir.lawnet.fordham.edu/cgi/viewcontent.cgi?article=5008andcontext=flr.
54. Hadfield and Rhode argue in favor of a single, national licensing authority for entities combined with certain state-based regulatory powers, notably for lawyers as individuals. Hadfield and Rhode, "How to Regulate Legal Services," 40–48.

55. The FTC should also feel emboldened by a 2016 OECD Issues Paper, which urges (if not exhorts) competition authorities to advocate "in favour of pro-competitive professional regulations that reflect market realities [including] advocating for the opening up of markets which may not yet be accessible to disruptive innovators." The Paper encourages competition authorities to undertake market studies "assessing the degree to which legal services professional regulations affect competition, and whether there are alternative regulatory approaches with fewer competition impacts." Organisation for Economic Co-operation and Development, "Protecting and Promoting Completion," 13, 14.

56. *North Carolina State Board of Dental Examiners v. Federal Trade Commission*, February 15, 2015, 6, http://www.supremecourt.gov/opinions/14pdf/13-534_19m2.pdf.

57. Ibid., 8.

58. Ibid., 2.

59. Ibid., 9.

60. See, for example, Hadfield and Rhode, "How to Regulate Legal Services," 6, 37-38. See also Ken Friedman, "Could Dental-Board Decision Unlock Lawyer Control of State Bar Regulations?" *Forbes*, March 4, 2015, http://www.forbes.com/sites/danielfisher/2015/03/04/dental-board-decision-could-unlock-lawyer-control/#75de2e7b68cf.; and Tamara Tabo, "What Lawyers Must Learn From Dentists About The Unauthorized Practice Of Law," *Above the Law*, March 2, 2015, http://abovethelaw.com/2015/03/what-lawyers-must-learn-from-dentists-about-the-unauthorized-practice-of-law/?rf=1.

61. At the time this book went to press, the SRA operated as the "independent regulatory arm" of the Law Society, but not as an independent legal entity. In November 2015, the Ministry of Justice announced that it will conduct a consultation with the view, in part, to complete the separation of the SRA from the Law Society. See Nick Hilborne, "Separation Would be Better for Both of Us, SRA Leaders Tell Law Society," *Legal Futures*, December 3, 2015, http://www.legalfutures.co.uk/latest-news/separation-would-be-better-for-both-of-us-sra-leaders-tell-law-society.

62. "Framework Document: Agreement Between the Ministry of Justice and the Legal Services Board." See also "LSB Framework Document," Legal Services Board, accessed August 22, 2015, http://www.legalservicesboard.org.uk/about_us/lsb_framework_document/index.htm.

## *Chapter Four*

# There is No Demonstrated Need, Demand, or Problem

Some have argued that there is no demonstrated need or demand for alternative structures in the United States.[1] They say "the case has yet to be made that there is a problem with the ability of American law firms to deliver legal services,"[2] that there is no "evidence that US law firms are hampered in serving their clients because they are prohibited from organizing alternative business structures,"[3] or that "alternative structures are a solution in search of a problem."[4]

Rejecting alternative structures on the grounds that there is no demonstrated need or demand for them is buggy whip mentality: That is, when cars were invented, no one was asking for a car and no one could have demonstrated a need for one; instead, you would have heard requests for a better buggy whip or, in words attributed to Henry Ford, requests for a faster horse. Similarly, at the time personal computers and cell phones were invented, no one could have demonstrated a need or demand for those, either. No one could have done so because very few people had ever conceived of the existence of such objects, or of how they could be used. The same is true in the case of alternative structures. But in this case, the challenge is even greater because alternative structures cannot be produced in three-dimensional prototypes for easy viewing and physical manipulation. Instead, they are an intellectual concept, and they require a significant intellectual investment in order to fully understand what they are and how they can be used. Those who have not (yet) made that intellectual investment (whether by choice or by lack of opportunity to do so) simply are not in a position to affirm or deny a need or demand for them, either expressly or implicitly. The argument that alternative structures should not be permitted because there is no demonstrated need or demand for them is based upon the false assumption that such structures are widely known and understood in the United States and have been widely rejected on the basis of that understanding.

Further, of those people who have made the intellectual investment necessary to understand alternative structures, many have expressed a need or a demand for them. Here are just some examples:

1. Responsive Law, a not-for-profit organization that "work[s] to make the legal system more affordable, accessible, and accountable to the people it is meant to serve,"[5] has formally commented on a number of occasions in support of alternative structures: twice to the ABA Commission on Ethics 20/20,[6] twice to the ABA Commission on the Future of Legal Services,[7] to the Task Force to Expand Access to Civil Legal Services in New York,[8] and, finally, to California's Civil Justice Strategies Task Force.[9] In its comments, Responsive Law states:

> [P]rohibitions on fee sharing between lawyers and nonlawyers have prevented much of the innovation that could result in more affordable legal services. There are numerous lawyers and nonlawyers who have ideas for improving the way legal services are delivered but who lack access to sufficient capital to implement those ideas.[10]
>
> [W]e can confirm that consumers nationwide would welcome the lower prices and new combinations of services that true innovation in the delivery of legal services would bring. . . . For example; if true MDP were allowed, partnerships between social workers and family lawyers or between financial advisors and tax lawyers could create new service models benefiting the large majority of the public that currently has limited access to the legal system.[11]

2. In her article "The Cost of Law: Promoting Access to Justice through the (Un)Corporate Practice of Law," Gillian Hadfield states that "as a matter of economic policy, it is essential that the legal profession abandon the prohibition on the corporate practice of law."[12] She argues that there is no humanly possible amount of legal aid and pro bono work that can satisfy the unmet need for legal services in the United States, and that it is only by permitting alternative structures that there is a chance of addressing the country's access to justice problem.

3. In her article "Democratizing the Delivery of Legal Services," Renee Knake argues not only that restrictions on the delivery of legal services by corporations violates the First Amendment as an unconstitutional restriction on free speech, but also that lifting the restrictions is necessary in order to make legal services available to the masses of people in the United States today who do not have access to them. She argues that it is only corporations, and not sole practitioners or law firms, who are in a position to develop rigorous processes and systems that can lower the cost and efficiency of "low-end" legal services, thus making them available to a much larger number of people. In sum, Knake argues, corporate ownership and investment in

legal services is a viable solution to the "dire access-to-justice problem facing the United States."[13]

4. In their 2000 article "Multidisciplinary Practice and the American Legal Profession: A Market Approach to Regulating the Delivery of Legal Services in the Twenty-First Century," John S. Dzienkowski and Robert J. Peroni argue that the ban on multidisciplinary practices is economic protectionism by the bar that is counter to the public interest. They propose a variety of models for multidisciplinary practices in the United States, and suggest how the rules of professional responsibility can be modified in order to accommodate multidisciplinary practices while still preserving the core values of the legal profession.[14]

5. In his article "Non-Lawyers Owning Law Firms," Steven Benathen calls for removing restrictions on nonlawyer ownership, arguing that the lack of opportunities for law graduates is due at least in part to the restrictive model under which lawyers are obliged to operate.[15] Because of dwindling work, partners are loathe to let new members into their ranks, as this will lower their incomes. More specifically, Benathen argues:

> Liberalizing firm ownership could change the playing field. . . . Psychologically in the work place, the vaunted status of equity partner might have a different meaning if nonlawyers could have ownership of the firm. Simply put, the expectations of young associates would be far different if firm ownership extended beyond the firm. Nonequity partnership would hardly carry the sting it seems to today. Firms could in turn divert their revenue more efficiently toward paying fixed salaries. If shares of law firms went on the market, equity partners might be enticed to cash out. As partners departed, associates advancing toward partnership could all be placed on a nonequity track with the option to purchase shares of the firm. The opportunity to obtain a share of the firm's revenue would still exist but without the superficial layer of prestige. Additionally, outside investing would presumably allow for businessmen to become part of the management of law firms. Excellent lawyers are not always excellent businessmen; management might actually find itself in more capable hands.[16]

6. A final example of an expressed need and demand for alternative structures: In 2011 the law firm Jacoby and Meyers brought litigation against authorities in New Jersey, New York, and Connecticut requesting that the enforcement of the "antiquated" ethical rule that restricts nonlawyer ownership of law firms be enjoined.[17] Among its multiple arguments, J&M asserted the rule violates the state constitutions, violates the separation of powers, is void for vagueness, and is an excessive burden on the flow of interstate commerce.

J&M argued that the rule prevented it from raising the capital necessary to pay for improvements in technology and infrastructure, to expand its offices, and to hire additional personnel. As a result of its restricted access to funding, suffered as well by other law firms, J&M argued that access to legal services for those otherwise unable to afford them was dramatically impeded. (In July 2014, the firm voluntarily dismissed its New Jersey litigation. In Connecticut, the litigation has been placed on hold pending resolution of the New York litigation. In July 2015, a lower New York federal court granted the defendants' motion to dismiss J&M's complaint, ruling that J&M's "constitutional challenges are entirely without merit."[18] J&M is appealing that decision.)

Finally, a demand for alternative structures is also demonstrated indirectly, in the contorted business and service models that companies have been obliged to adopt in order to not run afoul of the rules. Here are two examples:

Axiom Law: Axiom Law has on its roster over 500 lawyers that it offers to its customers for legal insourcing, outsourcing, and project management services. Axiom markets itself exclusively to large companies, and, more specifically, to the general counsel of large companies. In fact, Axiom will work only with in-house lawyers—it will not work with companies that do not have in-house lawyers.[19] The reason is that Axiom cannot claim to be a law firm or to provide legal advice. The reason it cannot make that claim is that a significant portion of Axiom's shares are held by nonlawyers—it has raised $33 million over two rounds of private equity funding. Axiom makes a strong point of its claim to not be a law firm—on its website, in response to the question of whether Axiom is a law firm, its response is "no way."[20] The reason for that, the website explains that "we were actually built on the premise that the current law firm model is broken so we don't mind being something completely new and different."[21] There is no reason for Axiom to categorically reject as customers all companies who do not have in-house counsel, beyond its fear of running afoul of Rule 5.4.

LegalZoom: LegalZoom has on its roster several hundred lawyers across most states of the United States. These lawyers offer their services as a complement to LegalZoom's document creation service. But the status of these lawyers is ambiguous. On the one hand, LegalZoom aggressively markets its "legal plan attorneys," offering to meet most of the legal needs of an individual or of a business at a low fixed monthly price. But on the other hand, LegalZoom takes pains to distance itself from those same lawyers, stating:

> LegalZoom does not endorse or recommend any lawyer or law firm who advertises on our site. We do not make any representation and have not made any judgment as to the qualifications, expertise or credentials of any participating lawyer. The information contained on this site is not legal advice. Any information you submit through this site may not be protected by attorney-client privilege. . . . Any arrangement made by you and your attorney is strictly between you and them.[22]

Because of Rule 5.4, when a LegalZoom customer seeks documents as well as attorney support, the customer's experience is fragmented, with the burden falling upon the customer to coordinate the two elements of the service, whether the customer wants to assume that burden or not. It is easy to imagine that many customers are not comforted by the disclaimer above, and that they would prefer a more integrated and streamlined service, notably with the support of LegalZoom's own in-house attorneys, such as what LegalZoom has been able to offer to its customers in the UK.

## NOTES

1. DRI—The Voice of the Defense Bar, 2; Murphy, "Comment: Issues Paper Regarding Alternative Business Stuctures [sic]."
2. Bruce A. Mann, "Comments on Proposed Amendments of Rules 1.5 and 5.4," February 24, 2012, http://www.americanbar.org/content/dam/aba/administrative/ethics_2020/ethics_20_20_comments/mann_alpschoiceoflawinitialdraftproposal.authcheckdam.pdf.
3. John Beisner, "Comments of the US Chamber Institute for Legal Reform on the Issues Paper Concerning Alternative Business Structures," June 1, 2011, 3, http://www.americanbar.org/content/dam/aba/administrative/ethics_2020/ethics_20_20_comments/uschamberinstituteforlegalreform_issuespaperconcerningalternativebusinessstructures.authcheckdam.pdf.
4. New Jersey State Bar Association, Comment Submitted to ABA Commission on Ethics 20/20, 2. See also Henry Mills Gallivan, "ABA Proposal in Alternative Business Structures."
5. Responsive Law, "Mission Statement," http://www.responsivelaw.org/index.php/about-us.
6. Thomas M. Gordon, "Comments on: Alternative Business Structures," May 31, 2011, http://www.americanbar.org/content/dam/aba/administrative/ethics_2020/ethics_20_20_comments/responsivelaw_issuespaperconcerningalternativebusinessstructures.authcheckdam.pdf, and Thomas M. Gordon, "Comments on: Alternative Law Practice Structures," January 30, 2012, http://www.americanbar.org/content/dam/aba/administrative/ethics_2020/ethics_20_20_comments/responsivelaw_alpsdiscussiondraft.authcheckdam.pdf (hereinafter "Responsive Law Testimony January 30, 2012").
7. Thomas Gordon, "Comments on: Issues Paper on the Future of Legal Services," December 10, 2014, http://www.americanbar.org/content/dam/aba/images/office_president/responsive_law.pdf; Thomas Gordon, "Comments On: Issues Paper Regarding Alternative Business Structures," May 2, 2016, http://www.americanbar.org/content/dam/aba/images/office_president/responsive_law_abs.pdf.
8. Thomas M. Gordon," Testimony On: Allowing Innovation to Meet Unmet Legal Needs," September 27, 2013, http://www.responsivelaw.org/files/Responsive_Law_-_NY_Task_Force_2013.pdf (hereinafter "Responsive Law Testimony September 27, 2013").
9. Thomas M. Gordon, "Comments on: Civil Justice Strategies Task Force 'New Group' Draft Recommendations," May 11, 2015, http://www.responsivelaw.org/images/testimony/Civil_Justice_Strategies_Task_Force_Comments.pdf.
10. Responsive Law Testimony September 27, 2013, 5.
11. Responsive Law Testimony January 30, 2012, 1–2.
12. Hadfield, "The Cost of Law," 43–63.
13. Knake, "Democratizing the Delivery of Legal Services," 1–46.
14. Dzienkowski and Peroni, "Multidisciplinary Practice," 83–207.
15. Steven Benathen, "Non-Lawyers Owning Law Firms," *Illinois Business Law Journal*, October 21, 2012, http://www.law.illinois.edu/bljournal/post/2012/10/21/Non-Lawyers-Owning-Law-Firms.
16. Ibid.

17. "Complaint for Declaratory and Injunctive Relief," *Jacoby and Meyers Law Offices LLP v. the Justices of the Supreme Court of New Jersey*, May 18, 2011, http://pdfserver.amlaw.com/nj/Jacoby_%20Meyers_complaint.pdf.

18. "Memorandum Opinion," *United States District Court, Southern District of New York, Jacoby and Meyers, LLP and Jacoby and Meyers USA II, PLLC v. the Presiding Justices of the First, Second, Third and Fourth Departments, Appellate Division of the Supreme Court, et. al.*, July 15, 2015, http://iln.isba.org/sites/default/files/blog/2015/07/judge-rejects-challenge-non-lawyer-ownership-law-firms/jacoby percent20 percent26 percent20meyers.pdf.

19. Richard Granat, "Is Axiom Law a Law Firm?", *eLawyering Blog*, April 8, 2013, http://www.elawyeringredux.com/2013/04/articles/outsourcing/is-axiom-law-a-law-firm/.

20. "What We're Not," Axiom Law, accessed August 20, 2015, http://www.axiomlaw.com/what-were-not/.

21. Ibid.

22. "Attorney Advertising Disclaimer," LegalZoom, accessed August 20, 2015, https://m.legalzoom.com/find-attorney-personal#.

## *Chapter Five*

# New Delivery Models Can Be Developed Without Changing Rule 5.4

Some have argued that alternative structures are not needed because new models for the delivery of legal services can be and have been developed without them. These arguments include:

- "[T]he desired increased efficiencies and competitiveness that external investment is designed to encourage abroad are already present in US firms based on those firms' responses to changing market pressures. Because the US legal market is already realizing and implementing many of the desired benefits that structural changes allow abroad, introducing such a substantial regulatory change at this time would not create sufficient benefits to offset the potential ethical costs."[1]
- "The idea that ABSs do not drive transformative change is consistent with developments in the United States, where there has been considerable innovation throughout the legal industry despite the absence of ABSs. [These innovations] are being driven by extant trends, such as rapid advances in technology and globalization, not ABSs."[2]
- "It is not clear that ABS can provide innovation in delivery of legal services that lawyers practicing in traditional firms cannot[3] . . . in recent years we have seen significant change. . . . This change has come about as a result of the efficiencies and exigencies of modern-day practice, not as a result of ABS."[4]
- "ABSs are not synonymous with [nonlawyer ownership]. There can be innovation in the law firm model, billing structures, or the delivery of legal services without changing the rules about ownership. Innovation in legal services is a laudable goal, but deregulation or the introduction of [nonlawyer ownership] is not a necessary precondition for such change."[5]

- "Without ABS, we can achieve all the benefits fatuously claimed as possible only through ABS."[6]

Following the same logic of this theoretical argumentation, with enough effort, many people with just one eye are able to see a great deal, and many people with just one arm are able to do a great deal. Those people are proof that a second eye or a second arm is a tool, or a resource, that is not strictly necessary. As discussed briefly in the Introduction to this book, as the world has evolved and grown more complex, so have the practice of law and the provision of legal services. Companies like LegalZoom, Axiom, RocketLawyer, Shake, Modria, Axess Law, Aluvion, and Conduit Law, to name a few, are proof that it is possible to develop new models for the delivery of legal services while remaining within the limitations of the existing rules.

However, if companies like the ones listed above have been able to do so, it is because, like persons with just one eye or just one arm, they had no choice but to do so. But also just like persons with just one eye or just one arm, they could do much more, much faster and with greater effectiveness, if they could have access to a full range of resources and tools.[7] This is the essence of the arguments that the literature described in chapter 4 advances, it is an essential motivation of the litigation Jacoby and Meyers brought against authorities in New Jersey, New York, and Connecticut, and it is an essential reason that LegalZoom sought ABS status in England and Wales (both discussed in chapter 4).

Indeed, empirical studies indicate that at least one of the ways that ABSs are doing more is with greater use of new information and communication technologies. When in 2015 the Council for Licensed Conveyancers (CLC, one of several "front-line" regulators in England and Wales) questioned the firms and businesses that it regulates (traditional firms as well as ABSs) with respect to their use of information and communication technologies, the results revealed that while 44.4 percent of ABSs provide clients "some form of online interactive service other than (and probably in addition to) e-mail," only 14.6 percent of traditional firms did the same. These results lead the CLC to conclude that there is "a substantial disparity in the use of innovative" technologies between traditional firms and ABSs.[8] These results of the CLC are comparable to those of a 2013 study and survey conducted by the LSB: 91 percent of the ABSs that responded to that survey indicated having a website that they used to deliver information and other services to their customers, including basic information, online case tracking, and feedback systems. In contrast, just 52 percent of traditional firms reported having a website that they used for advertising, and 6 percent used legal networks websites.[9] For the CLC, the results of these two studies are highly significant, in part because while information technology is certainly useful for commercial work (and particularly in bulk), "people—individual consumers—increasingly expect to be able to find, purchase, and monitor the progress of services online."

In their article "Life in a Law-Thick World: The Legal Resource Landscape for Ordinary Americans," Gillian Hadfield and Jaime Heine demonstrate on the basis of available data that on both a "macro" and a "micro" level, the resources available to ordinary Americans to address their legal matters are a fraction of those available to individuals in other countries. More specifically, on a "macro" level, Hadfield and Heine compare data for the United States and a selection of European countries—data such as total population, total expenditure on courts, public prosecution and legal aid, total number of criminal and civil cases, and total numbers of judges and lawyers. In analyzing this data, they find evidence of a "surprising fact":

> [A]lthough public expenditure, legal aid, numbers of judges and numbers of lawyers are comparable (or high) on a per capita basis, the much greater volume of cases in the US implies that the US devotes many fewer resources to supporting the legal system on a per case basis. That is, Americans choose or have no choice but to go through court-based processes at a much higher rate, but compared to other countries, there are fewer public dollars, judges and even lawyers available to them when they do so.[10]

On a "micro" level, Hadfield and Heine, after deploring the paucity of studies and data with respect to the legal resources available to ordinary Americans,[11] analyze the "small and disconnected bits"[12] that are available. On that basis, they conclude:

> What we find suggests that while Americans face legal needs at rates comparable to those faced by people in other countries, Americans are more likely to take no action to resolve these problems. When they do take action, they do so with fewer legal resources available to them. . . .[13]
>
> We identify here a troubling indication that Americans are led to "lump" their legal problems and do nothing about them at higher rates than is the case in these other countries. Looking closely at these studies suggests that one reason might be that Americans have fewer places to turn for legal help: environments in which people have more open regulatory systems that allow a wider variety of professionals to assist people with legal problems—not just lawyers, as is the case in the US—appear to be the ones in which people are significantly less likely to do nothing when trouble emerge. That is important: ignoring legal problems is likely to cause more problems. Moreover, both ignoring legal problems and muddling through them without legal help undermines our confidence that the complex legal rules and entitlements we have put in place are, in fact, accomplishing the objectives they are designed to achieve.[14]

Reports from the state of New York corroborate Hadfield and Heine's findings. More specifically, each year since 2010, the state's Permanent

Commission on Access to Justice (formerly called the Task Force to Expand Access to Civil Legal Services in New York) has "assisted in the preparation for four public hearings on civil legal services to assess the extent and nature of the current unmet civil legal needs of low-income New Yorkers throughout the State, and to identify the level of resources necessary to meet that need."[15] In connection with those hearings, each year the commission has collected the oral and written testimony of approximately 45 to 100 persons.[16] The witnesses come from a wide range of backgrounds, and include "business leaders, private and public residential property owners, bankers, local government officials, District Attorneys, labor leaders, medical providers, educators, providers of domestic violence prevention services, religious leaders, Judges, and clients."[17] On the basis of the hearings and the witness testimony, each year[18] the commission repeats its finding of a growing or "continuing crisis of the unrepresented in [the] State's courts and the continuing unmet need for civil legal services,"[19] and each year[20] the commission repeats the urgency of the "need for additional resources to bridge the justice gap."[21]

The work of the commission, together with that of Hadfield and Heine, shows that the resources available in the United States for "ordinary" and low-income Americans to meet their legal needs are not sufficient—they have access to some resources and tools, but that access is limited, and, for many, highly limited. The commission's work demonstrates that as a result of this lack of access, many persons are suffering, and their need for greater access to resources is urgent.

Considered in this context, theoretical arguments that the innovation in legal services necessary to meet these legal needs can take place in the United States without regulatory change are nothing but theoretical. In contrast to the theory, the reality is that in the absence of regulatory change, the necessary innovation is not happening at a sufficient level, and, concretely speaking, there are no grounds for believing that, absent regulatory change, it actually will happen at a sufficient level in the future.

## STORIES

### (PART V OR ONLINE)

*Monica Goyal, Founder and Principal, Aluvion Law* (Part V): Goyal explains that Aluvion could grow much faster if it could access outside capital.

*Peter Carayiannis, Founder and President, Conduit Law* (online): Carayiannis explains that the firm's growth and scalability as well as access to top talent are limited because the company can neither offer nonlegal services in combination with legal services, nor bring in IT, marketing, and other professionals into the firm's equity structure.

*Rubsun Ho and Joe Milstone, Founding Partners, Cognition LLP* (online): Ho and Milstone explain that lack of access to capital has limited the company's recruitment of lawyers and senior managers, slowed its deployment of technology, and discouraged its entry into other markets (including overseas).

## NOTES

1. Renee Rayne, "Do U.S. Firms Need External Equity Investments to Remain Competitive?" *Texas International Law Journal* 49 (2014): 560, http://www.tilj.org/content/journal/49/num3/Rayne559.pdf.
2. Perlman, "Towards the Law," 86–87.
3. Ontario Trial Lawyers Association, "Submission on Alternative Business Structures," 1.
4. Ibid., 10.
5. Jasminka Kalajdzic, "Memo to Linda Langston of the Ontario Trial Lawyers Association," December 1, 2014, 8, https://www.otla.com/index.cfm?pg=NonLawyerOwnership.
6. Bradley Wright, January 20, 2015 (12:53 pm), comment on Mitch Kowalski, "Anti-ABS Arguments Continue to Be Based on Emotion—Not Fact," *Slaw*, December 30, 2014, http://www.slaw.ca/2014/12/30/anti-abs-arguments-continue-to-be-based-on-emotion-not-fact/.
7. See, for example, Hadfield, "Legal Barriers to Innovation," 130–41.
8. Council for Licensed Conveyancers, "ABSs Leading the Way on Information Technology," *CLC Blog*, April 13, 2016, http://www.conveyancer.org.uk/CLC-Blog/April-2016/ABSs-Leading-the-Way-on-Information-Technology.aspx.
9. Legal Services Board, "Evaluation," 6.
10. Hadfield and Heine, "Life in the Law-Thick World," 3.
11. Ibid., 1–2.
12. Ibid., 3.
13. Ibid., 11.
14. Ibid., 4.
15. Task Force to Expand Access to Civil Legal Services in New York, "Report to the Chief Judge of the State of New York," November, 2014, ii, https://www.nycourts.gov/accesstojustice
commission/PDF/CLS%20TaskForce%20Report%202014.pdf.
16. Task Force to Expand Access to Civil Legal Services in New York, "Report to the Chief Judge of the State of New York," November, 2010, 3, https://www.nycourts.gov/accesstojusticecommission/PDF/CLS-TaskForceREPORT.pdf; Task Force to Expand Access to Civil Legal Services in New York, "Report to the Chief Judge of the State of New York," November, 2011, 15, https://www.nycourts.gov/accesstojusticecommission/PDF/CLS-2011TaskForceREPORT_web.pdf; Task Force to Expand Access to Civil Legal Services in New York, "Report to the Chief Judge of the State of New York," November, 2012, 7, https://www.nycourts.gov/accesstojusticecommission/PDF/CLS-TaskForceREPORT_Nov-2012.pdf; Task Force to Expand Access to Civil Legal Services in New York, "Report to the Chief Judge of the State of New York," November, 2013, 10, https://www.nycourts.gov/accesstojustice commission/PDF/CLS-TaskForceReport_2013.pdf; Task Force to Expand Access to Civil Legal Services in New York, "Report to the Chief Judge of the State of New York," November, 2014, 9, https://www.nycourts.gov/accesstojusticecommission/PDF/CLS%20TaskForce%20 Report%202014.pdf.
17. NY Report 2014, 9–10.
18. NY Report 2010, 1; NY Report 2011, 1; NY Report 2012, 1; NY Report 2013, 1; NY Report 2014, 1.
19. NY Report 2014, 1.

20. NY Report 2010, 8; NY Report 2011, 8, 10; NY Report 2012, 4, 7; NY Report 2013, 1, 11; NY Report 2014, 1, 10.
21. NY Report 2014, 10.

*Chapter Six*

# The Payment of Salary Is Adequate Compensation for Nonlawyers

Some have argued that they see no reason or need for nonlawyers to acquire ownership interest in law firms because firms are allowed to employ nonlawyers and pay them as generous a salary as they please, and that this compensation is largely adequate to retain them as employees, without any "operational need for them to acquire ownership interests."[1] Others have argued that US firms "have found ways to provide incentive compensation to their nonlawyer employees that they believe are consistent with the Model Rules,"[2] and, in this light, a change to the Model Rules is not justified. Stated more colorfully:

> If you want to benefit staff, give them bonuses based on either their performance or the performance of the firm or both. Do not sell them ownership. For Heaven's sake, how daft do we have to be to permanently and irreversibly harm our independence because some nitwit could not think of bonuses as a means to reward staff? Trust me, the staff receiving the bonus will be delighted.[3]

Nothing in this argumentation appears to take into account extensive research on the topic of employee ownership. The research dates back several decades,[4] and demonstrates that employee ownership can provide extensive benefits for an employer, especially if it is structured appropriately and implemented under the right circumstances.[5] The benefits include, in particular, significantly increased productivity and return on assets[6] (in one study, by 14.8 percent and 2.5 percent, respectively).[7] Further, for many small and medium-sized businesses, the offer of share ownership is considered important for attracting and retaining good employees.[8] According to the American Management Association, employee ownership:

- Improves organizational performance.
- Improves overall employee productivity.
- Increases firm profitability and revenue.
- Increases firm value.
- Provides diversification and an exit strategy/succession plan for principals.
- Increases optimism among employees that they will be financially prepared for retirement.
- Increases employee job satisfaction.
- Increases employee trust in the firm and its management.[9]

Two studies, both from the UK, are of particular interest:

The first study, published in 2014, looked at 49 employee-owned businesses (EOBs) and 204 non-EOBs in the UK over the period 2005 to 2011. These years corresponded to a general period of economic growth, followed by recession and prolonged "adverse economic conditions."[10] The study concluded that during a period of economic growth EOBs and non-EOBs are on par for profitability, but that EOBs:

- deliver higher employee sales contribution,
- show superior financial performance in knowledge and skill-intensive industries, and
- add more value to output and human capital than non-EOBs.[11]

The study further concluded that during a period of economic crisis, EOBs "far withstood the recession better than non-EOBs—not only at the onset of the downturn but even as the recession deepened."[12] They demonstrated this resilience with better financial performance, less sales variability, and increased hiring. The study explained these results in part as follows:

> [During a period of economic crisis, non-EOBs] are unable to maintain both top-line financial performance and employment levels while the EOBs seem to be better at doing this. The contrast can be attributed to the ownership culture of EOBs, which supports high employee engagement to deliver superior performance. For instance, EOBs are thus more likely to empower their front-line employees and to use feedback from them to pursue customer-oriented growth.
>
> EOBs support higher employment levels than non-EOBs. This is in line with findings that suggest that EOBs view employees as their biggest asset, and employee commitment as their central advantage. The increase in employee numbers in 2008–09 and 2009–10 points to the long-term orientation of

> EOBs and their ability to plan ahead for a time when the economy begins to look up. Research suggests that on account of preserving their social capital and knowledge base, they would be well positioned to bounce back strongly as the recession ends.[13]

The second study, published in 2015, was sponsored by (i) Fieldfisher, a UK-based law firm, (ii) the Chartered Management Institute, and (iii) the eaga Trust, a UK-based employee ownership organization. The study compares the survey responses of 1,019 people (managers and nonmanagers) working at 15 employee-owned companies[14] to the responses of a cross-sector control group of approximately 50,000 people.[15] The study's findings include:

- A strong suggestion that the culture, values, and ethics of employee-owned companies are significantly stronger than those with other forms of ownership: "[W]hen employees own their organisations, the culture is more human, less fearful and less bureaucratic . . . When people at work operate in a culture of fear and bureaucracy, customer focus and entrepreneurship suffer. This translates into lower revenues and profits and higher costs."
- As regards organizational hierarchy, the structure is much flatter and more collegiate in employee-owned companies: "Everyone has a stake in the company and therefore it is in everyone's benefit to care and treat colleagues on every level with respect."
- A conclusion that the values of employee-owned businesses are stronger than others: "Democratic, visionary, coaching and affiliative leadership styles are the norm here, compared with the coercive and demanding styles of competing forms of ownership."
- As regards leadership styles, 90 percent of people working in employee-owned companies report experiencing "high-performing visionary, democratic and coaching" leadership styles—compared to 58 percent in the control sample.[16]

In addition, the study's researchers asked people in the employee-owned companies questions about the effect of this ownership model on a number of specific cultural features, with the following responses:

- 95 percent of the respondents reported that the model has a positive effect on "people's commitment to the organization" (5 percent said it has no impact).
- 91 percent reported that the model has a positive impact on "the performance of the organization" (7 percent said it had no impact and 2 percent said it had a negative impact).

- 87 percent reported that the model has a positive impact on "the ability to attract new staff" (12 percent said it had no impact and 1 percent said it had a negative impact).
- 81 percent reported that the model has a positive impact on "the way people behave to each other" (16 percent said it had no impact and 3 percent said it had a negative impact).[17]

Returning to the United States, in their book *The Citizen's Share: Putting Ownership Back into Democracy*, Joseph R. Blasi, Richard B. Freeman, and Douglas K. Kruse begin by explaining the importance for the Founding Fathers of widespread property ownership.[18] While the likes of George Washington, Thomas Jefferson, James Madison, John Adams, and Alexander Hamilton disagreed on many issues of the time, the importance of widespread property ownership was one issue upon which they agreed, albeit each in his own way. For them, widespread property ownership was fundamental to a sustainable democracy because it gave citizens a stake in preserving the political and economic system, and avoided the concentration of ownership (and consequently, the concentration of wealth and political power) in the hands of a small aristocracy.[19] Adams stated that "property monopolized or in possession of a few is a curse to mankind."[20] Madison argued that "the proportion being without property or the hope of acquiring it, cannot be expected to sympathize sufficiently with its rights, to be safe depositories of power over them."[21] And Jefferson stated that "whenever there is in any country uncultivated lands and unemployed poor, it is clear that the laws of property have been so far extended as to violate natural right."[22]

Of course, for the Founding Fathers, property ownership meant real property. And their belief in the importance of its widespread ownership explains a variety of acts, most notably the ban on primogeniture[23] (which restricted property inheritance to the firstborn son rather than division among all offspring), the promulgation of the Northwest Ordinance of 1787 (which, rather than selling to the highest bidder, instead offered land for less than $1 per acre in what would later become Ohio, Indiana, Michigan, Illinois, Wisconsin, and part of Minnesota),[24] and the Louisiana Purchase (which vastly increased the amount of property available, albeit at the expense of the Native American population).[25]

And it was not just the Founding Fathers but also those who came later. In particular, the Homestead Act, adopted in 1862 during the Lincoln administration, gave ownership of 160 acres of undeveloped land west of the Mississippi River to families for a small fee and five-year residency if they built a house and worked the land, or for $1.25 an acre and minimal improvement with a six-month residency.[26] The House Speaker at the time, Galusha Grow, steered the act through Congress as promoting social and political equality, and as a means to "protect the rights of men."[27]

Eventually, of course, the land ran out. At the same time, Blasi, Freeman, and Kruse explain, manufacturing increasingly drove the economy, together with the exploitation of natural resources such as coal and oil. In the process of rapid industrialization, the nexus of wealth and power moved from land ownership to the ownership of capital, and, in particular, to the ownership of the huge corporate concentrations that developed.[28] Grow, still a member of the House of Representatives at the turn of the twentieth century, understood this shift. In his last speech before the House in 1902, he argued that large corporations, in themselves, were not the problem. Instead, the problem was that business and political leaders had not envisioned a way to organize the finances of corporations in a way that encouraged broadened ownership.[29]

Having established the historical roots of widespread property ownership in the United States, Blasi, Freeman, and Kruse then provide detailed examples and case studies of a number of present-day companies for whom broad-based share ownership, together with a culture of employee participation, are considered important elements in the companies' economic success. Their examples include small and medium-sized companies as well as large, high-profile companies, both public and private, such as Google, Procter and Gamble, Southwest Airlines, Microsoft, Apple, Exxon, Chevron, Amazon.com, IBM, Goldman Sachs, Cargill, Mars, Publix, Fidelity Investments, Bloomberg, S.C. Johnson & Sons, and Graybar Electric.[30]

The authors take care to caution that an employee share ownership program alone, especially if it is adopted outside a genuine culture of employee participation as well as basic good management, may very well fail, citing Enron, WorldCom, Lehman Brothers, and United Airlines as examples.[31] They also emphasize that because there is no guarantee that shares will increase in value—indeed, their value may very well decrease—the better programs grant (rather than sell) shares in addition to (not in lieu of) market rate wages and other compensation, notably profit sharing, and they facilitate diversified stock holdings.[32]

The authors describe the research of a number of others as well as their own several studies, with respect to employee share ownership. For example, one of the authors' studies involved over 40,000 employees at 14 large and small corporations, which they compared to a control group using data from the General Social Survey.[33] The study took into account employee share ownership as well as other forms of participatory compensation such as profit sharing and stock options, and compared, in a general manner, employees with high levels of employee stock ownership, profit sharing, and/or stock options (high-capitalist employees) to employees with low or no levels (low-capitalist employees). The results of this study led the authors to conclude the following:

- More likely to stay with their firms: 9 percent of high-capitalist employees reported that they were likely to look for a new job, as compared to 15 percent of low-capitalist employees.[34]
- Have greater loyalty and pride working for the firm: 58 percent of high-capitalist employees reported great loyalty to their companies, as compared to 46 percent of low-capitalist employees.[35]
- Express greater willingness to work hard: 36 percent of high-capitalist employees strongly agreed with the statement "I am willing to work harder than I have to in order to help the company I work for succeed," as compared to 30 percent of low-capitalist employees.[36]
- Make more suggestions: 26 percent of high-capitalist employees make a suggestion for improvement for their company at least once a month, as compared to 18 percent of low-capitalist employees.[37]

After presenting the results of these studies, the authors make the following concluding observations:

> The statistical evidence that firms in which workers have a property stake are more productive, induce more worker effort and responsibility, spur workers to innovate more, and produce diverse other benefits for workers and the corporation shows that a broad-based capitalist organizational form of capitalism can work. It pays off, at least for those firms and workers that choose it. The impacts are larger when the programs are larger . . . but the share idea is not simply about workers getting more money in the pocket. It is also about the firm and its employees developing a culture that supports employee participation and cooperation between management and employees over the long term. The corporations and workers that do best combine shares and workplace practices in the context of a participative ownership culture. Our analysis found that giving workers more responsibility, having more teams and problem-solving groups, having a less hierarchical workplace where supervision involved more coaching than control, paying workers at or above the market rate for their fixed wages, and providing workers with greater training were important parts of this culture.[38]

In sum, not only is widespread property ownership rooted in American democratic tradition, but, in addition, extensive research done over a number of years demonstrates that employee share ownership programs offer highly significant potential to improve an employer's competitiveness, profitability, and overall performance, as well as to improve employee attitudes and well-being. There are many reasons why an employer would want to offer ownership interests to one or more of its employees, and many reasons why the employer (and its employees) would benefit from doing so. There is nothing about law firms that make these reasons less pertinent for them. Seen in this context, arguments that there is no need for nonlawyers to acquire ownership interest in law firms because "firms are allowed to employ nonlawyers and pay them as generous a salary as they please," because there is no "operational need" for nonlawyers to acquire ownership interests, or because firms "have found ways to provide incentive compensation to their nonlawyer employees that they believe are consistent with the Model Rules" are, at best, highly uninformed.

## STORIES

### (PART V OR ONLINE)

*Oliver Jackson, Director of Strategy and Growth, Roberts Jackson* (online): Jackson argues that share ownership serves to align all the company's board members, lawyers and nonlawyers alike, and motivates them to ensure the success of the company.

*Andrew Grech, Group Managing Director, Slater and Gordon* (online): Grech explains that any member of the firm's staff may become a shareholder and that equity allows the firm to reward its employees for achieving long-term results.[39]

*Ursula Hogben, Practice Leader and General Counsel, Lega!Vision* (online): Hogben explains that for Legal Vision, the ability to offer shares to all team members—not just lawyers—is crucial because it allows the company to bring in high-quality people and it motivates them to work for the company's success.

*Adrian Powell, Partner, Proelium Law* (online): Powell explains that in partnering with nonlawyer Rich Stephens rather than paying him for work as an employee or a consultant, he will get the best from Stephens. As a partner, Stephens owns the issues and the success and that's a hugely important motivator.

*David Simon, Chair, Triton Global* (Part V): Simon describes Triton's employee share ownership program as a very important way to inspire and motivate its employees. Triton is so enthusiastic about its share ownership program, it became a member of the UK's Employee Ownership Association.

*Jenny Beck, Partner, Stephensons Solicitors LLP* (online): Beck explains how having different kinds of people around the partnership table has led to the development of new client services.

*Robert Camp, Stephens Scown LLP* (online): Camp explains that Stephens Scown became an ABS as part of its focus on a high level of customer service. More specifically, client service is dependent upon staff engagement, and employee ownership is an important component of staff engagement. Further, in the opinion of the firm's professional indemnity insurers, having employees more engaged in the business and having a stake in the outcome means that they will take risk more seriously.

*Martin Powell, OmniaLegal Limited* (online): Powell explains that OmniaLegal became an ABS in part in order to involve a person with nonlegal expertise as an owner. Law firms can benefit greatly from a fresh approach and attitude, Powell argues, and notably from people who have experience with providing high-quality customer care. However, Powell continues, you can't get the best out of those people without offering them management authority as well as the rewards of ownership.

## NOTES

1. New Jersey State Bar Association, "Comment Submitted to ABA Commission on Ethics 20/20," 1. See also Illinois State Bar Association, "Issues Paper Regarding Alternative Business Structures: Request for Comments," 2016, 3, http://www.americanbar.org/content/dam/aba/images/office_president/illinois_state_bar_association_abs.pdf; Mark R. Antonelli, "For Comment: Issues Paper Regarding Alternative Business Structures," April 27, 2016, 2, http://www.americanbar.org/content/dam/aba/images/office_president/mark_r_antonelli_abs.pdf.
2. Bruce A. Mann, "Comments on Proposed Amendments of Rules 1.5 and 5.4."
3. Bradley Wright, December 30, 2014 (6:28 pm), comment on Mitch Kowalski, "Anti-ABS Arguments Continue to Be Based on Emotion."
4. See, for example, Jon L. Pierce and Candace A. Furo, "Employee Ownership: Implications for Management," *Organizational Dynamics* 18 (1990): 32–43; Rhokeun Park, Douglas Kruse and James Sesil, "Does Employee Ownership Enhance Firm Survival?," in *Employee Participation, Firm Performance and Survival*, ed. Virginie Perotin and Andrew Robinson (*Advances in the Economic Analysis of Participatory and Labor-Managed Firms*, v.8) (Bingley, Washington: Emerald Group Publishing Limited, 2004) 3–33; Steven F. Freeman, "Effects of ESOP Adoption and Employee Ownership: Thirty Years of Research and Experience," Organizational Dynamics Programs Working Paper #07–01, January 4, 2007, http://repository.upenn.edu/cgi/viewcontent.cgi?article=1001andcontext=od_working_papers.
5. For a brief description of some of the relevant circumstances, see "When Workers are Owners: The Received Wisdom that Employee Ownership Is a Good Thing Comes with Caveats," *The Economist*, August 22, 2015, http://www.economist.com/news/business/21661657-received-wisdom-employee-ownership-good-thing-comes-caveats-when-workers-are; see also E. Han Kim and Paige Ouimet, "Broad-Based Employee Stock Ownership: Motives and Outcomes," *The Journal of Finance*, 69 (2014): 1273–1319, doi:10.1111/jofi.12150.
6. National Center for Employee Ownership, "Research on Employee Ownership, Corporate Performance, and Employee Compensation," http://www.nceo.org/articles/research-employee-ownership-corporate-performance.
7. National Center for Employee Ownership, "Key Studies on Employee Ownership and Corporate Performance," accessed August 20, 2015, http://www.nceo.org/articles/studies-employee-ownership-corporate-performance.
8. National Center for Employee Ownership, "A Conceptual Guide to Employee Ownership for Very Small Businesses," http://www.nceo.org/articles/employee-ownership-very-small-businesses.
9. Jerry L. Ripperger, "How Employee Ownership Benefits Executives, Companies, and Employees," July 21, 2014, http://www.amanet.org/training/articles/How-Employee-Ownership-Benefits-Executives-Companies-and-Employees.aspx.
10. Joseph Lampel et al., "Does Employee Ownership Confer Long-Term Resilience? A Follow-Up Study to 'Model Growth: Do Employee Owned Businesses Provide Sustainable Advantage?'" January 14, 2014, 2, http://www.cassknowledge.com/sites/default/files/article-attachments/Employee-Ownership-Report-January-14-2014.pdf.
11. Joseph Lampel and Ajay Bhalla, "How Employee-Owned Businesses Deliver Sustainable Performance in the UK?" January 28, 2015, 10, http://www.boeckler.de/pdf/v_2015_01_28_29_lampel_bhalla.pdf.

12. Lampel et al., "Does Employee Ownership Confer Long-Term Resilience?" 8.
13. Ibid.
14. Roger Steare et al., "The MoralDNA of Employee-Owned Companies: Ownership, Ethics and Performance," September 2015, 6, https://www.managers.org.uk/~/media/Files/MoralDNA/The_MoralDNA_of_Employee-Owned_Companies.pdf.
15. Ibid., 10.
16. Ibid., 7.
17. Ibid., 17.
18. Joseph R. Blasi, Richard B. Freeman, and Douglas Kruse, *The Citizen's Share: Putting Ownership Back into Democracy* (New Haven: Yale University Press, 2013), 1–56.
19. Ibid., 26–27.
20. Ibid., 46.
21. Ibid., 52.
22. Ibid., 49.
23. Ibid., 33–34.
24. Ibid., 30.
25. Ibid., 30–33.
26. Ibid., 39.
27. Ibid., 38.
28. Ibid., 42.
29. Ibid., 42–43.
30. Ibid., 57–101.
31. Ibid., 101–8.
32. Ibid.
33. Ibid., 174–77.
34. Ibid., 177–78.
35. Ibid., 178–79.
36. Ibid., 179.
37. Ibid., 179–81.
38. Ibid., 191–92.
39. Grech also explains the firm's experience with employee ownership in his article with Kristen Morrison, "Slater and Gordon: The Listing Experience," *Georgetown Journal of Legal Ethics* 22 (2009): 535–40.

## *Chapter Seven*

# No One in Their Right Mind Would Want to Invest in a Law Firm

Some have asked the question: "Who in their right mind would invest in a law firm?"[1] After all, a law firm is nothing more than a collection of lawyers, and they can leave at any time, with very little notice, taking their clients with them. Law firms do not retain earnings, so they have little to no excess cash, and they have little in the way of investable assets, such as intellectual property or equipment, and many if not most do not even own their own offices, let alone other real estate.

Perhaps Steven Davis, the former chairman of the law firm of Dewey and LeBoeuf, summed it up best, saying just months before the firm's collapse: "As far as I am concerned, if it is only money that holds a firm and its partners together, then there is really no glue at all."[2] Indeed, why would anyone want to invest in a traditional law firm? It is not clear just what the external investor would be investing in.

By the same token, if a traditional law firm partnership intends to carry on operating as a traditional law firm partnership, then outside of any potential tax advantages, it has little motivation to become an alternative structure. It would not need to as long as the firm's partners did not see the need or have the desire for a different management structure, for a different ownership structure, for external investment (private or public), or to offer a multidisciplinary service. In this light, it is easy to understand why in England and Wales a May 2014 study showed that:

- Approximately 33 percent of ABSs are new entrants—that is, they are newly created entities, not previously existing traditional law firms that have decided to change their status.[3]

- An additional 52 percent of ABSs are previously existing entities (40 percent law firms and 12 percent some other type of firm),[4] but each made significant changes to their business in connection with their status as an ABS. Those include changes to the way their business is structured (70 percent), the way their business is managed (69 percent), the services the business offers (23 percent), and/or some other "significant change" to their business (15 percent).[5]

In England and Wales, just 15 percent of the firms that become ABSs are previously existing law firms that do not make any significant change to the way their firm is structured or managed or to the services it offers.

It is the firms that are not operated as traditional partnerships that can be attractive to external investors, be they private or public. At a minimum, the firm needs to have in place a corporate structure, where the roles that each person plays—employee, executive/manager, equity owner—are clearly separated and where earnings are retained.

In addition, the firm ideally will have developed a clear plan for how the external investment will be used. That plan needs to show how the value of the firm is expected to increase, such as through the development of business and/or technological processes or services that will give the firm an advantage over its competitors, or allow the firm to scale (that is, to serve more clients at little or no additional marginal cost). In this manner, the firm is much more than just a collection of lawyers in a structure that could disintegrate at any moment. It becomes an enduring structure with distinct assets and potential for growth that it could make good sense to invest in.[6]

Neither the rules of England and Wales nor the rules of Australia require a firm to become an ABS or an ILP or to adopt a corporate structure—the rules simply provide the option to do so. The majority of firms in both countries continue to operate as traditional firms—either as sole practitioners or partnerships. Those seeking to invest in legal services, such as ABSs that have adopted a strategy of growth through acquisition and other external investors like private equity funds, have expressed frustration: They have complained that many law firm partners are "unwilling to embrace change" and that law firms either are "not ready" culturally or are not financially viable, for acquisition or for external investment.[7]

In early 2016, the UK-based online legal journal *Legal Futures* published an analysis of the value of investments in UK-based public companies that "have a strong legal element." The analysis found that over the prior year, they had been "good investments."[8] By far the best legal performer, the analysis found, was Redde plc, the accident management business that owns NewLaw Solicitors—its share price rose by 123 percent. In addition, the share price of Fairpoint Group, owner of the law firms Simpson Millar and

Colemans-ctts, increased by 15 percent, and the shares of the newly listed law firm Gateley increased by 7 percent.[9]

In sum, if the question is "Who would want to invest in a traditional law firm partnership?" then the response probably is "no one," or, at most, "not many." But if the question is "Who would want to invest in a corporate structure that offers legal services in a distinctive, sustainable, and scalable manner," then the response is quite different.

## STORIES

### (PART V OR ONLINE)

*Jordan Mayo, Managing Director, Smedvig Capital* (Part V): To date, private equity firm Smedvig Capital has invested in two legal services businesses, in large part because their models are scalable. Mayo explains that Smedvig is eager to invest in more, on the condition that the businesses have a clear plan for how they will use the money, and that their plans are distinctive and scalable.

*Jeff Winn, Managing Director, Winn Solicitors* (online): Winn explains that international investment company JZ International (JZI), which (together with Souter Investments) took a 60 percent shareholding in Winn Solicitors, are attracted to regulated sectors because their barriers to entry limit competition. Further, JZI foresaw consolidation in legal services in England and Wales, in favor of larger players who can streamline their processes and handle work more efficiently.

## NOTES

1. Murray Teitel, "A Dumb Idea Threatens Both Lawyers, Clients," *Lawyers Weekly*, September 26, 2014, 3, http://www.lawyersweekly-digital.com/lawyersweekly/3419?pg=4#pg4.
2. James B. Stewart, "The Collapse: How a Top Legal Firm Destroyed Itself," *The New Yorker*, October 14, 2013, http://www.newyorker.com/magazine/2013/10/14/the-collapse-2.
3. Solicitors Regulation Authority, "Research on Alternative Business Structures (ABSs): Findings from Surveys with ABSs and Applicants that Withdrew from the Licensing Process," May 2014, 10, http://www.sra.org.uk/sra/how-we-work/reports/research-abs-executive-report.page.
4. Ibid.
5. Ibid., 16–17.
6. See, for example, Nick Hilborne, "My 'Bog Standard Law Firm' Has Become a 'Roll-Out Specialist', Says High Street ABS Chief," *Legal Futures*, November 20, 2015, http://www.legalfutures.co.uk/latest-news/my-bog-standard-law-firm-has-become-a-roll-out-specialist-says-high-street-abs-chief.
7. Dan Bindman, "ABSs Frustrated by Acquisition Targets That Are Either Not Ready or 'Financial Basket Cases,'" *Legal Futures*, November 12, 2013, http://www.legalfutures.co.uk/latest-news/abss-frustrated-acquisition-targets-not-ready-financial-basket-cases. Some use this reticence as a reason to argue against changing Model Rule 5.4 in the United States, on the

grounds that "there is currently little evidence supporting the conclusion that ABSs are having a transformative effect on the delivery of legal services in the United Kingdom." See, for example, Perlman, "Towards the Law," 85.

8. Neil Rose, "Looking to Play the Markets? Then Invest in Law plc," *Legal Futures*, January 7, 2016, http://www.legalfutures.co.uk/latest-news/looking-to-play-the-markets-then-invest-in-law-plc.

9. Ibid.

*Chapter Eight*

# Alternative Structures Will Lead to a Consolidated Market Controlled by Large Firms

In an argument that is diametrically opposed to the argument that no one in their right mind would invest in a law firm, others contend that alternative structures should not be permitted because they will lead to consolidation in the legal services market, such that the market will be controlled by a small number of very large firms.[1] The result will be less choice in the marketplace, increased prices due to a loss of competition, and loss of independence for the legal profession as it will be beholden to the nonlawyer shareholders of the large firms.[2] One impassioned commentator from Ontario, Canada, wrote:

> ABS will not benefit the public . . . the "main" benefit of ABS is to allow access to capital to fund even more consolidations, do people not understand what that means? Consolidation means less competition and less competition means higher prices. People are dazzled by the new toy—ABS—but cannot seem to see dead obvious, major and irreversible problems with it. . . . Consolidations paid for by gargantuan companies with head offices half a world away or down south are guaranteed to worsen the situation.[3]

There are two levels of response to this argumentation, one with respect to markets in a general sense, and one with respect to the market for legal services specifically. With respect to markets in a general sense, this argumentation runs directly counter to a number of reports and papers that have been issued in recent years. These reports and papers call for the US and other governments to revise their economic policies and regulatory infrastructures in order to better support competition and growth, at local, national, and international levels. Two of the primary measures that they encourage are (i) the reduction of regulations that discourage capital investment, and (ii) the development of policies that promote greater levels of capital investment, particularly in small and medium-sized businesses. Examples of these papers, issued by American as well as overseas organizations, include:

1. "Fifty Ways to Leave Your Competitiveness Woes Behind: A National Traded Sector Competitiveness Strategy," issued by the think-tank Information Technology and Innovation Foundation. This report posits:

> The goal of a US traded sector competitiveness strategy should be to ensure that the United States offers the world's best traded sector environment, in part by ensuring that US traded sector firms have access to the world's best technology, talent, and infrastructure, but also the best business and regulatory environment. It should design the nation's business, regulatory, tax, and innovation policy environments to make the United States the world's most attractive location for R&D and business investment (including foreign direct investment) in manufacturing and other traded sectors.[4]

2. "Why Is Capital Investment Consistently Weak in the 21st Century Economy?" issued by The Aspen Institute. This report observes that since the dot-com bubble burst in 2000, capital investment in the United States "has not kept pace with the economic growth, profits, cash flows or virtually any other metric one could use to benchmark investment spending."[5] The report attributes this to a number of factors, including lack of investment opportunities and "the *relative* burden of regulation"[6] as compared to other countries. Reversing the trend of slowing investment in favor of increased investment, the report maintains, "should spur greater productivity growth and, ultimately, a higher rate of economic growth and living standard than we will have if we remain on the current path."[7]

3. "Driving Canadian Growth and Innovation: Five Challenges Holding Back Small and Medium-Sized Enterprises in Canada," issued by the think-tank Centre for Digital Entrepreneurship and Economic Performance. This report argues:

> [M]any smaller enterprises that would like to grow face serious hurdles. Removing these impediments and getting a larger share of the "untapped majority" on a growth trajectory may represent one of the most promising ways to lift employment and ensure a higher standard of living for all Canadians. . . .[8]
>
> In particular, five key challenges undermine the ability of small businesses to graduate into world-class firms with the capacity to expand their operations and contribute meaningfully to both employment and economic growth:
>
> a. a lack of incentives to pursue growth and international expansion;
> b. a shortage of management skills required to achieve high growth;
> c. under-investment in technology to enhance productivity and growth;

d. a lack of investment in R&D to drive innovation; and
e. insufficient access to capital to finance growth (including investments in technology, R&D and management capacity). . .

> [T]hese challenges require the urgent attention of policy-makers at all levels of government.[9]

The report cites research examining the relationship between firm size and productivity, reporting:

> The small size of companies in Canada, while often celebrated, is actually a drag on productivity and the wider economy. While Canadian data on the topic is sparse, the little research that exists demonstrates a clear relationship between firm size and productivity. One report shows that small Canadian manufacturing plants (less than 100 employees) are just 46 percent as productive as their larger (greater than 500 employees) counterparts . . . , while another finds that, compared to their small-sized counterparts, large manufacturing firms are 17 percent more productive, and medium-sized firms (100–500 employees) are 15 percent more productive. . . . Observing both manufacturing and non-manufacturing employers, [other researchers] similarly conclude that "relative to firms with 0–100 employees, firms with more than 500 employees are roughly 30 percent more productive and firms with between 100 and 500 employees are roughly 20 percent more productive." Further, they add, upwards of 18 percent of the productivity gap between Canadian and American firms is attributable to the smaller average size of Canadian firms.
>
> Of course, small firms and start-ups often contribute new ideas, processes, and resources to the economy—contributions that could end up making significant impacts on future growth and prosperity. However, these contributions would be greater still if small firms had both stronger incentives to pursue growth and a clearer runway to international expansion and success. Unfortunately, a combination of private ambition and public policy are dampening the growth aspirations of many Canadian small firms, thereby undermining Canada's economic performance on the global stage.[10]

4. "EPP Group Policy Paper: Five Building Blocks for Growth and Jobs," issued by the center-right EPP Group in the European Parliament. This paper states that "we have to improve our competitiveness and explore Europe's growth potential. We want to keep competitive industry producing in Europe instead of exporting . . . to other parts of the world."[11] Continuing, the paper posits that one of the "five building blocks for growth and jobs" in Europe is access to capital by small and medium sized companies.[12] This capital needs to come from more innovative forms of loan financing from banks, as well as from "modern financial instruments such as venture capital, crowd funding and project bonds."[13] The paper argues that "the EU needs to mobilise and set incentives for all sources of investment, public and private, ensuring SME access to capital."[14]

In sum, these reports and papers perceive greater access to capital investment, including foreign direct investment, as essential for increased competitiveness, as well as for increased productivity, economic growth, job creation, and overall increased standard of living. None of these reports or the paper perceives increased investment, whether from domestic or foreign sources, as something to be feared because it will or may lead to undesired market consolidations or diminished competition.

Interestingly, the Canadian report does expressly anticipate that increased investment will lead to increased firm size—but it perceives this as a positive and desired outcome because of the increased productivity that research cited in the Canadian report indicates will be the likely result.

This is not to say that vigilance is not required in order to guard against undesired consolidation or monopolization in any given market—undesired in the sense that it does lead to less real competition or less real choice for consumers in a way that truly is unfavorable for them (and not simply unfavorable for the less productive suppliers). Undesired consolidation or monopolization is of course theoretically possible in the legal services market, just as it is possible in nearly all, if not all, markets. However, in developed, Western countries, outside of the market for legal services, the response to this potential threat has not been a categorical ban on outside investment. Instead, it has been to adopt laws and regulations that place in the hands of competent regulators the authority and the tools both to monitor markets (all markets) for the potential creation of undesired consolidations or monopolies, and to take appropriate actions to halt their development (such as blocking a merger). In the event that, in any given country, these laws and regulations are not effective to halt the development of any specific undesired consolidation or monopoly, the appropriate course of action is to improve those laws and regulations to make them more effective. In this manner, all markets in that country can benefit from the improved regulation, rather than one or more specific markets being penalized by otherwise unnecessary and, in comparison, draconian measures like a blanket ban on outside investment.

With respect to the market for legal services specifically, the argument that alternative structures will lead to consolidation in the legal services market is probably correct. At least, it is probably correct with respect to certain segments of the market. Going further, for many who advocate alternative structures, consolidation in certain segments is a natural and desirable result.

Most segments of the legal services market today are the opposite of consolidated—they are highly fragmented. This is particularly true of the segments that serve individuals as opposed to corporations and governmental entities.

As discussed in the Introduction, the business model that law firms traditionally use for providing legal services—the "professional consultancy" or "solution shop" model—is difficult to scale. Under this model, lawyers solve problems by spending time working on the problems,[15] under the assumption that each problem requires a solution tailored especially for the specific client.[16] For lawyers to solve additional problems, they spend more time. This model is difficult to scale because (i) more clients can be served only by bringing in more lawyers, and (ii) in bringing in more lawyers, the marginal costs to serve more clients do not decrease. As a result, this model can be used to serve only a limited number of clients—only the clients that the lawyers have enough time in their day to serve and only the clients that are able to pay the high marginal costs. (In this manner, while the market for legal services is highly fragmented, at the same time it offers little real choice to consumers in that all the work is produced and delivered in exactly the same manner).

Contrast this to the "value chain" model. As applied to services, this model is used when the service provider identifies situations when a tailored solution is not necessary for each and every client—that some if not many clients can achieve their desired outcomes with a standardized—even automated—service, either in whole or in part. As Ray Campbell explains in his article "Rethinking Regulation and Innovation in the US Legal Services Market," two examples of this are a carpet cleaning franchise (it does not ask if the customer would be better off with a new carpet or with a restoration of the underlying floors), and Google Translate, which is both standardized and fully automatized.[17]

One (but not the only) advantage in permitting alternative structures is to facilitate the development of alternative business models to produce and deliver legal services: models that relieve lawyers of lower-level and routine tasks in order to have them carried out in a faster, less expensive, and/or less labor intensive manner. Or, in other words, models that move from the "solution shop" to the "value chain" model in whole or in part. An important, if not the entire, purpose of developing such models is to enable a larger number of clients to be served in less time and at a lower cost. If those models are devised successfully, then they will attract those clients, with the natural consequence of consolidation in the market, especially if few of the other competitors in the market have also modified their business models in order to accommodate a greater volume of clients at a lower cost.

In his book *Lawyers, Markets and Regulation*, Frank H. Stephen takes this analysis one step further. While he does not adopt the express terminology of "solution shop" or "value chain" models, he contrasts the two models in concept. Citing a 2002 UK study by Richard Moorhead and Avrom Sherr,[18] Stephen states that the record of "high street," or generalist practitioners, in providing accurate legal advice, in this case on the subject of social welfare law, "is not particularly good."[19] His explanation is that "high street" lawyers typically deal with relatively few cases in this area. The consequence is both an increased cost in dealing with them, as well as poor quality advice.[20] In contrast, Stephen posits:

> [A] national provider benefitting from economies of scope in using branch premises that exist for other services, as well as having centralized expertise in these areas is likely to face lower costs. The expertise will be enhanced by dealing with a much larger volume of cases in this field than a typical high street solicitor.[21]

The result, Stephen concludes, is that not only will the work be more profitable for the value-chain firm, but also the advice is likely to be better due to increased specialization.[22] In addition to the limitations of the solution shop model, there are two additional reasons why it is so hard to meet the legal needs of low and middle income persons: (i) because a firm's ability to take cases on a contingency basis is limited by its low capitalization and low appetite for risk, and (ii) because, in highly fragmented markets, it is difficult for consumers to understand where to go to find a legal services provider or how to select one. With access to outside capital, a law firm can address all these issues:

- It can invest in the development of business and technological processes to bring down marginal costs, enabling the firm to serve a greater number of persons at a reduced price.
- It can have the cash flow to litigate lengthy cases for lower income clients against defendants who often have deep pockets, it can fall back on a capital cushion in the event of losses, and it can spread the risk of contingency cases across a larger number of people.
- It can invest in wide-scale marketing and branding in order to educate consumers on their rights and options and to make their search process easier.

In this context, it is easy to understand not only why the adoption of alternative structures should lead to consolidation in certain market segments, but also why such consolidation is both natural and desirable.

The experiences of Australia and England and Wales bear this out. The most obvious example is Slater and Gordon. Slater and Gordon is an Australian-based law firm specializing in personal injury. Slater and Gordon has invested heavily in the development of business processes and technology to standardize and automate as much of its case management systems as possible. Slater and Gordon was the first law firm to publicly list its shares. When it did so in 2007, the firm had 12 sites in Australia, and annual revenue of about AUS$60 million (US$44.5 million). Since that time it has grown both through the opening of greenfield offices as well as through an aggressive acquisition campaign. Today, the firm has not only 70 sites in Australia but also just under 20 sites in the UK, and its annual revenue has grown to AUS$500 million (US$365 million). In 2007, Slater and Gordon's market share in the Australian personal injury market was estimated to be under 10 percent[23]—in 2015 it was estimated to be about 25 percent.[24] From 2012 to 2015, its UK market share grew from 0 percent to 12 percent.[25]

Slater and Gordon is not the only personal injury firm around which the personal injury market in Australia is consolidating. Two other firms, Shine and Maurice Blackburn, are Slater and Gordon's largest competitors, and the combined market share of the three firms for personal injury in Australia is estimated at about 40 percent.[26] (Shine is an ILP that went public in 2013; Maurice Blackburn is an ILP whose shares are held exclusively by approximately 25 of the firm's "Principal" lawyers).

Another example is Winn Solicitors. This UK-based, 300-employee ABS offers a one-stop service for accident management for individuals who are victims of traffic accidents. The service includes notifying the client's insurance company that an accident has occurred (without making a claim), pursuing payment from the insurer of the other vehicle directly, organizing the repair of the client's vehicle, and arranging for a replacement vehicle.

Winn Solicitors started in 2002 by targeting its services to wealthy clients who could afford to pay upfront fees for vehicle repair and replacement while waiting for compensation from the insurer. But today the ABS is able to offer its services to a much wider range of clients, thanks at first to its reinvestment of earnings and, in 2013, to a significant investment in the ABS's holding company, Winn Group, by the investment companies JZ International and Souter Investment Group.[27] This large capitalization enables another member of the Winn Group to offer interest-free loans to clients to pay the upfront costs while waiting to receive compensation from the insurer.

Winn Solicitors also invested heavily in the acquisition and development of software permitting the automation of its processes. At the same time, a 2013 change to UK law reduced from £1,200 to £500 the maximum fixed fee that can be charged for low-value accident claims. This change has had a dramatic impact on the law firms working in this sector—they have been obliged either to find solutions to dramatically reduce their costs, or, if not, to leave the market. In this context, Winn Solicitor's automated processes have proven to be particularly valuable. They have enabled the ABS to reduce its marginal costs and thereby, rather than closing, instead serve a large number of clients.[28]

These examples of Australia and England and Wales demonstrate that, at least in certain practices areas, consolidation of the market does indeed occur when alternative structures are allowed to enter the legal services market. These examples also demonstrate how such consolidation can be both natural and desirable.[29]

Here are some additional statistics from England and Wales that demonstrate the consolidation of that market:

- In 2006, 41 percent of all solicitors' firms were sole practitioners—in 2013 they were 29 percent.[30]
- There were 60 percent more law firm mergers in 2012 (the year the first ABSs were authorized) than there had been in 2008.[31]
- Between January 2013 and December 2014, about 500 firms exited the English and Welsh market. Most of those firms practiced in the areas of personal injury and conveyancing, and many made their exit by being acquired by a larger firm that had the resources to compete more effectively.[32]

There is nothing in the public record indicating that the consolidation process that is taking place in the personal injury market in Australia and England and Wales has caused harm to consumers or that consumers seeking personal injury representation in either country lack choice. There is no record of any complaint, negative observation, or warning in this regard having been made by a regulator or by a consumer association or other industry observer in either country.

What the public record does contain is a report issued by the Centre for Innovative Justice of RMIT University in Australia, "Affordable Justice: A Pragmatic Path to Greater Flexibility and Access in the Private Legal Services Market." The report describes Slater and Gordon's use of fixed fees in family law matters in order to "reduce consumer anxiety," and the firm's "Support Services, including a network of social workers, to whom lawyers can refer clients who need nonlegal assistance related to their claim, such as counselling, negotiation with social services, and advice regarding benefits."[33] The report also describes Shine's "no win no fee" arrangement, which it uses in all of its areas of practice and under which clients are not expected either to pay up front for third party costs or to take out a loan to fund litigation.[34] Finally, the report mentions that Maurice Blackburn has launched a free disability helpline to provide advice on issues such as employment, insurance, and superannuation and that Slater and Gordon offers a free Advice Line covering a wide range of areas.[35]

The public record also contains a December 2014 Consumer Impact Report on legal services in England and Wales, which states:

> Consumers are happier with the choice available to them. They shop around more and they're more satisfied with value for money.[36] . . . [A survey showed

that] 68 percent of recent users considered they had a great deal or fair amount of choice—up from 65 percent in 2011. Notably this rise has happened alongside consolidation within sections of the market. Therefore, even though the total number of law firms practicing in certain areas of law has reduced, this does not appear to have altered negatively consumer perceptions of choice. Indeed, since last year choice satisfaction has increased in conveyancing and personal injury—two markets where consolidation has taken place.[37]

The Solicitors Regulation Authority (SRA) has acknowledged the process of consolidation in the English and Welsh market, notably in its March 2014 paper "Magnetic Forces: Consolidation in the Legal Services Market." In this paper, the SRA states that a consolidated market, in itself, should not be seen as presenting more risk than a fragmented one. "The risks involved will be different, but market changes will also bring about opportunities and benefits. For example, the new market structure, and businesses within it, may perform better at broadening access to legal services for those who require them."[38]

In this paper, the SRA goes further, "[S]ome firms will experience consolidation as a crisis, while others will experience it as an opportunity. Benefits are most likely to be achieved by those that find means to access untapped demand. Firms that can manage their risks well will have an advantage as the market changes"[39]

Certainly alternative structures can pose a threat to sole practitioners and small firms that serve individual clients, and notably to those sole practitioners and small firms that have not identified ways to reduce their marginal costs in order to serve a greater number of clients. But this begs the questions: (i) for whom are legal services performed, and (ii) who is regulation of legal services intended to protect?

## STORIES

(PART V OR ONLINE)

*Tom Curran, CEO, Kings Court Trust* (Part V): Curran explains how the company's case management system allows the company to handle a large number of probate files. As a result of working on so many probate files, the company's lawyers develop a high degree of expertise in the area.

*Oliver Jackson, Director of Strategy and Growth, Roberts Jackson* (online): Jackson describes the importance of the company's IT processes and case management system in enabling the company to handle a high volume of cases (14,000 cases outstanding).

*Andrew Grech, Group Managing Director, Slater and Gordon* (online): Grech acknowledges that the international size and scope of the firm's operations and the consumer focus of its legal practice might at first glance appear counterintuitive. However, he explains why the firm's global growth has, in fact, better equipped the firm to act locally.

*John Briton, Former Legal Services Commissioner, Queensland* (online): Briton explains that consolidation in the personal injury market in Australia occurred naturally because, in a world of increasing specialization, being a small generalist firm is too hard. In Briton's opinion, consolidation has been beneficial for clients because the consolidated firms tend to be better managed.

## NOTES

1. Julius Melnitzer, "ABS Firm's Expansion Offers New Fodder for Ontario Debate," *Law Times*, April 20, 2015, http://www.lawtimesnews.com/201504204617/headline-news/abs-firm-s-expansion-offers-new-fodder-for-ontario-debate; Texas Association of Defense Counsel et al., "Comment and Opposition by Texas Association of Defense Counsel," 2.
2. Ontario Trial Lawyers Association, "Submission on Alternative Business Structures"; Paul Bennet, "Comment on Alternative Business Structures," April 25, 2016, http://www.americanbar.org/content/dam/aba/images/office_president/paul_w_bennett_abs.pdf; Brett A. Ross, Letter to Katy Englehart, April 28, 2016, http://www.americanbar.org/content/dam/aba/images/office_president/brett_a_ross_abs.pdf.
3. Bradley Wright, January 20, 2015 (9:19 pm), comment on Mitch Kowalski, "Anti-ABS Arguments Continue to Be Based on Emotion."
4. Stephen J. Ezell and Robert D. Atkinson, "Fifty Ways to Leave Your Competitiveness Woes Behind: A National Traded Sector Competitiveness Strategy," September, 2012, 5, http://www2.itif.org/2012-fifty-ways-competitiveness-woes-behind.pdf.
5. Thomas J. Duesterberg and Donald A. Norman, "Why Is Capital Investment Consistently Weak in the 21st Century Economy?" April, 2015, 1, https://www.mapi.net/system/files/attachments/files/Capital_Investment_4_0.pdf.
6. Ibid., 16.
7. Ibid., 1.
8. Dan Herman and Anthony D. Williams, "Driving Canadian Growth and Innovation: Five Challenges Holding Back Small and Medium-Sized Enterprises in Canada," May, 2013, 2, http://deepcentre.com/wordpress/wp-content/uploads/2013/03/DEEP-Centre-May-2013-Driving-Canadian-Growth-and-Innovation.pdf.
9. Ibid., 4–5.
10. Ibid., 5.
11. EPP Group in the European Parliament, "EPP Group Policy Paper: Five Building Blocks for Growth and Jobs," February 23, 2015, 5, http://www.eppgroup.eu/system/files_force/publications/2015/02/EPP_Policy%20Paper_Growth_148x210_EN_LR.rev_.11.02.105.pdf.
12. Ibid., 5.
13. Ibid., 9.
14. Ibid., 10.
15. See, for example, Mercer, "So Many Lawyers," 44–47.
16. Campbell, "Rethinking Regulation," 20.
17. Ibid., 19.
18. Stephen indicates a 2003 publication, but the version available online carries a publication date of December 4, 2002: Richard Lewis Moorhead and Avrom Sherr, "An Anatomy of Access: Evaluating Entry, Initial Advice and Signposting Using Model Clients," December 4, 2002, http://orca.cf.ac.uk/44851/1/modelclientpaper.pdf.
19. Stephen, 132.
20. Stephen, 133.

21. Ibid.
22. Ibid.
23. Slater and Gordon, "Prospectus: An Underwritten Offer of 35 Million Shares at an Offer Price of $1.00 per Share, Payable in Full on Application," April 13, 2007, 23, https://media.slatergordon.com.au/prospectus.pdf.
24. Farina Parsons, "The Consolidation of the Legal Services Profession is a Growth Opportunity for Slater and Gordon," *Morning Star Analysis Report*, July 10, 2015, http://analysisreport.morningstar.com/stock/research?t=SGHandculture=en-USandregion=ausandcur=AUDandproductcode=MLE.
25. Ibid.
26. Sam Haddad, "Shine Corporation (SHJ): Significant Growth for Well into the Future," *Bell Potter Analyst Report*, March 16, 2015, 2, https://www.bellpotter.com.au/media/148570/shj_20150316.pdf.
27. Neil Rose, "Private Equity Pair Take Majority Stake in Leading PI Firm," *Legal Futures*, September 3, 2013, http://www.legalfutures.co.uk/latest-news/private-equity-pair-take-majority-stake-leading-pi-firm.
28. Sam Chadderton, "Crash Course to Success," *The Lawyer*, February 4, 2013, http://www.thelawyer.com/analysis/market-analysis/crash-course-to-success/3000339.article.
29. See, for example, Hadfield and Rhode, "How to Regulate Legal Services," 34–36.
30. Solicitors Regulation Authority, "Magnetic Forces: Consolidation in the Legal Services Market," March, 2014, 3, http://www.sra.org.uk/risk/resources/magnetic-forces.page (hereinafter "SRA Magnetic Forces").
31. Ibid.
32. "Research and Markets: UK Legal Services Market Report 2015," Yahoo!Finance, February 12, 2015, http://finance.yahoo.com/news/research-markets-uk-legal-services-170800061.html.
33. Centre for Innovative Justice, "Affordable Justice—A Pragmatic Path to Greater Flexibility and Access in the Private Legal Services Market," October 2013, 18, 38, http://mams.rmit.edu.au/qr7u4uejwols1.pdf.
34. Ibid., 17.
35. Ibid., 33.
36. UK 2014 Consumer Impact Report, 3.
37. UK 2014 Consumer Impact Report, 12.
38. SRA Magnetic Forces, 3.
39. Ibid., 4.

## *Chapter Nine*

# Alternative Structures Cannot Help Those Who Cannot Pay for Legal Services

Some argue that alternative structures can be used only to provide legal services for payment—that they are of no use for providing free legal services to clients who are unable to pay.[1] For this reason, they argue that alternative structures will serve no valid purpose, since legal services for payment are already available. As one commentator wrote:

> [T]he changes spurred by nonlawyer ownership will not lead to significant access gains . . . persons in need of civil legal services frequently have few resources, are often involved in complicated cases, and commonly are not sophisticated at navigating either the legal services market or the legal system. Nonlawyer ownership provides few new options. . . . For these individuals, legal aid often will be the only way to address their legal service needs. The legal market, even a deregulated one, is unlikely to provide for these persons' legal needs because they do not have the money to purchase the frequently rather sophisticated legal services they require.[2]

There are two levels of response to this argument.

At the first level, as discussed in the Introduction, even if legal services for payment are already available, they are nevertheless out of reach for a large portion of the US population. This population includes people who are so poor that they cannot afford to pay anything for legal services, but it also includes the middle class, as well as start-ups and small and medium-sized businesses. Generally speaking, they are able to pay some amount. But they are not able to pay any amount—there are limits to how much they are able to pay, and they are not comfortable committing in advance to pay unknown amounts (the consequence of hourly billing). Further, both types of populations—those who can pay nothing and those who can pay something within limits—also struggle to access legal services for reasons not directly related to price. As also discussed in the Introduction, those reasons include not realizing their issue is a legal one, not knowing who can help them, not knowing where to go to find help, not knowing who they can trust to help them, and so forth.

If alternative structures offer a means to develop different ways to provide legal services in order to better reach the middle class and businesses, at affordable, predictable prices, is this not a legitimate and sufficient use of the structure? Or is the only legitimate use of an alternative structure to provide free legal services to those who cannot pay for them at all?

The second level of response to the argument is this: Alternative structures offer the means to provide free legal services to those who cannot pay for them at all. In addition, in contrast to traditional forms of legal aid, alternative structures offer the means to provide those services on a sustainable and scalable basis. There are examples of this from the present day as well as from the past. With respect to the present day, a good example is the "sister" corporations Salvos Legal and Salvos Legal Humanitarian. They are two Australian ILPs, both wholly owned by the Salvation Army:

- Salvos Legal is a commercial and property law practice whose lawyers have worked for prominent national and regional firms as well as in-house legal departments. Its clients are corporations, government agencies, and not-for-profits, including CBRA Australia, Commonwealth Bank, and Transport for New South Wales. Salvos Legal provides advice and legal assistance on a paid basis; the fees it collects, less expenses, are used to fund Salvos Legal Humanitarian.
- Salvos Legal Humanitarian is a full-service law firm that provides services to the "disadvantaged and marginalized" in a variety of areas, including family law, housing, migration and refugee matters, debt, and criminal law. The services of Salvos Legal Humanitarian are offered free of charge; the firm has a staff of lawyers whose salaries are paid from the income, less expenses, of Salvos Legal.

Salvos Legal Humanitarian receives no government funding, nor any funding from the Salvation Army—it is funded from the income earned by Salvos Legal, which serves commercial clients on a paid basis.[3] In 2014, Salvos Legal was named "Law Firm of the Year" by the Australian *Lawyers Weekly*.[4] In 2015 it was named "Corporate Citizen Firm of the Year" and "Boutique Firm of the Year" by *Australasian Lawyer*,[5] and it again won a *Lawyers Weekly* award, this time in the category "Pro Bono Program of the Year."[6] Since its founding in 2010, Salvos Legal Humanitarian has opened

16 offices across eastern Australia and, at the time this book went to press, had provided free legal services for approximately 16,000 matters.[7]

It is true that in the United States, a certain number of social service organizations provide free legal assistance. Many of them do this not with paid staff attorneys but in reliance upon volunteer attorneys who work on a pro bono basis.[8] However, some of these organizations have attorneys on staff who provide clients with direct representation—this is notably the case with respect to Catholic Charities, which provides this kind of representation in particular with respect to refugee and immigration matters.[9] At first glance, this model appears highly similar if not identical to the one of Salvos Legal Humanitarian. However, there is a fundamental difference: Catholic Charities is funded in part by donations from diocesan churches and in large part (about 65 percent)[10] by local and federal government donations. (One commentator has described Catholic Charities as "an arm of the federal welfare state."[11]) In contrast, again, Salvos Legal Humanitarian receives no government funding, nor any funding from the Salvation Army.

It is also true that in the United States lawyers are free to establish income-generating law firms and use the profits to fund free legal services. Indeed, any law firm whose lawyers provide pro bono services in any amount without a corresponding reduction in salary are arguably doing just that, albeit in the absence of a separate, formalized structure. However, as Hadfield explains in detail, the amount of pro bono services that are provided in this manner do not even scratch the surface of the number of hours that would be required to fulfill the unmet need for legal services in the United States.[12] Further, while it is certainly possible in theory, in reality it is rare indeed that one or more lawyers in the United States, acting independently and notably outside the context of a social services organization, have actually chosen to establish such structures, and notably without reliance upon government funding of any kind. While it is possible to speculate in many ways as to why this is so rare, some insight may be found in a 2013 letter from David Schraver, the president of the New York State Bar Association, to Jonathan Lippman, then chief judge of the State of New York: Objecting to a newly adopted rule that required New York attorneys merely to report the number of hours they spent on pro bono work (without imposing any minimum number of required hours), Schraver wrote that "the provision of legal services to the poor is a public responsibility."[13] That statement is in stark contrast to this explanation of Luke Geary, the managing partner of both Salvos Legal and Salvos Legal Humanitarian: "[T]he reason for [the] existence [of the two firms] is to serve people in need. They are an expression of the social work of the Salvation Army, in a justice sense."[14] In other words, rightly or wrongly, the provision of legal services to the poor and to people in need fits much more squarely within the purposes and objectives of a social services organization than it does with one or more lawyers acting independently of a social services organization. While certainly some lawyers go to law school with the intention of pursuing a career in public interest law, even those lawyers do not go to law school with the intention (let alone the ability) to work for free.

The model of Salvos Legal Humanitarian is a versatile one. It can be duplicated by any charitable or philanthropic organization as well by other types of organizations, like educational institutions and business incubators, in order to offer legal services in fulfillment of the organization's mission and objectives. One variation is the example of Salvos Legal—that is, the creation of two sister structures, one which provides legal services on a paid basis in order to fund the other, which provides legal services on a free basis. Another variation is where the structure providing free legal services is funded not by paid legal services but in some other manner—by other, nonlegal types of paid goods or services or through charitable donations or grants. (That being said, funding by charitable donations or grants would severely restrict the sustainability and scalability of the model—it is the reason why not-for-profit law firms in the United States, which rely heavily on donations and grants, struggle to expand their services).

The model of Salvos Legal Humanitarian is echoed in a proposal by two Canadian researchers: Myra Tawfik and James Hinton of the Centre for International Governance Innovation in Waterloo, Ontario. They propose that "entities such as a law school, an innovation hub or a philanthropic organization"[15] own pro bono clinics, and notably pro bono clinics offering services in entrepreneurship and IP. They explain that such clinics would benefit both start-up communities by providing them with support, as well as law students by providing them with training. And because such clinics would not need to rely upon public legal aid, they could operate in a more financially sustainable manner.[16] Tawfik and Hinton go even further—they argue that such structures are the means for the IP legal community to support the fulfilment of Ontario's and Canada's economic strategies—that they will allow Canada to "[shore] up our start-up and entrepreneurial capacity in order to grow our knowledge economy and to effectively compete on a global scale."[17]

Also in the present day, the model of Salvos Legal Humanitarian has been turned on its head—to use paid legal services to fund nonlegal charitable services. England and Wales offer two examples of this:

The first example is Aspire Law, a joint venture of Aspire, a spinal cord charity, and Moore Blatch, a personal injury law firm. Aspire Law specializes in persons with spinal cord injuries. It is different from its competitors in the personal injury legal services market in two manners: (i) it does not deduct fees from its clients' compensation awards (instead Aspire Law's fees are paid solely by the insurer that recorded the accident), and (ii) half of the profits earned by Aspire Law are paid to Aspire, the charity, which uses it to provide support, funding, and housing for persons with spinal cord injuries.

The second example is Castle Park Solicitors Community Interest Company, an ABS established and owned by Community Advice and Law Service (CALS). CALS is a Leicester-based not-for-profit organization and registered charity that provides advice, representation, and advocacy in the areas of debt, housing, and welfare benefits. CALS created Castle Park Solicitors in response to the UK's cuts in legal aid. It created the ABS for two purposes: (i) to serve at affordable rates low and middle income clients who would have been eligible for legal aid in the past, in the areas of family and immigration law, and (ii) in a manner akin to Aspire Law, to generate a sustainable income stream for CALS, so that it can continue to provide its services for free, but reduce its reliance on government funding and grants.[18] Castle Park Solicitors offers to certain low-income clients a reduction in fees of 50 percent and the possibility to pay in monthly installments. Castle Park Solicitors also offers free legal services, notably in the form of weekly drop-in clinics, at different locations such as the Family Court in Leicester, the Leicester Sikh Temple, and its own offices.

The present day offers another example in the form of Road Traffic Representation (RTR). This website, operated by the UK-based ABS Legalmatters Limited, provides an online legal advice service for road traffic offenses. In a first stage, a user accused of a traffic offense visits the site in order to respond online to a series of questions (the questions are posed on the basis of conditional logic). On the basis of the user's responses, the site assesses whether the authorities have followed the proper procedure (and thus whether any procedural or technical objections can be raised) and makes a diagnosis both of the likely penalties the client will face if convicted and of any defenses that may be asserted. These services are entirely automated as well as free of charge. Depending upon the complexity of the matter, that information may be sufficient for the user to adequately understand his/her rights and to make informed decisions about how to proceed.

As a next stage the user may, if he/she chooses, request a telephone call with a solicitor—in that case, the call is charged at a fixed price of £35 and is unlimited in time. Finally, at a third stage, the user may, for an additional fixed price, opt for representation in court. In this case, the system's automatic process triggers the allocation of a barrister to handle the case, notifies the user of the allocation, and generates a brief for the barrister to consult to obtain full information.[19]

Of course there already exist websites that provide generic information regarding traffic violations and a person's rights and options when they are faced with one. What differentiates RTR from those other websites is RTR's application of a rules-based expert system in order to offer advice that is tailored for the specific person and the specific offense. In this manner, a person seeking information, someone typically not trained in legal research, does not need to search for the information themselves, nor, once (if) they find it, do they need to wade through the generic information in order to determine for themselves what is and is not pertinent for them. In this way, RTR makes the information much more accessible and relevant, thus more likely to be used effectively.

RTR was named a finalist for the 2015 Legal Aid Practitioners Group's Legal Aid Lawyer of the Year awards, in the category of "Access to Justice through IT." The judges described it as "an interesting model which could be adapted to other areas of law."[20] Indeed, RTR's founder, Martin Langan, is currently exploring the development of RTR's software for use in the area of family law, notably in order to facilitate the offering of unbundled services with respect to divorce and child custody matters.

The past also offers important examples of how alternative structures have been used to provide free legal services to low-income persons. These examples are important not only from a historical perspective, but also from a modern-day one in that they can be replicated more or less closely today. Further, these examples come not from a foreign country, but from the United States itself:

In her 2015 book *Women and Justice for the Poor: A History of Legal Aid, 1863–1945*, Felice Batlan unveils an otherwise unknown but exceptionally rich history of how free legal assistance was provided to poor and disadvantaged persons, and, in particular, to poor and disadvantaged women in the United States, over a period of decades. This assistance was not provided by traditional law firms, by the organized bar, or by legal aid organizations in the manner we know legal aid today. Instead, it was provided by a number of women's social services organizations, the most active of which included the Protective Agency for Women and Children in Chicago[21] and the Women's Educational and Industrial Union in Boston.[22]

At Batlan explains, while some of these organizations saw themselves primarily as providing legal aid, many of them performed a wide range of reform work as well as providing services to poor women.[23] In that manner, legal assistance was integrated on a continuum with other types of assistance, such as help to find employment, housing, or clothing and to enrich the cultural and spiritual lives of their communities.[24] (In today's parlance, we might describe it as "multidisciplinary.")

The organizations that offered these services were not owned, controlled, or managed by lawyers. They were charitable or not-for-profit organizations that were founded and run by, for the most part, middle- or upper-class women.[25] Further, the women who provided legal assistance were, for the most part, not professional lawyers in that they did not have a formal legal education and were not admitted to the bar.[26] This does not mean, however, that they did not have legal knowledge or experience. To the contrary, as

Batlan explains, many of these "lay lawyers" acquired extensive knowledge and experience, and were accepted and even respected by professional lawyers and judges.[27] Going further, Batlan states, "[T]here is no evidence that, historically, the work of nonlawyers was inferior to that of lawyers."[28]

Batlan has estimated that in a given year, one of these organizations would have handled anywhere from a couple of hundred to a couple of thousand cases or more.[29] That being said, because precise records were not always kept, it is not possible to know exactly how many of these organizations existed.[30] (Batlan's research focused on organizations founded by white, Christian women in the Midwest and Northeast of the United States. She exhorts others to pick up the mantle of her research, in order to gain a better understanding of comparable organizations in other parts of the country as well as of comparable organizations founded by others, and notably by African-Americans and by immigrants.[31])

By the 1930s, these organizations ceased to exist. While several factors contributed to their demise, Batlan explains that the principal factor was the professionalization of legal aid, on the one hand, and of social work, on the other. With respect to legal aid, professional lawyers, in nearly all cases men, created legal aid societies that worked to progressively take over the legal work done by the women's social services organizations. These men believed both that only professional lawyers could provide the relevant services and that only men should be professional lawyers. At the same time, social work was undergoing a professionalization process of its own, creating a profession in which one would attend school and learn the new discipline of social work. As a result of these dual processes, women "lay lawyers" working in social services organizations lost their place. They became sandwiched between professional lawyers, who were nearly exclusively men, and professional social workers, who were nearly exclusively women.[32]

In addition to losing their place, these women were written out of the history of legal aid. Batlan explains how this happened: Our source of knowledge about the history of legal aid comes principally from the 1919 book *Justice and the Poor*, by Reginald Heber Smith.[33] At the time Smith was doing research for his book, he visited fourteen cities and met with many people, including a limited number of women lay lawyers.[34] To his shock, Batlan explains, he discovered that these women knew what they were doing: They knew the law, they followed cases through, and their work was effective.[35] The problem was that their model was radically different from the model that matched his vision for legal aid. For him, legal aid needed to look like any other law firm, which meant that legal services could be provided only by professional, male lawyers.[36] He and his colleagues saw no role for women to play, believing that their mere presence would diminish the prestige of legal aid.[37] For these reasons, in writing his book, Smith deliberately deleted references to them.[38]

Because generations of scholars have accepted *Justice and the Poor* as an accurate account of the history of legal aid,[39] one consequence of the book was to render the legal work of the social services organizations invisible.[40] As a result, the real-life examples they provide have also been invisible—examples of how alternative structures not only have been but also can again today be used to provide free legal services. And, again, these examples come not from a foreign country but from the United States. More specifically, these examples, as finally brought to life in Batlan's book, show how social service, charitable and other not-for-profit organizations could once again provide legal services to poor and underprivileged persons, as they did a hundred years ago. But to see that requires a rejection of Smith's highly restrictive view of what legal aid (and, indeed, legal services more generally) is and how it must be provided in favor of a view that is more flexible, expansive, and open to a variety of different models.

## STORIES

### (PART V OR ONLINE)

*Luke Geary, Managing Partner, Salvos Legal and Salvos Legal Humanitarian* (Part V): Geary describes how Salvos Legal Humanitarian has provided free legal services with respect to 16,000 cases to date and counting, without funding from the government or from the Salvation Army.

*Chris Byron, Managing Director, Aspire Law* (online): Byron describes how Aspire Law both represents its spinal cord injury clients for a reduced fee and provides an income stream to Aspire, the charity, which uses it to help persons with spinal cord injuries in a variety of ways.

*Glenda Terry, Practice Manager, Castle Park Solicitors* (online): In a model similar to that of Aspire Law, Terry describes how Castle Park Solicitors provides legal services to low-income clients at a reduced fee and channels its profits to the charity Community Advice and Law Service for use in supporting its activities.

*Martin Langan, Founder, Road Traffic Representation* (online): Langan describes how Road Traffic Representation's automated system provides to persons charged with a traffic offense a certain amount of free legal services together with options for additional telephone information and in-person representation at low, fixed prices. Langan also describes how RTR's system can be adapted for use in other areas, notably family law.

*Felice Batlan, Professor of Law, IIT Chicago-Kent College of Law* (online): Batlan describes in greater detail the legal aid work of women's social services organizations in the late nineteenth and early twentieth centuries and explains how these organizations offer examples for legal aid today.

*Jenny Holloway, Associate Dean, Nottingham Law School and Nick Johnson, Pro Bono Director, Nottingham Law School Legal Advice Centre* (Part V): Holloway and Johnson describe how as an ABS, Nottingham Law School's Legal Advice Centre can charge below market rates for certain legal services and use those amounts to fund the Centre's free legal services.

## NOTES

1. See, for example, Gillian Hadfield and Larry Fox, "Regulating the Future Delivery of Legal Services," webinar, 39:45, http://bcove.me/la7z1w1b. See also Goldfinger Personal Injury Law, "Alternative Business Structures and the Legal Profession in Ontario," *Toronto Injury Lawyer Blog*, April 16, 2015, http://www.torontoinjurylawyerblog.com/2015/04/alternative-business-structures-and-the-legal-profession-in-ontario.html; and David Wiseman, "Alternative Business Structures and Access to Justice … for Whom?," *Slaw*, August 28, 2014, http://www.slaw.ca/2014/08/28/alternative-business-structures-and-access-to-justice-for-whom/.
2. Robinson, "When Lawyers Don't Get All the Profits," 41.
3. Salvos Legal, "The 2010–2014 Media Collection," 3, accessed August 21, 2015, https://fliphtml5.com/qokx/mguh.
4. Leanne Mezrani, "Legal Stars Shine Light on What Is Possible," *Lawyers Weekly*, August 12, 2014, http://www.lawyersweekly.com.au/news/15615-legal-stars-shine-light-on-what-is-possible.
5. Samantha Woodhill, "Australasian Law Awards Winners Announced," *Australasian Lawyer*, May 22, 2015, http://www.australasianlawyer.com.au/news/australasian-law-awards-winners-announced-200668.aspx.
6. Felicity Nelson, "Australian Law Awards Winners Revealed," *Lawyers Weekly*, September 18, 2015, http://www.lawyersweekly.com.au/news/17171-australian-law-awards-winners-announced.
7. Salvos Legal maintains an online counter of the number of matters for which it has provided free legal assistance since 2010: https://slh.salvoslegal.com.au/counter.
8. See, for example, Catholic Charities Archdiocese of Washington, "Catholic Charities Legal Network Annual Report 2015," https://www.catholiccharitiesdc.org/file/Legal_Networkbreak _Annual_ReportFY2015.pdf.
9. See, for example, "Immigration Legal Services," Catholic Charities Archdiocese of Washington, accessed April 25, 2016, https://www.catholiccharitiesdc.org/ILS.
10. Kelly Riddell, "Catholic Church Collects $1.6 Billion in U.S. Contracts, Grants Since 2012," *The Washington Times*, September 24, 2015, http://www.washingtontimes.com/news/2015/sep/24/catholic-church-collects-16-billion-in-us-contract/?page=all. See also, for example, "Immigration Legal Services," Catholic Charities Archdiocese of Washington: This webpage explains that "[t]he generous support of Maryland Legal Services Corporation, Montgomery County, MD, and individual and law firm donors enables our Immigration Legal team to continue to offer in-depth comprehensive services to our clients."
11. Riddell, "Catholic Church Collects."
12. Hadfield, "The Cost of Law," 45–46; Hadfield, "Innovating to Improve Access," 5.
13. David M. Schraver, "Mandatory Reporting of Pro Bono Service and Contributions," June 26, 2013, 1, http://nylawyer.nylj.com/adgifs/decisions/062813letter.pdf.
14. Luke Geary, interview with author, December, 2014.
15. Myra Tawfik and James Hinton, Letter to the Law Society of Upper Canada's Working Group on Alternative Business Structures, December 23, 2014, 3, http://www.lsuc.on.ca/uploadedFiles/Centre%20for%20International%20Governance%20Innovation%20(CIGI).pdf.
16. Ibid.
17. Ibid.

18. Dan Bindman, "Not-for-Profit's Groundbreaking ABS Eyes Expansion," *Legal Futures*, June 4, 2014, http://www.legalfutures.co.uk/latest-news/abs-lives-not-profits-groundbreaking-abs-eyes-expansion.
19. The founder of Road Traffic Representation, Martin Langan describes the service in this video: "Martin Langan—AI Law," Reinvent Law Channel, n.d., https://vimeo.com/72383554.
20. Legal Action Group, "Legal Aid's 2015 Roll Call of Honour," June, 2015, http://www.lag.org.uk/magazine/2015/06/legal-aid%E2%80%99s-2015-roll-call-of-honour.aspx.
21. Felice Batlan, *Women and Justice for the Poor: A History of Legal Aid, 1863–1945* (New York: Cambridge University Press, 2015), 49–81.
22. Ibid., 36–46.
23. Ibid., 47–84.
24. Ibid.
25. Ibid., 4
26. Ibid.
27. Ibid., 5.
28. Ibid., 14.
29. Felice Batlan, interview with author, November, 2015.
30. Ibid.
31. Batlan, *Women and Justice for the Poor*, 11.
32. Ibid., 123–53.
33. Reginald Heber Smith, *Justice and the Poor* (New York: Carnegie Foundation, 1919).
34. Batlan, *Women and Justice for the Poor*, 140.
35. Ibid., 142.
36. Ibid., 142–43.
37. Ibid., 148.
38. Ibid., 143.
39. Ibid., 6.
40. Ibid., 4.

# *Chapter Ten*

# Alternative Structures Will Make Things Harder for Un- and Underemployed Lawyers

Some argue that it is a mistake to open the market for legal services to the participation of nonlawyers when there are many licensed lawyers who are either unemployed or underemployed. Those arguments include:

- "[A]lternative business structures would cause difficulties with the legal profession and would dilute the value of current attorneys' investment in their legal education."[1]
- "It is a disservice to the public and to our profession to allow nonlawyers to dispense legal advice especially when we have countless thousands of newly admitted and established colleagues who are not able to make a decent living as a practicing lawyer."[2]
- "[The focus should be less] on broadening who can offer legal services as opposed to how do we help people who are already licensed . . . to deliver those services."[3]
- "With a significant number of new licensees remaining unemployed, or underemployed, we have a natural concern that by allowing nonlicensees into the equation, those unemployed licensees will now be forced to compete with the 'other talent' that may have more investing power."[4]
- "[We are concerned] about the large scale delivery of services as limiting practice options for general practitioners in smaller communities."[5]

In recent years, many have bemoaned the high rate of un- and underemployment of lawyers. This has been particularly the case with respect to recent law school graduates, whose situations are often acute because many graduate with a high level of debt.[6] On the other hand, some dispute that there is a problem, arguing that even if a greater number of lawyers than before are un- or underemployed, the overall unemployment rate for lawyers is significantly lower than the unemployment rate for the population as a whole (in 2010, the unemployment rate for lawyers was 1.5 percent, as compared to 9 percent for the population as a whole).[7] At the same time, as discussed in part III, so many people (as well as businesses) in the United States lack meaningful access to legal support that the problem is considered by some to constitute a human rights crisis.

An important explanation for this disconnect between lawyers and people (as well as businesses) that need legal services is the professional consultancy or "solution shop" model that is most typically used. As discussed in chapter 8, regardless of how many lawyers there may be, this model severely limits the number of people that can be served, and especially it severely limits the number of low and middle income persons that can be served. This is because under this model, lawyers solve problems by spending time working on the problems. For lawyers to solve additional problems, they spend more time. In working this way, there is little or no reduction in marginal costs. Additional work incurs additional marginal costs, such that increased volume cannot result in lower prices. Aggravating this problem is the use of hourly billing, because it incentivizes the delegation of as much work as possible to lawyers, and discourages the development of processes that would relieve lawyers of lower-level and routine tasks in order to have them carried out in a less expensive or less labor intensive manner. Finally, hourly billing combined with the high level of fragmentation of the legal market also make it difficult to access legal services—difficult to know in advance how much the service will cost, to know where or how to look, to judge quality, to know who to trust.

In this manner, it does not matter how many "surplus" lawyers there may be—as long as the principal delivery model used is the professional consultancy or "solution shop" model and as long as the market remains so fragmented and reliant upon hourly billing, there will always be a significant portion of the population that simply cannot access legal services, because they cannot afford them, because they need price certainty, because they cannot find them, or for all those reasons.

Alternative structures offer the means to address this gap. They offer the means to bring together people with different but complementary skills, expertise, and resources that, when combined, enable the development and implementation of new methods to deliver legal services—methods that can address the deficiencies of the professional consultancy model and reach a larger number of people who need legal services. If it were possible for lawyers, and notably for "surplus" lawyers, acting alone, to develop and implement such methods on the large scale that is needed, would they not have already done so?

At any rate, alternative structures, while they may utilize lawyers in a different way, cannot exclude them entirely. To the contrary, they must include them—they cannot operate without them. In the first place, lawyers are needed for practical reasons: Investors can bring cash, IT experts can bring IT expertise, business process experts can bring business process expertise, project management experts can bring project management expertise, marketing experts can bring marketing expertise, etc. None of those persons can bring the legal expertise that the alternative structure will also require if it is to effectively and credibly provide legal services.

In the second place, in Australia and in England and Wales, the regulations require that lawyers be included. In England and Wales, each ABS is required to appoint a Compliance Officer for Legal Practice (COLP), and in Australia, each Incorporated Legal Practice (ILP) is required to appoint one or more "authorised principals" (AP) or Legal Practitioner Directors (LPD). In each case, these persons must be qualified lawyers, and they bear principal (but not sole) responsibility for the legal services provided by the alternative structure, and notably that the structure complies with ethical rules.

If there are a large number of un- and underemployed lawyers, and notably of recent law graduates, it is because the legal services market as it is structured today does not offer them opportunities. The lawyers are not needed by existing law firms, and the challenges of practicing on their own, under a professional consultancy model, are great. Keeping alternative structures out of the market will not increase their opportunities. To the contrary, alternative structures offer new, as yet untapped, opportunities to lawyers—either to join with others to found an alternative structure, or to join one as an employee. (The opportunities that alternative structures offer to lawyers are more fully explored in part II.)

Finally, the argument that alternative structures should be opposed because there are already a large number of un- and underemployed lawyers begs the questions: Who are legal services for? What is their purpose? Why are they regulated? Are legal services performed for the benefit of lawyers, with the purpose of regulation to ensure they are employed (and see a return on their legal education)? Or are legal services performed for the benefit of the public—with the purpose of enabling individuals and organizations to understand their rights and obligations and to protect their rights? If the response is that legal services are performed not for the benefit of lawyers but for the benefit of the public, then is the argument that alternative structures will makes things harder for un- and underemployed lawyers relevant to the debate?

## STORIES

(PART V OR ONLINE)

*Rod Cunich, National Practice Group Leader, Slater and Gordon* (online): Cunich explains that many lawyers at the firm who are of retirement age are delaying retirement because for the first time in a long time they are enjoying practicing law.

*Nadia Haque Associate, Radiant Law* (online): Haque explains that because Radiant is a new company and is still evolving, she feels that the firm offers her many opportunities.

*Dina Tutungi, General Manager—Personal Injury Victoria, Slater and Gordon* (Part V): Tutungi describes the opportunities for lawyers at the firm as "endless."

## NOTES

1. Beal Law Firm, "Comment in Opposition to Alternative Business Structures," April 28, 2016, http://www.americanbar.org/content/dam/aba/images/office_president/beal_law_firm_abs.pdf; see also Ross, Letter to Katy Englehart, 1; and Jack E. Truitt, "ABA's Commission on the Future of Legal Services—Alternate Business Structures for Law Firms," April 25, 2016, http://www.americanbar.org/content/dam/aba/images/office_president/jack_e_truitt_abs.pdf.
2. Paris P. Eliades, "Testimony to the ABA Commission on the Future of Legal Services," February 7, 2015, 3, http://www.americanbar.org/content/dam/aba/images/office_president/paris_eliades.pdf.
3. Andrew Schpak, Video Testimony to the ABA Commission on the Future of Legal Services, 4:55, February, 2015, http://bcove.me/ntiu0oxy.
4. Lorne Berndt et al., "Alternative Business Structure Call For Input," December 20, 2014, 2, https://www.lsuc.on.ca/uploadedFiles/BRENDT,%20Lorne%20and%20group.pdf.
5. Ontario Bar Association, "Alternative Business Structures and the Legal Profession in Ontario," n.d., 8, https://www.lsuc.on.ca/uploadedFiles/Ontario%20Bar%20Association.pdf.
6. Mark Koba, "No New Lawyers! Economy Can't Handle Them," *The Fiscal Times*, March 21, 2013, http://www.thefiscaltimes.com/Articles/2013/03/21/No-New-Lawyers-Economy-Cant-Handle-Them.
7. Ilya Somin, "Challenging the Conventional Wisdom About the Job Market for Lawyers," The Volokh Conspiracy, October 17, 2011, http://volokh.com/2011/10/17/challenging-the-conventional-wisdom-about-the-job-market-for-lawyers/.

## *Chapter Eleven*

# The Burden of Proof Has Not Been Met

Some have argued that alternative structures should not be allowed because those who advocate in their favor have not met their burden of proof. For some, the argument is a simple: "[T]he burden should be on those who desire such a fundamental change to Rule 5.4 to make the case for it, and they have failed to do so."[1] For others, the argument is more complex: "[T]he 'burden of proof' must remain on proponents of ABS to show that nonlawyer ownership . . . is necessary to achieve wider access to justice, and that ABS both helps the public and protects it."[2]

Meeting this burden is especially important, they argue, because the change will be permanent and irreversible: "One of the major problems is that, once you sell ownership of the legal profession, you can never get it back. You cannot undo ABS once it is allowed. It is irreversible and permanent. That is reason enough not to entertain it. . . . The onus is on those who want to make a permanent, irreversible gargantuan change to show that overturning centuries of independence will not result in harm."[3] Or, phrased more mildly, "We'd like to see more of a track record of client protection being paramount so there are no divided loyalties."[4]

Those in favor of alternative structures take the opposite perspective: They argue that, generally speaking, people and companies are free to raise capital in the United States. If the ability to raise capital is restricted, then there needs to be a very good reason to do so. Thus, those who oppose alternative structures have the burden to prove that there is a very good reason to prohibit them.

An argument such as this one, attempting to assign a burden of proof, is caricatural among lawyers.

For lawyers, and especially in the context of litigation, the concept of "burden of proof" is an important one—it clarifies which side in a trial is the "default" or assumed position and which side is not. The side that is not has the burden to produce evidence that is sufficient both to support its position and to refute the default position. The "default" side has no obligation to produce evidence in support of its position, and the "default" side will prevail if the other side's evidence is insufficient. In the context of litigation, in most cases it is clear which side bears the burden of proof, and it is (more or less) clear what level of evidence that side needs to produce in order to meet that burden—those questions have been decided in advance either by statute or by precedent case law. A stereotypical example is a criminal trial where the defendant is (or at least should be) presumed to be innocent, and the prosecution is required to refute that presumption "beyond a reasonable doubt." While evidence of the defendant's innocence is certainly nice to have, the defendant is not required to produce it.

The debate over alternative structures is not occurring in the context of litigation. There is no statute or precedent case law that dictates or even suggests which side is presumed to be correct and which side is presumed to be incorrect, and thus which side has the burden to produce sufficient evidence in support of its position and which side can "win its case" even if it produces no evidence at all.

In other words, the debate of burden of proof in relation to alternative structures is being held outside of the normal context (litigation) and in the absence of the normal indicators (statutes and precedent case law). For these reasons, it is not surprising that the debate is difficult if not impossible to resolve.

In this debate, it is also not clear just what needs to be proved. Is it necessary to prove that alternative structures are "better" than traditional structures in all contexts and for all situations? Is it possible to prove that? Is it necessary to prove that no "harm" will result from alternative structures? Is it possible to prove that? Harm to whom? What quantity or level of proof would be sufficient? Should there also be a requirement to prove that the current restrictions on alternative structures do not cause harm? Has that ever been proven?

The assertion that allowing alternative structures is "irreversible and permanent" is not clear, either. If the rules can be changed to allow for alternative structures, then why can't they be changed back to restrict them again? Admittedly, if such a restriction were applied to pre-existing structures, there could be claims of deprivation of property. However, if those existing structures proved to be as detrimental as feared, then the rules should allow for regulatory intervention to address those problems, including the ability to liquidate the structures (this is the case in England and Wales and Australia) and to block mergers (as standard competition regulations permit).

Raising at this time the issue of burden of proof invites this question: At the time that restrictions on nonlawyer ownership and multidisciplinary practices were first imposed in the early twentieth century, what burden of proof was met in order to justify the restrictions? A small number of corporate practices had formed in the early 1900s, about a decade before the first restrictions were imposed. At the time the first restrictions were imposed, nothing in the public record indicates that any proof of harm caused by those existing structures was required.

To the contrary, while the court decisions from that time describe at length hypothetical evils that might result from the corporate practice of law, none cite any actual evils that did occur during the short period when corporate practices were in existence. This 1910 decision of a New York appellate court provides a typical example of the justifications that were considered sufficient for imposing the restrictions:

> The practice of law is not a business open to all, but a personal right, limited to a few persons of good moral character, with special qualifications ascertained and certified after a long course of study, both general and professional, and a thorough examination by a state board appointed for the purpose. The right to practice law is in the nature of a franchise from the state conferred only for merit. It cannot be assigned or inherited but must be earned by hard study and good conduct. It is attested by a certificate of the Supreme Court, and is protected by registration. No one can practice law unless he has taken an oath of office and become an officer of the court, subject to its discipline, liable to punishment for contempt in violating his duties as such, and to suspension or removal. It is not a lawful business except for members of the bar who have complied with all the conditions required by statute and the rules of the courts. As these conditions cannot be performed by a corporation, it follows that the practice of law is not a lawful business for a corporation to engage in. As it cannot practice law directly, it cannot indirectly by employing competent lawyers to practice for it, as that would be an evasion which the law will not tolerate. . . .[5]
>
> The relation of attorney and client is that of master and servant in a limited and dignified sense, and it involves the highest trust and confidence. It cannot be delegated without consent, and it cannot exist between an attorney employed by a corporation to practice law for it, and a client of the corporation, for he would be subject to the directions of the corporation, and not to the directions of the client. There would be neither contract nor privity between him and the client, and he would not owe even the duty of counsel to the actual litigant. The corporation would control the litigation, the money earned would belong to the corporation, and the attorney would be responsible to the corporation only. His master would not be the client but the corporation, conducted it may be wholly by laymen, organized simply to make money and not to aid in the administration of justice which is the highest function of an attorney and counselor at law. The corporation might not have a lawyer among its stockholders, directors, or officers. Its members might be without character, learning or standing. There would be no remedy by attachment or disbarment to protect the public from imposition or fraud, no stimulus to good conduct from the traditions of an ancient and honorable profession, and no guide except the

> sordid purpose to earn money for stockholders. The bar, which is an institution of the highest usefulness and standing, would be degraded if even its humblest member became subject to the orders of a moneymaking corporation engaged not in conducting litigation for itself, but in the business of conducting litigation for others. The degradation of the bar is an injury to the state.[6]

In the early 1900s, the organized bar's interest in the unauthorized practice of law, notably by corporations, and its attempts to ban it, were sporadic and unfocused. The Great Depression changed that. In a 1950 publication, James Willard Hurst, a professor at the University of Wisconsin Law School, explained that the ABA "gave no vigorous attention to the problem until it appointed a committee in 1930."[7] By 1940, he continued, "over 400 bar association committees had been appointed to consider the unauthorized practice of law."[8] Professor Hurst explained this intensified interest in the topic as follows:

> The depression of the 1930's stimulated the first really widespread and organized concern of the bar with its lay competition. This coincidence of events ill fitted claims that this activity was moved simply by regard for protecting the public against the incompetent or unscrupulous. The speedy development of the drive against "unauthorized practice," set against the circumstances of the time, suggested that the movement was born more of an emotional desire to do something in the face of social catastrophe, than out of any deeply reasoned analysis. Evidence of this was found in the almost complete lack of any scientific fact gathering out of all the sudden bustling of committees and associations.[9]

In sum, there is nothing in the public record to suggest that at the time the organized bar sought to ban the corporate practice of law in the early twentieth century, it at any time produced any evidence in support of its position that could be credibly characterized as meeting a burden of proof.

In the larger context, does it really matter who has the burden of proof? Does the question of which side has the burden of proof have any bearing upon the ultimate questions of the (un)desirability and (in)utility of alternative structures? Is the debate over burden of proof a red herring—a debate that unnecessarily distracts from the real issues of economic policy, open competition, access to justice, and human rights? Is the question of burden of proof a debate that only lawyers could love?

## STORIES

(PART V OR ONLINE)

*John Ray, Senior Consultant, Law Firm Consulting Group* (online): Ray observes that, in general, people and companies are free to raise capital in the United States. He argues that if we are going to restrict the ability of anyone, law firms included, to raise capital, then we need a really good reason to do so. As regards law firms, he states, there is no good reason.

*Kristin Dangerfield, CEO, The Law Society of Manitoba* (online): Dangerfield explains that the Benchers of the Law Society of Manitoba didn't see how whether there exists proof that something necessarily will or will not occur is a compelling enough argument to hold Manitoba back.

## NOTES

1. Chandler et al., "Comments of Nine General Counsel," 3.
2. New York State Bar Association, "New York State Bar Association's Comments," 7.
3. Bradley Wright, February 9, 2015, comment on Colin Lachance, "ABS D.O.A? Idk," *Slaw*, February 6, 2015, http://www.slaw.ca/2015/02/06/abs-d-o-a-idk/.
4. William C. Hubbard, President of the ABA, quoted in Elizabeth Olson, "A Call for Law Firms to Go Public," *New York Times*, February 18, 2015, http://dealbook.nytimes.com/2015/02/18/a-call-for-law-firms-to-go-public/?_r=1.
5. In re Co-operative Law Co., 198 NY 479 (1910) 479–86, 483, https://casetext.com/case/matter-of-co-operative-law-co.
6. Ibid., 483–84.
7. James Willard Hurst, *The Growth of American Law: The Law Makers* (Boston: Little, Brown and Company, 1950), 323.
8. Ibid.
9. Ibid.

# *Part II*

# The Opportunities Offered by Alternative Structures

Alternative structures raise objections—the preceding pages are evidence of that. But they also present opportunities—for lawyers and the profession, for legal service providers, for regulation, for legal aid, for downstream markets, and for the economy as a whole.

## *Chapter Twelve*

# Opportunities for Legal Aid

Few (if, indeed, anyone) would claim that legal aid is sufficiently funded. To the contrary, many assert, and assert on a repeated basis, that legal aid is woefully underfunded. Two noteworthy examples include:

1. The Conference of Chief Justices (CCJ): This organization, founded in 1949, brings together the highest judicial officer of each state, as well as of the District of Columbia and certain territories. It is governed by a board of directors, it works through a variety of standing, temporary, and special committees, and it often works in close collaboration with the Conference of State Court Administrators (COSCA). The principal output of the CCJ is resolutions proposed by a specific committee and adopted by the CCJ as a whole, often jointly with the COSCA.[1]

Between 2002 and 2015, the CCJ adopted no less than eight resolutions calling for increased funding of legal aid. Most of these resolutions call specifically upon the US Congress to provide greater funding to the Legal Services Corporation;[2] others call upon the members of the CCJ to do more on a state level to attract greater funding for legal aid.[3]

In addition to the no less than eight resolutions, in March 2012 the CCJ and the COSCA jointly issued and shared with Congress a Position Paper entitled "The Importance of Funding for the Legal Services Corporation from the Perspective of the Conference of Chief Justices and the Conference of State Court Administrators."[4] In this seven-page paper, the CCJ and the COSCA explain to Congress the importance of equal justice, the extent of the "justice gap" in the United States, the importance of legal aid for meeting that gap, and, as a consequence, the importance of adequate funding for legal aid. The paper concludes with an appeal to Congress for increased funding for legal aid.

2. The ABA: Near the top of the page of its website entitled "Civil Legal Services," the ABA states:

> Adequate funding for the federal Legal Services Corporation is one of the ABA's highest legislative priorities.
>
> The ABA strongly supports a significant funding increase for the Legal Services Corporation. ABA advocacy seeks to gain or reinforce Congressional Members' support for LSC, to get their signature on a letter in support of LSC's funding increase and to keep them involved on behalf of LSC funding throughout the appropriations process.[5]

On another page of its website, entitled "Civil Legal Aid Funding," the ABA states:

> Financial resource limitations remain one of the largest barriers preventing civil legal aid providers, even with their pro bono allies, from addressing the needs of low-income client communities.[6]

The ABA has created a "Resource Center for Access to Justice Initiatives." The home page for the center states that the center's "two main focuses" are "supporting the growth and development of state-based Access to Justice Commissions," and "collecting and analyzing data on the various sources of funding for civil legal aid."[7]

The center has developed a two-page document entitled "Supreme Court Leadership on State Legislative Funding for Civil Legal Aid" (ABA Best Practice Document). The document lists and describes "best practices" for a state's highest court to follow in seeking to attract greater funding for legal aid, including:

- "Create a high-powered [Access to Justice (ATJ)] commission . . . ATJ commissions have been instrumental in obtaining or increasing state funding."
- "Speak and write publicly on behalf of the funding."
- "Call for and/or host hearings."
- "Visit with legislators."
- "Find funding sources. Helping campaign leadership and legislators identify the most appropriate sources of state funding for legal aid."
- "Administer the funds."[8]

The ABA Best Practice Document provides examples from the states of Texas, New York, and Wyoming, as follows:

> Example of Texas:
>
> *The Role of the Supreme Court*: Funding for basic civil legal services is included in the supreme court's budget, and the court actively advocates for

additional funding. There is a bipartisan consensus on this key principle: that providing assistance for those who cannot afford a lawyer is a critical part of the justice system and essential to the integrity of the rule of law. The chief justice and individual members of the court play a public role, making the case for legal aid funding by giving speeches, visiting with individual legislators, meeting with newspaper editorial boards and authoring op-ed pieces.

*The Result*: In 2013, Texas legal aid programs received approximately $20.8 million in funds through appropriations and court fees and fines, almost 300 percent more than the $5.4 million received 10 years ago.

Example of New York:

*The Role of the Chief Judge*: The current chief judge, when he was appointed in 2009, made increasing funding for civil legal aid a priority. He created the Task Force to Expand Access to Civil Legal Services, which includes leaders from the bench, bar, law schools, and legal aid, as well as legislators and representatives of unions, corporations, foundations and the medical community. He conducts annual public hearings to assess the unmet civil legal aid needs throughout the state. The task force prepares an annual report, based on the hearings and other research, which the chief judge then uses to make his case to the legislature and the governor.

*The Result*: New York's state funding has increased more than any other state over the past 12 years, going from $4.6 million in 2003 to $85 million for 2015.

Example of Wyoming:

*The Role of the Supreme Court*: An ATJ commission was established by the court in 2008. The chief justice designated an associate justice to chair the commission, and he worked tirelessly to lead the effort to document the need for civil legal aid and then find additional funding. Community meetings were held throughout the state, gathering documentation of the unmet need. The commission took responsibility for both leading the campaign and doing the hard day-to-day work to get the legislation passed and signed by the governor.

*The Result*: Wyoming obtained its first-ever state funding, through a filing fee surcharge, in 2010. It generates about $1,250,000 annually, making Wyoming fifth in the country in terms of state dollars per poor person, and more than doubling the total amount of funding available for civil legal aid in the state.[9]

Indeed, the CCJ was sufficiently impressed with the ABA Best Practice Document that one of the most recent of its eight resolutions mentioned above was to encourage its members (as well as the members of the COSCA) to consider it "as a worthy guide for their own endeavors to obtain increased funding for civil legal services."[10]

Given the severity of the unmet need for legal services in the United States (discussed in detail in part III), it is difficult to find fault with these and the many other calls that are repeatedly made for greater public funding for legal aid. At the same time, these calls are remarkable in the way that they focus nearly exclusively on the allocation of greater public funds by the US Congress and/or by state legislatures. These calls seem to be premised upon the (for the most part) unstated assumption that the only possible source of funding for legal aid, or at least the only potentially adequate source, is public funds. (Other sources of funding, such as Interest on Lawyers Trust Accounts [IOLTA], of course exist, and private donations are certainly encouraged and accepted, but there is no pretense of the adequacy of these other sources.) On the basis of this unstated assumption, neither the CCJ nor the ABA (nor nearly any other individual or organization that calls for greater funding for legal aid) suggests or even appears to have considered the potential of alternative structures as a viable complement to increased public funding. This failure is puzzling, for two reasons.

The first reason is that as desirable as increased public funding is, it can never come close to being enough. As discussed in detail in part III, today total public spending for the Legal Services Corporation and other legal aid, combined with charitable donations for legal aid, is about $3.7 billion per year,[11] whereas Professor Gillian Hadfield's research estimates that $50 billion per year would be required to secure one hour of legal assistance for households with unmet dispute-related needs.[12] An increase in public funding for legal aid by $46.3 billion—not just once but on an annual basis—would, at a minimum (taking inspiration from the ABA Best Practice Document), require highly intensive, nonstop, long-term lobbying efforts at the federal level as well as at the level of each and every one of the 50 states, the District of Columbia, and the territories. And it still would not be enough.

The second reason is that other options for funding legal aid exist—options that do not require the allocation of public funds and that, at the same time, are sustainable and scalable. An evident example is the Australian "sister" corporations Salvos Legal and Salvos Legal Humanitarian, both wholly owned by the Salvation Army. As described in detail in part I, Salvos Legal is a commercial and property law practice that serves corporate clients. Salvos Legal Humanitarian is a law firm that provides services to the "disadvantaged and marginalized" in a variety of areas, including family law, housing, migration and refugee matters, debt, and criminal law. The services of Salvos Legal Humanitarian are offered free of charge; the firm has a staff of lawyers whose salaries are paid from the income, less expenses, of Salvos Legal. Salvos Legal Humanitarian receives no government funding, nor any funding from the Salvation Army—it is funded from the income earned by Salvos Legal, which serves its corporate clients on a paid basis. As also noted in part I, at the time this book went to press, Salvos Legal Humanitarian had provided free legal services for approximately 16,000 matters across its 16 offices in eastern Australia.[13] In addition to the number of awards that Salvos Legal and Salvos Legal Humanitarian have won (as detailed in part I), Luke Geary, the managing partner of both firms, was listed in Pro Bono Australia's Impact 25, which recognizes the social sector's most influential people of 2015. Pro Bono Australia described Luke Geary as having "managed to create a self-sufficient law firm that helps some of the most needy people in the community." In doing so, Pro Bono Australia continued, "he has changed the face of the funding of pro bono legal services in Australia."[14] There is just one thing that prevents the Salvation Army, and, indeed, any other charitable organization that is so inclined, from creating comparable structures in the United States—that is the regulations that restrict nonlawyer ownership and control of law firms.

Another example is the website Road Traffic Representation (RTR), operated by the UK-based ABS Legalmatters Limited. Also described in detail in part I, RTR provides an automated online legal advice service for road traffic offenses. After posing the user, accused of a traffic offense, a series of questions, the service assesses whether the authorities have followed the proper procedure (and thus whether any procedural or technical objections can be raised) and makes a diagnosis both of the likely penalties the client will face if convicted and of any defenses that may be asserted. The service provides that information to the user free of charge—payment is requested only if the user requests additional assistance either in the form of a phone call with a solicitor or in-person representation in court.

Additional examples, perhaps less evident but no less compelling, can be found in Felice Batlan's book *Women and Justice for the Poor: A History of Legal Aid, 1863–1945*.[15] As discussed in part I, this book details how, over a period of decades in the late nineteenth and early twentieth centuries, a number of women's social services organizations in the United States provided free legal services to the poor. They did this sometimes with the assistance of professional lawyers, but, in most cases, with "lay lawyers"—that is, with women who did not have a formal legal education and were not admitted to the bar, but who did have extensive legal knowledge and experience. In either case, the services were provided free of charge (as well as, in many cases, in combination with other, nonlegal services, such as help to find employment, housing, or clothing), yet also without any allocation of public funding.

Today women's social services organizations no longer play the role in society that they once did. That does not mean, however, that the types of legal issues that they dealt with or the types of causes that they championed have disappeared. To the contrary, they are still very much alive and championed in a large variety of community organizations and advocacy groups that seek to help poor and disadvantaged persons with respect to housing, labor conditions, domestic violence, an so forth. While these organizations of course provide information to their members and constituents, to the extent that the information is legal in nature, and certainly to the extent it is tailored for any specific individual or case, the organizations enter a gray area where their activities could be characterized as the unauthorized practice of law. There is just one thing that prevents these organizations from providing to their members and constituents the legal aid that they so desperately need—and doing so without public funding—that is the regulations that restrict nonlawyer ownership and control of law firms.

Lifting such regulations in order to allow community organizations to provide legal services to their members and constituents, and, in particular, to the poor and disadvantaged, is one of the first recommendations that was made by the Commission on Legal Empowerment of the Poor. This independent international organization, hosted by the United Nations Development Programme, was established in 2005 as the "first global initiative to focus on the link between exclusion, poverty, and the law."[16] The commission was co-chaired by Madeleine Albright, former US Secretary of State, and Hernando de Soto, Peruvian economist and founder of the Institute for Liberty and Democracy, and its members were made up of policy makers and practitioners from around the world, including:

- Anthony Kennedy,[17] US Supreme Court Justice,
- Lawrence Summers, former president of Harvard University and former US Secretary of the Treasury,
- Mary Robinson, former president of Ireland and former United Nations Commissioner for Human Rights,
- Fernando Henrique Cardoso, former president of Brazil and former president of the Club of Madrid, and
- Lloyd Axelworthy, former Minister of Foreign Affairs of Canada.[18]

During a period of three years, the members of the commission and other contributors for its five working groups conducted 22 national consultation processes with representatives from local governments, academia, civil society, and grassroots movements.[19] In 2008, the commission published its two-volume report entitled *Making the Law Work for Everyone*.

The report of the first working group, "Access to Justice and Rule of Law," contains a number of observations and recommendations with respect to "reforms to the law and justice sector that will provide poor people with the institutional environment, the protections, and the incentives they need to realise their full capabilities and reap the maximum potential return of their existing assets."[20] Among other topics, those observations and recommendations address the unauthorized practice of law, as well as community-based organizations and advocacy groups.

On the topic of the unauthorized practice of law, the working group writes:

> [A] potential problem [in the supply of legal services] may arise when countries adopt stringent "unauthorised practice of law" rules—that is, when countries mandate that certain legal services can only be offered by certain legal professionals, such as licensed attorneys . . . While these restrictions may arise from the purist of motives—such as the desire to maintain minimum quality standards and to protect consumers from exploitation—they often have the effect of conferring a monopoly on a particular set of legal service providers. This drives up the price of legal services to the disadvantage of consumers in general and poor consumers in particular . . . .
>
> There is a small but growing body of empirical research—most of it, admittedly, conducted in rich countries—that indicates that nonlawyers (especially paralegals) and lay people can perform a variety of "legal" services as effectively as lawyers, and that market mechanisms and less intrusive regulation can be effective in protecting consumers from exploitation. This evidence, though suggestive rather than conclusive, indicates that liberalisation of the market for legal services—in the form of weakening restrictions on who can provide particular legal services—is likely to improve access to justice for the poor substantially, while imposing relatively few costs on society so long as alternative quality-control institutions are in place.
>
> A major attraction of [this reform strategy] is that, compared to many other legal reform strategies, it may require fewer government or donor expenditures, at least in the medium- to long-term. Instead of compensating for a market distortion through continuous payments to individuals, the liberalisation strategy focuses on curing a market distortion through a change in the regulatory scheme.[21]

On the topic of community-based organizations and advocacy groups, the working group writes:

> The use of local community-based organizations [can be expanded to allow individuals to pool their risks, as a form of emergency legal insurance]. For example, labor unions can—and often do—provide legal services on behalf of their members. . . . Tenants' associations can provide emergency legal assistance to contest evictions; similarly, while landlords' associations can offer emergency legal assistance to take action against unruly or destructive tenants. The advantage of relying on small community-based representative groups to provide emergency legal insurance is that these groups may be able to better monitor and police their members and to apportion insurance costs in proportion to risk.[22]

In sum, no matter how intensive or extensive any lobbying efforts for increased public funding for legal aid may be over any period of time, they will never lead to an allocation of funding at a level sufficient to close the justice gap in the United States. At the same time, the Australian sister corporations Salvos Legal and Salvos Legal Humanitarian and the UK-based website Road Traffic Representation provide compelling present-day examples of how legal aid (free legal services) can be provided without public funding. In addition, Felice Batlan's book, *Women and Justice for the Poor: A History of Legal Aid, 1863–1945*, provides a multitude of equally compelling examples from the past of how community organizations can provide free legal services without public funding—examples that remain fully relevant today. Finally, a global initiative hosted by the United Nations and led by high-profile policymakers, including US Supreme Court Justice Anthony Kennedy, has recommended the liberalization of the regulation of legal services in order to allow nonlawyers and community-based organizations and advocacy groups to provide legal services to the poor, stating that "it is likely to improve access to justice for the poor substantially while imposing relatively few costs on society," and that a "major attraction" of such liberalization is that it may require "fewer government or donor expenditures."[23]

In short, it is clear that alternative structures offer a real and meaningful opportunity for legal aid: the opportunity to provide free legal services without the allocation of public funds. What is less clear is why the CCJ, the ABA, and other organizations continue to focus so much of their limited attention and resources on seeking increased public funding—and call on others to do the same—rather than devoting some of that attention and resource to changing the regulations in order to allow for alternative means of providing legal aid and, as a consequence, to also allow for alternative means of funding.

## STORIES

### (PART V OR ONLINE)

*Luke Geary, Managing Partner, Salvos Legal and Salvos Legal Humanitarian* (Part V): Geary explains how Salvos Legal Humanitarian provides free legal services in Australia without funding from either the government or the Salvation Army.

*Martin Langan, Founder, Road Traffic Representation* (online): Langan describes how Road Traffic Representation's automated system provides to persons charged with a traffic offense a certain amount of free legal services. Langan also describes how RTR's system can be adapted for use in other areas, notably family law.

*Felice Batlan, Professor of Law, IIT Chicago-Kent College of Law* (online): Batlan describes how for decades in the late nineteenth and early twentieth centuries, women's social services provided legal aid without government funding.

# NOTES

1. See, generally, "Conference of Chief Justices," Conference of Chief Justices, accessed August 27, 2015, http://ccj.ncsc.org/.

2. "Resolution 9: In Support of Continued Funding for the Legal Services Corporation Commensurate with Its Vital Role in the Administration of Justice," January 24, 2002, http://ccj.ncsc.org/~/media/Microsites/Files/CCJ/Resolutions/01242002-Support-Continued-Funding-Legal-Services-Corporation-Administration-Justice.ashx; "Resolution 11: In Support of Increased Federal Funding for the Legal Services Corporation," August, 2009, http://ccj.ncsc.org/~/media/Microsites/Files/CCJ/Resolutions/08012009-In-Support-of-Increased-Federal-Funding-For-the-Legal-Services-Corporation.ashx; "Resolution 9: In Support of the Federal Funding Legal Services Corporation," August 3, 2011, http://ccj.ncsc.org/~/media/Microsites/Files/CCJ/Resolutions/08032011-In-Support-of-the-Federal-Funding-Legal-Services-Corporation.ashx; "Resolution 1: In Support of Continued Federal Funding for the Legal Services Corporation," February 1, 2012, http://ccj.ncsc.org/~/media/Microsites/Files/CCJ/Resolutions/02012012-In-Support-of-Continued-Federal-Funding-for-the-Legal-Services-Corporation.ashx; "Resolution 1: In Support of Continued Federal Funding for the Legal Services Corporation," July 25, 2012, http://ccj.ncsc.org/~/media/Microsites/Files/CCJ/Resolutions/07252012-In-Support-of-Continued-Federal-Funding-for-the-Legal-Services-Corporation.ashx; "Resolution 7: Reaffirming the Critical Importance of Adequate Funding of the Legal Services Corporation," 2015, http://ccj.ncsc.org/~/media/Microsites/Files/CCJ/Resolutions/07252015-Reaffirming-Critical-Importance-Adequate-Funding-Legal-Services-Corporation.ashx.

3. "Resolution 7: In Support of State Supreme Court Leadership in Increasing Funding for Civil Legal Assistance," July 28, 2010, http://ccj.ncsc.org/~/media/Microsites/Files/CCJ/Resolutions/07282010-In-Support-of-State-Supreme-Court-Leadership-in-Increasing-Funding-for-Civil-Legal.ashx; "Resolution 4: In Support of the Statement of Best Practices for State Funding of Civil Legal Aid Prepared by the ABA Resource Center for Access to Justice Initiatives," 2015, http://ccj.ncsc.org/~/media/Microsites/Files/CCJ/Resolutions/07252015-Support-Statement-Best-Practices-State-Funding-Civil-Legal-Aid.ashx.

4. Conference of Chief Justices and Conference of State Court Administrators, "The Importance of Funding for the Legal Services Corporation from the Perspective of the Conference of Chief Justices and the Conference of State Court Administrators," 2012, http://www.ncsc.org/~/media/Files/PDF/Services%20and%20Experts/Government%20Relations/Final%20CCJCOSCA%20white%20paperonLSCFunding33012CleanVersion1%20w%20resolution.

5. "Civil Legal Services," American Bar Association, accessed December 30, 2015, http://www.americanbar.org/groups/legal_aid_indigent_defendants/initiatives/civil_legal_services.html.

6. "Civil Legal Aid Funding," American Bar Association, accessed December 30, 2015, http://www.americanbar.org/groups/legal_aid_indigent_defendants/initiatives/resource_center_for_access_to_justice/resources---information-on-civil-legal-aid-funding.html.

7. "Resource Center for Access to Justice Initiatives," American Bar Association, accessed May 21, 2016, http://www.americanbar.org/groups/legal_aid_indigent_defendants/initiatives/resource_center_for_access_to_justice.html.

8. ABA Resource Center for Access to Justice Initiatives, "Supreme Court Leadership on State Legislative Funding for Civil Legal Aid," July 15, 2015, 1, http://www.americanbar.org/content/dam/aba/images/legal_aid_indigent_defendants/ls_SC%20Best%20Practices.pdf.

9. Ibid., 2.

10. "Resolution 4: In Support of the Statement of Best Practices for State Funding of Civil Legal Aid Prepared by the ABA Resource Center for Access to Justice Initiatives," 2015, 2, http://ccj.ncsc.org/~/media/Microsites/Files/CCJ/Resolutions/07252015-Support-Statement-Best-Practices-State-Funding-Civil-Legal-Aid.ashx.

11. Hadfield, "The Cost of Law," 45.

12. Ibid. See also Hadfield and Rhode, "How to Regulate Legal Services," 3–4.

13. Salvos Legal maintains an online counter of the number of matters for which is has provided free legal assistance since 2010: https://slh.salvoslegal.com.au/counter.

14. "Luke Geary," Pro Bono Australia Impact 25, accessed December 30, 2015, http://www.pbaimpact.com/#!luke-geary-/oinwt.
15. Batlan, *Women and Justice for the Poor*.
16. Commission on Legal Empowerment of the Poor (CLEP), *Making the Law Work for Everyone, Volume I: Report of the Commission on Legal Empowerment of the Poor* (New Jersey: Toppan Printing Company America, 2008), 16.
17. Interestingly, Justice Kennedy later authored the US Supreme Court's 2015 decision *North Carolina Board of Dental Examiners v. FTC*, described in part I.
18. Ibid., v–vi.
19. Ibid., 2.
20. Commission on Legal Empowerment of the Poor (CLEP), *Making the Law Work for Everyone, Volume II: Working Group Reports* (New Jersey: Toppan Printing Company America, 2008), 2.
21. Ibid., 29–30.
22. Ibid., 33.
23. Ibid., 30.

*Chapter Thirteen*

# Opportunities for Downstream Markets and the Economy as a Whole

Certain US-based (as well as Canada-based) commentators have examined the regulation of legal services generally, and alternative structures more specifically, in an economic context. Some of the more prominent examples include US-based Gillian Hadfield as well as Clifford Winston, Robert W. Crandall, and Vikram Maheshri, and Canada-based Edward Iacobucci and Michael Trebilcock.

Hadfield, in particular, has published a number of groundbreaking and highly compelling pieces, and they are essential reading for anyone interested in the topic. Two examples include:

1. "Legal Barriers to Innovation: The Growing Economic Cost of Professional Control Over Corporate Legal Markets," in which Hadfield argues:

> [A] great deal of legal work is, and should be appreciated as, economic activity that contributes to the effective functioning of a market economy. As a result, the extensive regulation imposed upon this market by the profession has substantial economic costs. [1]

The most significant effect of the heavy regulation of legal services, Hadfield argues, is on innovation, which in most other markets is a primary source of not just cost reductions but also improvements in quality. [2]

Hadfield states that a distinction should be made between the "political/democratic" and the economic spheres of the legal system. The former relates to "normative goals of equality, dignity, fairness and individual well-being," whereas the latter relates to "the profit-making endeavors of the entities upon which a market economy relies for the invention, production, distribution and pricing of most good and services."[3] When it comes to the latter, she argues:

> [O]ur primary concern in the design of regulation should be the efficiency of the legal markets and their capacity to promote the efficiency of other markets. Here a vigorous market that releases the capacity to deliver more effective and lower-cost legal inputs, channeling market pressures into innovation rather than spiraling hourly rates, should be the goal.[4]

2. "Legal Infrastructure and the New Economy," in which Hadfield reports on the problems that in-house counsel at "leading innovative firms" complained to her that they face in seeking legal services. Hadfield states that while the persons she interviewed did mention spiraling legal fees and litigation costs, their primary focus was on their difficulties in finding the types of legal help that they need.[5]

For example, Hadfield recounts that in-house counsel of Google bemoaned the difficulties they have in convincing their outside counsel to streamline the contracting process, as well as the difficulties they have in finding legal service providers who have in-depth experience with compliance issues such as privacy, intellectual property, and defamation, and who can address them on an international basis in a sufficiently integrated manner.[6] As another example, the general counsel of Cisco Systems complained that he was unable to find litigation counsel who could think about litigation strategy not only in the strict context of the litigation itself, but also in the larger context of the company's public and investor relations concerns.[7]

Hadfield argues that the principal reason why the legal services market is unable to fill the needs of clients such as these (who, it is probably safe to assume, would not have a problem paying for it) is that the regulations governing the legal services market insulate the market from market pressures and do not allow for innovative or different services to be developed.[8] Hadfield continues:

> The transformation in legal demand wrought by the attributes of a new globally networked web-based economy—facing high degrees of heterogeneity, high velocity and pervasive uncertainty—are clearly outstripping the capacity of our legal infrastructure to keep pace. The gaps and frictions and missing bridges identified by general counsel in leading innovative firms reflect the growing inadequacy of the set of legal inputs available to them to structure and regulate their economic relationships and environment. The primary legal infrastructure available to them is excessively document-based and human capital intensive, and insufficiently diversified, flexible and responsive to change and cost. . . .[9]
>
> Only lawyers will find anything remarkable in the proposal that markets for legal goods and services should operate as most other markets do, with decisions about who can provide what goods and services where, with what

> training, in what organizational form and with what financing left largely to the market, subject only to the level of regulation necessary to make such a market reasonably competitive and responsive to social welfare. Lawyers will argue that these are matters of professional ethics—but they are not. They will argue that these are matters of consumer protection—but they are not. They are matters of economic policy.[10]

In their book *First Thing We Do, Let's Deregulate All the Lawyers*, Winston, Crandall, and Maheshri use empirical data to argue that lawyers in the United States enjoy a substantial earnings premium: For example, in 2004, of a total annual spend on lawyers in the United States of about $170 billion, they estimate that the earnings premium was about $64 billion (about 38 percent), or $71,000 per practicing lawyer.[11] In more recent years, they estimate the premium to have reached about 50 percent.[12] For the authors, the premium cannot be attributed to any one or more particular skills or other personal characteristics.[13] Instead, it is principally due to a combination of two factors: Government policies "generate massive demand for legal services,"[14] while, at the same time, "occupational licensing requirements"[15] constrain the supply of lawyers and, thus, of legal services. The authors offer as examples of policies that "generate massive demand" regulations intended to curb market power and to address externalities such as pollution, liability rules to settle civil wrongs, enforcement of criminal laws to protect the public, and legal guidelines to facilitate commercial and residential property transactions.[16] The constraining "occupational licensing requirements" are, the authors explain, the need to pass a state bar examination, and, most especially, the need to attend an ABA-accredited law school in order to be able to provide legal services.[17]

In making these arguments, the authors echo Hadfield's and Heine's expression that we live in a "law-thick" world[18]—indeed, the authors' list of policies that "generate massive demand" are only a sampling of the types of policies that are essential for any country that values the rule of law. By restricting the supply of the services that are intended to assist with the enforcement of these policies, the authors argue, lawyers are able to earn premiums "that result not merely from lump-sum transfers but also in a substantial deadweight loss to the US economy from inflated prices for legal services."[19]

The solution to this inefficiency, the authors argue, is to "deregulate" entry into the legal profession. This should be done both by allowing individuals who are not licensed lawyers to provide legal services, as well as by allowing nonlawyer entrepreneurial organizations to enter the market and compete with law firms.[20] The many benefits that would result from this would include a reduction of the "deadweight loss associated with lawyers' earnings premiums" as well as greater competition that would cause law firms to offer innovative new services and products.[21]

In their paper "An Economic Analysis of Alternative Business Structures for the Practice of Law," Iacobucci and Trebilcock examine in detail different forms of legal practice—sole proprietorships, partnerships, limited liability partnerships, and, finally, business corporations, with and without nonlawyer ownership. In doing so, they consider the "potential economic benefits and costs of different structures." Notably, considering these benefits and costs principally from the perspective of lawyers and law firms, they conclude:

- "There is no single structure that is optimal across all contexts": there are trade-offs with respect to each type of structure, and the best resolution of those trade-offs depend upon the circumstances, such as the nature of the firm's clients and of the services the firm provides.[22]
- "[F]rom an economic perspective, there are potential gains from opening up options for business structures and associated capital structures," and that gains from liberalization are "most likely to materialize where a large capital investment is necessary for a firm to realize certain gains."[23]
- "Even if liberalization of the choice of form of legal practice led to the demise of certain business structures, it would not necessarily be a bad thing, especially in the longer run for the lawyers at such doomed structures."[24]

These works of these US and Canada-based authors make important contributions to our understanding of the regulation of legal services in an economic context.[25] As vital as their contributions are, however, they are not complete. This is because they rest upon the assumption that a more liberal regulatory regime and greater competition in the legal services market will more or less necessarily result in economic benefits for those who seek legal services, without exploring that assumption in any level of detail or attempting to demonstrate resulting economic benefits with empirical evidence. The assumption can be seen, for example, in Iacobucci and Trebilcock's statements such as "Greater efficiency means greater potential gains for lawyers, clients and investors alike,"[26] and "it is probable that economic efficiencies realized as a result of liberalization would be passed on to clients and prospective clients."[27]

To examine this assumption in greater detail, and thus to complete our understanding, we need to look outside North America to Europe, where since 1989 a number of studies have been carried out demonstrating with empirical evidence that liberalization of the regulatory regime does, not just in theory but also in fact, result in economic benefits—for individuals and organizations that purchase legal services, for downstream markets, and for the economy as a whole. These studies include the following:

1. A 1989 study in England and Wales by Simon Domberger and Avrom Sherr: Prior to the mid-1980s, solicitors in England and Wales held a monopoly over conveyancing (this term refers to the legal work involved with the purchase and sale of real property). Domberger and Sherr explain that during the 1970s and early 1980s, consumers expressed increasing dissatisfaction with the high cost of conveyancing and the length of time required to complete a typical transaction.[28] An intense public debate ensued, during which the legal profession, through the Law Society (which at that time played a dual representative and regulatory role) mounted a strong defense of its monopoly. It argued that the underlying laws were complex and so necessitated a fully qualified professional, that if the monopoly were lost other legal services would suffer because they were unprofitable as compared to conveyancing, and that as a result many offices would close down because they were profitable only as a result of their conveyancing activity.[29]

In spite of these arguments, in early 1984 the government gave an undertaking that it would liberalize the provision of conveyancing services by removing the state-supported monopoly. What followed over the course of the mid-1980s was a series of regulatory changes that included, among other liberalizations, reduced restrictions on advertising by solicitors (a change adopted in October 1984) and the creation of a new "para-profession" of licensed conveyancers who were allowed to compete with solicitors for conveyancing work. The first licensed conveyancers began to practice in May 1987.[30]

Domberger and Sherr examined the effects of these regulatory changes by issuing a questionnaire to members of the UK-based Consumers' Association who had changed address between 1983 and 1986, the large majority of whom had bought and/or sold real property rather than moving from one rental accommodation to another. The questionnaire contained approximately 75 questions and addressed a wide range of topics relating to fees, lengths of time to complete tasks, and the client's perception of the quality of the service provided.[31]

Given that the full implementation of the regulatory changes was not complete until 1987, the study did not analyze their full effect, but rather, the effect of the reduced restrictions on advertising combined with the threat of new entrants to the market.

Domberger and Sherr's analysis of the responses to the questionnaire led them to conclude that "the threat of competition has yielded significant welfare benefits. Price discrimination has been reduced, conveyancing costs have fallen in real terms, and there has been a measurable improvement in consumer satisfaction."[32] More specifically, they concluded:

> The emergence of a threat of new entry into the field was sufficient to set in motion strong competitive forces within the profession. Fees started to fall in 1984, following the policy announcement to liberalise conveyancing, and a full three years before licenced conveyancers entered the market. By 1986 the discriminatory element in the combined fees charged for sales and purchases of property had fallen by one third—from £6 to £4 per £1,000 of property value. . . .
>
> [T]he impact of competition has been far more pronounced in the conveyancing of property sales than of purchases. In particular, there has been a perceptible improvement in satisfaction ratings which suggests that the scope for improving the service is greater in the case of sales because the work involved is routine and subject to greater control by the solicitor than that associated with purchases.[33]

A later study on the effect of the same regulatory changes in England and Wales was published in 1994. That study concluded that the changes noted by Domberger and Sherr, and notably the reduction in prices, were short-lived: By 1992, licensed conveyancers "were pricing rather like solicitors."[34] In fact, at that time, a greater liberalization of the legal services market in England and Wales had yet to take place: In the early 1990s, licensed conveyancers effectively shared a monopoly with solicitors in that others, and notably nonlawyers through alternative business structures, were not yet allowed to enter the conveyancing market. In this light, and as the 1994 study concludes, "[T]he post-entry behaviour of licensed conveyancers is not too surprising. Even more than for solicitors, the conveyancing market is the focus of their business. They, just like solicitors, will benefit from implicit collusion."[35]

In fact, neither this subsequent study nor the passage of time since the original 1989 study has diminished the significance of Domberger and Sherr's work. It continues to be cited today in discussions regarding the liberalization of regulatory regimes for legal[36] as well as for other professional services.[37] For example, the French Commission d'Etude des Effets de la Loi Pour la Croissance et l'Activité[38] refers to the study four times in their 2015 paper in support of abolishing pricing schedules, geographic installation, certain licensing requirements, and other regulatory restrictions placed upon certain categories of licensed legal service providers in France, most notably notaries and bailiffs (*huissiers de justice*). The panel cites the 1989 study as an example where quality of service did not diminish as a result of opening the market to additional service providers—to the contrary, it increased.[39] In addition, the panel observes that the fact that price reductions did not persist in the long term indicates that partial reforms that still have the effect of limiting new entrants may not produce the desired effects on prices.[40]

2. A 2014 study by Erik Canton, Daria Ciriaci, and Irune Solera (Canton Study). This study focuses on four professional services activities—legal, accounting, architectural, and engineering—in certain European Union countries over the period 2008–2011.[41] It observes that as a consequence of the adoption of two EU Directives, the Professional Qualifications Directive[42] in 2005 and the Services Directive[43] in 2006, certain regulatory reforms with respect to these activities were implemented across the European Union Member States.[44] The reforms included reducing restrictions on access to the professions, on cooperation between professions, on legal form of practice and on advertising, and abolishing tariff restrictions.[45]

Using OECD regulatory indicators and Eurostat Structural Business Statistics (in combination with business demography data) as its main data sets,[46] the Canton Study measures the impact of the regulatory reforms in a two-step approach. As a first step, it measures the impact of the reforms on business dynamics, defined as the entry and exit of firms. As a second step, it measures the impact of the reforms on, on the one hand, "allocative efficiency," defined as the extent to which productive factors are allocated to their most efficient use, and, on the other hand, "sectoral profitability," which the study "proxies" by the gross operating rate, defined as the ratio of gross operating surplus to turnover.[47] The study finds that less strict regulation does result in intensified business dynamics in these professions, which, in turn, results in improved allocative efficiency and in reduced "observed larger-than-average profitability."[48] In other words (that is, in plain English), the study finds:

> [A] decrease of the level of regulation positively affects both birth and death rates and, through them, favours a better within sector allocation of resources and decreases profits. Stated simply, reducing barriers to the reallocation of capital and labour within sectors helps ensuring that the most productive firms can achieve their growth potential and that less efficient ones leave the industry (or get restructured).[49]

In concluding, the Canton Study stresses that the full economic impact of the regulatory reforms is expected to be much larger than the findings of this particular study. This is in part because, the study states:

> [D]eregulation could generate additional indirect benefits in the sense that, as shown by our analysis, professional services constitute an important intermediate input to down-stream sectors such as manufacturing. Therefore, efficiency gains will disseminate and spread to the rest of the economy through their backward and forward linkages.[50]

3. A 2011 study by Guglielmo Barone and Federico Cingano (Barone Study): This study seems to anticipate the Canton Study's final remarks in

that it examines whether countries with less anticompetitive regulation see better economic performance in manufacturing industries that use less-regulated services more intensively.[51] The Barone Study draws upon OECD databases and indicators that measure economic productivity as well as regulatory settings—the extent to which regulations promote or inhibit competition in that product market—and including the STructural ANalysis (STAN) data set. In this case, the data cover 17 OECD countries and 15 manufacturing industries.[52] The study focuses upon the regulatory settings for four upstream service activities: energy (electricity and gas), communication (telecommunication and postal services), transportation (air, road, rail transportation services), and professional services (including accountants, architects, engineers, and legal services).[53] In quantifying the relevant regulatory settings, the study considers barriers to entry, vertical integration, and market conduct regulation.[54] Conduct regulation, more specifically, encompasses "restrictions on prices and fees, advertising, the form of business, etc."[55] However, the study clarifies, the data available with respect to professional services is more limited as compared to the data available for the other types of upstream services.[56] For this reason, the study does not look back further than 1996.[57]

Making use of the available data and indicators, the Barone Study conducts a number of measurements, notably: "exposure" of manufacturing industries to services regulation, cross-country services regulation,[58] and level of dependence of each specific industry on each type of service.[59] On the basis of these measurements, the study discerns:

1. Lowering anti-competitive regulation in the provision of services has a "significant and positive effect on growth" in the downstream industries. Further, the greater a given downstream industry's dependence upon upstream services, the greater the positive effect on growth. The median growth rate for the countries and industries examined was 1.8 percent per year.[60]
2. Lower regulation (combined with higher financial development) translates into lower prices in service-intensive manufacturing industries.[61] (The study mentions pulp, paper, and printing as an industry whose service dependence is relatively high at the 75th percentile, and fabricated metal products as an industry whose service dependence is relatively low at the 25th percentile.[62])
3. Service regulation has a significant impact on the growth rate of value added per worker in service-intensive industries. The median productivity growth rate for all industries combined was 2.2 percent per year—for service-intensive industries, it was 0.9 percent greater.[63]
4. Service regulation is an important determinant of comparative advantages and international specialization: Exports by service-intensive in-

dustries tend to grow disproportionately more in countries with low levels of service regulation. In the bulk of industries studied, the increase is about 1 percent following a reduction in regulation.[64]

5. The positive effects of lower service regulation are stronger in larger countries, due to the larger extent of the demand by downstream industries. Indeed, the Barone Study states, larger countries should expect "substantial payoffs" from competition policies.[65]
6. Lowered regulations with respect to two types of services in particular—professional services and energy—offer the greatest opportunities for increasing downstream value-added growth rates. Specifically with respect to lowered regulations with respect to professional services, depending upon the country and the industry, the additional growth rate could be as much as 0.8 percent (in addition to the median growth rate of 1.8 percent per year).[66]

With these observations, the Barone Study concludes:

> [S]ervice regulation has a significant negative impact on the growth rate of value added, productivity and exports of service dependent industries. . . . [T]he impact of regulation appears to be particularly relevant in the case of . . . energy supply and professional services. . . . Also, our findings suggest the payoffs from lower service regulation would be more significant the larger the extent of the domestic market.[67]

4. A 2013 study by Renaud Bourlès et al. (Bourlès Study). The Bourlès Study builds upon the Barone Study, also seemingly in anticipation of the Canton Study's final remarks. The Bourlès Study focuses on the extent to which weak competition in upstream markets, notably by reason of restrictive regulations, curbs productivity and efficiency growth in downstream markets. This study considers 15 OECD countries (including the United States but not including the UK) for the period 1985 to 2007.[68] The study's examination encompasses a total of 20 downstream industries together with "intermediate inputs," such as energy (gas and electricity), transport (rail, road, and air) and communication (post, fixed, and cellular telecommunications), retail distribution, and professional services[69] (which includes legal services, as well as other professional and business services, such as accounting and architectural services, and the rental of machinery and equipment).[70]

The Bourlès Study collected data from a variety of sources, including, like the Barone Study, the OECD international product market regulation database (with a focus on nonmanufacturing regulation indicators), the OECD productivity database by industry, and the STAN database for industrial analysis.[71] Principal measurements, quantifiers, and concepts used in the study include:

- "Multifactor productivity (MFP) growth,"[72] which measures the changes in value added of downstream markets per unit of combined labor and capital inputs.
- The "regulatory burden indicator," which quantifies the "trickle-down" effect of nonmanufacturing regulations on all industries of the economy.[73]
- The "technological frontier," which refers, for any given industry, to that industry's most productive, economical, or sophisticated technology.[74]
- "Observation," which refers to each of the study's unbalanced panel of 4,629 "country-industry-period triads" for 15 countries and 20 industries over the 1985–2007 period.[75]

On the basis of the available data and using these measurements, quantifiers, and concepts, the Bourlès Study presents several regression models and simulations, notably:

i. The "Impact on Downstream MFP Growth of a One Unit Increase in the Indicator of the Burden of Upstream Regulations for Downstream Industries":[76] This regression model examines the estimated impact on multifactor productivity growth in downstream industries per one unit increase of the regulatory burden indicator in upstream industries. The model exposes that in a large majority—87 percent—of the cases observed, the impact of the regulatory burden indicator is negative. The model clarifies, however, that for 39 percent (of the 87 percent) the negative impact is not statistically significant. On the other hand, the model also clarifies that for the remaining 48 percent where the negative impact is statistically significant, this occurs with respect to observations that are closer to the technological frontier.[77] On the basis of this regression model, the study observes:

> [W]hen regulation restricts competition in industries that supply intermediate inputs, the incentives to improve efficiency are weaker in downstream industries the more intensively these industries use the regulated products. Moreover, the positive effect of competition on efficiency improvement is strongest for observations that are close to the global technological frontier.[78]

ii. "The Impact of Upstream Regulation on Downstream MFP Growth Depending on Distance to Frontier and Regulatory Settings":[79] This simulation examines what the effect on multifactor productivity growth would be if all anticompetitive regulations in upstream industries were instantaneously eliminated. The simulation examines this using estimation results over the entire period of 1985 to 2007, as well as for two subperiods of 1985–1994 and 1995–2007. The simulation exposes that when the entire period of 1985–2007 is considered, for the average technological gap (64 percent of the technology leader), and for the average level of regulation, the effect would be to increase multifactor productivity growth by 1 percent per year.[80]

A closer examination of the results for the two subperiods is even more interesting. For the first period of 1985–1994, the average impact of the regulatory burden indicator is positive for 63 percent of the observations and nonsignificant for 17 percent. In stark contrast, for the second period of 1995–2007, the average impact of the regulatory burden indicator is negative for 99 percent of the observations and significant for 73 percent. During the second subperiod, for the average technological gap (65 percent of the technology leader), and for the average level of regulation, the effect would be to increase multifactor productivity growth by 1.7 percent per year.[81]

After stressing that "these estimated effects are purely illustrative, as they would correspond to radical and sudden changes in regulatory settings that are unlikely to be politically implementable in practice,"[82] the Bourlès Study observes:

> The increasingly negative impact of regulation on MFP growth over time needs to be investigated further, but one interpretation is related to two sources of structural change affecting the global economy during this period: globalization and the diffusion of new technologies. With increased integration of the world economy in the context of the diffusion of new technologies, competition has become tougher downstream and [technology] adoption and the corresponding reorganization of production processes have become more compelling for maintaining market shares. At the same time, new entry by innovative firms has become a more important source of productivity improvements. Thus, the erosion of returns from efficiency improvements by regulated upstream industries is increasingly more damaging for incentives to enhance productivity, and possible barriers to entry generated by regulation in upstream industries are increasingly reflected in a drag on industry-level productivity performance. It is important to note that these different effects of regulation depending on the period studied should not be understood as coming from different levels of development (for example, from smaller average distance to frontier) as the effects appear to change over time at each given level of technological gap. They therefore necessarily originate from structural changes in the global economy.[83]

iii. "Simulation of Annual Gains in MFP Growth in Selected Countries from Adopting in 2000 the Lightest Practice Observed in 2007 in the Upstream Industries":[84] This simulation examines what the effect on multifactor productivity growth in nonfarm business industry would be if, in 2000, the 15 countries had adopted the "lightest practice" regulation observed in the upstream industries in 2007. The study defines "lightest practice" as, in each upstream industry, the average of the three lowest levels of anticompetitive regulation observed among the countries in the data set.[85] The study explains that "a switch to lightest practice means a pervasive and important easing of anticompetitive regulations in every nonmanufacturing industry covered in our data set. It is therefore an extreme example of structural policy reform."[86]

The study observes that in 2000, the countries where regulation was the "friendliest" were Sweden, Australia, the Netherlands, and the United States, and the countries where it was the most restrictive were France, Austria, Italy, and Greece. Seven years later (in 2007), regulatory environments had changed such that the friendliest countries were Denmark, Sweden, the Netherlands, and Australia. However, France, Austria, Italy, and Greece remained the most restrictive.[87]

The simulation demonstrates that from the year 2000 to 2007, there is a significant increase in multifactor productivity growth in each country studied. The increase peaks in 2001 and declines subsequently each year, which the study explains as a "declining catch-up effect," as well as reductions in regulatory burdens that took place in the relevant countries as compared to the baseline.[88] While for each country the increase in multifactor productivity growth is significant, they vary widely across the countries, depending upon the country's starting point. The increase for 2001 (that is, after the first year of adopting the "lightest practice") ranges from 0.5 percent (Denmark) to 2.25 percent (Italy).[89] The increase for the entire seven-year period ranges from 3 percent (Denmark and Netherlands) to 11 percent (Italy) and 12 percent (Belgium). The simulated increase for the United States for the seven-year period is 5 percent.[90] The study specifically observes that the highest gains occur with respect to retail and professional services and the lowest gains with respect to financial intermediation and communication. The study attributes the large cross-country differences to four factors: (a) the excess regulatory burden relative to lightest practice in each upstream industry, (b) the initial distance to the frontier of productivity in downstream industries, (c) the intensity of intermediate consumption of products from regulated upstream industries, and (d) the composition effect due to differences in industry structure across countries (as reflected in differences in value added shares of downstream industries).[91] On the basis of the regression models and simulations presented, the Bourlès Study concludes:

> Regulations that bridle access to otherwise competitive markets and unnecessarily constrain business operations can be a drag on productivity growth. While most analyses of this issue have focused on the effects of these regulations on the productivity of the firms or industries directly concerned, the main point of this paper is that such regulations can also have powerful indirect depressing effects on the productivity of other industries through input-output linkages. . . . [The main channels through which these effects happen are] reduced access to key intermediate inputs that curb competition downstream and rent seeking by intermediate input providers, both reducing incentives to improve productivity downstream . . . that differences in regulation of non-manufacturing industries providing intermediate inputs are indeed quite relevant in explaining the variance of multifactor productivity growth rates in our sample, with upstream regulation curbing such growth rates significantly in a

> large share of observations. Moreover, we showed that the closer that MFP is to the technological frontier, the higher is the estimated negative impact of upstream regulation on productivity growth. Interestingly, the estimated negative impact has increased over time with deepening globalization and diffusion of ICT [information and communications technology].[92]

Like the Barone Study, the Bourlès Study establishes clear cause and effect links between anticompetitive regulations in upstream services markets and downstream manufacturing and other markets that rely upon the upstream services. The Bourlès Study goes further than the Barone Study, in demonstrating that the cause and effect link is especially strong for developed countries where, notably in recent years, most downstream industries are increasingly involved in global competition. The study's explanation for this especially strong link is that for these industries, the few opportunities for increased efficiency that remain are with respect to their intermediate service inputs—inputs that, commonly, are "protected from extensive trade pressures."[93] With these upstream industries accounting for rising shares of total intermediate inputs, the study explains, the effects of lack of competition there are no longer limited to those industries themselves. Instead, the effects "propagate throughout the economy."[94]

5. A 2014 study by Cristina Mocci et al. (Mocci Study). This study confirms the general findings of both the Barone and the Bourlès Studies with a focused examination of Italy. More specifically, the Mocci Study examines the extent to which regulatory "liberalizations" that were adopted in the Italian services sector resulted in "sectoral value added" for 45 "overall sectors" and 25 manufacturing sectors of the Italian economy.[95] The services considered are telecommunications, the professions (legal, accounting, engineering, and architecture), energy, air, and transport.[96] The study examines the period 1995 to 2008, and, based upon the available data, breaks the period up into five time spans of 1995, 1998, 2001, 2004, and 2007.[97] The Mocci Study draws upon much of the same OECD indicators and databases as the Barone and the Bourlès Studies, most notably with respect to product market regulation.[98] The Mocci Study also draws upon data made available by the Italian National Institute of Statistics, most notably Input-Output tables, which "illustrate flows between the sales and purchases (both final and intermediate) of industry outputs or the sales and purchases (both final and intermediate) of product outputs,"[99] and include "the supply and use of goods and services, both imported and domestically produced, showing the value added produced by each sector."[100]

On the basis of those and other data, the Mocci Study performs a regression analysis of a panel of three-year averages of real and nominal value added as a measure of economic performance, for the manufacturing sectors and for the economy as whole, and the relevant product market regulation indicators. The analysis generates statistically significant results linking the overall liberalization of all the services considered to value added for both the manufacturing sector as well as for the economy as a whole, with coefficients of –0.14 and –0.29, respectively. Singling out specific services, the link is especially strong for professional services, which generates a coefficient of –0.26 for the manufacturing sector and a coefficient of –0.20 for the economy as a whole. (The next strongest link was energy, which generates a coefficient of –0.10 for the manufacturing sector and a coefficient of –0.21 for the economy as a whole).[101] The Mocci Study concludes:

> [T]he results prove that in Italy the sectoral liberalization played a relevant role in increasing value added in general and in the manufacturing sector. The effects of higher regulation in utilities, communication, energy, transport and professions sectors . . . is negative. Under the economic point of view, this result is in line with the idea that liberalization in [services regulation] determines positive effects on growth in downstream sectors.[102]

The studies described above are not the only ones of their kind. Others that offer empirical evidence to demonstrate the economic benefits of reduced anticompetitive services regulations for downstream markets and economies as a whole include:

- A 2010 study by Emanuele Forlani: Focusing on France, this study demonstrates that a low level of competition in services sectors, notably due to anticompetitive regulation, has negative effects on the productivity of downstream manufacturing firms.[103]
- A 2011 study by Jens M. Arnold, Beata S. Javorcik, and Aaditya Mattoo: Focusing on the Czech Republic, the study finds a "positive strong relationship between services sector reform and the productivity of local producers relying on services as intermediate inputs."[104]
- A 2014 study by Emilio Fernández Corugedo and Esther Pérez Ruiz: This EU-focused study uses its finding of "important multiplier effects of greater efficiency" in services for the rest of the economy to argue in favor of a "renewed impulse to the liberalization process" and an "enhancing of the advocacy role" of national competition authorities "in interpreting the notion of public interest underpinning existing regulations."[105]
- A 2014 study by Gilbert Cette, Jimmy Lopez, and Jacques Mairesse: Analyzing country and industry data for 14 OECD countries and 18 industries, this study examines the effects of anticompetitive regulations governing both services as well as labor markets, concluding that "nearly all countries could expect sizeable gains in multifactor productivity from deregulation reforms."[106]
- A 2015 study by Oliver Arentz et al.: This study applies the methodology of the Mocci Study to demonstrate that in Germany, also, regulation of the

services sector has a significant effect on the manufacturing sector as well as on the overall economy.[107] With a particular preoccupation with the manufacturing sector, this study observes:

> The structure of the German economy changed drastically over time. The decline of the proportion of gross value added of the manufacturing sector at the expense of the services sector is often cited as an indicator for this structural change. However, this shift is not necessarily an indication of a decreasing importance of the manufacturing sector, but rather it points to a fundamental change of the gross value added process in manufacturing. Within the manufacturing process, business services and product-related services are growing in importance in development, production, marketing, and sales as well as in customer relations and maintenance.
>
> With the increasing importance of intermediate inputs of the business services sector, the interest in the regulatory framework for the provision of these services and the resulting welfare effect is also increasing. Inappropriate regulation can, inter alia, lead to the waste of resources in the production process and to unexploited innovation potential. Negative effects would especially occur in the downstream domestic production areas, which compete internationally and, therefore, need competitive services. Conversely, the reduction of unnecessary regulation and trading-barriers can release unused growth potential not just in the services sector, but also in the manufacturing sector.[108]

Granted, none of these studies focus specifically on regulations that restrict nonlawyer ownership or multidisciplinary practices. Instead, to the extent they include legal services in their scope, they do so in a more general manner, and are constrained by the scope of the relevant OECD regulatory indicators. This does not, however, diminish the importance of these studies. Taken together, they are highly compelling in their use of empirical evidence to demonstrate that real reductions in any kind of anticompetitive regulations that govern legal (as well as other types of) services will result in significant economic benefits not just for the legal services market itself, but also for downstream markets and the larger economy. Further, as the Bourlès and the Barone Studies, respectively, point out, these benefits will be greater for:

- Those industries and those countries that are close to the "technological frontier" (that is, which use the most productive, economical, or sophisticated technology), because immediate service inputs (such as legal services) are one of the few opportunities for increased efficiency that remain open to them.[109]
- Larger countries, because of the larger extent of the demand for intermediate service inputs by downstream industries.[110]

In other words, the economic benefits of reduced anticompetitive regulations should be especially great for a country like the United States, to the extent that it qualifies both as having many downstream industries that operate at the technological frontier, and as being a larger country.

## STORIES

### (PART V OR ONLINE)

*Alexander Hamilton, CEO, Radiant Law* (Part V): Hamilton describes how Radiant, applying a combination of legal judgment, technology, design, and streamlined processes, improves for its clients the quality, consistency, and speed to conclusion of their high-volume contracts.

*Karl Chapman, Chief Executive, Riverview Law* (online): Chapman explains how Riverview's technology and operating model helps businesses to manage large volumes of legal documentation, information, and data quickly and efficiently, with the result of improving how the business operates.

*Ursula Hogben, Practice Leader and General Counsel, LegalVision* (online): Hogben explains how LegaiVision has developed business and IT processes that enable the capture and retention of unique knowledge gained by one person in order that everyone in the firm may use it afterwards to the benefit of all the firm's clients.

*Elisabeth Davies, Chair, Legal Services Consumer Panel* (Part V): Davies explains that while it is still early days in England and Wales, the panel's research already demonstrates that there has been a large amount of activity as regards new business models. In addition, consumers are becoming more empowered, notably by shopping around more and by the increased use of fixed fees.

## NOTES

1. Hadfield, "Legal Barriers to Innovation," 130.
2. Ibid., 130–31.
3. Ibid., 143.
4. Ibid.
5. Gillian Hadfield, "Legal Infrastructure and the New Economy," *I/S: A Journal of Law and Policy for the Information Society* 8 (2012): 2, http://ssrn.com/abstract=1567712.
6. Ibid., 3.
7. Ibid., 4.
8. Ibid., 9.
9. Ibid., 57.
10. Ibid., 59.
11. Winston, Crandall, and Maheshri, *First Thing We Do*, 55.
12. Ibid., 36.
13. Ibid., 24–72.
14. Ibid., 59.

15. Ibid., 9.
16. Ibid., 14–16, 60.
17. Ibid., 9–14.
18. Hadfield and Heine, "Life in the Law - Thick World."
19. Winston, Crandall, and Maheshri, *First Thing We Do*, 73.
20. Ibid., 82–89.
21. Ibid., 94.
22. Iacobucci and Trebilcock, "An Economic Analysis," 59.
23. Ibid.
24. Ibid., 3.
25. That being said, Benjamin Barton advises reading the second half of Winston, Crandall, and Maheshri with a grain of salt, notably their arguments that "the demand for lawyers in the public and private sector has experienced continual growth, thanks in part to government policies that require private firms to retain legal counsel or encourage them to engage in litigation." Barton describes these arguments as a "frontal assault on much of the recent law and regulation protecting consumers and the environment." Benjamin H. Barton, "Economists on Deregulation of the American Legal Profession: Praise and Critique," *Michigan State Law Review* 2011 (2011): 11–13, http://ssrn.com/abstract=2008942.
26. Iacobucci and Trebilcock, 60.
27. Ibid., 61.
28. Simon Domberger and Avrom Sherr, "The Impact of Competition on Pricing and Quality of Legal Services," *International Review of Law and Economics* 9 (1989): 41–56, 41.
29. Ibid., 42–43.
30. Ibid., 43.
31. Ibid., 47.
32. Ibid., 55.
33. Ibid.
34. Frank H. Stephen, James H. Love, and Alan A. Paterson, "Deregulation of Conveyancing Markets in England and Wales," *Fiscal Studies* 15 (1994): 102–18, 116.
35. Ibid.
36. See, for example, Camille Chaserant and Sophie Harnay, "The Regulation of Quality in the Market for Legal Services: Taking the Heterogeneity of Legal Services Seriously," *The European Journal of Comparative Economics* 10 (2013) 267–91, http://eaces.liuc.it/18242979201302/182429792013100208.pdf.
37. See, for example, Daniel Bennett and Wesley Yin, "The Market for High-Quality Medicine: Retail Chain Entry and Drug Quality in India," NBER Working Paper No. 20091, November 17, 2014, http://home.uchicago.edu/~dmbennett/chainentry.pdf.
38. Commission for the Study of the Effects of the Law for Growth and Activity. This was a panel of economists and other subject matter experts appointed by the government of Prime Minister Manuel Valls in order to study the effects of a series of business-friendly laws promoted by the Minister of the Economy Emmanuel Macron. As explained on the second page of the panel's paper, the panel's objectives included: (i) encouraging "dynamism" in professional services, notably through innovation and increased availability, in order to better accompany the development of French enterprise, "notably internationally," and (ii) improving the competitiveness of French businesses.
39. Commission d'Etude des Effets de la Loi Pour la Croissance et l'Activité, "Réformes des Professions Réglementées du Droit," January, 2015, 6, 10, http://www.strategie.gouv.fr/sites/strategie.gouv.fr/files/atoms/files/fiche-professions_0.pdf.
40. Ibid., 9.
41. Erik Canton, Daria Ciriaci, and Irune Solera, "The Economic Impact of Professional Services Liberalisation," European Commission Economic Papers 533, September 2014, 5 ("Canton Study"), http://ec.europa.eu/economy_finance/publications/economic_paper/2014/pdf/ecp533_en.pdf.
42. Directive 2005/36/EC on the Recognition of Professional Qualifications, September 7, 2005, http://eur-lex.europa.eu/legal-content/EN/TXT/?uri=celex percent3A32005L0036.

43. Directive 2006/123/EC on Services in the Internal Market, December 12, 2006, http://eur-lex.europa.eu/legal-content/EN/TXT/?uri=celex percent3A32006L0123.
44. Canton Study, 7–8.
45. Ibid., 9.
46. Ibid., 15.
47. Ibid., 5, 19.
48. Ibid., 1.
49. Ibid., 25.
50. Ibid., 29.
51. Guglielmo Barone and Federico Cingano, "Service Regulation and Growth: Evidence from OECD Countries," *The Economic Journal* 121 (2011): 931 ("Barone Study"), http://dx.doi.org/10.1111/j.1468-0297.2011.02433.x.
52. Ibid., 936.
53. Ibid.
54. Ibid., 936–37.
55. Ibid., 931, 937. The Barone Study does not provide any additional explanation with respect to these "anti-competitive restrictions." However, other OECD publications indicate that their scope is relatively limited. For example, an OECD Economics Department Working Paper explains that the expression "form of business" addresses the extent to which incorporation, either public or private (and as opposed to sole proprietorship), is allowed. In this context, nonlawyer ownership is considered only partially and indirectly insofar as the expression addresses public companies. See, for example, Isabell Koske, Isabelle Wanner, Rosamaria Bitetti, and Omar Barbiero, "The 2013 Update of the OECD's Database on Product Market Regulation: Policy Insights For OECD and Non-OECD Countries," OECD Economics Department Working Papers No. 1200, March 31, 2015, 44, 70, http://dx.doi.org/10.1787/5js3f5d3n2vl-en.
56. Barone Study, 937.
57. Ibid., 938.
58. Ibid., 936.
59. Ibid., 937.
60. Ibid., 938–39.
61. Ibid., 941–43.
62. Ibid., 931–32.
63. Ibid., 943.
64. Ibid.
65. Ibid., 949–50.
66. Ibid., 950–53.
67. Ibid., 953.
68. Renaud Bourlès et al., "Do Product Market Regulations in Upstream Sectors Curb Productivity Growth? Panel Data Evidence for OECD Countries," *The Review of Economics and Statistics* 95 (2013): 1750 ("Bourlès Study").
69. Ibid., 1755. Due to a lack of data, for the intermediate inputs of professional services and retail were considered only for the years 1998, 2003, and 2007. Ibid., 1756.
70. The Bourlès Study uses the United Nation's International Standard Industrial Classification (ISIC) codes, Revision 3. Renaud Bourlès, Gilbert Cette, Jimmy Lopez, Jacques Mairesse, and Giuseppe Nicoletti, "Do Product Market Regulations in Upstream Sectors Curb Productivity Growth? Panel Data Evidence For OECD Countries: Supplementary Web Appendix," 2013, 6, http://www.mitpressjournals.org/doi/suppl/10.1162/REST_a_00338/suppl_file/REST_a_00338_esupp.pdf. More specifically, the Bourlès Study uses code 74 of Revision 3, which encompasses legal, accounting, bookkeeping and auditing activities, tax consultancy, market research and public opinion polling, business and management consultancy, architectural, engineering and other technical activities, advertising, and business activities not elsewhere classified. See "Detailed Structure and Explanatory Notes - ISIC Rev. 3 Code 74," United Nations Department of Economic and Social Affairs, accessed December 26, 2015, http://unstats.un.org/unsd/cr/registry/regcs.asp?Cl=2andLg=1andCo=74.
71. Bourlès Study, 1754.

72. Ibid., 1750.
73. Ibid., 1754.
74. See, for example, Greg B. Falker and Charles Weiss, Jr., "An Analytic Framework for Measuring Technological Development," in *The Emerging Technological Trajectory of the Pacific Rim*, ed. Denis Fred Simon (New York: M.E. Sharpe, 1995), 385–400, 388.
75. Bourlès Study., 1753
76. Ibid., 1760.
77. Ibid.
78. Ibid.
79. Ibid., 1760–62.
80. Ibid., 1760.
81. Ibid., 1762.
82. Ibid.
83. Ibid.
84. Ibid., 1762–66. The lowest values of anticompetitive regulation indicators are observed in 2007, so the 2007 lightest practices are also the lightest practices for the whole period. Jimmy Lopez, email message to author, January 7, 2016.
85. Bourlès Study, 1762.
86. Ibid.
87. Ibid.
88. Ibid., 1764.
89. Ibid.
90. Ibid., 1765.
91. Ibid., 1764.
92. Ibid., 1766.
93. Ibid., 1750.
94. Ibid.
95. Cristina Mocci, Stefania Pozzuoli, Francesca Romagnoli, and Cristina Tinti, "Deregulation and Growth in Italy," Government of the Italian Republic (Italy), Ministry of Economy and Finance, Department of the Treasury Working Paper No. 3, May, 2014, 10, http://ssrn.com/abstract=2445863.
96. Ibid., 9–10.
97. Ibid., 10. Again, however, the data available with respect to professional services is available only for the years 1998, 2003, and 2007. Ibid.
98. Ibid., 7–10.
99. Ibid., 8.
100. Ibid.
101. Ibid., 10–13.
102. Ibid., 12.
103. Emanuele Forlani, "Competition in the Service Sector and the Performances of Manufacturing Firms: Does Liberalization Matter?" CESifo Working Paper Series No. 2942, February, 2010, http://ssrn.com/abstract=1553654.
104. Jens M. Arnold, Beata S. Javorcik, and Aaditya Mattoo, "Does Services Liberalization Benefit Manufacturing Firms? Evidence from the Czech Republic," *Journal of International Economics* 85 (2011): 136–46, 145, http://www.sciencedirect.com/science/article/pii/S0022199611000523.
105. Emilio Fernández Corugedo and Esther Pérez Ruiz, "The EU Services Directive: Gains from Further Liberalization," IMF Working Paper No. 14/113, July, 2014, 1, http://ssrn.com/abstract=2475012.
106. Gilbert Cette, Jimmy Lopez, and Jacques Mairesse, "Product and Labour Market Regulations: Production Prices, Wages and Productivity," NBER Working Paper No. w20563, 2014, 1, http://ssrn.com/abstract=2505868.
107. Oliver Arentz et al., "Services Liberalisation in Germany Overview and the Potential of Deregulation: A Study by the Institute for Economic Policy at the University of Cologne," Otto-Wolff-Institut Discussion Paper 1b/2015, March 2015, 24–25, https://iwp.uni-koeln.de/fileadmin/contents/dateiliste_iwp-website/publikationen/DP/dp01b_2015.pdf.

108. Ibid., II.
109. Bourlès Study, 1760.
110. Barone Study, 949–50.

## *Chapter Fourteen*

# Opportunities for Lawyers

It is estimated that only two-thirds of graduating law students are able to find jobs in the legal field.[1] Of those who do find work in law firms, 57 percent have left law firm work by their fifth year of practice.[2] The numbers are even bleaker for women and minorities—women make up 47 percent of law graduates, but they make up just 33 percent of the legal profession, and just 15 percent of equity partners in law firms.[3] By mid-career, nearly 40 percent of women have left the legal profession all together.[4]

Minorities (men and women) make up 18.1 percent of law firm associates, but just 5.4 percent of partners; minority women make up 10.1 percent of law firm associates and just 1.7 percent of law firm partners.[5] The situation for minority women is the most acute: More than 75 percent leave law firms within five years.[6]

Of all employed lawyers, 45 percent are dissatisfied with their jobs,[7] and fewer than half describe themselves as happy.[8] Lawyers are two times as likely as the general population to suffer from drug or alcohol abuse, and they have one of the highest rates of depression compared to other professions, as well as one of the highest rates of suicide.[9]

The ABA Commission on Lawyer Assistance Programs recently stated: "Our research indicates that lawyers and law students use and abuse alcohol at rates far higher than the public in general and suffer from mental health disorders, particularly depression and anxiety, leading to both debilitation and suicide in inordinate numbers."[10]

What is happening in the legal profession? What is happening to all these lawyers, either who cannot find jobs or who, once they have them, leave in droves, often by killing themselves?[11]

Many rationales have been offered for such high levels of discontent in the profession: Lawyers are by nature pessimistic and so prone to depression, the adversarial nature of law makes it a stressful profession with enormous pressure to win at all costs, negative attitudes of the public toward lawyers, a bad economy.[12] Brian Clarke, now assistant professor at Charlotte School of Law, explained his 11 years in practice like this:

> Practicing law is hard. The law part is not that hard (that was the fun part for me), but the business side of law is a bear. Finding clients, billing time, and collecting money, are just a few aspects of the business of law of which I was not a big fan. Keeping tasks and deadlines in dozens (or hundreds) of cases straight and getting everything done well and on time is a constant challenge. The fear of letting one of those balls drop can be terrifying, especially for the type A perfectionist who is always terrified of making a mistake or doing a less than perfect job. Forget work-life balance. Forget vacations. Every day out of the office is another day you are behind.[13]

What we know about opportunities in the legal profession in the United States is this:

- There are far fewer available jobs in the law than there are people seeking them. This is true at all levels, but the situation is acute for law graduates looking to start their careers as they leave law school with high debt.
- Traditional law firms operate under the same basic business model, called a "leveraged pyramid," where the money the partners make depends upon the number of hours their associates bill. Under this model, in order to keep partner profits high, there is pressure to keep the ratio of associates to partners high, as well as pressure for associates to bill as many hours as possible.
- This model necessarily places a limit on the number of people that can make partner. Most who do not make partner are expected to leave—some stay for an often temporary period under a reduced status commonly referred to as "of counsel."
- A partner's compensation is dependent upon the billings that are attributable to that partner's clients. The number of clients a partner controls also determines the ease with which a partner can move to another firm. For these reasons, partners are often reluctant to share important responsibilities and client relationships with other partners as well as associates in the firm (one consequence of this is that the lawyer's "brand" is just as important, if not more important, than the brand of the firm).
- While there are many barriers and challenges for white men to make partner, the statistics above demonstrate that the barriers and challenges for women and minorities to make partner are, for most, insurmountable.
- Becoming a sole practitioner is a viable Plan B only for a few: Since 1988, the average compensation of solo practitioners has declined sharply. In 1988, the average solo practitioner earned 190 percent of what the average

US worker earned. In 2012, that percentage had fallen to 110 percent. One estimate suggests that the median earnings for solo practitioners in the United States may be less than $35,000 per year.[14]

More generally, some have described a growing "sense of disillusionment,"[15] notably from young lawyers who, even when offered equity partnership, refuse it. One commentator described this as a "common occurrence" that is "causing havoc with growth, succession and transition plans."[16] He explains:

> [W]hile they want to be lawyers they do not want to take the financial and other business risks nor make the other work commitments such as working nights, weekends, and the 24-hour commitment that has historically been the requirements for equity partners in law firms.[17]

Some of the frustrations with the practice of law that lawyers typically express are:

- The need to be salespersons, to become "rainmakers": Most lawyers do not go to law school because they want to become proficient at marketing legal services. But, once in practice, they discover that, large firm or small, a successful career often depends in large part upon their marketing abilities.[18]
- Lack of control: Those who do not become proficient rainmakers (that is, who have not succeeded in recruiting and retaining a critical mass of clients or business) work in deference to the rainmakers. They have little control over the work they do or the schedule that they work under, often at the sacrifice of their personal lives. As they progress in their careers, they can move to other firms only with great difficulty as most firms will bring on new partners only that can bring a "book of business" with them.
- Law firm management and administration: In large firms, managers are often described, at best, as untrained and ineffective and, at worst, as abusive. (Certainly no one has ever held up a law firm as an exemplary model for management).[19]
- Small firms, and sole practitioners in particular, are overloaded with administrative matters that they didn't sign up for when they decided to go to law school: recording time, billing and collecting, file and calendar management, maintaining accounts.[20]
- Large firm or small, boredom with mundane and repetitive work: Litigation as well as corporate work often involves long hours in front of a computer spent in tedious document review, routine document preparation, and socially isolating research.[21]

Women experience additional frustrations. The reasons that women typically give for leaving the profession are:

- Business models that value billable hours over productivity.
- Either flexible working arrangements are not available or, if they are, they are stigmatized positions that compromise the careers of those that ask for them.
- They experience discrimination, both (i) before they have children, because there is a risk that they might have them, as well as (ii) after they have children, because, regardless of whether they ask for flexible working arrangements or not, there is an assumption that if they have children, they are less committed to and less interested in their work.[22]

One woman, noticing that her East Coast firm did not have any minority women partners who were married with children, decided to leave the firm for a government position. She described her reasons for leaving in this way:

> I didn't want to take the gamble of altering the course of my life for these people—and if they didn't make me partner, then what did I do? That, coupled with the fact that I am black and female, I thought it made my chances for being partner less, and I didn't want to take that risk.[23]

Even if they make partner, conditions can be difficult for women in traditional law firm partnerships: In its 2015 survey of 73 of the country's largest firms, the National Association of Women Lawyers (NAWL) reports that, among other discriminatory practices, men outpace women in obtaining rainmaking credits, and there is a gender gap in revenues generated from client billings, even as women partners report higher working hours.[24] This reporting is borne out in lawsuits brought by former woman partners against, for example, the Richmond, Virginia-based law firm of LeClairRyan,[25] and, in another lawsuit, the Miami, Florida-based law firm of Greenberg Traurig.[26] In both lawsuits, the former partners alleged that the women partners at the respective firms are, again among other discriminatory practices, denied their fair share of origination credit and internal referrals, and are frozen out of the firm's high-level management positions[27] and executive and compensation committees.[28] In light of these and a host of other discriminatory measures systematically practiced against both women and minorities over a period of many years, the NAWL report describes the situation as "a story of institutional failure."[29]

In other words, the traditional law firm operating under the traditional law firm business model is an inhospitable place for many, many lawyers—a place where their success depends not upon their skills as a lawyer but upon their abilities in areas in which they have no training, interest, or aptitude, as well as upon their gender and the color of their skin; a place that requires them to sacrifice their personal lives; a place where they do not feel valued or fulfilled in their work; a place where opportunities are denied to them and only a very small number can reach positions of success. As a result, they leave. Some leave for positions in government agencies, in-house, or not-for-profits, and others simply leave the legal profession altogether. They leave not because they are poor lawyers or have poor legal skills—they leave because there is no place for them in the traditional law firm partnership model. Self-employment as a sole practitioner is a viable option for only a few; in the words of an article in the *Illinois Bar Journal* (a publication of the Illinois State Bar Association) "The bottom line is that to be successful as a solo, you must want to be a solo."[30]

But besides the traditional law firm partnership or self-employment as a sole practitioner, what other business models does Rule 5.4 allow?

While no one can know what reason(s) drove Mark Levy to suicide, his story bears telling. A graduate of Yale Law School, Levy was of counsel at Kilpatrick Stockton in Washington, DC. He was chair of the firm's US Supreme Court and appellate advocacy practice, and was considered one of the most skilled appellate lawyers in the Unites States.[31] He had argued before the Supreme Court 16 times, and had won his most recent Supreme Court appeal with a unanimous (9–0) court decision.

In late April 2009, Levy was told that he was one of 24 lawyers that the firm was laying off. He was asked to vacate his office within a few days. On the morning of Thursday, April 30, his last day at Kilpatrick Stockton, Levy went to his office and shot himself. An article in the *ABA Journal* explains that while Levy loved the practice of law, there were elements that he struggled with. In particular, he did not relish marketing. One of Levy's clients explained that Levy "was not the kind of guy who made a hard sell trying to get work. He was more collegial. He was more interested in the issues."[32]

The article explains that throughout Levy's career—at Kilpatrick Stockton as well as at other law firms—he was highly dependent upon other lawyers in his firm to refer work to him, but that those lawyers often were reluctant to lose control over their files, even to a talented colleague. As a result, the firms Levy worked for felt he had underachieved, and Levy felt unsupported and underutilized. Despite his high rate of success in the cases he worked on, he was highly vulnerable in the legal partnership world, where "rainmaking is often valued over skill and judgment. For all his prestige, he had little real power behind his formidable status."[33]

In the months leading up to his layoff, Levy had approached several firms to see if they had a place for him, and also sought a political appointment in the Justice Department, but all proved to be dead ends. The day before his suicide, he had a 30-minute phone call with a close friend, who described him as "concerned about what he was going to do."[34]

Why are some lawyers, like Levy, killing themselves? Patrick Krill, a lawyer and the director of the Legal Professional Program at Hazelden Betty Ford Foundation, proposes this response:

> Despite whatever preconceptions or judgments many people may have of lawyers and the work they do, there are some facts about the practice of law that can't be denied: It's tougher than most people think and frequently less fulfilling than they would ever believe.
>
> The psychologist Rollo May famously defined depression as "the inability to construct a future." And, unfortunately for many attorneys who define their existence by a hard-earned membership in the legal profession, the powerful despair they experience when that profession overwhelms and demoralizes them doesn't leave them much psychological real estate for constructing a future they can believe in.
>
> Not a future where the practice of law will be what they hoped for, not a future where their lives will have balance and joy, and not a future where their relationships will bring fulfillment and their stresses will seem manageable. They just can't see it. Unable or unwilling to extract themselves from the psychological, financial and personal mire they never would have expected years of hard work and discipline to bring them, many lawyers then find themselves sinking into a funk, a bottle or a grave.[35]

Model Rule 5.4 essentially operates to allow for just one kind of business model for legal services: the traditional law firm partnership. But as we've seen, many good lawyers are not able to work within the confines of such a structure—either it places too much pressure and too many demands on them, and they leave it voluntarily, or they are not able to conform to its expectations, with the consequences that they are rejected from it. But once they leave, there are very few places for them to go. Model Rule 5.4 operates to deny to so many lawyers the ability to construct a future. Alternative structures permit lawyers to construct alternative futures. That is, they permit the creation of legal service firms:

- Where lawyers who are either not skilled or not interested in marketing would not need to do marketing: The marketing work would be done by professionals trained and skilled in marketing, and the legal work would be done by professionals trained and skilled in law.
- Where lawyers who do not want their jobs to depend upon billing a high number of hours would not need to bill a high number of hours: Under a corporate structure, there would be no "leveraged pyramid" for partner compensation, fixed prices would be determined by professionals skilled in the pricing of legal services, and the lawyers' jobs would depend upon their productivity.
- Where small firm lawyers who are overwhelmed by administrative tasks would not need to do them: They could join a franchise, which, benefitting

from external investment, would have the resources to develop and offer to a large number of small firms streamlined IT infrastructure, billing, marketing and file management, advertising, and a branded name and logo, freeing the lawyers to practice law.

- Where lawyers who are demoralized by the mundane and repetitive elements of legal work would not need to do them: They would be done either by an automated process and/or by appropriately trained staff in accordance with a carefully developed procedure (all financed by external investment).

At the time of his death, one of Levy's former law school classmates was quoted as saying: "If someone like him cannot prosper in law practice, you wonder what law practice has become."[36]

What if, at the time Levy was laid off from Kilpatrick Stockton, alternative structures had existed in the United States? What if one of those structures placed all sales and marketing responsibility with a sales and marketing team? Not a team of lawyers doing marketing on the side, but a team of professionals trained and experienced in sales and marketing, who only do sales and marketing? And what if it also had another team—one trained and experienced in customer relations, who only do customer relations? Those teams would not jealously guard their files from someone like Levy—to the contrary, since they were not lawyers themselves, they would need someone like Levy—someone with the technical legal expertise to provide the underlying legal services. And they wouldn't care about Levy's aptitude for marketing or even for customer relations—they'd just need him to address the legal issues.

Those are a lot of what-ifs, of course. We cannot wind back the clock and replay Levy's life in order to know for sure if such a structure would have offered an opportunity to him—a chance for him to remain employed in the law and able to contribute his obviously considerable legal talents in a manner that enabled him to feel valued and fulfilled. But we do not need to know for sure. We only need to know that it could have offered him such an opportunity; that the possibility is real.

And we know that Levy was not alone in his frustrations. For all of the lawyers like Levy who take the drastic step of suicide at least in part due to lack of professional opportunities—to their "inability to construct a future"—how many more lawyers experience the same frustrations? How many of them feel trapped—in an inhospitable and inflexible business model that requires them to be something they are not (skilled at marketing) and does not value what they are (technical lawyers)? How many of them leave the profession as a result, depriving the market of their contributions when we know that the market is in desperate need of more accessible legal services?

It would be unrealistic to expect alternative structures to be a panacea—a utopia or a universal remedy for all unhappy lawyers, or even for all good lawyers who are not suited for the traditional law firm model. But the potential they offer to many of those lawyers is real—the ability to construct a future outside of the traditional law firm model.

## STORIES

### (PART V OR ONLINE)

*Rod Cunich, National Practice Group Leader, Slater and Gordon* (online): Cunich explains why, in his opinion, a corporate structure offers a better working environment as compared to a traditional partnership. In particular, it promotes better decision making and more professional behavior, and everyone, including the company's employees, benefits from that.

*Adrian Powell, Partner, Proelium Law* (online): Powell finds the ABS structure beneficial because it allows him to rely upon different kinds of work, not just legal work, to earn a living, and it also allows him to work in a way that makes him happy.

*William Robins, Operations Director, Keystone Law, and Warren Kalinko, CEO, Keypoint Law* (online): Robins and Kalinko describe how the lawyers of Keystone and its subsidiary, Keypoint, work flexibly and without minimum billing targets. They also work without the pressure of financial responsibilities of law firm partnership, and without the administrative responsibilities of a sole practitioner.

*Ken Jagger, CEO, AdventBalance* (Part V): Jagger describes how, by working on a project basis, AdventBalance lawyers are able to take time off between projects without the fear of losing their jobs or being set back in their careers.

*Andrea Pierce, Legal Services Director, Kings Court Trust* (online): Pierce explains that KCT does not track time, and it employs marketing and sales specialists who are responsible for bringing business to the company. In this context, the lawyers at KCT are not evaluated on the basis of either their billable hours or the business they bring in. Instead, they are evaluated on the basis of defined key performance indicators such as meeting service level requirements and deadlines.

*Nadia Haque, Associate, Radiant Law* (online): Haque explains that even if she is ambitious and wants to succeed, she does not want to do so in the environment of a traditional law firm and its focus on billable hours. For her, Radiant, as a nontraditional structure, is a place where she can be happy and where she can work flexibly and without politics.

*Tamyn Hearne, Associate, Radiant Law* (online): Hearne describes how Radiant's business model speaks directly to her frustrations with a traditional firm and explains that she has learned more with Radiant than she has anywhere else.

*Dina Tutungi, General Manager—Personal Injury Victoria, Slater and Gordon* (Part V): Tutungi describes the many and varied opportunities in different roles she has had at the firm. She explains that the firm offers a high degree of working flexibility to parents, and notably to women returning from maternity leave. Tutungi herself was promoted when she was out on her second maternity leave.

*Sue Bence, Head of M & A Operations and Integration—UK, Slater and Gordon* (online): Bence explains the variety of roles she has had with the firm in both Australia and the UK, and the highly unique experience she is gaining in her role as head of M & A. She states that she finds working in a nontraditional structure to be liberating and inspiring.

## NOTES

1. Marco Rabinowitz, "Legal Profession in Crisis? Law School Bubble, Weak Job Market Signal Precarious Changes," *Benzinga*, May 2, 2012, http://www.benzinga.com/trading-ideas/short-ideas/12/05/2553116/legal-profession-in-crisis-law-school-bubble-weak-job-market#ixzz3jfT9aBq4.
2. Marlisse Silver Sweeney, "The Female Lawyer Exodus," *Daily Beast*, July 31, 2013, http://www.thedailybeast.com/witw/articles/2013/07/31/the-exodus-of-female-lawyers.html.
3. Ibid.
4. Susan Smith Blakely, "Why Do Women Lawyers Leave?," *Ms. JD*, April 24, 2014, http://ms-jd.org/blog/article/why-do-women-lawyers-leave.
5. Gita Z. Wilder, "Are Minority Women Lawyers Leaving Their Jobs? Findings from the First Wave of the After the JD Study," The NALP Foundation for Law Career Research and Education and the National Association for Law Placement, Inc., 2008, 4, http://www.nalp.org/assets/1280_ajdminoritywomenmonograph.pdf.
6. Debra Cassens Weiss, "Why More than 75 percent of Minority Female Lawyers Leave Law Firms Within 5 Years," *ABA Journal*, July 22, 2009, http://www.abajournal.com/news/article/why_more_than_75_of_minority_female_lawyers_leave_law_firms_within_5_years/. See also Liane Jackson, "Minority Women are Disappearing from BigLaw—and Here's Why," *ABA Journal*, March 1, 2016, http://www.abajournal.com/magazine/article/minority_women_are_disappearing_from_biglaw_and_heres_why.
7. Stephanie Francis Ward, "Pulse of the Legal Profession," *ABA Journal*, October 1, 2007, http://www.abajournal.com/magazine/article/pulse_of_the_legal_profession.
8. Lawyers' Assistance Program, "The Happy Lawyer: The Path from Stress to Well-Being," Presentation for Continuing Legal Education Credit, April 13, 2015, on file with author ("The Happy Lawyer").
9. The Happy Lawyer; see also Ashby Jones, "In Down Times, Depression Taking Hold Among More Lawyers," *Wall Street Journal*, May 5, 2009, http://blogs.wsj.com/law/2009/05/05/in-down-times-depression-taking-hold-among-more-lawyers/. See also MP McQueen, "The Legal Profession's Drinking Problem Is Worse Than We Thought," *The American Lawyer*, February 4, 2016, http://www.americanlawyer.com/id=1202748847326/The-Legal-Professions-Drinking-Problem-Is-Worse-Than-We-Thought#ixzz41lu34mta; Patrick R. Krill, Ryan Johnson, and Linda Albert, "The Prevalence of Substance Use and Other Mental Health Con-

cerns Among American Attorneys," *Journal of Addictive Medicine* 10 (2016): 46–52, doi: 10.1097/ADM.0000000000000182.

10. ABA Commission on Lawyer Assistance Programs, "Proposed Resolution Regarding Model Regulatory Objectives," October 28, 2015, http://www.americanbar.org/content/dam/aba/images/office_president/lawyer_assistance_programs.pdf.

11. The situation of lawyers in Canada appears to be comparable to the United States. See, for example, Megan Seto, "Killing Ourselves: Depression as an Institutional, Workplace and Professionalism Problem," *Western Journal of Legal Studies* 2 (2012) http://ir.lib.uwo.ca/cgi/viewcontent.cgi?article=1053andcontext=uwojls. See also Fiona M. Kay, Stacey Alarie, and Jones Adjei, "Leaving Law and Barriers to Re-entry: A Study of Departures from and Re-entries to Private Practice," A Report to the Law Society of Upper Canada , April 2013, http://www.lsuc.on.ca/WorkArea/DownloadAsset.aspx?id=2147494539; Lindsay Scott, "Young Lawyers, Read This LSUC Report" *Canadian Lawyer*, May 20, 2013, http://www.canadianlawyermag.com/4660/Young-lawyers-read-this-LSUC-report.html; Michael Dempster, "The Hurting Profession," *National*, April-May 2012, 12–20, http://cbanational.rogers.dgtlpub.com/2012/2012-05-31/pdf/Lawyers_in_crisis.pdf; Anastasia Jogal, "Less Than Half of All Law Grads Find Work After Call: Survey," *Canadian Lawyer Magazine*, January 11, 2016, http://www.canadianlawyermag.com/5885/Less-than-half-of-law-grads-find-work-after-call-survey.html. Also, see complaints brought against one of Canada's most prestigious firms, McCarthy Tetrault: Kenneth Kidd, "Woman's Fight Opens Legal Titans' Secret Files," *The Star*, September 3, 2009, http://www.thestar.com/news/gta/2009/09/03/womans_fight_opens_legal_titans_secret_files.html. A 2015 study of recent graduates of Canadian law schools has been cited as demonstration that Canadian lawyers are more satisfied than US lawyers, in spite of a similar regulatory environment. However, this study is limited to persons who are newly admitted to the bar (four years or less), who were employed upon admission to the bar (the study does not encompass unemployed law graduates), and it addresses lawyers in all professional contexts, including government positions. The study reveals that the rate of satisfaction of lawyers in government positions is significantly higher than the rate of lawyers in private practice. The rate of satisfaction of solo lawyers is particularly low for lawyers just two years out of law school—at just 71 percent, it begs the question of how 29 percent became disillusioned in such a short period of time. The study also shows low levels of satisfaction with respect to working conditions for beginning lawyers in medium and large law firm settings. Ronit Dinovitzer, "Law and Beyond: A National Study of Canadian Law Graduates," May 27, 2015, 37–39, 41, http://dx.doi.org/10.2139/ssrn.2615062.

12. See, for example, Martin E. P. Seligman, "Why Are Lawyers So Unhappy?," *Lawyers with Depression*, November 16, 2012, http://www.lawyerswithdepression.com/articles/why-are-lawyers-so-unhappy/; Susan Swaim Daicoff, *Lawyer, Know Thyself* (Washington, DC: American Psychological Association, 2004), 5.

13. Brian S. Clarke, "Law Professors, Law Students and Depression . . . A Story of Coming Out," *Journal of Law* 4 (2014): 219–34, 223, http://journaloflaw.us/5%20The%20Post/4-2/JoL4-2,%20TP4-2,%20Clarke.pdf.

14. Paul Campos, "The Collapsing Economics of Solo Legal Practice," *Lawyers, Guns and Money*, May 25, 2015, http://www.lawyersgunsmoneyblog.com/2015/05/the-collapsing-economics-of-solo-legal-practice.

15. John W. Olmstead, "Best Practice: The Equity Partner Problem," *Illinois Lawyer Now*, January 6, 2016, http://iln.isba.org/blog/2016/01/06/best-practice-equity-partner-problem.

16. Ibid.

17. Ibid.

18. See, for example, Silvia Hodges, "I Didn't Go to Law School to Become a Salesperson—The Development of Marketing in Law Firms," *Georgetown Journal of Legal Ethics*, 26 (2013): 225–60, http://ssrn.com/abstract=2343341.

19. See, for example, Deena Shanker, "Why are Lawyers Such Terrible Managers?," *Fortune*, January 11, 2013, http://fortune.com/2013/01/11/why-are-lawyers-such-terrible-managers/; Dale B. Evans, "Why Lawyers Can't Manage," *Law Practice Management*, 19 (October, 1993): 26, http://evans-legal.com/dan/manage.html.

20. Suzanne Meehle, "10 Things I Hate About Being A Solo Practitioner (and Why I'm Still Happy Being Solo!)," *Solo Practice University Blog,* March 24, 2011; http://solopracticeuniversity.com/2011/03/24/10-things-i-hate-about-being-a-solo-practitioner-and-why-im-still-happy-being-solo/.

21. David Cheng, "Why So Many Lawyers Are Unhappy with Their Jobs," *Business Insider*, August 29, 2013, http://www.businessinsider.com/why-lawyers-are-unhappy-at-work-2013-8#ixzz3jieKXqLN.

22. See, for example, Marlisse Silver Sweeney, "The Female Lawyer Exodus," *Daily Beast*, July 31, 2013, http://www.thedailybeast.com/witw/articles/2013/07/31/the-exodus-of-female-lawyers.html.

23. Jill Schachner Chanen, "Early Exits," *ABA Journal*, August 6, 2006, http://www.abajournal.com/magazine/article/early_exits.

24. National Association of Women Lawyers, "Report of the Ninth Annual NAWL National Survey on Retention and Promotion of Women in Law Firms," October 27, 2015, 3, http://www.nawl.org/p/cm/ld/fid=82#reports (hereinafter NAWL Report").

25. Neil Gluckman, "Complaint Alleges Gender Discrimination at LeClairRyan," *The American Lawyer*, January 7, 2016, http://www.americanlawyer.com/id=1202746570645/Complaint-Alleges-Gender-Discrimination-at-LeClairRyan?mcode=0andcurindex=0and curpage=ALL.

26. Cindy Krischer Goodman, "Why Aren't Women Lawyers Reaching the Top of Their Firms in Pay and Respect?" *Miami Herald*, April 12, 2012, http://miamiherald.typepad.com/worklifebalancingact/2012/12/do-law-firms-discriminate-against-women.html.

27. Ibid.

28. *Michele Burke Craddock v. LeClairRyan*, Complaint, In the United States District Court for the Eastern District of Virginia, January 6, 2016, 4, http://amlawdaily.typepad.com/CraddockComplaint.pdf. In both cases, the woman partners reported that the firm defended compensation differences with the explanation that the men partners needed the money because they have families to support. Debra Cassens Weiss, "$200M Class Action Claims 'Boys Club' at Greenberg Traurig Hogs Work and Origination Credit," *ABA Journal*, December 3, 2012, http://www.abajournal.com/news/article/class_action_claims_boys_club_at_greenberg_traurig_hogs_work_and_originatio/; and *Michele Burke Craddock v. LeClairRyan*, Complaint, 6–7.

29. NAWL Report, 2.

30. "Solos' Incomes Take a Deep Dive," *Illinois Bar Journal* 103 (August, 2015): 49.

31. Jonathan Turley, "D.C. Lawyer Mark Levy Reportedly Dead by Suicide at His Kilpatrick Stockton Office," *Jonathan Turley Blog*, April 30, 2009, http://jonathanturley.org/2009/04/30/dc-lawyer-mark-levy-reportedly-killed-himself-at-his-kilpatrick-stockton-office/.

32. Richard B. Schmitt, "A Death in the Office," *ABA Journal*, November 2, 2009, http://www.abajournal.com/magazine/article/a_death_in_the_office/.

33. Ibid.

34. "Mark I. Levy," *Wikipedia*, last modified September 22, 2014, https://en.wikipedia.org/wiki/Mark_I._Levy.

35. Patrick Krill, "Why Lawyers are Prone to Suicide," *CNN*, January 21, 2014, http://edition.cnn.com/2014/01/20/opinion/krill-lawyers-suicide/.

36. Schmitt, "A Death in the Office."

*Chapter Fifteen*

# Opportunities for In-House Legal Departments in the Private and Public Sectors

Model Rule 5.4 allows a lawyer to be employed as in-house counsel for a company owned by one or more nonlaywers, but on the condition that the lawyer provides legal services only to that company—the lawyer cannot provide legal services to third parties on behalf of the company. In other words, a company that has one or more nonlawyer shareholders may not, via one or more lawyers in its employ, engage in the corporate practice of law.

Many in-house counsel are overwhelmed with the amount of legal work generated by their employers, and they cannot imagine being in a position to provide legal services to anyone else. But this is not the case of all in-house counsel—some have developed unique skills and expertise in the delivery of legal services—skills and expertise that are valued by their internal clients, that external law firms may find difficult to match, and that the in-house department would like to offer to external, fee paying clients.

In England and Wales, a number of these in-house legal teams—in the private as well as the public sector—have or are planning to take advantage of the ABS structure in order to offer their unique skills and expertise to external clients. In doing so, they have transformed their legal departments: They are revenue generators rather than mere cost centers, and they enhance client service for their corporate, associative, or government employers rather than detract from it. Here are a few examples:

*BT Law Ltd.*: BT, one of the largest telecommunications providers in the UK, has a large fleet of repair and other vehicles. Just because of the sheer size of the fleet—many thousands of vehicles—it is probable that on any given day at least one of its vehicles will be involved in an accident. In this context, BT's in-house legal team has developed an expertise in motor claims—an expertise particular to a large company that needs to resolve such claims not on an individual, isolated basis but by taking a larger picture, and notably the company's brand, into account. This unique expertise was recognized not only by the legal department's internal clients at BT, but also by opposing parties—other companies who appreciated how BT's in-house legal team handled a given claim, and asked if they would do the same for their companies. These kinds of requests led BT's in-house legal department to apply for an ABS license. Since BT Law received its ABS license in 2013, it has expanded its service offering from motor claims to also include public liability, employers' liability, and employment law. Most of its clients are other large companies that generate many claims, such as Network Rail and EDF Energy.

*BPIF Legal*: The British Printing Industries Federation is a trade association representing members of the UK's print, printed packaging, and graphic communications industry. The BPIF offers support and advice to its members in the areas of human resources, health, safety and environment, quality, marketing, sales, and finance. In 2014, BPIF Legal received an ABS license and in doing so added legal to its list of support services that BPIF offers to its members. BPIF's in-house legal team is able to draw upon its experience in the industry sector to provide advice and support to the association's members in employment, intellectual property, contract and commercial law, and administrative matters.

*BMA Law*: The British Medical Association (BMA) is a trade association of about 160,000 members, representing doctors and student doctors in the UK. In addition to its collective bargaining and other advocacy activities, BMA also offers career support and guidance to its members. ABS BMA Law, created in 2015, offers support and advice to members of the BMA and their families in the areas of corporate and commercial, contracts (such as partnership agreements and doctor network and federation agreements), competition, regulatory, estate planning and probate, conveyancing, mediation, personal injury, and immigration.

*Oracle Family Office*: Oracle Capital Group is a multi-family office and wealth consultancy specializing in emerging markets. Its clients are companies and individuals whose origins are in Eastern Europe and who come to the UK for business or to live. The Group's in-house counsel was often approached by the Group's clients with requests to help them with legal matters, but, as in-house counsel, they were obliged to refuse those requests. In 2014, the in-house legal team formed Oracle Family Office, which received its ABS license in 2014. Oracle Family Office is now able to fill the role of in-house counsel to the Group as well as assist the Group in providing legal services to its clients.

*Kent Legal Services*: Kent County is one of the largest municipal authorities in England. Kent Legal Services (KLS) is its in-house legal department. In 2000, KLS introduced private sector principles and practices to its in-house legal team, by giving internal clients the choice to seek legal services externally but also the requirement to pay for the services if they chose to obtain them internally, and by setting income targets for its in-house lawyers. At the same time, KLS adopted IT-based case management systems and a client portal for real-time access to their files. Based upon this model, KLS expanded its client base to over 600 other public sector bodies across the country. KLS grew from 25 lawyers in 2000 to 125 lawyers in 2015, and in 2014 KLS generated for Kent County a profit of £2.5 million.

KLS is in the process of creating an ABS whose sole shareholder will be Kent County Council. Using a loan from the council, the ABS will invest significantly in order to develop state-of-the-art IT systems and to bring on staff specialist skills and expertise in business finance and business development. The ABS will provide services to public sector bodies across the country, in the mainstream areas of property, commercial and contracts, planning, and employment as well as in areas niche to the public sector, such as adult social welfare, child protection, highways, asylum, mental health, public sector housing, specialist police and fire. Geoff Wild, director of KLS, has stated that if the ABS is successful, it not only will continue to generate a surplus, but, over a decade or so, will develop into a capital asset for the council that, Wild estimates, will be valued between £40 to £60 million.[1]

These are just five examples of how alternative structures can be used to expand opportunities for in-house legal departments. In fact, depending upon the sector and the in-house legal department's experience and expertise, there is a multitude of ways by which an in-house legal department can use an alternative structure to expand its opportunities and/or to enhance the service offerings of its owner.

## STORIES

### (PART V OR ONLINE)

In part V or online, a representative from each of the five ABSs described above explains in greater detail the evolution of their respective in-house legal departments.

*Archana Makol, Director, BT Law Ltd.* (Part V): Makol explains that the shift that BT Law took is not a big shift: The department went from offering certain services to internal clients to offering the same services to other, external clients.

*Anne Copley, Head of Legal, BPIF Legal* (online): Copley explains that clients come to BPIF Legal because of its expertise in the industry—an expertise that traditional law firms cannot match.

*Viv Du-Feu, Director of Legal Services, BMA Law* (online): Du-Feu explains that BMA Law both offers its clients a highly specialized knowledge of and experience with the specific legal needs of doctors and permits the BMA to keep its finger on the political pulse of its members.

*Yuliya Andresyuk, Founding Partner, Oracle Family Office* (online): Andresyuk explains how the ABS structure has allowed her and her colleagues to think about how they work in a different way, to provide better client service, and simply to serve more clients.

*Geoff Wild, Director, Kent Legal Services* (online): Wild explains that while the ABS structure is not a panacea for the public sector, it offers a means to develop high-quality legal services at a lower cost. For Wild, sometimes the only restrictions are in your head.

## NOTE

1. Geoff Wild, interview with author, May 2016.

## *Chapter Sixteen*

# Opportunities for an Improved Regulatory Approach

As discussed in the introduction and part I, neither in England and Wales nor in Australia were alternative structures adopted in isolation of other regulatory changes. To the contrary, they were adopted in the context of extensive changes to their regulatory frameworks as a whole. This chapter will focus on two of the most significant changes: (i) adopting entity-based regulation, and (ii) moving away from proscriptive, rules-based regulation toward what has been termed, in the case of England and Wales, outcomes-focused regulation (OFR), in the case of Australia, proactive, management-based regulation (PMBR), and, in the case of Canada, compliance-based regulation.[1]

England and Wales did this firstly by requiring firms, as well as individuals practicing as sole practitioners, to submit a detailed application[2] with the SRA (at the time this book went to press, the application form was 13 pages in length. Prior to October 2015, the form was 30 pages). In the case of ABSs, the application is for authorization by the SRA, and in the case of traditional structures such as partnerships and sole practitioners, the application is for simple recognition. In either case, operation of the ABS or other structure may not commence until the application procedure is completed.[3]

Each firm, whether an ABS or a traditional structure, is required to appoint both a Compliance Officer for Legal Practice (COLP) and a Compliance Officer for Finance and Administration (COFA). The COLP is responsible for ensuring that the firm has in place the systems and controls needed to comply with the applicable ethical and professional standards, and the COFA is responsible for ensuring that the firm complies with the SRA's accounting rules. These persons bear principal responsibility for the firm's compliance, and they are obliged to report to the SRA material noncompliance.[4]

The second step that England and Wales took was to implement OFR. With this approach, the regulations move away from proscriptive rules that state what a firm (or an individual lawyer) may or may not do. Instead, specific outcomes are required, and each firm is responsible for designing and implementing its own systems and processes that will ensure those outcomes are achieved. The rationale for this is that practices and their clientele are different, and the systems and processes that are appropriate for one type of firm are not the same systems and processes that are appropriate for another. OFR, the SRA explains, offers to a firm more flexibility in how it achieves the right outcomes for its clients, but, at the same time, requires greater judgment from the firms.[5] One commentator described it as a "more demanding form of regulation which requires greater thought."[6]

In Australia, an incorporated legal practice (ILP) must file notifications with the competent regulatory authority before it begins to engage in legal practice. In contrast to England and Wales, the Australian filings are merely notifications—no express authorization by any authority is required.

As explained in chapter 1, in New South Wales and Victoria, each "principal" of a legal service provider (ILP or not) can be held responsible for the compliance of the firm, and, in Queensland and the other Australian states, ILPs are required to appoint at least one lawyer to serve as "Legal Practitioner Director" (LPD). In New South Wales and Victoria, if the ILP fails to respect any rule, the principal "is taken" to have done the same, if the principal "knowingly authorized or permitted" the act (or omission), or if the principal "was in or ought reasonably to have been in a position to influence"[7] the relevant conduct of the ILP. In Queensland and the other Australian states, the obligation placed upon the LPD is less equivocal: The LPD is responsible for ensuring that the firm has appropriate management systems in place that enable the firm to provide legal services in accordance with the applicable ethical rules. And, in the event of a violation by the firm and/or by any employee of the firm, the LPD as well as the firm itself can be held responsible:[8] Not only can the LPD lose his/her practicing certificate (that is, be disbarred) but the entire ILP can be liquidated.

The website of the Queensland Legal Services Commission contains a 39-page self-assessment audit form for an ILP to use in order to determine if it has appropriate management systems in place.[9] All ILPs in Queensland are required to complete a self-assessment and submit the self-assessment form to the Legal Services Commission. Some examples of the elements contained on the self-assessment form are:

- In each matter, a working plan exists, which deals, among other things, with client communication including time frames for return of telephone calls, responses to correspondence, and responses to emails.[10]

- A system for ensuring that the working plan in each matter is adhered to and that the file contains all appropriate file notes or time records or other evidence that the plan has been adhered to.[11]
- Procedures for regular review of files, checklists, and a firm-wide diary system, which may or may not be computer based.[12]

For each of the elements on the form, an ILP: (i) indicates which arrangements are already in place and where the evidence of that is located, and (ii) describes what improvements are still needed. On its website, the Queensland Legal Services Commission comments on the self-assessment process in this manner:

> We don't expect legal practitioner directors necessarily to rate the systems their firm has in place when they first receive the self-assessment form but the systems they have in place when they complete and return the form—we count the self-assessment process a success if it causes them to make improvements. The purpose of the exercise is not to catch anyone out but to help law firms develop and maintain management systems and workplace cultures that nurture and sustain best practice.
>
> Certainly we hope and expect that legal practitioner directors will approach the exercise not as an administrative burden but as a positive opportunity to review their firm's systems and to take stock. We want them to engage with the exercise and to candidly identify any gaps or shortcomings that require or might benefit from improvement.[13]

In light of these comments, it is unlikely that the Commission will take action against an ILP that is making good faith efforts to put appropriate management systems in place. On the other hand, in egregious cases the Commission can decide to audit an ILP and, if it is noncompliant, to force it into administration or liquidation.

As also discussed in part I, certain provinces in Canada have been closely studying these regulatory changes in England and Wales and Australia, and they are taking actions in turn. Notably (and as also described in part I):

1. In 2013, the Nova Scotia Barristers' Society embarked on a multi-year program to shift to "a new model of regulating legal services, in a manner that is risk-focused, proactive, principled and proportionate."[14] Previously existing legislation already granted to the Society a certain level of authority to regulate entities.[15] Today, the Society is using that authority as a building block in the implementation of a 19-point Policy Framework that includes:

- The regulation of the delivery of legal services by lawyers as well as by legal entities, "which include lawyers, law firms, law corporations, law departments and other similar entities."

- Regulation that requires "each law firm and legal entity" to designate an individual who will be responsible for the entity's compliance with its regulatory requirements, and to ensure that all persons associated with the entity who deliver or assist in the delivery of legal services comply with the applicable code of conduct.
- Regulation that will require "each law firm and legal entity" (i) to establish and maintain a management system that promotes competent and ethical legal practice, and (ii) to undertake to self-assess and report to the Society on its management system.
- Amendments to the applicable code of conduct "to eliminate barriers to fee sharing with nonlawyers."[16]

The Society is in the process of consulting with members of the legal profession and other stakeholders, with the expectation that in mid- or late 2016 it will be in a position to propose to the Nova Scotia legislature the legislative amendments that will be needed in order for the Society to be able to fully implement the Policy Framework.[17] In addition, the Society has developed a "Management System for Ethical Legal Practice" self-assessment tool.[18] In May 2016, it announced that it would conduct a pilot project to test the tool with 50 volunteer lawyers and firms during the period July 2016 to April 2017.[19]

For the moment, the work underway in Nova Scotia barely mentions alternative structures, save for an indirect reference with the expression of elimination of "barriers to fees sharing with nonlawyers." But this does not mean that alternative structures are not up for consideration in Nova Scotia—to the contrary, designing and implementing a regime to regulate entities and developing a framework for PMBR is laying the groundwork that will permit Nova Scotia to allow for the creation and operation of alternative structures.

2. In November 2015, and in conformity with the recommendations of the Law Society of Manitoba (LSM),[20] the Legislative Assembly of Manitoba enacted[21] amendments to the province's Legal Profession Act in order, among other changes: (i) to grant to the LSM the power to regulate law firms in addition to individual lawyers, and (ii) to define law firm broadly enough to include any entity that provides legal services, regardless of whether or not it is owned or managed, in whole or in part, by nonlawyers.[22] The amendments did not have the immediate result of allowing for alternative structures in Manitoba—instead, they have established a framework that will enable the LSM, as the regulator, both to adopt rules that allow for alternative structures, and to define the conditions under which they will be permitted to operate.

Further, Manitoba is not working alone but in collaboration with the other Canadian "Prairie provinces" of Saskatchewan and Alberta. Most notably, as discussed in part I, the law societies of the three provinces together issued a discussion paper describing a joint approach to the three "components" of "entity regulation, compliance-based regulation and ABS,"[23] and in May 2016 they commenced a consultation process.[24]

3. In January 2016, the Compliance-Based Entity Regulation Task Force of the Law Society of Upper Canada (LSUC—Ontario) launched a consultation process with respect to "compliance-based entity regulation."[25] In describing the process, the task force stated that it is "seeking input from lawyers, paralegals and others on options for a proactive approach to regulation."[26] The task force issued an accompanying consultation paper[27] and a call for comments by a deadline of March 31, 2016.[28] At the time this book went to press, the task force was expecting to issue a report in mid-2016.[29]

4. In October 2015, the Law Firm Regulation Task Force of The Law Society of British Columbia issued its own consultation brief, calling for comments and also conducting an online survey of members of the legal profession on the topics of "law firm regulation" (described as "a limited form of 'entity regulation'")[30] and "proactive regulation."[31] As a next phase, in 2016 the task force held "face-to-face consultation with the profession."[32] Herman Van Ommen, the chair of the task force, has observed that "once a regulator develops the tools it needs to regulate law firms, it's much easier to take the next step and move to regulate other entities, too."[33]

A February 2016 article in the Canadian newspaper *Financial Post* captured the significance of the work being done in these provinces in this way: "Entity regulation might seem dull to outsiders. But this seemingly mundane discussion may very well set the course of a modern legal services industry in Canada."[34] In the United States, lawyer conduct is regulated on an individual basis: Nearly every rule of the ABA Model Rules is directed expressly toward "a lawyer," as an individual, and places responsibilities only on "a lawyer," as an individual, for his/her own conduct.[35]

Two exceptions are Model Rules 5.1[36] and 5.3[37]—rules first adopted in 1983 as recognition by the ABA of the increased prevalence and importance of law firms as opposed to sole practitioners. Taken together, these two rules require a law firm partner and lawyer(s) having managerial responsibility in a law firm to take "reasonable efforts" to ensure that the firm has in effect "measures" that give "reasonable assurance" that the other lawyers as well as nonlawyers in the firm act in conformity with the rules. Under Model Rules 5.1(c) and 5.3(c), a lawyer is responsible for the conduct of another person—lawyer or nonlawyer—in the firm if either (i) the lawyer ordered the conduct or knowingly ratified the conduct, or (ii) the lawyer, in a partnership or managerial role, or with "a direct supervisory authority," knew of the conduct at a time when its consequences could have been avoided or mitigated but failed to take reasonable remedial action.

Save for in New Jersey and New York, however, Model Rules 5.1 and 5.3 still regulate individual lawyers and not entities. They differ from the other

Model Rules only in that they attempt to place responsibility on individual lawyers not for their own conduct but for the conduct of other individuals, lawyers as well as nonlawyers, over which they arguably have control through a hierarchical relationship in a law firm. (New Jersey and New York have adopted alternate versions of Model Rule 5.1(a) that extend the responsibility to law firms as well. In this manner, the National Organization of Bar Counsel has argued that these two states "have already laid the groundwork for PMBR entity regulation," albeit with few examples of enforcement to date).[38]

In any state, neither Rule 5.1 or 5.3 actually requires that a firm have appropriate policies and procedures in place—as the comments to Model Rule 5.1(a), explain, all that is required is that "lawyers with managerial authority" make "reasonable efforts" to establish internal policies and procedures designed to provide "reasonable assurance" that the lawyers and nonlawyers in the firm act in conformity with the rules.[39] There is no requirement to actually establish any such policies and procedures and no requirement to ensure that they function appropriately.

Further, the comments to Model Rule 5.1 make a clear distinction between partners and "junior lawyers," implying that if policies and procedures are needed, it is principally, if not exclusively, in order to control the conduct of junior lawyers, under the implied assumption that there is little to no risk that senior lawyers will violate the rules.[40] Accordingly, Rule 5.1 is ambiguous regarding the extent to which a partner might bear responsibility for the conduct of another partner, and arguably the rule does not create this responsibility at all, given that one of the comments to the rule reads, "In a small firm of experienced lawyers, informal supervision and periodic review of compliance with the required systems ordinarily will suffice."[41]

To date, enforcement of these two rules is considered to be minimal, and few disciplinary proceedings have been brought under either of them. A reason offered for this is that in most law firms, managerial responsibility is usually too diffuse—it is often not clear just who has any given responsibility—for disciplinary authorities to be able to make a case for violation of either rule.[42]

In the opinion of Canadian Adam Dodek, "the proper question is not 'Why should law firms be regulated?' but 'Why do they largely escape . . . regulation?'"[43] The rationale for entity-based regulation is that lawyers do not work in a vacuum; they work in the setting of a firm, be it large or small. And the ethical compliance of an individual lawyer depends in part, and perhaps in large part, upon the environment in which they work and upon the systems and processes that the firm has in place to ensure compliance.[44] Indeed, disciplinary complaints bear this out: Many of them relate to misconduct that very well may have been avoided if appropriate firm management systems had been in place. This demonstrates, in the words of Dodek, that there is a "regulatory gap."[45]

Taking Illinois as an example: The 2015 Annual Report of that state's Attorney Registration and Disciplinary Commission (ARDC) states that of the 5,648 investigations docketed by the ARDC in that year, 38 percent of the charges involved "neglect of the client's cause," and 12 percent of the charges involved "failure to communicate with the client."[46]

A well-publicized case originating in the neighboring state of Iowa sheds light on what "neglect of the client's cause" and "failure to communicate with the client" can mean: In this case, an attorney, Cameron A. Davidson, represented Deere and Co. as a defendant in an employment lawsuit. The plaintiff was a former Deere employee who had been fired from her job on the grounds that she had violated the company's travel expense policy, but she claimed her termination resulted from age discrimination. In a series of interrogatories and requests for production of evidence including motions and orders to compel disclosure, Davidson delayed providing responses and failed to arrange for depositions. As a result of these failures, on three different occasions over the course of 2012 to 2013, Deere was sanctioned by the court and ordered to pay attorney's fees to the plaintiff's counsel. On each of those three occasions, Davidson arranged for his firm, Lane and Waterman (a firm of about 40 lawyers), to pay the sanctions, and Davidson then billed Deere for reimbursement.[47]

In reporting his conduct to the Iowa Supreme Court Attorney Discipline Board, Davidson stated that, as regards the first of the three sanctions, he believed that he had discussed with Deere the motions and the orders to compel, but that his files "did not reflect" that he had. As regards the other two sanctions, Davidson admitted that he did not inform the client of either the motions or the orders to compel, and that the client "was not aware of the seriousness of the discovery dispute."[48]

The public documentation does not explain how Davidson's partners at Lane and Waterman finally became aware of the existence of the motions and the orders, or of Davidson's failure to inform the client, but they eventually did become aware. When they did, they informed Deere, and also requested the court to amend the sanctions in order that they be imposed solely against Lane and Waterman and not against the client.[49]

As the Illinois ARDC statistics show, attorney neglect of their client's causes and failure to communicate with clients are common occurrences. On the other hand, billing a client for reimbursement of sanctions that are imposed as a result of that neglect is not a common occurrence, and it is for that reason that this case received more publicity than other cases of neglect and failure to communicate typically receive.[50]

However, what is equally, if not more, remarkable with this case is that Davidson failed to respond to motions and court orders, was sanctioned on that basis, failed to inform the client, and billed the client for reimbursement—all not just once but on *three different occasions* over the course of at least one year, before his fellow law firm partners became aware of what was happening and took action. On this basis, it seems safe to conclude either that Davidson's firm did not have in place policies and procedures to ensure that all lawyers in the firm conduct themselves ethically, or, if they did have such policies and procedures in place, that they were ineffective. Indeed, given that nothing in the public record indicates that either the firm Lane and Waterman or any of its partners were, themselves, sanctioned by the Iowa disciplinary authorities—or even threatened with sanctions—in relation to this matter, and given that not a single commentator on this case raised the question of the responsibility of the firm or any of the firm's partners, it is clear that Model Rules 5.1 and 5.3 are not sufficient to motivate, much less to compel, firms to establish effective policies and procedures to protect clients from ethical violations.[51]

Contrast this situation to that of an ILP in Australia that has declared itself to the regulatory authorities, has designated a LPD to be responsible for the ILP's management systems, has completed an obligatory self-assessment in order to ascertain if it has appropriate management systems in place, and has made adjustments in those areas where the firm deemed it was not compliant. While taking such steps cannot guarantee that no one at the ILP will ever act unethically, it will reduce the likelihood that they will and, importantly, will increase the likelihood that violations will be caught and corrected before they reach the egregious level that they did at Lane and Waterman. That is the rationale for entity-based regulation.[52]

The rationale for proactive, management-based regulation (PMBR) is that rules-based, proscriptive regulation such as that applied in the United States is not sufficient to protect consumers. Rules-based, proscriptive regulation is a reactive process. It focuses on serious misconduct, in contrast to simply unsatisfactory conduct. And it acts merely by sanctioning serious misconduct after the fact, in contrast to fostering the adoption of proactive measures that would reduce the likelihood that serious misconduct occurs.

Rules-based regulation is conducted in an adversarial setting that is often described as "quasi-criminal" in nature.[53] A burden of proof must be met, an often difficult challenge given that many of the Model Rules (and notably Rules 5.1 and 5.3) apply reasonableness standards. Investigating and prosecuting complaints is resource intensive, but the responsibility for it falls upon disciplinary agencies that have highly limited resources.

In this restrictive context, disciplinary agencies focus on the most egregious cases, on the cases where violations are blatant and relatively easy to demonstrate. As a result, less egregious cases, cases for which it is difficult to meet the burden of proof, and certainly cases that constitute merely unsatisfactory conduct without amounting to professional misconduct, go unsanctioned, if not entirely unchecked. It is for this reason that rules-based, proscriptive systems like that of the United States are criticized as offering little in the way of consumer protection.[54]

In contrast, a proactive, management-based approach, building upon entity-based regulation, places the burden upon entities to develop and implement systems and processes whose purpose is to minimize the occurrence not only of egregious rule violations, but also of failures in customer service that aggravate clients without amounting to sanctionable ethical breaches.[55]

This burden is placed on entities not in a diffused manner by simple reference to "partners" or lawyers "with managerial responsibility," but in a direct and accountable manner, by requiring the entity to appoint by name one or more specific persons (LPD, COLP, etc.) whose explicit responsibilities include ensuring that the entity has developed and implemented the appropriate management systems.

PMBR, as well as OFR, also differ from rules-based, proscriptive regulation in that they do not dictate or impose any particular system or process—instead, they only require outcomes (such as timely communications with clients, meeting of deadlines, maintenance of confidential information). PMBR and OFR leave to the entity the freedom, as well as the responsibility, to determine the means. Finally, empirical evidence of the benefits of PMBR in Australia has not gone unnoticed in the United States. As the National Organization of Bar Counsel describes:

> [E]ntity regulation reduces the number of complaints made against law-practice entities and improves practice management. In 2008, a research study by Dr. Christine Parker of the University of Melbourne Law School in conjunction with the [New South Wales] regulator assessed the impact of ethical infrastructure and the self-assessment process in NSW to assess whether the process is effective and whether the process is leading to "better conduct" by firms required to self-assess. The research focused on the number of complaints relating to incorporated legal practices after incorporation and comparing this with prior to incorporation. The research found that complaints rates for incorporated legal practices were two-thirds lower than nonincorporated legal practices after the incorporated legal practice completed their initial self-assessment. The research also revealed that the complaints rate for incorporated legal practices that self-assessed was one-third of the number of complaints registered against similar nonincorporated legal practices.[56]

The repeated ethical breaches that Cameron Davidson committed at Lane and Waterman could happen with any lawyer and with any firm. But it is much easier to imagine them happening in a regulatory environment that is rules based, proscriptive, and focused on the individual, than it is to imagine them happening in a regulatory environment that is proactive, management based, and focused as much on the entity as on the individual.

This explains, at least in part, the interest that regulatory authorities in Colorado and Illinois have expressed, if not (yet) explicitly in entity regulation, than at least in PMBR. As explained in part I, in late 2015, the Office of Attorney Regulation Counsel of the Colorado Supreme Court formally announced that "Colorado is studying an approach to attorney regulation that is centered on prevention, not solely discipline" that, if enacted, "would be the first of its kind in this country."[57] The program is called the "Colorado Proactive Management Based Regulation (PMBR) program," and the announcement describes its benefits as including "improve[ed] management and culture of law firms," "prevent[ing] client and public harm" rather than focusing on discipline after the fact, and "improve[ing] the relationship between the regulator and the regulated because the regulator focuses on helping to improve the practice as a whole and reduce complaints while shifting the regulatory focus away from discipline alone."[58] Notably, the announcement describes the research of Hofstra professor Susan Saab Fortney, which "revealed that lawyers who completed the self-assessment process ended up revising their firm systems, policies and procedures, or adopting new ones, and thereby strengthened their firm management through such self-assessment."[59]

In the absence of the either prior or simultaneous implementation of PMBR and, especially, entity regulation, it is difficult to imagine that Model Rule 5.4 could be modified in order to permit alternative structures. On the other hand, the reverse is quite easy to imagine. That is, entity regulation as well as PMBR can be adopted without taking the extra step of also permitting for alternative structures. This is because PMBR and, especially, entity regulation are natural and necessary elements in a shift toward permitting alternative structures. In addition, neither entity regulation nor PMBR appear to raise the same polemical objections that alternative structures do. That is, while it would be incorrect to claim that they were adopted in England and Wales and in Australia without any controversy at all, the discussions were not nearly as impassioned as they were on the topic of ABSs in, most notably, England and Wales.[60]

It is likely that regulators in Nova Scotia and Colorado (and perhaps also Illinois) have recognized this, and it is why, for the time being, they are focused on the development and implementation of PMBR (and, in Nova Scotia, also entity regulation) without, for the most part if at all, even mentioning the incendiary term "ABS" or its synonyms. In all likelihood, they see two benefits in proceeding in this manner: (i) in developing and implementing PMBR and entity regulation independently, their jurisdictions can enjoy their benefits—and enjoy them sooner—without their progress being held hostage by a contentious debate around alternative structures, and, at the same time, (ii) because PMBR and, especially, entity regulation are prerequisites to the adoption of alternative structures, they can move their jurisdictions that much closer to their eventual adoption.

In contrast, the law societies of the "Prairie provinces" of Manitoba, Alberta, and Saskatchewan have not demonstrated the same hesitation in expressly connecting entity regulation and PMBR to alternative structures. In their jointly issued discussion paper "Innovating Regulation: A Collaboration of the Prairie Law Societies," they explicitly link the three and state they are "intimately connected."[61] The consultation website they created further reflects this approach, in that it also addresses all three topics at the same time. That being said, the law societies of the Prairie provinces have demonstrated at least some caution: In a first stage, their consultation process addresses only compliance-based regulation and entity regulation. It addresses alternative structures only in an indirect manner, in that, in contrast to opening full consultations on the other two topics, the website opens only a "discussion forum" on the topic of alternative structures.[62] The law societies explain their two (or more) stage consultation process as follows: "[T]he Prairie law societies will not consider ABSs until an entity regulation system is put in place.[63] . . . We will reserve a more fulsome discussion of ABS in a subsequent round of consultation, if and when the proposition is brought to the table."[64]

It could be said that Ontario is in the process of learning the hard way. In September 2012, the Law Society of Upper Canada established an "Alternative Business Structures Working Group."[65] For a period of three years, this group examined a possible change to the Ontario regulations in order to permit alternative structures. Their work involved "extensive research, . . . including meetings with lawyers and paralegals, consulting with experts and reviewing research and related literature."[66] Most notably, in September 2014, the LSUC issued a discussion paper "seeking input from the public, the legal community and other interested parties on alternative business structures (ABS) as a means for delivering legal services in Ontario."[67] While the discussion paper mentioned entity regulation and PMBR very briefly in passing, it did not explain or develop either topic.

The activities of the working group, and, especially its September 2014 discussion paper calling for comments with respect to four potential models for nonlawyer ownership, triggered an avalanche. The working group received 41 written submissions in response to the discussion paper, of which 21 expressed opposition,[68] and, in many cases, very strong opposition to the introduction of alternative structures in Ontario (10 expressed support[69] and 10 either expressed no position or their position was not clear[70]). The discussion paper also spurred an intensified discussion of alternative structures in the legal press and on social media, one example being a December 2014 post on *Slaw* ("Canada's online legal magazine") by the commentator Mitch Kowalski entitled "Anti-ABS Arguments Continue to Be Based on Emotion—Not Fact."[71] Over a 29-day period from December 2014 to January 2015, his post generated just under 100 comments, many of them extraordinarily lengthy (well over 3,000 words), and, especially, many of them impassioned. Just a few examples of the statements made include:

- "There is nothing that is claimed for ABS that cannot be achieved without ABS. We would be far better off if we put our talents and resources into achieving those benefits without resorting to the bottomless hell-hole of profit-motivated, bean-counter remote ownership of the legal profession. . . . Every real benefit foolishly attributed to the ersatz panacea of ABS can be achieved . . . without resorting to the myopic and irreversible blunder of selling the ownership of the legal profession to mostly remote bean-counters."[72]
- "We stumble around like drunks attacking the modest cost of wills and work assiduously at being bootlicks to big business by offering to sell them our profession. . . . Are we completely daft? Are we that blindly and brainlessly cavalier?"[73]
- "[ABS] is poison. It is immeasurably harmful. It is like communism once was—a superficially appealing philosophy that garnered a number of adherents even in the West, but which, as history has proven, engenders and spreads harm like an ebola virus sneezed into a classroom. You may not appreciate it but I am trying to prevent you and the other misguided sponsors of this evil from later garnering for yourselves the scorn of history."[74]
- "ABS is an irreversible blunder of stunning proportions that will do nothing for the public except to harm them. . . . It should be seen for what it truly is—the worst idea to hit the profession in centuries . . . [ABS] assuredly will prove to be the most colossal, short-sighted, cynical, profiteering at the expense of the public, and unnecessary blunder in the history of the legal profession dating back 800 years."[75]

This impassioned argumentation exposes how controversial the topic of ABS became in Ontario. Understood in this context, the decision of the working group in late September 2015 to not further examine "any majority or controlling nonlicensee ownership models for traditional law firms in Ontario"[76] is not a surprise. Nor was its explanation that "such nonlicensee ownership levels do not appear to be warranted based on current information when the potential benefits to such external ownership levels are weighed against the regulatory risks and regulatory proportionality."[77]

Also not a surprise is that just over two months later—early December 2015—the Compliance-Based Entity Regulation Task Force of the Law Society of Upper Canada announced its decision to conduct a consultation process with respect to compliance-based entity regulation.[78] It is absolutely no surprise that neither the document announcing the process nor the consultation paper[79] issued subsequently makes any reference to alternative structures or ABS.

In sum, the adoption of entity-based regulation, ideally accompanied by proactive, management-based (or outcomes-focused or compliance-based) regulation, are natural and necessary steps toward the adoption of alternative structures. Adopted together, the two regulatory changes create the opportunity to completely re-work the relationship between the regulator and the regulated, regardless of whether alternative structures are also ultimately adopted or not. While they can be adopted simultaneously with the adoption of alternative structures, they can also be adopted as a preliminary step, and the examples of Nova Scotia, the Prairie provinces, and Ontario suggest that this is likely the least controversial way to proceed.

## STORIES

### (PART V OR ONLINE)

*John Briton, Former Legal Services Commissioner, Queensland* (online): Briton describes PMBR as a way for the regulator to get to the cultural influences that have an impact on the behavior of lawyers in law firms—influences that are just as much if not more important in determining how an individual performs than that individual's knowledge and character.

*Darrel Pink, Executive Director, Nova Scotia Barristers' Society* (online): Pink states both that regulating lawyers on an individual basis only no longer reflects the way that many lawyers work, and that it is not possible to discuss alternative structures without first addressing the regulation of entities in addition to the regulation of individuals.

*Kristin Dangerfield, CEO, The Law Society of Manitoba* (online): Dangerfield explains why the Benchers of Manitoba have concluded that, with entity regulation, Manitoba can move toward permitting lawyers to partner with nonlawyers, and allowing law firms to accept capitalization from other sources.

*Ross Earnshaw, Chair, Task Force on Compliance-Based Entity Regulation and Margaret Drent, Policy Counsel, Law Society of Upper Canada* (online): Earnshaw and Drent explain that compliance-based regulation may have the effect of increasing client satisfaction and reducing the incidence of complaints and claims.

*Herman Van Ommen, Chair, Law Firm Regulation Task Force, Law Society of British Columbia* (online): Van Ommen explains that law firm regulation offers a real chance to reduce the number of complaints that the public make about lawyers.

*James Coyle, Attorney Regulation Counsel, Colorado Supreme Court* (online): Coyle explains that the best way for regulators to improve the provision of legal services in Colorado is to help attorneys to have the tools they need to build an ethical infrastructure, and notably to develop a self-assessment form for attorneys who are in private practice.

*James J. Grogan, Deputy Administrator and Chief Counsel, Illinois ARDC* (online): Grogan explains that for him, PMBR is a way to help lawyers, and sole practitioners in particular, to have successful careers so that the ARDC doesn't have to deal with them.

## NOTES

1. For a more detailed description of these regulatory innovations in Australia and England and Wales, see Grech and Tahlia Gordon, "Modern Law Firm Management." With respect to England and Wales, see also Hadfield and Rhode, "How to Regulate Legal Services," 20–32.

2. Solicitors Regulation Authority, "FA1—Firm Authorisation Application Form," Version 22, last modified January 25, 2016, accessible at http://www.sra.org.uk/solicitors/firm-based-authorisation/authorisation-recognition.page.

3. In England and Wales, there are a number of different legal services professions in addition to solicitors, as well as a number of different regulators in addition to the SRA. Most notably, in addition to the SRA, three other "front-line" regulators also have the authority to license ABSs: the Council for Licensed Conveyancers (CLC), the Institute of Chartered Accountants in England and Wales (ICAEW), and the Intellectual Property Regulation Board (IPReg). Further, at the time this book went to press, the Bar Standards Board, which regulates barristers, had submitted to the Legal Service Board (LSB, the oversight regulator) an application for comparable authority. For the sake of simplicity, this chapter focuses on solicitors and the SRA, as the largest group of legal services professionals and the largest regulator, respectively.

4. Further information about COLP and COFA is available on the SRA's website: "COLPs and COFAs," http://www.sra.org.uk/solicitors/colp-cofa.page.

5. Further information about OFR is available on the SRA's website: "Outcomes-Focused Regulation at a Glance," http://www.sra.org.uk/solicitors/freedom-in-practice/ofr/ofr-quick-guide.page#ofr-3-1.

6. Hilborne, "COLPs Failing to Report."

7. Legal Profession Uniform Law (New South Wales), 2014, Section 35(1), http://www5.austlii.edu.au/au/legis/nsw/consol_act/lpul333/s35.html.

8. See, for example, Queensland Legal Services Commission, "Obligations of LPDs."

9. Queensland Legal Services Commission, "Incorporated Legal Practices Self-Assessment Audit," accessed December 31, 2015, https://www.lsc.qld.gov.au/__data/assets/pdf_file/0005/97781/ILP-Self-Assessment-Audit-Form-Version-4.pdf. For a general discussion of the self-assessment form pioneered in New South Wales, see Grech and Tahlia Gordon, "Modern Law Firm Management," 5–6.

10. Ibid., 11.

11. Ibid., 13.

12. Ibid., 13, 26.

13. "Self-Assessment Audits," Queensland Legal Services Commission, last modified November 11, 2013, https://www.lsc.qld.gov.au/compliance/compliance-audits/self-assessment-audits.

14. "Legal Services Regulation," Nova Scotia Barristers' Society, accessed May 16, 2016, http://nsbs.org/legal-services-regulation. For an in-depth discussion, see Victoria Rees, "Transforming Regulation and Governance in the Public Interest," paper prepared for Council of the

Nova Scotia Barristers' Society, October 15, 2013, https://nsbs.org/sites/default/files/cms/news/2013-10-30transformingregulation.pdf.

15. Legal Profession Act. 2004, c. 28, as amended by S.N.S. 2010, c 56, accessed December 3, 2015, http://nsbs.org/sites/default/files/cms/menu-pdf/legalprofessionact.pdf.

16. Nova Scotia Barristers' Society, "Legal Services Regulation: The Policy Framework."

17. Darrel Pink, interview with author, November, 2015.

18. "A Management System for Ethical Legal Practice (March 2016)," Nova Scotia Barristers' Society, accessed May 16, 2016, http://nsbs.org/sites/default/files/cms/page/2016-03-29_revisedmselpselfassessment.pdf.

19. "Transforming Regulation: Will You Volunteer for Pilot Project?," Nova Scotia Barristers' Society, accessed May 16, 2016, http://nsbs.org/news/2016/04/transforming-regulation-will-you-volunteer-pilot-project.

20. Clearwater, "President's Report."

21. Fourth Session, Fortieth Legislature," The Legislative Assembly of Manitoba, accessed December 31, 2015, https://web2.gov.mb.ca/bills/40-4/index.php.

22. 40th Legislature of Manitoba, Government Bill 19, "The Legal Profession Amendment Act," 2015, https://web2.gov.mb.ca/bills/40-4/pdf/b019.pdf.

23. "Innovating Regulation: A Collaboration of the Prairie Law Societies," 2.

24. "Innovating Regulation," The Law Societies of Alberta, Manitoba and Saskatchewan, accessed May 16, 2016, http://www.lawsocietylistens.ca/.

25. "Compliance-Based Entity Regulation," The Law Society of Upper Canada, accessed February 2, 2016, https://www.lsuc.on.ca/better-practices/. See also Law Society of Upper Canada Compliance-Based Entity Regulation Task Force, "Report to Convocation," December 4, 2015.

26. "Compliance-Based Entity Regulation," The Law Society of Upper Canada, accessed February 2, 2016, https://www.lsuc.on.ca/better-practices/.

27. Compliance-Based Entity Regulation Task Force, "Call for Input Consultation Paper: 'Promoting Better Legal Practices,'" January 2016, https://www.lsuc.on.ca/uploadedFiles/compliance-based-entity-regulation-consultation-paper.pdf.

28. "Compliance-Based Entity Regulation," The Law Society of Upper Canada, accessed February 2, 2016, https://www.lsuc.on.ca/better-practices/.

29. Law Society of Upper Canada Compliance-Based Entity Regulation Task Force, "Report to Convocation," December 4, 2015, 274.

30. Law Firm Regulation Task Force, "Law Firm Regulation Consultation Brief." 11.

31. The Law Society of British Columbia, "Law Firm Regulation Consultation: FAQs," n.d., https://www.lawsociety.bc.ca/docs/newsroom/highlights/FirmRegulation-FAQ.pdf.

32. "Law Firm Regulation Consultation, Phase Two," The Law Society of British Columbia, January 28, 2016, https://www.lawsociety.bc.ca/newsroom/highlights.cfm#c4191.

33. Mitch Kowalski, "Entity Regulation Comes to Canada."

34. Ibid.

35. Semple refers to this as the "professionalist-independent tradition of legal services regulation" and states that it survives today primarily in North America. One chapter of his book, *Legal Services Regulation at the Crossroads: Justitia's Legions*, is devoted to describing the "regulatory failure" that results from this tradition and another chapter to describing how it impedes access to justice. Semple, *Legal Services Regulation*, 4, 93–182.

36. "Rule 5.1: Responsibilities of a Partner or Supervisory Lawyer," American Bar Association, accessed August 23, 2015, http://www.americanbar.org/groups/professional_responsibility/publications/model_rules_of_professional_conduct/rule_5_1_responsibilities_of_a_partner_or_supervisory_lawyer.html.

37. "Rule 5.3: Responsibilities Regarding Nonlawyer Assistant," American Bar Association, accessed August 23, 2015, http://www.americanbar.org/groups/professional_responsibility/publications/model_rules_of_professional_conduct/rule_5_3_responsibilities_regarding_nonlawyer_assistant.html.

38. National Organization of Bar Counsel, "Entity Regulation: Frequently Asked Questions," July 14, 2015, 10–11, http://www.nobc.org/docs/Global%20Resources/Entity%20Regulation/Entity.Regulation.Committee.FAQs.FINAL.07142015.(00000003).pdf.

39. "Comment on Rule 5.1," American Bar Association, accessed August 23, 2015, http://www.americanbar.org/groups/professional_responsibility/publications/model_rules_of_professional_conduct/rule_5_1_responsibilities_of_a_partner_or_supervisory_lawyer/comment_on_rule_5_1.html.

40. Ibid.

41. Ibid.

42. See, for example, Schneyer, "The Case for Proactive Management-Based Self-Regulation," 256–61.

43. Adam M. Dodek, "Regulating Law Firms in Canada," *Canadian Bar Review* 90 (2012): 387, http://dx.doi.org/10.2139/ssrn.1984635.

44. For a detailed exploration of these issues with respect to Canadian but also US law firms, see Ibid., 388–404.

45. Ibid., 393.

46. Attorney Registration and Disciplinary Commission, "Annual Report of 2015," April 27, 2016, 11–13, https://www.iardc.org/AnnualReport2015.pdf.

47. *Iowa Supreme Court Attorney Disciplinary Board v. Cameron A. Davdison*, Order of Public Reprimand no. 14–0878, August 18, 2014, http://www.abajournal.com/images/main_images/Davidson.pdf.

48. Debra Cassens Weiss, "Lawyer Who Billed Corporate Client for His Sanctions is Reprimanded," *ABA Journal*, September 2, 2014, http://www.abajournal.com/news/article/lawyer_who_billed_corporate_client_for_his_sanctions_is_reprimanded_partly.

49. Ibid.

50. See, for example, Brian Wellner, "Q-C Attorney Reprimanded for Mishandling Deere Case," *Quad-City Times*, August 29, 2014, http://qctimes.com/news/local/crime-and-courts/q-c-attorney-reprimanded-for-mishandling-deere-case/article_c6f6f209-93df-59dd-896b-40a4765efb57.html; Associated Press, "Iowa Discipline Board Reprimands Attorney," *KCRG.com*, August 31, 2014, http://www.kcrg.com/subject/news/iowa-discipline-board-reprimands-attorney-20140831; Keith Lee, "What's Worse than Billing a Client for Bottled Water? Billing Them for Sanctions," *Above the Law*, September 5, 2014, http://abovethelaw.com/2014/09/whats-worse-than-billing-a-client-for-bottled-water-billing-them-for-sanctions/; Joseph A. Corsmeier, "Ethics Alert—Iowa Supreme Court Reprimands Lawyer who Billed Corporate Client for Costs of Sanctions Which 'Resulted From His Own Lack of Diligence and Communication,' " *Lawyer Ethics Alert Blogs*, September 5, 2014, https://jcorsmeier.wordpress.com/tag/lawyer-failure-to-communicate/.

51. For additional, if less recent, examples, see Schneyer,"Professional Discipline for Law Firms," 1–3.

52. Two Canadian regulators have linked entity regulation to the Panama Papers. More specifically, Malcolm Mercer, a Bencher and chair of the Law Society of Upper Canada's Professional Regulation Committee, wrote:

> Much has been written about the Law Societies' complaints-driven and reactive approach to regulating professional conduct. As the Panama Papers case (and the GM, Volkswagen, Enron, Watergate and other cases) makes clear, this reactive complaint-driven regulatory approach simply does not work where lawyers facilitate unlawful client conduct. Where client misconduct is somehow found out, the question is often "Where were the lawyers?" Our reactive complaint-driven regulatory approach increases the risk that, time and time again, we will have to ask the same question. Malcolm Mercer, "Yet Again the Question Is 'Where Were the Lawyers?'" *Slaw*, May 5, 2016, http://www.slaw.ca/2016/05/05/yet-again-the-question-is-where-were-the-lawyers/.

In response to Mercer, Darrel Pink, executive director of the Nova Scotia Barristers' Society, wrote:

> [In learning about the Panama Papers, my] immediate reaction was that this is but one other reason why an "entity regulation" approach to regulation has become

> absolutely essential. The public interest requires that "law firms" be subject to regulatory oversight and be held responsible for their local and global behavior. . . . The entity/proactive compliance based regulation work now being undertaken . . . by the [Canadian] law societies will move us much closer to truly being able to advance the public interest in overseeing what lawyers and their firms actually do and how they do it. (Darrel Pink, May 5, 2016 [8:17 am], comment on Mercer, "Yet Again the Question Is 'Where Were the Lawyers?'")

53. Kenneth M. Mogill, "Trying an Attorney Discipline Case," *Michigan Bar Journal*, March, 2014, 44–45, 44, http://www.michbar.org/file/journal/pdf/pdf4article2351.pdf.

54. James C. Turner and Suzanne M. Mishkin, "Time for a Whupping: Across the Country, Attorney Discipline Systems Disgrace the Profession," *Legal Times*, August 18, 2003, http://www.turnerhome.org/jct/Clips/turner-legal-times-08-18-03.pdf

55. For a discussion of this issue in a Canadian context, see Amy Salyzyn, "What If We Didn't Wait?: Canadian Law Societies and the Promotion of Effective Ethical Infrastructure in Law Practices," *Canadian Bar Review* forthcoming, Ottawa Faculty of Law Working Paper No. 2015-15, March, 2015, http://ssrn.com/abstract=2533229.

56. National Organization of Bar Counsel, "Entity Regulation: Frequently Asked Questions," 12, citing Parker, Gordon, and. Mark, "Regulating Law Firm Ethics Management."

57. Jim Coyle, "A New Model of Attorney Regulation?"

58. Ibid.

59. Ibid., referencing Fortney, "Promoting Public Protection," 1–12; and Fortney, "The Role of Ethics Audits," 112–49.

60. The comments submitted in response to the January 2016 Consultation Paper issued by the Law Society of Upper Canada Compliance-Based Entity Regulation Task Force demonstrate comparably little passion. See these two links: https://www.lsuc.on.ca/uploadedFiles/CBER%20Submissions%20-%20Legal%20Organizations.pdf and https://www.lsuc.on.ca/uploadedFiles/CBER%20Submissions%20-%20Individuals.pdf.

61. "Innovating Regulation: A Collaboration of the Prairie Law Societies," 2.

62. "Innovating Regulation," Law Societies of Alberta, Manitoba and Saskatchewan, accessed May 16, 2016, http://www.lawsocietylistens.ca/.

63. "Alternative Business Structures," The Law Societies of Alberta, Manitoba and Saskatchewan, accessed May 16, 2016, http://www.lawsocietylistens.ca/abs-discussion-forum/forum_topics/alternative-business-structures1.

64. Innovating Regulation Team, n.d., reply to comment by Chad Brown, "Alternative Business Structures," The Law Societies of Alberta, Manitoba and Saskatchewan.

65. "Alternative Business Structures," Law Society of Upper Canada, accessed January 2, 2016, http://www.lsuc.on.ca/ABS/.

66. Ibid.

67. Alternative Business Structures Working Group, "Alternative Business Structures and the Legal Profession in Ontario: A Discussion Paper," September, 2014, http://www.lsuc.on.ca/uploadedFiles/abs-discussion-paper.pdf.

68. The submissions can be consulted at this link (accessed January 2, 2016): http://www.lsuc.on.ca/ABS/. The 21 submissions that can be characterized as more or less clearly in opposition are those of The Advocates' Society, Barrie Real Estate Lawyers Association, Blair Botsford, Brendt, Lorne and Group, Ken Chasse, The County District Lawyers Presidents' Association, County of Carleton Law Association, Janis Criger, Criminal Lawyers Association, Essex Law Association, Nicholas Gehl, Gordon Harris, McLeish Orlando, Ontario Bar Association, Ontario Trial Lawyers Association, Southwest Region Women's Law Association, Stewart Title, Murray Teitel, Thunder Bay Law Association, Waterloo Region Law Association, and Women's Paralegal Association of Ontario.

69. The 10 submissions that can be characterized as more or less clearly in support are those of Julie Audet, Julie Audet and Nathalie Picard, Centre for International Governance Innovation, Cognition LLP, Conduit Law, Joseph Granton, Mitch Kowalski, Devon LaBuik, Liam Ledgerwood, and Baruch Lipinski.

70. The 10 submissions that can be characterized either as expressing no position or their position was not clear are those of Lee Akazaki, James Ball, Canadian Defense Lawyers, Equity Advisory Working Group on ABS, Federation of Asian Canadian Lawyers, John Hollander, Law Students' Society of Ontario, LawPRO, Ontario College of Social Workers and Social Service Workers, and David Wiseman.

71. Mitch Kowalski, "Anti-ABS Arguments Continue to Be Based on Emotion."

72. Bradley Wright, December 30, 2014 (6:28 pm), comment on Mitch Kowalski, "Anti-ABS Arguments Continue to Be Based on Emotion."

73. Bradley Wright, January 2, 2015 (1:43 pm), comment on Mitch Kowalski, "Anti-ABS Arguments Continue to Be Based on Emotion."

74. Bradley Wright, January 7, 2015 (10:31 am), comment on Mitch Kowalski, "Anti-ABS Arguments Continue to Be Based on Emotion."

75. Bradley Wright, January 23, 2015 (5:38 pm), comment on Mitch Kowalski, "Anti-ABS Arguments Continue to Be Based on Emotion."

76. Law Society of Upper Canada Professional Regulation Committee, "Report to Convocation," September 24, 2015, 111, http://www.lsuc.on.ca/uploadedFiles/For_the_Public/About_the_Law_Society/Convocation_Decisions/2015/convocation-september-2015-prc.pdf.

77. Ibid.

78. Law Society of Upper Canada Compliance-Based Entity Regulation Task Force, "Report to Convocation," December 4, 2015.

79. Compliance-Based Entity Regulation Task Force, "Call for Input Consultation Paper: 'Promoting Better Legal Practices.'"

## *Chapter Seventeen*

# Opportunities for Failure

Alternative structures are not immune to the risks that all businesses face. Should those risks be realized, an alternative structure can, like other businesses, fail. Both England and Wales and Australia provide examples of this.

## HACKING ASHTON

Hacking Ashton received its ABS license in March 2013. It gave two reasons for seeking to become an ABS: (i) in order to make one of its nonlawyer executives a partner, and (ii) in order to secure external funding. Jim Hickey, one of the firm's partners, stated that ABS status will enable the firm to benefit from a larger infrastructure and wider coverage.[1] Hickey further stated, "What also drove this forward was that we didn't think that smaller firms would be able to manage all the new compliance and regulatory requirements. ABS will allow the fee-earners to concentrate on the law."[2]

However, by October 2013, the firm had entered liquidation, owing £1.1 million to unsecured creditors.[3] The firm's demise was attributed to a dramatic fall in income, blamed upon increased competition from fixed-fee and online service providers, cuts in legal aid, and the departure of a number of partners over the summer of 2013.[4] The firm sought a buyer for the business, but was unsuccessful. The final nail in the firm's coffin was its inability to pay the £300,000 due to renew its professional indemnity insurance—without insurance, the firm was forced to wind down.[5]

## ILH GROUP LTD.

ILH Group Ltd. listed on the Australian Securities Exchange in 2007, shortly after Slater and Gordon. The group originally focused on legal services, owning a variety of practices like Rockwell Olivier, Signet Lawyers, Civic Legal, and Law Central. Later the group expanded into wealth management (Capricorn Investment Partners, acquired in 2013) and corporate advisory services (Eaton Capital Partners, acquired in 2012). In 2013 to 2014, ILH reportedly had "a horror" 12 to 18 months, with net profit loss after tax of 540 percent.[6] In the year ended June 30, 2014, the company declared after-tax loss of AUS$8.9 million.[7] The losses were blamed in part on sharp falls in legal revenues in Perth after an exodus of senior staff, and in part on the poor performance of Eaton Capital.[8] In August 2014, ILH sold Eaton Capital to Symon Capital Pty, a company controlled by Stephen Moss, Eaton Capital's chairman.[9] By the end of 2014, ILH found that it was unable to meet the terms of its AUS$12.6 million loan. In December 2014 the company went into administration and its shares were delisted.[10]

## QUINDELL LEGAL SERVICES AND SLATER AND GORDON

Another troubled structure was the ABS Quindell Legal Services. Its parent company, Quindell plc, was listed on the UK's Alternative Investment Market (AIM). Beginning in 2009, Quindell plc embarked on an acquisition spree of legal as well as other businesses,[11] eventually establishing five operating divisions in technology, solutions, legal services, medico-legal reporting, claims outsourcing, and telematics. It housed its legal services division in its Quindell Legal Services Limited, which received its ABS authorization in 2012.

In April 2014, a US group called Gotham City Research, having shorted Quindell stock, issued a report, "Quindell plc: A Country Club Built on Quicksand."[12] Claiming that the company's shares were overpriced, the report described a variety of problems with the Quindell group, claiming that "42 percent–80 percent" of its profits were "suspect," that a large percentage of its revenues came from companies owned by Quindell's CEO and other undisclosed related parties, that many of its acquisitions lacked economic substance, and that the company had negative operating cash flow.[13] As regards Quindell Legal Services, Gotham stated that recent changes in the law to ban referral fees would have made redundant the business models of many of the law firms it had acquired, yet Quindell refused to explain how it operated both in conformity with the new laws and at a profit.[14] In this context, Gotham concluded that Quindell Legal Services was operating unethically, and that the principal purpose of its ABS was to side-step the ban on referral fees.[15] While Quindell issued a statement rejecting Gotham's claims, Quindell plc's shares nevertheless went into a free fall, down 40 percent in one day.[16]

Even though Quindell plc, and notably Quindell Legal Services, reported revenue gains over the course of 2014, the company still faced increased scrutiny. During the final months of 2014, many of Quindell's senior executives resigned, including its founder and chair Rob Terry,[17] and the chief executive of Quindell Legal Services, Phil Hodgkinson.[18] PwC was asked to perform an independent review of Quindell plc's business, and the company spoke with a number of potential buyers. In May 2015 the sale of Quindell Legal Services to Australia-based (and also publicly held) Slater and Gordon was completed in what appeared to be a fire sale.[19]

But that did not end the story: Following the purchase of Quindell, the shares of Slater and Gordon declined dramatically, losing 90 percent of their value between April and December 2015.[20] This was attributed in part to questions over the accuracy of financial statements made in connection with the purchase of Quindell, and in part for other reasons, such as the anticipated impact of proposed legislative changes affecting the personal injury legal market in the UK.[21] In February 2016, the company voluntarily suspended trading of its shares while it finalized its midyear financial statements.[22] When trading resumed a few days later, share value immediately plummeted again.[23] Trading at a high of AUS$8.07 in April 2015, in early March 2016 the share price had fallen as low as AUS$0.23.[24] At the time this book went to press, at least two other law firms, Maurice Blackburn and ACA Lawyers, were preparing shareholder class action lawsuits.[25]

On the other side of the Atlantic, Slater and Gordon's stumbles did not go unnoticed. A commentator for Canada's *Financial Post* characterized the situation as an "accounting scandal," and predicted that because of it, the "proposal to let nonlawyers own Canadian law firms is probably toast."[26] After all, the commentator continued, Canadian legal industry observers look to Slater and Gordon as an example of what the Canadian profession could look like if ownership was opened to nonlawyers, and opponents to ABS in Canada are "seizing on Slater and Gordon as an example of all that is wrong with ABS."[27]

Other commentators immediately rejected that Slater and Gordon's troubles should make a difference for the debate in Canada (or indeed for anywhere else). In the first place, they argued, in recent years there have been a number of examples of traditional law firms experiencing financial mismanagement—the high-profile collapses of Dewey and LeBoeuf in the United States and Halliwells[28] in the UK being prime examples. When those failures occur, no one suggests that law firm partnerships should be banned because they are flawed as a concept.[29] In the second place, there has been no suggestion that Slater and Gordon has engaged in professional misconduct. More specifically, there were "no improper pressures or practices imposed by non-lawyer owners, no clients mistreated or ripped off."[30] In fact, the commentators argued, the situation demonstrates that the regulatory system for ABSs works quite well—"the scandal was identified quickly and is being promptly investigated in a transparent and public manner," which is a far better situation than the regulatory situation in Canada, where "client complaints are shrouded in secrecy and take an excruciatingly long time to be completed."[31]

These examples demonstrate that operating as an alternative structure does not guarantee success. The example of Hacking Ashton shows that alternative structure or not, there must be a viable business model. The example of Quindell shows that alternative structure or not, the business cannot appear to operate unethically, regardless of whether it actually is operating unethically or not. And a company's status as a public company arguably makes it even more vulnerable, as a potential target of short sellers. Finally, the examples of ILH and Slater and Gordon show that alternative structure or not, sound business and financial decisions are required. In the end, as one commentator observed, "ABS is just a means to an end; it is no golden bullet for business success."[32]

## NOTES

1. "Top Media Firm and Regional Practice Seeking External Cash Help Take ABS Total to Over 100," *Legal Futures*, March 5, 2013, http://www.legalfutures.co.uk/latest-news/top-media-firm-regional-practice-seeking-external-cash-help-take-abs-total-100.
2. Ibid.
3. Edward Devlin, "Hacking Ashton Partners Set for Shortfall," *Insider Media*, December 9, 2013, http://www.insidermedia.com/insider/midlands/104420-hacking-ashton-partners-set-shortfall/.
4. Ann King, "North Staffordshire Law Firm Hacking Ashton Closes Down," *The Sentinel*, October 2, 2013, http://www.stokesentinel.co.uk/North-Staffordshire-law-firm-Hacking-Ashton/story-19872528-detail/story.html#ixzz3jjNbftYm.
5. Devlin, "Hacking Ashton."
6. Justin Whealing, "ILH's Future under a Cloud," *Lawyers Weekly*, December 19, 2014, http://www.lawyersweekly.com.au/news/15962-ILH-s-future-under-a-cloud.
7. Chris Merritt, "Integrated Legal Holdings Calls for Reprieve on $12.6m Loan Repayments," *The Australian*, September 12, 2014, http://www.theaustralian.com.au/business/legal-affairs/integrated-legal-holdings-calls-for-reprieve-on-126m-loan-repayments/story-e6frg97x-1227055657940.
8. Ibid.
9. "ILH Group Ltd Says Sale of Eaton Capital Partners," *Reuters*, August 15, 2014, http://www.reuters.com/finance/stocks/ILH.AX/key-developments/article/3050863.
10. Sean Smith, "Administrators Called in to ILH," *West Australian*, December 18, 2014, https://au.news.yahoo.com/thewest/a/25810173/administrators-called-in-to-ilh/.
11. Neil Rose, "ABSs to the Fore as Quindell Claims 15% of PI Market and Countrywide Sees Profits Rise," *Legal Futures*, February 22, 2013, http://www.legalfutures.co.uk/latest-news/abss-fore-quindell-claims-15-pi-market-countrywide-sees-profits-rise/.
12. Gotham City Research, LLC, "Quindell PLC: A Country Club Built on Quicksand," April, 2014, https://www.scribd.com/fullscreen/219517633?access_key=key-11nxwoeikqzat6ii6aclandallow_share=trueandescape=falseandview_mode=scroll.

13. Ibid., 4.
14. Ibid., 54–58.
15. Ibid., 57.
16. Harriet Mann, "What Was the Cause of Quindell's Share-Price Slump?," *Interactive Investor*, April 23, 2014, http://www.iii.co.uk/articles/161814/what-was-cause-quindells-share-price-slump.
17. Neil Rose, "Terry Quits as Chairman of Ailing Quindell," *Legal Futures*, November 18, 2014, http://www.legalfutures.co.uk/latest-news/terry-quits-chairman-ailing-quindell.
18. Neil Rose, "Exclusive: Quindell Legal Services Chief Departs," *Legal Futures*, January 6, 2015, http://www.legalfutures.co.uk/latest-news/exclusive-quindell-legal-services-chief-departs.
19. "Gateley Set to Raise £30m from AIM Listing, as Slater and Gordon's Acquisition of Quindell Completes," *Legal Futures*, May 29, 2015, http://www.legalfutures.co.uk/latest-news/gateley-set-to-raise-30m-from-aim-listing-as-slater-gordons-acquisition-of-quindell-completes.
20. Nick Hilborne, "Slater and Gordon Tight-Lipped as Australian Law Firms Recruit Shareholders for Group Actions," *Legal Futures*, December 24, 2015, http://www.legalfutures.co.uk/latest-news/slater-gordon-tight-lipped-as-australian-law-firms-recruit-shareholders-for-group-actions; Jonathan Shapiro, "Slater and Gordon Shares Suspended Ahead of Earnings," *The Sydney Morning Herald*, February 24, 2016, http://www.smh.com.au/business/markets/slater--gordon-shares-suspended-ahead-of-earnings-20160223-gn1yy5.html.
21. Neil Rose, "Slater and Gordon's Share Price Collapses in Response to Autumn Statement," *Legal Futures*, November 26, 2015, http://www.legalfutures.co.uk/latest-news/slater-gordons-share-price-collapses-in-response-to-autumn-statement.
22. Michael Roddan, "Slater and Gordon Shares Suspended," *The Australian*, February 24, 2016, http://www.theaustralian.com.au/business/legal-affairs/slater--gordon-shares-suspended/news-story/936f361f1dbbcce7ed048b7ebbbf503c.
23. Ryan Newman, "Why the Slater and Gordon Limited Share Price was Slammed Another 33% Today," *The Motley Fool*, March 1, 2016, http://www.fool.com.au/2016/03/01/why-the-slater-gordon-limited-share-price-was-slammed-another-33-today/.
24. "Slater and Gordon Ltd." Financial Times Equities Markets, accessed March 2, 2016, http://markets.ft.com/research/Markets/Tearsheets/Summary?s=SGH:ASX; see also Neil Rose, "UK Litigation Funder to Back Shareholder Class Action Against Slater and Gordon," *Legal Futures*, March 2, 2016, http://www.legalfutures.co.uk/latest-news/uk-litigation-funder-to-back-shareholder-class-action-against-slater-gordon.
25. David Hellier, "Slater and Gordon Targeted by Aggrieved Investors for Potential Class Action," *The Guardian*, February 29, 2016, http://www.theguardian.com/business/2016/feb/29/slater-and-gordon-law-firm-targeted-investors-potential-class-action.
26. Drew Hasselback, "Why That Proposal to Let Non-Lawyers Own Canadian Law Firms Is Probably Toast," *Financial Post*, August 12, 2015, http://business.financialpost.com/legal-post/drew-hasselback-that-proposal-to-open-canadian-law-firm-ownership-to-non-lawyers-is-probably-toast.
27. Ibid.
28. Neil Rose, "Ex-Halliwells Partners Win Immunity from Liquidator Claims," *Legal Futures*, October 29, 2014, http://www.legalfutures.co.uk/latest-news/ex-halliwells-partners-win-immunity-liquidator-claims.
29. Neil Rose, "Why the Fuss Over Quindell and Slater and Gordon?" *Legal Futures*, August 14, 2015, http://www.legalfutures.co.uk/blog/why-the-fuss-over-quindell-and-slater-gordon.
30. Ibid.
31. Mitch Kowalski, "Why One Scandal Shouldn't Doom a New Twist on Law Firm Ownership," *Financial Post*, August 17, 2015, http://business.financialpost.com/legal-post/why-one-scandal-shouldnt-doom-a-new-twist-on-law-firm-ownership.
32. Neil Rose, "The Sorry Tale of a Fallen Giant," *Legal Futures*, March 2, 2016, http://www.legalfutures.co.uk/blog/the-sorry-tale-of-a-fallen-giant.

# *Part III*

# Access to Justice

One of the most polarizing discussions regarding alternative structures has been in relation to the issue of access to justice. Those in favor of alternative structures argue that they are an important if not primary means to increase access to justice in the United States.[1] Those opposed to alternative structures argue that they will have the opposite effect[2] or, at best, that there is no empirical evidence that alternative structures have increased access to justice in either England and Wales or Australia.[3] Given the potential dangers that alternative structures pose, the argument continues (echoing the debate over burden of proof), they should not be permitted in the absence of such empirical evidence.

## NOTES

1. See, generally, Hadfield "The Cost of Law." See also, for example, ABA Standing Committee on Professionalism, "Standing Committee on Professionalism Comment on Issues Paper Regarding Alternative Business Structures," May 5, 2016, 1, http://www.americanbar.org/content/dam/aba/images/office_president/professionalism_abs.pdf.

2. John Beisner, "Comments of the US Chamber Institute for Legal Reform on the Issues Paper Concerning Alternative Business Structures," June 1, 2011, 3, http://www.americanbar.org/content/dam/aba/administrative/ethics_2020/ethics_20_20_comments/uschamberinstituteforlegalreform_issuespaperconcerningalternativebusinessstructures.authcheckdam.pdf; Christian Ellis, "Comment on Future of Legal Services," April 28, 2016, http://www.americanbar.org/content/dam/aba/images/office_president/christian_ellis_abs.pdf.

3. Ontario Trial Lawyers Association, "Submission on Alternative Business Structures," 2–10; DRI — The Voice of the Defense Bar, 2.

## *Chapter Eighteen*

# Unacknowledged Complexity

The issue of access to justice in the context of alternative structures is highly complex—much more complex than most of the debates on the issue take into account. In spite of the complexities, is it nevertheless possible to demonstrate evidence of access to justice?

## MOTIVATIONS FOR THE REGULATORY CHANGES IN ENGLAND AND WALES AND AUSTRALIA

The importance of the question of access to justice in the debate in the United States is interesting in the context of the history of and motivations for the regulatory changes in England and Wales and Australia.

In England and Wales, the Clementi Report reveals that while, for Clementi, improving access to justice is an important regulatory objective, his primary motivations were not focused on the issue. Clementi's primary motivations were different: (i) to design a better regulatory system, (ii) to improve the complaints system, and (iii) to remove barriers to competition, notably by the introduction of alternative structures. Further, Clementi's perspective on the question of access to justice was a broad one, encompassing not only disadvantaged persons who cannot pay anything for legal services, but also the public at large, who needed "cost-effective service" provided in a consumer-friendly way.[1]

The motivations for the regulatory changes in Australia were entirely focused on the removal of barriers to competition. Increasing access to justice was never expressed as a motivation behind or an objective for the changes.

The fact that the primary objectives of the regulatory changes in England and Wales and Australia did not include increasing access to justice of course does not mean that the changes did or did not have that effect—it just means that it was not a primary objective, and, indeed, in Australia was not an objective at all, at least not in a direct manner.[2]

This history explains at least in part why there exists little empirical evidence that alternative structures have increased access to justice in either Australia or England and Wales. Rightly or wrongly, the primary focus of the regulations as well as of the regulators has been on other issues, and notably on removing barriers to competition.

## WHAT IS ACCESS TO JUSTICE?

Again, in the debate about alternative structures, many people raise the issue of access to justice, usually to make one of three arguments: either they will lead to increased access to justice, they will not, or there is not enough evidence either way. In this debate, rarely does anyone explain what they mean by access to justice, or suggest how it can be effectively measured.[3] What is access to justice? What are its elements?

Does it encompass just court procedures, or also other dispute resolution mechanisms, legal advice and information, contracts, document preparation, and representation in negotiations or before government agencies? Does it encompass only services tailored for a specific person, or also services that are not tailored, such as information on a website or in a leaflet? Is it more relevant for certain areas of the law or certain types of legal issues and less relevant for others? Is it relevant only for poor people, or also for middle class? Is it relevant for wealthy persons? Is it relevant only for disadvantaged populations (handicapped persons, minorities, women) or for all populations? Is it relevant for entrepreneurs, start-ups, small and medium-sized companies? Is it relevant for large companies? For the public sector? Is it relevant only with respect to the availability of free legal services, or also paid legal services? Is it relevant only with respect to the dollar amount charged for legal services? Or it is also relevant to issues such as fixed pricing, the variety of services available, search costs, confidence or trust in the provider, customer service, and value for money? Who gets to answer these questions?

As can be gleaned from these questions, access to justice can mean (many) different things to (many) different people. One commentator has stated that the term "def[ies] precise definition."[4] As Deborah Rhode explains, what it means often depends on perspective, making it practically impossible to agree upon even a common core definition:

> The organized bar worries about the economic effects of procedural simplification and nonlawyer competition. Government officials focus on how much the public values subsidized legal assistance in comparison with other needs.

> Judges and court administrators are interested in efficiency: how to clear dockets and promote confidence in judicial decision making. Legal services providers focus on resources: how to secure the staff and support structures necessary for addressing unmet needs. Clients and the nonprofit groups that represent them care about both procedural and substantive fairness; they want processes and outcomes that will secure their rights and address their social and economic disadvantages.[5]

But, without a clear and shared understanding of what access to justice means, can debates about alternative structures and access to justice have meaning? If it were shown that alternative structures increase access to justice with respect to only some elements, but not all, would that mean that the prohibition should remain in place? If it were shown that alternative structures increase access to justice with respect to some elements, but decrease access with respect to others, would that mean that the prohibition should remain in place? Exactly what would need to be shown in order to convincingly demonstrate a positive (or not) correlation between alternative structures and access to justice? How many different showings would be required? Again, who gets to answer these questions?

## HOW CAN ACCESS TO JUSTICE BE MEASURED?

Generally speaking, the way to measure access to justice will depend in large part upon how the expression is defined—what elements are included and what elements are excluded from consideration. Whatever the definition that is chosen, there will be challenges in measurement: (i) how to determine what changes were caused by alternative structures as opposed to some other cause(s)? (ii) will measurement be based upon existing data or will new data be collected? and (iii) either way, who will conduct and who will pay for the study? An attempt to measure access to justice in England and Wales will have its own particular challenges, for these reasons:

1. At about the same time that ABSs came into existence in England and Wales, funding for public legal aid as well as funding for litigation were drastically reduced, along with other public sector funding. To the extent it is possible to measure changes in access to justice in England and Wales, it may not be possible to know with certainty what caused which changes.
2. The SRA did not begin accepting applications for ABSs until late 2011, and the first ABSs were not authorized until March 2012. The SRA's authorization process is a daunting one—simply completing all of the application requirements requires significant time and resources. The SRA has stated that the authorization process is intended

> to deter from even applying those firms that would not meet the SRA's standards.[6] The SRA has been severely criticized for how it has handled applications: that it has taken too long to process them (in some cases as long as two years) and that it has shown great reluctance in granting licenses to "new, unfamiliar approaches that have the potential to open the market to more consumers."[7] The LSB has openly criticized the SRA for demonstrating an "inherent cognitive bias"[8] in its approach to licensing. For the LSB, if ABSs have not yet lived up to their potential to increase access to justice, it is not because that potential does not exist but because the SRA's approach to licensing has been too conservative, with the result of keeping out of the market the firms with the most potential to increase access to justice. The SRA itself has admitted openly that it "made such a hash [of processing applications] in the first few years," and has apologized for it.[9]

In addition to its criticism of the SRA for its conservatism in granting ABS licenses, the LSB has petitioned the government of England and Wales to make certain changes to the Legal Services Act that would make it easier to approve and to regulate ABSs. The LSB has explained that the changes are necessary in order to remove certain requirements placed upon ABSs that assumes "without evidence—that ABSs are more risky than other types of providers, thereby imposing higher costs and burdens on them."[10]

In spite of these challenges in measuring access to justice, the LSB has voiced its intention to conduct a study over the course of 2015 to 2016. The LSB appears to understand the complexity of the task as in 2012 it published a 44-page paper explaining how it plans to approach its measurements of access to justice.[11]

## WHAT EVIDENCE IS THERE?

In the absence of both an agreed definition of access to justice as well as empirical evidence that alternative structures have increased access to justice in Australia and in England and Wales, we can look to the commentary and observations of industry observers in the two countries:

### Australia

In its October 2013 report, "Affordable Justice: A Pragmatic Path to Greater Flexibility and Access in the Private Legal Services Market," the Centre for Innovative Justice (CIJ) of RMIT University in Australia observes that "some practitioners have developed new and innovative ways of facilitating [access to justice]."[12] However, the CIJ also deplores that "the majority of the population feel shut out" of the legal system.[13]

But as the CIJ's report as well as a paper by Tahlia Gordon and Steve Mark ("Access to Justice: Can You Invest in It?") reflect, many of the firms that are taking steps to increase access to justice in Australia are ILPs (corporate structures). Gordon and Mark define "access to justice" broadly—as "the notion of not only access to a lawyer and access to courts but also access to legal information, legal education, non-court-based dispute resolution mechanisms, participation in law reform and basic problem-solving."[14] Going further, for Gordon and Mark, "[t]he term 'access to legal services,' rather than 'access to justice,' better reflects this broader concept."[15]

Both the report and the paper take special note of Slater and Gordon, the world's first publicly listed law firm, together with Shine, another publicly listed firm.

They describe that Slater and Gordon has increased access to justice by:

- Acquiring a certain number of firms that were going to close. In acquiring those firms, they provided an exit strategy to the partners and also kept the firm and its services operating for its clients.[16]
- Opening a number of new offices in suburban and regional locations, thus increasing the number and variety of access points for those needing legal assistance.[17]
- Applying in those firms and offices Slater and Gordon's centralized management systems, which brought increased efficiency and cost effectiveness, and reduced the administrative burden on the local staff, enabling them to focus more on the provision of legal services rather than administrative tasks.[18]
- Adopting fixed fees for family law matters[19] (the CIJ report cites fee certainty and transparency as an important element of access to justice[20]).
- Offering a free advice line on a wide range of areas of the law.[21]
- Offering support services, including a network of social workers, to whom lawyers can refer clients who need nonlegal assistance related to their claim, such as counselling, negotiation with social services, and advice regarding benefits.[22]

They describe that Shine has increased access to justice by:

- Expanding into practice areas that other law firms were reluctant to explore.[23]
- Offering "no-win, no-fee" arrangements in all its areas of practice, which include personal injury as well as coal seam gas claims, human rights, and environmental matters (clients are not expected to pay up front for third party costs, or to take out a loan to fund the litigation).[24]

The CIJ's report also takes note of the "sister" corporations, Salvos Legal and Salvos Legal Humanitarian, both wholly owned by the Salvation Army.[25] Owned by the Salvation Army and described in detail above, Salvos Legal provides commercial law legal services on a paid basis, and its income, less expenses, is used to fund the operations of Salvos Legal Humanitarian, which provides legal services to the "disadvantaged and marginalized" on a free basis.

## England and Wales

In its December 2014 "Consumer Impact Report," the Legal Services Consumer Panel begins by saying:

> Judging whether the legal services reforms have been a success was never going to be straightforward. There are too many different interests and perspectives to agree something definitive. . . . [V]iewed from the consumer perspective there's no doubt that there has been significant progress. Consumers are happier with the choice available to them. They shop around more and they're more satisfied with value for money, perhaps due to the rise in fixed fee deals. They find it less difficult to compare lawyers and are less likely to go back to the lawyer they used for their previous transaction. . . . [But] our evidence is all too clear that consumer experiences of legal services differ far too much across different sections of the population.[26]

The panel continues:

> All types of law firm can deliver responsive services, but the growth in ABS matters given its implications for the diversity of supply and the benefits that external investment can bring. . . . Commentators are divided about the extent of the impact of ABS and it is difficult to separate the impact of the competition reforms from other drivers of change such as economic conditions, changes to legal aid availability and litigation funding reforms. . . . Looking back, there have been a wide range of striking developments—diversity of supply, technology, investment—that added together have the potential to make a significant impact, even if there hasn't so far been one change that has transformed the way in which people consume legal services. In many ways the level of innovation to date has been quite remarkable considering the relatively short timescale the reforms have been operating.[27]

Echoing the comments of the LSB regarding the SRA's conservative approach to licensing, the panel also states:

> Even so, there has been frustration about the take up of ABS, particularly the small numbers of multi-disciplinary practices. There have been criticisms directed towards the SRA over the speed of its licensing process . . . and a cautious attitude towards unfamiliar business models like MDPs.[28]

In sum, access to justice in the context of alternative structures is a highly complex issue, for a number of reasons: There is no clear and commonly shared definition of access to justice, the reforms of Australia and of England and Wales were not adopted with the specific purpose of increasing access to justice, many factors can have an impact on access to justice—it is difficult to isolate them in order to definitively know which factor had which effect, we do not yet have the results of empirical studies, and so forth. In spite of this complexity, however, the reports of the Centre for Innovative Justice and the Legal Services Consumer Panel refute any argumentation that ABSs in England and Wales and ILPs in Australia have not had a positive effect on access to justice.

## STORIES

(PART V OR ONLINE)

*Elisabeth Davies, Chair, Legal Services Consumer Panel* (Part V): Davies states that, according to the panel's research, ABSs have gone for the areas of law where there is significant unmet need, and have provided access to services that previously people didn't have access to at all.

*Robert Cross, Project Manager (Research), Legal Services Board* (online): Cross states that arguments that ABSs have not increased access to justice miss the point. For him, the point is that there is a large unmet need for legal services, and it is in the public interest to do something about it. It's a complex problem, and regulatory reform and ABSs are one part of a mixed economy.

*Kristin Dangerfield, CEO, The Law Society of Manitoba* (online): Dangerfield states that for her, whether or not there is evidence that alternative structures will increase access to justice is irrelevant. What is relevant is that alternative structures offer the flexibility that is needed to meet the needs of the public. For that reason, because the Law Society's mandate is to protect the public interest, it would be counterintuitive to not allow them.

## NOTES

1. Clementi Report, 5.

2. Semple explains that both England and Wales and Australia have, as a general manner, adopted an approach towards the regulation of legal services that prioritizes competition and consumer (as opposed to client) interests. Semple, *Legal Services Regulation*, 5, 75–90.

3. In a comparable vein, some, such as Andrew Perlman, examine the extent to which ABSs in England and Wales have demonstrated a "transformative effect." Perlman does not explain with any precision what evidence would constitute "transformative effect," beyond a listing of (i) changing how a firm markets itself, (ii) changing its target client base, and (iii) changing its practice areas. This examination is exceedingly narrow, in the first place because it

relates only to pre-existing firms that converted to ABS status (as opposed to newly created ABSs, which would not have anything to change from) and because it does not examine to what extent "transformation" might occur outside of this short list of three elements. At any rate, Perlman concludes that there is "limited data on the transformative potential of ABSs." Perlman, "Towards the Law," 83–87.

4. Louis Schetzer, Joanna Mullins, and Roberto Buonamano, "Access to Justice and Legal Needs: A Project to Identify Legal Needs, Pathways and Barriers for Disadvantaged People in NSW, Background Paper," Law & Justice Foundation of New South Wales, August 2001, 5, http://www.lawfoundation.net.au/ljf/site/articleIDs/012E910236879BAECA25706000 7D13E0/$file/bkgr1.pdf.

5. Deborah L. Rhode, "Whatever Happened to Access to Justice," *Loyola of Los Angeles Law Review* 42 (2009): 872, http://digitalcommons.lmu.edu/cgi/viewcontent.cgi?article=26 70andcontext=llr.

6. Crispin Passmore, interview with author, March 2014.

7. Robert Cross, "Balancing Regulatory Risk," presentation at UCL International Access to Justice Conference, London, England, June 20, 2014, 24, https://research.legalservices board.org.uk/wp-content/media/UCL-AtoJ-Conference-presentation-20-June-2014.pdf.

8. Ibid., 25.

9. Monidipa Fouzder, "SRA Says 'Sorry' Over ABS Application Delays," *The Law Society Gazette*, April 21, 2015, http://www.lawgazette.co.uk/practice/sra-says-sorry-over-abs-applica tion-delays/5048340.fullarticle.

10. See Neil Rose, "Legal Regulators Urge Government to Ease Burdens on ABSs," *Legal Futures*, July 21, 2015, http://www.legalfutures.co.uk/latest-news/legal-regulators-urge-government-to-ease-burdens-on-abss; see also Nick Hilborne, "Gove Poised to Back Call for Less Overbearing Regulatory Regime for ABSs," *Legal Futures*, November 19, 2015, http://www.legalfutures.co.uk/latest-news/gove-poised-to-back-call-for-less-overbearing-regulatory-regime-for-abss.

11. Legal Services Board, "Evaluation: How Can We Measure Access to Justice for Individual Consumers? A Discussion Paper," September 2012, https://research.legalservices board.org.uk/wp-content/media/Evaluation-measuring-A2J-11-09-12-Discussion-paper -FINAL-FORMATED.pdf.

12. Centre for Innovative Justice, "Affordable Justice," 4.

13. Ibid.

14. Tahlia Gordon and Steve Mark, "Access to Justice: Can You Invest in It?" April, 2015, 2, http://legal.opaxweb.biz/wp-content/uploads/2015/05/Access-to-Justice-ABS-GordonMark-Final.pdf.

15. Ibid.

16. Ibid., 23.

17. Ibid.

18. Ibid., 23, 27.

19. Centre for Innovative Justice, "Affordable Justice," 18.

20. Ibid., 14, 19.

21. Ibid, 33.

22. Centre for Innovative Justice, "Affordable Justice," 38; Gordon and Mark, "Access to Justice," 35–36.

23. Gordon and Mark, "Access to Justice," 28.

24. Centre for Innovative Justice, "Affordable Justice," 17; Gordon and Mark, "Access to Justice," 29–30.

25. Centre for Innovative Justice, "Affordable Justice," 33.

26. UK 2014 Consumer Impact Report, 3.

27. Ibid., 14.

28. Ibid.

## *Chapter Nineteen*

# Access to Justice Comes in All Shapes and Sizes, Sometimes Obvious and Sometimes Not

As mentioned above, a common argument made in relation to alternative structures is that there is no evidence they increase access to justice.[1] A work that is often cited in support of this argument is that of Canadian professor Jasminka Kalajdzic. In her 2014 paper commissioned by the Ontario Trial Lawyers Association, she examines "the empirical literature in the UK and Australia with a view to identifying any data that would speak to these five metrics": reduced cost of legal services, increased number of represented litigants, greater availability of legal services in smaller city centers, fewer unmet legal needs, and better quality of work performed.[2] Applying these five metrics in her examination of the available literature, she concludes that there is "a dearth of empirical evidence to support any of the contentions" that alternative structures lead, directly or indirectly, to an increase in access to justice.[3] As also mentioned above, it is true that there is no "empirical" evidence that alternative structures increase access to justice. However, that does not mean that there is no evidence at all.

In the excerpts below, founders, managers, and employees of England and Wales, Australia, and Washington, DC-based alternative structures describe how their their structures work (or, in the last excerpt, how they plan it will work in the future). These excerpts expose a multitude of examples of access to justice, in a large variety of shapes and sizes. Sometimes the example is obvious from the excerpt, but sometimes it is less obvious (but no less significant), and for that reason the excerpt requires attentive reading.

*Jenny Beck, Partner with UK-based ABS Stephensons Solicitors*, explains how, using fixed prices, unbundling, and technology, the firm makes its services accessible on a number of levels:

> Some of our services remain eligible for legal aid; those that are not are provided at a fixed price, so people need not fear the uncertainty of not knowing what the service will cost them . . . ; We offer modular [unbundled] services, so that we can put together bespoke packages that suit everyone's pocket; We offer extended services by phone and email, so that people who do not want to come into an office don't need to (whether it's because they are simply busy or because they've been subjected to violence and prefer to remain in a place where they know they are safe); We offer flexible hours, including evenings and weekends; We demystify law by talking to clients in plain English . . .
>
> The Constant hub provides free access to legal support and many client loyalty benefits. Constant is unique in its offering to clients who can access a helpline open 24-hours a day / 365 days a year for 30 minutes of free legal help. Constant includes additional extras relevant to a client's legal needs, such as access to a network of counsellors and advice on managing the media. Finally, the Constant hub also offers access to a range of guides [and] DIY legal advice videos. . . . Constant provides a person with the assurance that their lawyer is ready to work with them at all times, delivering this message in a client-friendly way.

*Andrea Pierce, Legal Services Director of UK-based ABS Kings Court Trust*, explains how the company's case management processes and software enable a high volume of client matters to be handled faster as well as with fewer errors and provide clients with greater visibility:

> [A]t any given moment we have in excess of 500 open files. In contrast, in a traditional structure, typically a lawyer would deal with 10, 20 maximum, probate files a year. . . . While the client has one point of contact, there are at least five, if not six, pairs of eyes that work on a file until it is completed. From a risk perspective, this offers a great advantage. In private practice, typically only one person oversees a file from start to finish—potentially something could be overlooked. . . . Another advantage we offer clients is a shorter life cycle for a file. This happens in part because of our project management software which has allowed us to build in efficiencies into our processes, and in part because of the way we structure our work—each person who works on a file is highly specialized and is able to provide solutions very quickly. . . . [Finally,] technology is a very important part of driving our cases forward. In treating a file, we've broken the process into ten stages, and each stage has certain required components. With our technology, everyone knows what stage a file is in, and everyone knows what work they need to be doing. And the best part is that everything that we see in-house, our clients see too—it is fully transparent—they can track their files as we do.

*Dina Tutungi, General Manager—Personal Injury Victoria, for Australia-based ILP Slater and Gordon*, describes how the firm's automated case management system allows the firm to handle a high volume of cases at the same time that it reduces errors and increases transparency:

> We have created a "flow" for every type of matter that we handle in personal injury. It anticipates different combinations and permutations for how that matter can progress. It is like a "choose your own adventure" because it can go off in so many different ways by using prompts and checklists.
>
> For example, it will prompt questions such as: Are you pursing a common law or statutory claims for damages, or both? Do you have a medical report? Will you make a claim for lost wages? Did you want to get a police report? Do you want to speak with witnesses? Do you need updated medicals?
>
> There are thousands of these interactions in each "flow." No, it will not teach you how to take a witness statement, or how to provide great customer service or how to manage your client's expectations or undertake high level legal analysis. But it does minimize risk and improve efficiency, expertise and client service in a busy practice. And it is really empowering for the legal assistants because they can see exactly where the matter is at, keep the clients well informed and plan and manage their workload.

*Tamyn Hearne, Associate of UK-based ABS Radiant Law*, explains how the firm uses technology to systematize the collection and internal transmission of knowledge about its clients, and how the firm uses that technology to provide greater value added:

> We create what we call a "Playbook." This is a live document which captures client-specific information and evolves as we develop a deeper and more practical understanding of the client and its operations. Depending on the work stream (client's needs, type and complexity of an instruction), we refer to the information and/or processes within the client's Playbook . . . some of the Playbooks contain a substantial amount of information, and we avoid client information sitting specifically within the knowledge realm of one person. We are always looking at ways to see how technology can assist in capturing an employee's real time knowledge and ensure the quick and easy dissemination of Playbook information.
>
> Compare this to how a traditional law firm typically serves its clients: One or more lawyers in the firm may or may not invest time to get to know the client. If they do, it would be exceptional that they would make the investment to get to know a client in the depth that we do, and unheard of to record their knowledge in a systematic and easily transferable way like we do. What's more, traditional firms often shift responsibility for a client from one lawyer to another, especially from one junior lawyer to another, but without the necessary transfer of knowledge about the client and its specific needs. This is very frustrating for the client, and it limits the value that the firm may add to the client.

*Karl Chapman, Chief Executive of UK-based ABS Riverview Law*, describes how the company's technology simplifies and accelerates the analysis of large volumes of contracts:

> [I]magine you are [an in-house] lawyer . . . and you have all the contracts relating to a particular area of [your company's] business. Imagine that all those contracts need to be re-negotiated to be sure they are in compliance with new regulations and a new company risk profile. And we also have to consolidate the number of suppliers that we have. How on earth do you start such a task? You have to find the contracts, you have to analyze them, you have to decide the strategy. . . . [W]e can put all of the contracts in front of you on your screen, showing you how they connect, and suggesting which ones needs to be re-negotiated first. The lawyer then needs to review it and decide if that is, in fact, the right way to do it. What we are doing is short circuiting the decision making process, and making it better. You don't take out the human interaction—quite the opposite—what we do take out is the foundation work that comes before, in order to present it to the lawyer in a way that they can interpret it and make the analytical decisions.

*Jeff Winn, Managing Director of UK-based ABS Winn Solicitors*, explains how the firm's brand reduces client search costs and provides clients with peace of mind—because Winn Solicitors is a multidisciplinary practice, its clients need to deal with only one service provider:

> What clients like about us, and why they come to us, is that we [offer a] one-stop-shop. . . . Our clients know us as the place to go if the accident was not your fault—as the place that will take care of everything.

*Julia Hulme, Managing Director of UK-based ABS Omnia Strategy*, a multidisciplinary firm, explains how the firm's clients are comforted from the knowledge that they will get a consistent message from a variety of professionals and experts:

> [As an] ABS . . . we can assemble the entire team that the client needs. Take high-profile litigation for example: Normally, a client needs to hire a law firm for the litigation itself, a government relations firm for government advocacy, a communications firm for reputational and communications issues, and a strategy firm to help with how to move forward. With us, it's a one-stop shop. The client can pick up the phone and speak to just one person, who understands all of the different work streams, and from whom they can be confident they will receive a consistent message.

*Martin Langan, founder of UK-based Road Traffic Representation* (RTR, operated by the ABS Legalmatters Limited), explains that RTR is different from other services because RTR provides specific information and advice, tailored to the individual situation of each user:

> The difference between RTR and other sites is that RTR offers much more than just generic information—it offers a diagnosis of the user's case and information specifically tailored for that user, and it offers that for free. . . . For a great many people, the free advice is all they want or need. It provides them with reassurance as to where they stand and what might happen to them.

*Keith Arrowsmith, Partner of UK-based ABS Counterculture Partnership*, explains how the multidisciplinary nature of his firm enables him to reach clients who need legal services but would otherwise not seek them out:

> There are clients who talk to me now because I am sitting with them wearing a Counterculture badge that wouldn't dream of walking through the door of what they see as a law firm. There is something about the perception of being in this more comprehensive structure that allows them to be more comfortable in engaging with me. Some of it might be related to concerns about cost, but I think that the real reason is that because I am wearing a Counterculture badge, I can begin conversations that otherwise I never would have been able to have. Many people in the arts start with the premise that their world and the legal world are so far apart, a lawyer could never understand them. With Counterculture, I am able to communicate with clients in a much more open way because they don't see us as a traditional law firm.

*Randy Price, Co-Founder and Managing Partner of Washington, DC-based Tandem Legal Group*, explains how his fellow co-founder and CEO Mike McDevitt reassures the firm's clients for the very reason that he is not a lawyer:

> It is because of Mike that Tandem has been able to grow so quickly. He brings a combination of assets to the firm . . . he is able to reassure our young CEO clients. Young CEOs are much more inclined to not trust lawyers than they are to trust them; with Mike sitting at the table, there is an immediate trust factor. Mike helps new clients to become comfortable with us much faster than with another law firm.

*Ursula Hogben, Practice Leader and General Counsel of Australia-based ILP Legal Vision*, explains that many of the businesses that are clients of her firm had never worked with a lawyer before:

> For clients, their first point of contact with us is usually our website, because it provides a vast amount of information. Their next point of contact is usually with our client care team. . . . We do not charge for initial consultations or for preparing quotes and we offer fixed fees where possible. Our quotes include consultations and rounds of amendments to help us take the time to explain the advice or documents to our client. . . . [I]t's about honesty and certainty. . . . Many of our clients have never used a lawyer before. It 's not because there was no lawyer in their locality, or because they couldn't have gone into a city to use a lawyer. It's because for some reason they did not engage those law-

yers, whereas they did engage us. So, even if those clients theoretically had access to business law services before, they had not accessed those services.

*Anne Copley, Head of Legal of UK-based BPIF Legal*, explains how the ABS uses specialized industry knowledge and a privileged relationship to provide enhanced services to its clients:

> Our [SME] members come to us because of our expertise in the industry. They do not have to explain to us how the industry works, they do not have to explain the terminology, the production methods, the processes. We know what our members are and we can ask questions that other lawyers might not know to ask because we know frontwards and backwards what goes on in a printing company. In addition, the relationship we have with our members is different than the one a traditional law firm would have with them. For lack of a better word, the relationship is more intimate. Since they are members, they consider that they have some ownership of us, rather than coming to us cap in hand. And since we liaise with the other services in our organization, we have a much more rounded view of their businesses.

*Viv Du-Feu, Director of Legal Services, BMA Law*, explains how in providing legal services to the members of the British Medical Association, BMA Law is able to learn about the types of issues they are facing and communicate that to the association's leaders, who can then take that into account in formulating the association's positions and policies:

> [O]ur "core" activities are done in-house and . . . our "core" expertise is located in-house. This is because the work they do is on the matters that keep our members awake at night. By having the lawyers that do that work in-house, I can keep my finger on the political pulse—I can feed into the association's committees and management the types of things that the members are worried about. It's a conduit for information and a virtuous circle.

*Chris Byron, Managing Director of UK-based ABS Aspire Law*, explains how the firm offers its clients with spinal cord injuries both a reduced fee as well as the opportunity to support a charity that helps others with spinal cord injuries:

> Aspire Law provides to clients a better choice when they seek representation for spinal cord injury. They can go with firms like Irwin Mitchell or Slater and Gordon, or they can go with Aspire Law. If they go with Aspire Law, they know that a large contribution will be made to a charity that supports others who are in their circumstances. They also know that they can retain all of their compensation, rather than just 75 percent or less.

*Jenny Holloway, Associate Dean, Nottingham Law School and Nick Johnson, Pro Bono Director, Nottingham Law School Legal Advice Centre,* explain how the law school's newly created ABS can be used to create a research center focused on developing new models for the delivery of legal services:

> We can become a research establishment, experimenting with different ways of providing legal services. Like other university departments that research developments in science, we can research and develop new methods of delivering legal services and access to justice that could be exploited commercially later on. Universities do that—they develop things, and the good ideas are used by the rest of society, and help people in that way. For example, what about a short module on how to conduct your own litigation, that is available to people for a fee, like car mechanics classes?

Some of the above examples of access to justice are those that are commonly predicted by advocates of alternative structures: business models that facilitate reduced and fixed price legal services and/or unbundling, technology that enables standardization and improved processes to handle large volumes of cases or contracts, branding that reduces the client's search costs and increases their level of trust, and multidisciplinary services that significantly ease the client experience notably because they do not need to assemble or coordinate different streams of work.[4] Other examples are not so commonly predicted (if, indeed, they are predicted at all), yet are no less significant: business models that facilitate *free* legal services, the use of nonlegal (notably industry and business) knowledge and experience to increase client trust in and comfort with the firm and with legal services more generally, the collection of knowledge about the legal issues of individual clients in the same industry for use by a trade association to assist and defend the rights of all in that industry on a collective basis, a severely injured client's reassurance and comfort in knowing that in selecting a certain legal services provider the client is not just receiving highly specialized advice but also benefitting an association that helps others with the same type of severe injury, and the development of a legal research establishment for experimentation with different ways of providing legal services. Indeed, this second set of examples steps far outside the five metrics that Kalajdzic applied in her research of secondary literature, and these examples demonstrate that alternative structures can operate to increase access to justice in ways that were not predicted, that do not lend themselves easily to metrics or empirical research, and that seemingly are limited only by creativity and imagination.

Could any or even all of these examples be developed by traditional structures, without changing the regulations to allow for alternative structures? Surely some of them could be, at least theoretically. Of course, as already mentioned, the theory of what traditional structures could do and the reality of what they actually are doing (and appear likely to do in the future) are very different things. The examples in this chapter demonstrate that alternative structures open quite wide a very large spectrum of possibilities with respect to access to justice—possibilities that today we can easily predict, as well as ones that only the future and our own creativity will reveal. And the examples in this chapter demonstrate that, with alternative structures, these possibilities can become very real.

## NOTES

1. These are excerpts from the stories that appear in Part V of this book and/or online at www.notjustforlawyers.com.
2. Kalajdzic, "Memo to Linda Langston," 6.
3. Ibid., 14.
4. Again, a number of persons have made these predictions, as detailed in the notes to the Introduction to this book.

## *Chapter Twenty*

# Unmet Need as Human Rights Crisis

A variety of studies and surveys evidence that while large organizations, such as corporations and public sector bodies, and high net worth individuals are able to obtain legal assistance, most low and middle income individuals as well as small businesses are all but shut out of the legal market. In particular, it is estimated that 80 percent of the legal needs of low-income persons in the United States are not met.[1]

The average market rate for lawyers in the United States has been estimated at $200 to $350 per hour,[2] and it is difficult to find lawyers that charge less than $150 per hour.[3] From this perspective, it is easy to see how most Americans, not just the poor but also middle class and many businesses, simply cannot afford a lawyer.

The source of the problem of unmet need is often seen as lack of monetary resource: that many people cannot afford legal services. Accordingly, the solutions most often proposed are more legal aid from government sources in order to pay lawyers (a topic discussed in detail in part II), and more pro bono (free or volunteer) work from lawyers. But to the extent such solutions are available, they are available only to the most impoverished—they are not solutions made available to the middle class, let alone to entrepreneurs and small businesses, even though those populations also suffer from a huge unmet need for legal services.

Gillian Hadfield has explained that given the huge amount of unmet legal need in the United States, neither more legal aid nor more conventional pro bono offers even a remote solution:

> Increased public funding of legal aid is clearly not feasible as a means of meeting the demand for legal help: at the rates estimated for solo and small firm practitioners, it would cost on the order of $50 billion annually just to secure one hour of legal help for all the American households with an unmet

> dispute-related need; the current total expenditure on legal aid in the US, counting both public funds and charitable donations, is less than 10 percent of that figure: $ 3.7 billion annually. . . . Even those living in poverty, who are eligible for civil legal aid, often are unable to obtain assistance: the Legal Services Corporation estimated that in 2009, half of those seeking assistance from LSC-funded services were turned away. . . . As for pro bono work: American lawyers average about 30 hours of pro bono work per year. That's less than 2 percent of all legal effort. If every American lawyer in the country did an additional 100 hours per year, that would be enough to secure less than 30 minutes per dispute-related problem per household. . . . There is simply no way for the pervasive need for legal services experienced by ordinary Americans to be met through the conventional means advocated by the legal profession.[4]

At the time he was head of the Department of Justice's Access to Justice Initiative, Laurence Tribe described Americans' access to justice as a "dramatically understated crisis."[5]

While the unmet need for legal services affects virtually every person of low and middle income, it disproportionally affects women and racial minorities. A 2014 report to the United Nations Committee on the Elimination of Racial Discrimination[6] explains that this occurs for two reasons. The first reason is because women and racial minorities are more likely to experience poverty in the United States, and because they are more likely to experience discrimination that gives rise to legal claims.[7] The second reason, the report explains, is that such groups make up a disproportionate number of litigants without representation.[8] The 2014 report also explains:

> [E]xisting studies indicate that lack of legal representation dramatically impairs the ability of low-income people to effectively navigate the court system and attain successful outcomes. Represented parties enjoy statistically more favorable results in housing, family law, child welfare, small claims, and employment-related civil rights cases. Those who are represented by an attorney before administrative agencies governing such vital issues as social security, immigration, and unemployment also have higher success rates—in some cases up to two or three times higher—than those who are unrepresented in comparable cases. In a survey of trial judges from thirty-seven states, the majority reported that pro se [unrepresented] litigants were ineffective in their self-advocacy because they failed to present necessary evidence, committed procedural errors, or were unable to properly examine witnesses.[9]

In fact, the extent of the unmet legal need in the United States is so high, it is considered a human rights crisis by some,[10] with the result that the United States is in breach of its obligations under a number of human rights treaties,[11] which require the United States, for example, to provide effective remedies to rights violations,[12] to guarantee equal treatment before the tribunals and other organs administering justice,[13] and to protect against discrimination and provide equal protection under the law.[14]

The United States itself has acknowledged the problems, stating to the United Nations Committee on the Elimination of Racial Discrimination that:

> [T]he United States faces challenges in . . . its provision of free and affordable civil legal services to the poor and middle class. We recognize that these challenges are felt acutely by members of racial and ethnic minorities.[15]

The access to justice problem in the United States in also made acutely apparent in The World Justice Project *Rule of Law Index* for 2015. While on a general basis this index ranks the legal system of the United States 19th out of 102 countries,[16] on the specific question of affordable and accessible civil justice, the United States is ranked 65th out of 102 (behind countries such as Russia and Kyrgyzstan, Mongolia, and Ukraine),[17] and is ranked last out of the regional group of North America and Western Europe, behind countries such as Romania and Bulgaria (the report places Mexico in the region of Latin America and the Caribbean). Commenting on the United States, the prior year's (2014) report stated, "Civil legal assistance is frequently expensive or unavailable, and the gap between rich and poor individuals in terms of both actual use of and satisfaction with the court system is significant."[18]

The repercussions of the failure to meet this pervasive need for legal services are not limited to the individual themselves. It hurts other litigants: For example, when only one party to a matter is represented by counsel, the result is typically a higher legal bill for that party. It hurts the court system: Unrepresented litigants unschooled in procedure clog the courts, consuming the time of court staff, producing delays, and creating dilemmas for judges who may wish to help but who must also remain neutral and fair to both sides.[19]

And it hurts society as a whole: Access to legal services is "a catalyst for change in discriminatory and prejudicial societal structures."[20] If all citizens do not have the means to resolve their claims, then individuals as well as companies "can take advantage of one another without much fear of recourse, resulting in an inequitable and immoral society."[21] It is a Canadian who has perhaps summed it up best: "Being without a lawyer means being without power in our society."[22]

What it means to be without power—and the unmet need for legal services as a human rights crisis—is illustrated in the story of Lauren McConniel, as told by a decision of the Court of Appeals of Indiana[23]:

Born in October 2004, Lauren was not yet two years old in July 2006 when her parents, Ryan McConniel and Amber Huggins, separated. After the separation, Amber and Lauren (together with Lauren's older sister Kaylynn) moved from Indiana to Tennessee, and Ryan moved to Arkansas. In November 2006, Ryan filed for divorce in Arkansas. Ryan was represented by an attorney. Amber sought representation, but legal aid in Tennessee could not represent her because the case was out of state, and legal aid in Arkansas could not represent her because she was not an Arkansas resident. Because Amber could not afford to pay attorney's fees, she was obliged to represent herself.[24]

The divorce was final in May 2007. At the time of the divorce proceedings, both children were living with Amber, and Amber's fitness as a mother was not questioned. Nevertheless, custody of both was awarded to Ryan, and Amber was ordered to pay Ryan $104 per week in child support. However, Ryan and Amber verbally agreed that Lauren would remain with Amber and that Amber would not pay child support. During the time that Amber had custody of Lauren, Lauren was described as a healthy child who was toilet trained and was well behaved and talkative.

In October 2007, Ryan married Brittany McConniel, the stepdaughter of Ryan's cousin Robert Lee. At the time of the marriage, Brittany had a one-year-old son, and she and Ryan later had a daughter. After their marriage, Brittany pressured Ryan to enforce against Amber the order for payment of child support, and Brittany told Ryan that he was "a worthless piece of crap" because he did not enforce his right for custody of Lauren.

Lauren lived with Ryan and Brittany from December 2007 to June 2008 and then again from October to December 2008. When Amber picked up Lauren in December 2008, Amber discovered that Lauren had bruises on many parts of her body. In addition, Lauren was withdrawn and had reverted to peeing in her pants. Amber called child protective services to report what she had observed; later Ryan called Amber to ask her if she had called child protective services. After Amber affirmed that she had, Ryan asked Amber if she would like to keep Lauren with her "like forever." During her time with Amber, Lauren returned to being toilet trained.

In March 2009, Ryan and Brittany moved to Indiana, first to Winchester and, three or four months later, to Farmland. In Indiana, they lived with Robert Lee, his wife Angela Lee, and their daughter Samra—at that time, Brittany disclosed to Ryan that Robert Lee has molested her as a child. Brittany continued to pressure Ryan to enforce the order for payment of child support, stating that they needed the money and that Ryan was a worthless father who did not love his daughter because he let her stay with Amber.

At some point, Brittany called a 911 center in Tennessee to "have a welfare check on Lauren." She told the Tennessee authorities that Ryan was custodial parent and that Amber refused to give the child back. She then pressured Ryan to drive to Tennessee to collect Lauren, which Ryan did, in August 2009. Without informing Amber of his intentions, he arrived at her house with the custody order and two law enforcement officers. At the time that Ryan took Lauren from Amber's house in Tennessee to Indiana, Lauren was healthy, toilet trained, outgoing and did not demonstrate any eating disorders. Ryan initiated an action for back payment of child support from May 2007, and Amber was given Ryan's former address in Winchester, Indiana, as a contact address.

Shortly after bringing Lauren to Indiana, Ryan, Brittany, Robert Lee, Angela Lee, and the children moved from Farmland to Muncie, Indiana. Amber was not provided with the new address or with any telephone number. Amber tried different ways to reach Ryan, but she was only able to make contact with Brittany, who lied to her by saying that they were living in Winchester, that Amber should pay the back child support, and that Amber should not attempt to reach them again.

Amber threatened to seek contempt charges if the girls did not telephone her. In December 2009, Amber received a call from a restricted number, and for eight minutes she was able to speak with both girls. The call ended when Amber heard Brittany say "you've talked long enough," and the line was cut. At the end of January 2010, Amber traveled from Tennessee to Winchester, Indiana, to try to find her daughters, but found the house at the address she had been given to be empty.

Over the period from August 2009 to March 2010, Lauren suffered greatly at the hands of Robert Lee and Brittany. As Ryan later reported, he observed Robert Lee and Brittany hit Lauren with a stick on the palms of her hands and the soles of her feet. Immediately after being beat on the feet, Lauren was forced to do jumping jacks for anywhere from 5 to 50 minutes at a time, often not stopping until she was vomiting. Lauren was also forced to run, or to hold up heavy objects, for long periods of time without being allowed to stop. Robert Lee and Brittany would hit Lauren on the backs of her legs with wet rags or hand towels, later explaining that this way there would not be bruising. Brittany force-fed Lauren, which led to more vomiting and then more beatings. Brittany forced Lauren to take Benadryl at night, in order that she would sleep. In December 2009, when Ryan returned home from work, Lauren's hands were full of feces, and she tried to smear the feces on Ryan and the other children in the house. Lauren was taken to the emergency room on more than one occasion, with various problems such as a red and painful eye, broken fingers, and a vaginal area that did not "look normal." After one medical exam, she retracted into a defensive position and hit herself repeatedly on the forehead with her fists.

On March 3, 2010, Ryan took Lauren to the emergency room again. At her arrival, she was described as "malnourished," "emaciated," "dehydrated and . . . extremely lethargic." She weighed just 28 pounds; her bones, ribs, and clavicle were pressing against her skin, and she had little or no subcutaneous fat. When she cried, she did not have any tears, and the mucous membranes in her mouth were dry, indicating that she was dehydrated. She had multiple bruises on her face and extremities and a laceration on her thigh.

Her sodium level was very high, and her blood pressure was very low. Lauren was dying, and, indeed, on March 4, 2010, she became nonresponsive, developed multi-organ failure, and was likely brain dead. A few days later she was taken off the ventilator, and on March 9, 2010, she died.

One of Ryan's relatives contacted Amber when Lauren was admitted to the hospital. Amber drove from Tennessee, arriving at the Indiana hospital shortly before Lauren's death. It is clear that many people let Lauren down—her father Ryan, the other people who lived in the house with Robert Lee and Brittany and who visited the house and observed her abuse, child protective services, the health care workers on Lauren's prior emergency room visits—all of them had opportunities to intervene and try to stop the abuse but none did.

It would be easy (and facile) to stop there. It would be easy (and facile) to say that because of the failings of all those others, our legal system could not—should not—also be blamed. It would be easy (and facile) to say that, but it would also be wrong. It is not because others are also guilty that our legal system is less so. Any assertion that it is can only serve to perpetuate the problem, dooming cases like Lauren's to be repeated.

At the time Amber and Ryan divorced, Ryan was able to pay for his own attorney, but Amber was not, and legal aid was not available to her. At the time of the divorce, both daughters were living with Amber, and there was no suggestion that she was an unfit mother. The statements that Ryan made later suggest that he never wanted custody of the girls, and there is no indication that he was ever concerned with Lauren's welfare. There is no reason to explain why he was awarded custody except that he was represented by an attorney who understood how to navigate the court system in order to obtain custody for his client, while Amber was not.

In her 2012 testimony before the Task Force to Expand Access to Civil Legal Services in New York, District Attorney Kathleen Rice described the link between the civil access to justice gap and public safety in this manner:

> Access and quality representation for all those in front of the court is at the heart of a preventative, front-end public safety strategy. As a [District Attorney], without such a strategy and without such civil court access and representation, I can tell you that our communities will be more dangerous and [we] will . . . continue to repeat public policy failures at great financial and human cost.[25]

New York Chief Judge John Lippman echoed this connection between access to civil justice and public safety when he stated: "If what happens inside this courthouse or any courthouse . . . is anything short, even by the smallest amount, of promoting equal justice . . . [t]he most vulnerable in our society, they're the ones who have suffered the most."[26]

In his book *Children, Courts and Custody: Interdisciplinary Models for Divorcing Families*, Andrew Schepard explains the challenges that divorcing parents face when they are unable to secure representation:

> Divorcing parents must resort to a complicated court system to settle their differences. Yet the system does not provide them with the lawyers they need to navigate it, treating representation as a privilege for the wealthy or as charity for a small number of the very poor.
>
> The increase in *pro se* [unrepresented] representation poses special challenges for the child custody court. At their best, lawyers can guide parents through a mystifyingly complex system at a time of great emotional turmoil, identify problem-solving strategies to help their children, encourage them to participate in education and mediation, and prepare and present their cases in court with full knowledge of the formal rules of procedure. *Pro se* parents do not get the benefit of this help. As a result, they suffer serious disadvantages in the legal system. Substantial numbers of *pro se* parents have difficulty finding out where to file court papers, understanding and completing forms and obtaining evidence to support their position in court. Parents with representation are more likely to be awarded physical custody than parents without representation. Where both parents are represented, they received joint legal custody 92 percent of the time, as compared to 50 percent of the families where neither parent was represented.[27]

A 2013 report to the Arkansas Access to Justice Commission confirms this situation specifically for self-represented litigants in Arkansas, where Amber and Ryan were divorced. After explaining the difficulties that poor persons have to obtain legal services, the report states that in Arkansas, self-represented litigants are, for the most part "left on their own and flounder."[28] For example, very few Arkansas lawyers provide limited scope representation and, in particular, no family law lawyers do so: Either they handle the entire matter from start to finish, or they decline representation.[29] Further, the report states, in Arkansas almost every family law matter has at least one unrepresented party.[30] Those unrepresented parties are at a huge disadvantage because, among other reasons, many judges require self-represented litigants to perform as if they were lawyers; if they do not, they are denied the relief they request.[31] In a survey of judges, 80 percent reported that self-representation has a negative impact on case outcomes, with one judge stating that "there have been times [self-represented litigants] prevailed, but very, very seldom."[32] Understood in this context, Amber never had a chance. And if she didn't, neither did Lauren.

In order to help self-represented litigants in Arkansas, the report advocates for a number of changes, including the greater use of limited scope representation,[33] the wider development and availability of forms and document assembly technology,[34] the "repurposing" of the Supreme Court Library as the center of a network of court-based services for self-represented litigants,[35] improved court case management systems,[36] and the promulgation of clear policy guidelines for judges, clerks, and librarians on how to work with self-represented litigants.[37] These are all worthwhile proposals, of course, that should be put in place. They will benefit many persons. But the report contains no allusion that, alone, they will be sufficient to close Arkansas's access to justice gap.

In Australia, the ILP Salvos Legal Humanitarian provides, among other services, family law services. In the late nineteenth and early twentieth centuries in the United States, a number of social service organizations provided free legal assistance for divorce and child custody matters. What if a service like Salvos or those social service organizations had existed in Arkansas, Tennessee, or Indiana when Lauren McConniel was still alive? What if such a service had represented Amber Huggins in her divorce from Ryan McConniel, and had succeeded in maintaining Amber's custody of Lauren? Or, what if such a service had been able to represent Amber Huggins when she first noticed that Lauren was bruised, so that Amber could have obtained custody at that time?

Those are a lot of what-ifs. We cannot wind back the clock and replay Lauren's short life, in order to know with certainty whether such a structure would have effectively provided a lifeline to her—if it would have successfully represented Amber in order that she could protect Lauren from her suffering and death at the hands of Robert Lee and Brittany McConniel. But we do not need to know for sure. We only need to know that it could have offered Lauren such a lifeline; that the possibility is real. And that it can offer a lifeline to parents and children in the future who find themselves in situations comparable to Amber's and Lauren's. We need to see in those structures real-life examples of how alternative structures can be used to help to meet the huge unmet need for legal services in the United States and, in doing so, end real suffering of real people. If we are unable—if we refuse—to see this, how are we different from all the others who observed Lauren's abuse yet took no action to stop it?

Lauren McConniel had the right to not be tortured to death. That right was violated in a horrific manner. If Lauren's mother had had access to civil legal services at the time of her divorce, it is more than possible that Lauren would be alive and well today. Lauren's story illustrates in a dramatic fashion how the unmet need for legal services in the United States constitutes a human rights crisis. The examples of Salvos Legal Humanitarian and the late nineteenth- and early twentieth-century social service organizations illustrate the potential for alternative structures to help (certainly, along with other solutions such as those mentioned in the Arkansas report) to alleviate the crisis. To be clear—it is only a potential—there is no guarantee that they will do so. As alternative structures will not offer a panacea for lawyers, neither will they offer one for poor persons. That is, they will not offer a utopia or a universal remedy for all poor persons who are otherwise unable to obtain legal services. But the potential that they will help some people is real, and merely the fact this potential exists is highly significant. The story of Lauren McConniel (and others like her) places upon us a moral obligation to pursue this potential fully. It is too late for Lauren McConniel, but it is not too late for the other Laurens that will surely come after her.

And it is not just children that experience the unmet need for legal services as a human rights crisis. Another example is that of the many persons in the United States who are incarcerated because of their inability to pay a fine. This occurs when someone with few resources is, most typically, cited for a traffic offense. Because of their limited resources, they do not seek legal counsel. Then, they do not attend the court hearing—because they fear arrest because of their inability to pay the fine,[38] because they are unable to get time off from work, because they are unable to make arrangements for child care for the time they would be at court, because they do not realize that it is possible to challenge the ticket, even if they believe the ticket was issued unfairly.

And that is when their troubles really start—when they do not show up at court, additional fines are issued, court costs are assessed, and a warrant is issued for their arrest—all not because of the underlying violation, but because of the resulting failure to appear at court. Once arrested under the warrant and incarcerated, their lives enter a downward spiral of loss of access to jobs and housing—the very stability that they need to be able to pay the increasing fines. A typical scenario is that a person enters and leaves prison on several occasions over a period of several years as they struggle and fail to pay ever increasing fines and court costs, all originating from the same traffic offense.[39]

Today there are estimated to be thousands of such persons incarcerated across the United States. All are low income, and nearly all are members of racial minorities. Certainly this outcome is a result of a multiple of factors—underfunded municipalities and courts under pressure for additional sources of revenue, the increased use of private probation companies who seek their fees from offenders rather than from the state, and racial profiling that results in the ticketing of minorities for traffic violations at a higher rate—factors that cannot be addressed (at least not directly) by changes to the way legal services are regulated.

But one important factor can be addressed by changing the manner by which legal services are regulated—the lack of legal information: not knowing if it is better to appear in court or better to not appear, because if you do and you are unable to pay the fine, you will necessarily be incarcerated, not knowing whether it is possible to request a more convenient court date in order to maintain employment, not knowing if children are allowed in the courtroom and not having access to child care, not knowing if the citation itself can be challenged, and, if so, how. Unable to access legal representation or advice, this ignorance is prevalent and is an important factor in the suffering—imprisonment, job loss, homelessness—that results.

England offers us an example of how persons in this situation could be helped, both free of charge as well as for a low, fixed fee. That example is Road Traffic Representation (RTR), a web-based service that is operated by the ABS Legalmatters Limited. Described in detail in part I, RTR provides an online legal advice service for road traffic offenses. After posing the user, accused of a traffic offense, a series of questions, the service assesses whether the authorities have followed the proper procedure (and thus whether any procedural or technical objections can be raised) and makes a diagnosis both of the likely penalties the client will face if convicted and of any defenses that may be asserted. It is easy to imagine that the information offered by the service could be adapted to address additional topics, such as whether and how a hearing date could be rescheduled, what is likely to happen if the user is unable to pay the fine, whether payment arrangements may be available, and whether restrictions on the presence of children at a hearing may apply.

A service like RTR would not offer a panacea to the thousands of Americans whose lives face a downward spiral after they are issued a traffic ticket. A mere website, even one applying a sophisticated rules-based expert system, cannot solve the myriad of underlying problems, like the underfunding of courts and municipalities, the conflict of interest when private probation companies receive their revenue from offenders, or the targeting of racial minorities for traffic stops. But RTR demonstrates in a concrete manner how technology can be used to fill an unmet need for legal services, in this instance, to help someone faced with a traffic offense to quickly obtain basic but pertinent information at little or no cost, in order to understand his/her specific rights, obligations, and options.

## NOTES

1. William C. Hubbard, "Remarks of William C. Hubbard, President of the American Bar Association" (presentation to Meeting of American College of Trial Lawyers, Miami, Florida, February 28, 2015), http://www.americanbar.org/groups/leadership/office_of_the_president/selected-speeches-of-aba-president-william-c--hubbard/american-college-of-trial-lawyers--february-2015-.html. See also Ethan Bronner, "Right to Lawyer Can Be Empty Promise for Poor," *New York Times*, March 15, 2013, http://www.nytimes.com/2013/03/16/us/16gideon.html?pagewanted=alland_r=1. See, generally, Legal Services Corporation, "Documenting the Justice Gap in America—The Current Unmet Civil Legal Needs of Low-Income Americans: An Updated Report of the Legal Services Corporation," September, 2009, http://www.lsc.gov/sites/default/files/LSC/pdfs/documenting_the_justice_gap_in_america_2009.pdf.

2. Deborah Beth Medows, "Justice as a Luxury?: The Inefficacy of Middle Class Pro Se Litigation and Exploring Unbundling as a Partial Solution," October 28, 2013, 11, http://dx.doi.org/10.2139/ssrn.2346267.

3. Nathan Koppel, "More Strapped Litigants Skip Lawyers in Court," *Wall Street Journal*, July 22, 2010, http://www.wsj.com/news/articles/SB100014240527487042290045753713415

07943822?mg=reno64-wsj&url=http%3A%2F%2Fonline.wsj.com%2Farticle%2FSB1000142 4052748704229004575371341507943822.html.

4. Hadfield, "The Cost of Law," 45–46.

5. Channing Turner, "Tribe: Gap in Justice a 'Dramatically Understated' Crisis," *Main Justice*, June 18, 2010, http://www.mainjustice.com/2010/06/18/tribe-gap-in-justice-a-%E2 %80%98dramatically-understated%E2%80%99-crisis-2/.

6. Columbia Law School Human Rights Institute and Northeastern University School of Law Program on Human Rights and the Global Economy, "Equal Access to Justice: Ensuring Meaningful Access to Counsel in Civil Cases, Including Immigration Proceedings—Response to the Seventh and Ninth Periodic Reports of the United States to the Committee on the Elimination of All Forms of Racial Discrimination," July, 2014, http://web.law.columbia.edu/ sites/default/files/microsites/human-rights-institute/files/equal_access_to_justice_-_cerd _shadow_report.pdf.

7. Ibid., 4.

8. Ibid.

9. Ibid., 2–3

10. Carrie Johnson, "Rights Advocates See 'Access to Justice' Gap in U.S.," NPR, March 10, 2014, http://www.npr.org/sections/thetwo-way/2014/03/10/288225649/rights-advocates-see-access-to-justice-gap-in-u-s.

11. See, generally, Zachary H. Zarnow, "Obligation Ignored: Why International Law Requires the United States to Provide Adequate Civil Legal Aid, What the United States is Doing Instead, and How Legal Empowerment Can Help," *Journal of Gender, Social Policy and the Law* 20 (2011): 273–309, http://ssrn.com/abstract=2090054. See also Kristel Jüriloo, "Free Legal Aid—A Human Right," *Nordic Journal of Human Rights* 33 (2015): 203–19, http:// dx.doi.org/10.1080/18918131.2015.1066143.

12. *International Covenant on Civil and Political Rights*, December 16, 1966, Art. 2(3)(a), http://www.ohchr.org/en/professionalinterest/pages/ccpr.aspx. See also *The Universal Declaration of Human Rights*, Art. 8, http://www.un.org/en/documents/udhr/.

13. *International Convention on the Elimination of All Forms of Racial Discrimination*, December 21, 1965, Art. 5(a), http://www.ohchr.org/EN/ProfessionalInterest/Pages/CERD .aspx.

14. *International Convention on the Elimination of All Forms of Racial Discrimination*, Art. 6. See also *The Universal Declaration of Human Rights*, Art. 7.

15. United States of America, "Periodic Report of the United States of America to the United Nations Committee on the Elimination of Racial Discrimination Concerning the International Convention of the Elimination of All Forms of Racial Discrimination," June 12, 2013, 37, http://www.state.gov/documents/organization/210817.pdf.

16. The World Justice Project, *Rule of Law Index 2015*, 6, 20.

17. This ranking is derived from the data (xls) that is available for download from the World Justice Project website.

18. The World Justice Project, *Rule of Law Index 2014*, 2014, 57, http://worldjusticepro ject.org/sites/default/files/files/wjp_rule_of_law_index_2014_report.pdf.

19. See, for example, Terry Carter, "Judges Say Litigants Are Increasingly Going Pro Se—At Their Own Peril," *ABA Journal*, July 12, 2010, http://www.abajournal.com/news/article/ judges_say_litigants_increasingly_going_pro_se--at_their_own_/; and "More People Acting as Their Own Lawyers: Courts Clog Up as Americans Represent Themselves, Even in Complex Cases," *NBC News*, November 24, 2008, http://www.nbcnews.com/id/27894755/ns/us_news-crime_and_courts/t/more-people-acting-their-own-lawyers/#.VdijULKqqkp.

20. Jüriloo, "Free Legal Aid," 203–4.

21. Medows, "Justice as a Luxury," 5.

22. Julia H. Bass, W. A. Bogart, and Frederick H. Zemans, *Access to Justice for a New Century: The Way Forward* (Toronto, Ontario, Canada: Law Society of Upper Canada, 2005), 12.

23. *Brittany L. McConniel v. State of Indiana*, In the Court of Appeals of Indiana, Opinion for Publication, September 11, 2012, http://www.in.gov/judiciary/opinions/pdf/091112 01ebb.pdf (hereinafter "Court of Appeals of Indiana").

24. Facebook, Inc. "Remembering Lauren McConniel, 10/3/2004 - 03/09/2010," accessed May 21, 2016, https://www.facebook.com/pages/Remembering-Lauren-McConniel-1032004-03092010/128472153894713?sk=infoandtab=page_info.

25. Task Force to Expand Access to Civil Legal Services in New York, "Report to the Chief Judge of the State of New York," November, 2012, 9, https://www.nycourts.gov/accesstojusticecommission/PDF/CLS-TaskForceREPORT_Nov-2012.pdf.

26. Ibid., 4.

27. Andrew I. Schepard, *Children, Courts and Custody: Interdisciplinary Models for Divorcing Families* (Cambridge, UK: Cambridge University Press, 2004), 41.

28. John M. Greacen, "Services for Self-Represented Litigants in Arkansas: A Report to the Arkansas Access to Justice Commission," July 26, 2013, 3, http://www.arkansasjustice.org/sites/default/files/file%20attachments/Arkansas%20Final%20Report%207-26-13.pdf.

29. Ibid., 17–18.

30. Ibid., 10.

31. Ibid., 16.

32. Ibid., 11.

33. Ibid., 20–21, 31–32.

34. Ibid., 20, 25–26, 27.

35. Ibid., 29–31.

36. Ibid., 22–26.

37. Ibid., 28–29.

38. See, for example, Shaila Dewan, "A Surreptitious Courtroom Video Prompts Changes in a Georgia Town," *New York Times*, September 5, 2015, http://www.nytimes.com/2015/09/05/us/a-surreptitious-courtroom-video-prompts-changes-in-a-georgia-town.html?_r=0.

39. See, generally, Chrissy Brown, "How to Go From Citizen to Criminal in Under 10 Minutes," *Thoughts On Liberty*, July 23, 2013, http://thoughtsonliberty.com/how-to-go-from-citizen-to-criminal-in-under-10-minutes; Casey Smith and Carey A. Spinwall, "Increasing Number Going to Jail for Not Paying Fines: Inability to Pay Costs Plenty for All," *Tulsa World*, November 13, 2013, http://www.tulsaworld.com/news/local/increasing-number-going-to-jail-for-not-paying-fines/article_8b8d2229-c7ad-5e7f-aea2-baeb13390880.html; Hannah Rappleye and Lisa Riordan Seville, "The Town That Turned Poverty Into a Prison Sentence," *The Nation*, March 14, 2014, http://www.thenation.com/article/town-turned-poverty-prison-sentence/; "Without Funds to Pay Fines, Minor Incidents Can Mean Jail Time," *PBS Newshour*, April 12, 2014, http://www.pbs.org/newshour/bb/without-funds-pay-fines-minor-incidents-can-mean-jail-time/; Radley Balko, "How Municipalities in St. Louis County, Mo., Profit From Poverty," *Washington Post*, September 3, 2014, https://www.washingtonpost.com/news/the-watch/wp/2014/09/03/how-st-louis-county-missouri-profits-from-poverty/; "ArchCity Defenders Municipal Courts White Paper," 2014, http://s3.documentcloud.org/documents/1279541/archcity-defenders-report-on-st-louis-county.pdf.

*Part IV*

# The (Non) Regulation of Legal Services and the World Stage

This book calls for fundamental changes in the way that lawyers and legal services are regulated in the United States. In doing so, it begs the questions of who regulates legal services in the United States, and how and in what larger context they do so.

There is no clear or simple answer to the question of who regulates legal services in the United States, or how they do so. All that is clear is that the process is highly complex, that what is supposed to occur in theory is rarely what occurs in practice, and that much of the process occurs behind closed doors (literally and figuratively) involving decision makers who are unknown, and, in many cases, unknowable, to both the legal profession as a whole as well as to the general public.

In contrast, as regards the question of the larger context of the regulation of legal services in the United States, the response is clear and relatively simple, if disheartening: As a signatory to a number of international treaties and commitments, the United States has promised to protect the human rights of its citizens, and it has promised to do so, in part, by ensuring "equal access to justice for all." In spite of these promises, the United States continues to allow its legal profession to exercise a monopoly on legal services in the United States. While the monopoly may not be a perfect one, it is sufficient to exclude from the market a great many actors—individuals as well as alternative structures—who offer a real potential for addressing the access to justice gap. As long as the lawyer monopoly on legal services (as imperfect as it may be) remains in place, the United States will never be able to fulfill the commitments it has made on the world stage to protect the human rights of all its citizens and to ensure equal access to justice for all.

# *Chapter Twenty-One*

# Abdication of Regulatory Power

Part I of this book contains a general discussion of the extent to which the legal profession in the United States is self-regulated, and the implications of self-regulation with respect to the adoption of alternative structures. That general discussion includes a brief examination of the roles—both de facto and de jure—of the ABA and of state supreme courts, in the regulation of legal services.

The purpose of this chapter is to take that discussion further by examining three specific examples, one on a state level and the other two on a national level. In doing so, this chapter exposes more fully both the nature of the relationships among state supreme courts, the ABA, state and local bar associations, law firms, and practicing members of the bar, as well as the immense significance of those relationships for the regulation of legal services in the United States today. It is important to have a good understanding of those relationships and their significance for the regulation of legal services today, because, without it, any attempt to change how legal services are regulated in the future cannot succeed.

## ONE EXAMPLE ON A STATE LEVEL

In 1997 the ABA established the "Ethics 2000" Commission with the mandate to conduct a comprehensive review of the Model Rules of Professional Conduct. By way of reminder, the Model Rules were developed by the ABA and form the basis for the regulatory framework that governs lawyers (and, by default, also legal services more generally) in 49 of the 50 states (the exception is California).

The justifications for the review were (i) to address a growing disparity among the various state ethical codes, and (ii) to address the influence that technological developments were having on the delivery of legal services. The Commission's work took place over a number of years, culminating with a report to the House of Delegates. The House of Delegates considered the report in meetings held in 2001 and 2002, and, after taking input from other ABA committees, in 2002 it adopted a series of modest amendments to the Model Rules.[1]

In 1999, two years after the Ethics 2000 Commission began its work, the Illinois State Bar Association (ISBA) "established a Special Committee on Ethics 2000 to monitor the work of the Ethics 2000 Commission and undertake consideration of recommendations for changes to the current Illinois Rules of Professional Conduct."[2] In 2002, the ISBA created a joint committee with the Chicago Bar Association (CBA) in order to "continue and complete the mission."[3] In April 2004, this Special Committee issued a report that was approved by the governing boards of the two bar associations and submitted to the Illinois Supreme Court.[4]

As explained in a press release later issued by the Illinois Supreme Court,[5] over the course of the next few years, the Illinois Supreme Court Committee on Professional Responsibility (the PR Committee) carried out its own study, culminating with the PR Committee's February 2007 report[6] to the Illinois Supreme Court Rules Committee (the Rules Committee). In addition, the same press release states, "important input also was received from the Attorney Registration and Disciplinary Commission and the Illinois Supreme Court Rules Committee."[7] At the request of the PR Committee, two public hearings were held, each chaired by practicing attorney John Nicoara, as chair of the Rules Committee. It was only upon the completion of that entire process that "the proposal then received several reviews by the Supreme Court with additional revisions and refinements occurring as a result."[8]

Based upon the description in the Supreme Court press release, four groups played the instrumental roles in the process to amend the Illinois rules: the ISBA, the CBA, the PR Committee, and the Rules Committee. Let's take a look at the composition of those groups:

- The ISBA is a voluntary association, with membership of approximately 30,000 attorneys and law students.
- The CBA is also a voluntary association, with membership of approximately 22,000 attorneys and law students.
- The PR Committee is appointed by the supreme court for the purpose of advising and making recommendations to the court on matters relating to legal ethics and professional responsibility. Its members are practicing attorneys. The supreme court press release mentions two members of the committee by name: Steven F. Pflaum,[9] at that time a partner with McDermott, Will and Emery in Chicago, and Richard A. Redmond,[10] at that time

a partner with Holland and Knight, also in Chicago. (Underscoring the identification of the PR Committee with the practicing bar, the PR Committee's report to the Rules Committee was issued on Holland and Knight letterhead[11]).

- The Rules Committee is appointed by the supreme court for the purpose of studying and recommending new supreme court rules or modifications to existing rules. Its members are also practicing attorneys. The supreme court press release mentions one by name, Chair John Nicoara,[12] at that time a partner with Nicoara and Steagall, in Peoria.

In other words, the persons that played the instrumental roles in this process to amend Illinois's rules to align them with the revised ABA Model Rules were four groups of practicing attorneys. The only other group to have input in the process was the Attorney Registration and Disciplinary Commission (ARDC), the regulatory body to whom the Illinois Supreme Court has delegated responsibility for attorney registration and discipline. There is nothing in the supreme court press release that suggests the ARDC played anything more than a minor role, or that expertise other than legal expertise (such as economic policy, human rights, competition, consumer affairs, etc.) played any role at all.

Indeed, the supreme court press release quotes the chief justice himself giving effusive recognition of the critical roles played by the bar associations and the two committees, as well as other practicing attorneys:

> These new rules reflect the effort of the bar associations, the Supreme Court Committee on Professional Responsibility and the Supreme Court Rules Committee as well as many other lawyers who gave their input along the way," said Chief Justice Thomas R. Fitzgerald. . . .
>
> The Court, Illinois lawyers and the public that they serve are grateful for the efforts of those who worked long and hard to bring the ethical rules for Illinois attorneys up to date with twenty-first century practice.[13]

The Illinois Supreme Court adopted the new rules in 2009, with effect January 1, 2010. In most respects, the rules that the supreme court adopted conform to the ABA Model Rules. There are deviations, but most are minor, and most of them track nearly to the letter those recommended to the supreme court by the ISBA and CBA and the two committees.[14]

This example from Illinois is a concrete and powerful illustration of how state supreme courts with a voluntary bar abdicate their regulatory powers firstly to the ABA (and in particular to its House of Delegates) and then to state and local bar associations and other practicing attorneys. The entire process was initiated, organized, and controlled by groups of practicing attorneys, first nationally in the form of the ABA, and then locally in the form of the ISBA, the CBA, and the two committees. To the extent there was meaningful participation by the Illinois Supreme Court independent of the practicing bar, it occurred only at the very end of the process, when the court officially adopted the new rules, in the form approved by the ISBA, the CBA, and the committees.

There was never any genuine question as to whether Illinois would, as a general matter, adopt the ABA's amended Model Rules. Of course it would. There was never any genuine question as to whether Illinois would tinker with the ABA Model Rules before adopting them. Of course it would. But at the same time, there was also never any genuine question that the tinkering would be just that—tinkering rather than substantial changes. And that it would be controlled not by the supreme court, but by the state and local bar associations and other groups of practicing attorneys. At the end, there was never any question that the Illinois Supreme Court would adopt the rules that resulted from that tinkering. Of course it would.

This example from Illinois is illustrative for two additional reasons. The first reason is the manner by which it both explains and exposes the immense power and authority that the ABA Model Rules carry across the country. The 2004 joint report issued by the ISBA and CBA contains, and the 2007 report issued by the PR Committee repeats nearly word-for-word the same language, as follows:

> Early in its deliberations, the Committee determined that it would recommend adoption of each ABA Model Rule of Professional Conduct unless there was a compelling reason not to do so. There are at least three reasons for following the ABA Model Rules as the template for revising the Illinois Rules.
>
> First, the Model Rules are the de facto national standard for ethics rules, a standard that has already been recognized in Illinois. Like most states, Illinois requires that all applicants for admission to the bar, either by examination [Supreme Court Rule 703(b)] or on motion [Supreme Court Rule 705(a)], have a first degree in law from a law school approved by the ABA. Law schools have been required to teach the Model Rules to all students to achieve accreditation by the ABA since the late 1970s. In addition to their study of the Model Rules in law school, applicants for the Illinois bar must know the Model Rules to take the Multistate Professional Responsibility Examination. This examination, usually called the MPRE, is based on the ABA Model Rules. Applicants by examination [Supreme Court Rule 704(c)] as well as applicants on motion [Supreme Court Rule 705(c)] are required to have passed the MPRE.
>
> A second substantial argument for following the Model Rules is to achieve a higher level of uniformity and consistency with the rules of other jurisdictions. As noted above, 44 jurisdictions including Illinois have adopted some form of the 1983 version of the Model Rules. Since the publication in 2002 of the Ethics 2000 version of the Model Rules, at least three states (Arizona, Delaware, and North Carolina) have adopted new rules of professional conduct based on those rules. Virtually every other United States jurisdiction is currently reviewing its ethics rules in light of the Ethics 2000 revisions to the Model Rules.

> The value of national uniformity and consistency in ethics rules is clear. The practice of law is no longer a purely local matter. Although exact figures on the extent of multiple admissions are unavailable, it is apparent that many thousands of lawyers admitted in Illinois are admitted in one or more other states as well. From information provided by the ARDC (James J Grogan on September 25, 2003), its records show that more than 9,300 lawyers registered with the ARDC who are resident in Illinois also report another admission outside Illinois. In addition, there are almost 14,000 nonresident lawyers registered with the ARDC who are admitted in other jurisdictions as well as Illinois. The ARDC's 2002 Annual Report shows a total of 75,421 registered lawyers as of October 31, 2002. Thus, at least 30 percent of the lawyers registered with the ARDC in 2002 were also admitted in another jurisdiction. These figures confirm that the ethics rules of Illinois will have an effect beyond the state's borders . . . [15]
>
> The advent of multijurisdictional practice dictates the need for lawyers to have a clear understanding of their responsibilities in the various jurisdictions in which they practice. The benefits to clients and the public from a coherent system of rules that guide lawyer conduct and ensure compliance, while upholding the ethical standards of the profession, are obvious.
>
> A third important rationale for following the ABA Model Rules absent a compelling reason is that amending well-known and commonly-used standard language will have consequences. At a minimum, unnecessary changes will cause confusion. Even minor stylistic amendments will inevitably cause lawyers consulting the Illinois Rules to speculate why the Illinois language was changed from the original ABA text. [16]

The second reason why this example from Illinois is illustrative is its demonstration that in the formulation and review of the rules governing lawyers and legal services, only lawyers—indeed, only very specific and select groups of lawyers—had a voice in the process. At no point in the process was the input, opinion, or expertise of anyone outside the legal profession sought or obtained, let alone taken into account (economic policy, human rights, competition, consumer affairs, etc.). In this manner, in describing the US process as "a monologue rather than a dialogue,"[17] the two Canada-based commentators Richard Devlin and Ora Morison were entirely accurate.

In sum, this example from Illinois demonstrates with powerful detail: (i) the extent to which state supreme courts (without mentioning the legislature[18]) abdicate their de jure power to regulate legal services, opening the path for the de facto power of the ABA, state and local bar associations, and even individual law firms and practicing attorneys, (ii) the full import of the ABA Model Rules, and consequently the enormous regulatory power of the ABA, (iii) the exclusion from the process of any kind of input, opinion, or expertise from anyone outside the legal profession.[19]

In the absence of national legislation, the ABA Model Rules serve as the default mechanism for national harmonization of the rules that govern legal services across the United States. Whether they should serve that purpose, and whether the lawyers that decide upon the content of the Model Rules should have that power—those are separate questions.

As powerful and pervasive as the ABA Model Rules are, there is a recent example of one state whose supreme court, acting independently of any corresponding ABA Model Rule, adopted a significant change to its rules governing who may practice law. That example is Washington State, which in 2015 began licensing a new category of persons who may provide legal services, called Limited License Legal Technicians (LLLTs).[20] In a manner comparable to lawyers, persons (only individuals, not companies) seeking to qualify and practice under this title are required to fulfill certain educational requirements, must pass a qualifying exam, are subject to disciplinary and ethical rules and procedures, and are required to hold malpractice insurance. Once licensed, they may carry out certain—limited—activities for clients in certain—limited—areas of the law, without the supervision of a lawyer. This rule change did not come easily—it took 11 years of study and debate. The work was piloted by the Practice of Law Board (POLB), established as an independent entity under the Washington State Supreme Court. Even if the Washington State Bar Association (WSBA) did partially fund the POLB, the structure was intended to free it from the undue influence of the WSBA.[21]

During that 11-year period, on three separate occasions, once in 2006 and twice in 2008, the WSBA formally opposed the change. In 2009 the supreme court published the proposed rule change for public comment, and in both 2010 and 2011 it placed the rule on its agenda for a vote, but each time the vote was postponed. In February 2012, the rule was revised to address some of the concerns of the WSBA (which remained opposed to the rule), and in June 2012 the supreme court finally voted to adopt the rule. It went into effect in early 2015, and the first LLLTs were sworn in later that same year.[22]

However, the story did not end there: In November 2015, nearly the entire membership of the POLB resigned in protest, complaining that the WSBA had made their continued service untenable. In their resignation letter, they described in detail various attacks the WSBA made on the POLB in the WSBA's efforts to defeat the proposed rule creating LLLTs, concluding with this summary:

> The treatment of the Practice of Law Board over the last three years is a textbook study on how to discourage and disempower a board comprised of volunteers: oppose their mission; cut their budget; withhold meaningful staff support; personally attack and seek to oust the volunteers who disagree with you; conduct secret meetings to discuss the future of the group without informing its volunteer members or inviting them to participate; dismiss or reject out of hand the volunteers' concerns; and replace the group's members and leadership team. There is no surer way to demoralize a group of volunteers and undermine their good intentions.[23]

This example demonstrates that it is possible for a state supreme court to override (at least in part) the opposition of the state and local bar associations and adopt a rule change, but that the path is long and difficult and by no means assured.

## TWO EXAMPLES ON A NATIONAL LEVEL

There are two recent examples of how the competent governing authorities abdicate their regulatory power to the ABA on a national level. The first example relates to the Conference of Chief Justices (CCJ). By way of reminder, the CCJ brings together the highest judicial officer in each state, typically the chief justice. The chief justice presides over the state's supreme court, which is the entity that, generally speaking, holds de jure (actual) regulatory power.

At its midyear meeting on February 3, 2016, the CCJ adopted "Resolution 9: Recommending Consideration of ABA Model Regulatory Objectives for the Provision of Legal Services."[24] In this resolution, the CCJ begins by explaining that the ABA Commission on the Future of Legal Services "concluded that the development of regulatory objectives is a useful step to guide state supreme courts and bar authorities as they assess the existing regulatory framework and identify and implement regulations related to legal services beyond the traditional regulation of the legal profession."[25] The resolution then repeats the list of Model Regulatory Objectives that had been developed and proposed by the ABA Commission,[26] and recommends that the members of the CCJ (that is, state supreme court justices) consider the objectives in the manner intended by the commission (that is, "as a means to help assess the state's existing regulatory framework and to help identify and implement regulations related to legal services beyond the traditional regulation of the legal profession"[27]).

While there is nothing inherently objectionable to this encouragement on behalf of the CCJ, the resolution makes glaringly obvious both that the CCJ itself failed to develop model regulatory objectives for adoption by its members, and that this failure is shared by most of the state supreme courts themselves (the notable exception being Colorado[28]).

The second example relates to the National Organization of Bar Counsel (NOBC). The NOBC is an organization "*whose members work in the regulation of the practice of law*."[29]

In October 2015, the same ABA Commission on the Future of Legal Services released an "Issues Paper Concerning New Categories of Legal Service Providers."[30] In the Issues Paper, the commission asks (i) whether the concept and definition of "legal services providers" should include lawyers and nonlawyers; and (2) whether state judicial authorities should be encouraged to create new categories of judicially authorized and regulated legal services providers (individuals, not organizations) to perform discreet and limited legal tasks in an effort to facilitate greater access to justice.[31]

In its December 21, 2015, response to the Issues Paper, the NOBC first writes that it "takes no position on the specific issues presented."[32] Then the NOBC goes further—it states that "it is appropriate for the ABA to play a leadership role in evaluating and guiding the manner in which the delivery of legal services will be regulated so that all US jurisdictions can make informed decisions."[33] Stated another way, an organization made up of persons who "*work in the regulation of the practice of law*" has decided that it is more appropriate for an entirely different organization to take the lead in the work of regulation. And that entirely different organization, composed of people that practice law, has made no secret that its "Goal 1" is to serve its own members.[34]

## NOTES

1. Commission on the Evaluation of the Rules of Professional Conduct ("Ethics 2000"), "Chair's Introduction," August 2002, http://www.americanbar.org/content/dam/aba/administrative/professional_responsibility/e2k_chair_intro.authcheckdam.pdf.
2. ISBA/CBA Joint Committee on Ethics 2000, "Revised Final Report," January 8, 2004 (Corrected April 1, 2004), 4, http://www.illinoiscourts.gov/supremecourt/public_hearings/rules/2007/isbacbafinalreport.pdf.
3. Ibid.
4. Illinois Supreme Court, "Supreme Court Adopts New Rules of Professional Conduct for Lawyers," July 1, 2009, http://www.illinoiscourts.gov/media/pressrel/2009/070109.pdf.
5. Ibid.
6. Richard A. Redmond, Letter to John Nicoara, Chair, Supreme Court Rules Committee, February 20, 2007, http://www.illinoiscourts.gov/SupremeCourt/Public_Hearings/Rules/2007/ProfRespReport.pdf.
7. Illinois Supreme Court, "Supreme Court Adopts New Rules," 3.
8. Ibid.
9. Ibid., 2.
10. Ibid.
11. See http://www.illinoiscourts.gov/SupremeCourt/Public_Hearings/Rules/2007/ProfRespReport.pdf (accessed May 29, 2016).
12. Illinois Supreme Court, "Supreme Court Adopts New Rules," 3.
13. Ibid., 1.
14. Robert A. Creamer, "Get Ready for Illinois' New Rules of Professional Conduct," *Illinois Bar Journal* 97 (October 2009): 500, http://www.isba.org/ibj/2009/10/getreadyforillinoisnewrulesofprofes.
15. ISBA/CBA Joint Committee on Ethics 2000, "Revised Final Report," 5–6.
16. Ibid., 7.
17. Devlin and Morison, "Access to Justice," 527.
18. The fact that the legislature in Illinois as well as in any other state rarely, if ever, appears to contemplate playing a role is not surprising. It could do so only with great determination, given that the ABA repeatedly expresses strong opposition to any legislative role in the regulation of the legal profession. See, for example, "Independence of the Legal Profession," American Bar Association, accessed February 8, 2016, http://www.americanbar.org/advocacy/governmental_legislative_work/priorities_policy/independence_of_the_legal_profession.html.

Moliterno puts it this way: "In some respects, American legislatures speak for the legal profession, usually by not speaking at all. . . . By remaining quiet, the legislatures have said something on behalf of the profession: they have supported the self-governance claims made by the organized bar." Moliterno, *The American Legal Profession in Crisis,* 15.

19. Barton offers detailed reasons for this abdication in his article "An Institutional Analysis," 1167–250.

20. Gene Johnson, "Washington Experiments with More Affordable Legal Advice," *Seattle Times*, September 27, 2015, http://www.seattletimes.com/seattle-news/washington-experiments-with-more-affordable-legal-advice/. See also Hadfield and Rhode, "How to Regulate Legal Services," 47–50.

21. Victor Li, "Board Members Quit, Blast Washington State Bar in Fight over UPL, Legal Technicians," *ABA Journal*, November 9, 2015, http://www.abajournal.com/news/article/Board_members_quit_blast_Washington_State_Bar_in_fight_over_UPL.

22. Robert Ambrogi, "Washington State Moves Around UPL, Using Legal Technicians to Help Close the Justice Gap," *ABA Journal*, January 1, 2015, http://www.abajournal.com/magazine/article/washington_state_moves_around_upl_using_legal_technicians_to_help_close_the/ ; Gene Johnson, "Washington Experiments with More Affordable Legal Advice."

23. Scott A. Smith et al., Letter to Washington Supreme Court Justices, November 9, 2015, 10, http://www.abajournal.com/files/Letter_to_Supreme_Court_Explaining_Resignations.pdf.

24. Conference of Chief Justices, "Resolution 9: Recommending Consideration of ABA Model Regulatory Objectives for the Provision of Legal Services," February 3, 2016, https://richardzorza.files.wordpress.com/2016/02/ccj-2016-res-9.pdf.

25. Ibid., 1.

26. Ibid., 1–2.

27. Ibid., 2.

28. See "[Draft] Regulatory Objectives of the Supreme Court of Colorado," November 12, 2015, http://www.americanbar.org/content/dam/aba/images/office_president/supreme_court_of_colorado.pdf; see also Joan C. Rogers, "ABA Commission Suggests Overall Regulatory Objectives," *BNA News*, October 21, 2015, http://www.bna.com/aba-commission-suggests-n57982062517/.

29. "Mission Statement," National Organization of Bar Counsel, accessed May 21, 2016, http://www.nobc.org/index.php/about-us/mission-statement.

30. ABA Commission on the Future of Legal Services, "Issues Paper Concerning New Categories of Legal Services Providers," October 16, 2015, http://www.americanbar.org/content/dam/aba/images/office_president/delivery_of_legal_services_completed_evaluation.pdf.

31. Ibid., 11–12.

32. National Organization of Bar Counsel, "Comments to 'Issues Paper Concerning New Categories of Legal Services Providers,'" December 21, 2015, http://www.americanbar.org/content/dam/aba/images/office_president/lspcomments_national_organization_of_bar_counsel.pdf.

33. Ibid.

34. "ABA Mission and Goals," American Bar Association, accessed February 11, 2016, http://www.americanbar.org/about_the_aba/aba-mission-goals.html. Indeed, and as detailed in part I, chapter 3, a number of persons, including two members of the ABA's House of Delegates, harshly reprimanded the ABA Commission on the Future of Legal Services for appearing to have overlooked that very fact, for the simple reason that in April 2016 the commission released an Issues Paper on the topic of alternative structures.

## *Chapter Twenty-Two*

# International Obligations and Commitments

As discussed in part III, in several international human rights treaties the United States has undertaken to guarantee to its citizens a number of rights and protections, and notably:

- to provide effective remedies to rights violations,[1]
- to guarantee equal treatment before the tribunals and other organs administering justice,[2] and
- to protect against discrimination and provide equal protection under the law.[3]

Further, the United States has undertaken to "take the necessary steps . . . to adopt such laws and other measures"[4] as may be necessary to give effect to these rights and protections. And these obligations of the United States have recently been intensified: As a signatory of the United Nations 2030 Agenda for Sustainable Development (adopted on September 25, 2015, on the occasion of the UN's 70th anniversary[5]), the United States has committed to the implementation of certain goals and targets by 2030, including these:

> Goal 16: Promote peaceful and inclusive societies for sustainable development, provide access to justice for all and build effective, accountable and inclusive institutions at all levels . . .
>
> 16.3: Promote the rule of law at the national and international levels and *ensure equal access to justice for all* . . .
>
> 16.6: *Develop effective, accountable and transparent institutions at all levels.*[6]

With these goals, the United States is under even greater pressure, not only to address the problem of unmet need for legal services in the United States, but also to develop the "effective, accountable and transparent institutions at all levels" that are necessary in order to do so.

## "ENSURE EQUAL ACCESS TO JUSTICE FOR ALL"

The Agenda for Sustainable Development declares that "sustainable development cannot be realized without peace and security,"[7] and that there is a "need to build peaceful, just and inclusive societies that provide equal access to justice and that are based on respect for human rights."[8] Accordingly, as a signatory to the Agenda, the United States has committed to "ensur[ing] equal access to justice for all."

However, today this is simply a commitment on the part of the United States—it is far from a reality. As discussed in part III, the unmet need for legal services in the United States is so great, it is considered by some to be a human rights crisis. The United States is considered to be in violation of international treaty obligations and the government of the United States has expressly acknowledged "challenges" in this regard. Certainly the government of the United States has already taken steps to try to address the problem of unmet need for legal services. The most prominent examples are the federally funded Legal Services Corporation and the Department of Justice's Access to Justice Initiative. These programs are important and necessary. But, even taken together with other programs, they are not, nor can they ever be, sufficient to address the huge unmet need.

As discussed above, total public spending for the Legal Services Corporation and other legal aid, combined with charitable donations for legal aid, is about $3.7[9] billion per year. This number does not even come close to the $50 billion per year that Professor Hadfield's research estimates would be required to secure one hour of legal assistance for households with unmet dispute-related needs.[10] It is possible, but unlikely, that Congress will vote to increase funding for legal aid by an additional $46.3 billion annually.

Additional pro bono work by lawyers in private practice is also important and necessary. But, like public funding and charitable donations for legal aid, it cannot ever come close to being enough. Professor Hadfield's research estimates that each American lawyer would need to provide at least 900 hours of pro bono work per year in order to provide some measure of assistance to all households with legal needs.[11] The current average amount of pro bono work per lawyer per year is about 30 hours, and 900 hours represents approximately half a year of billable hours for the average lawyer.[12] It seems highly unlikely that each lawyer in the United States will agree to work for free for half of each year.

## "EFFECTIVE, ACCOUNTABLE AND TRANSPARENT INSTITUTIONS AT ALL LEVELS"

The Agenda for Sustainable Development also declares that there is a "need to build peaceful, just and inclusive societies that . . . are based on . . . effective rule of law and good governance at all levels and on transparent, effective and accountable institutions."[13] Accordingly, as a signatory to the Agenda, the United States has committed to developing "*effective, accountable and transparent institutions at all levels*."

Chapter 21 contains a detailed study of the de facto regulatory power exercised by certain members of the legal profession. A superficial examination would suggest that this power extends over the legal profession only. However, a closer look reveals that this power extends much further: Because (as discussed in greater detail below) the legal profession exercises a monopoly over legal services in the United States, this de facto power to regulate the legal profession necessarily then also encompasses the power to regulate legal services as a whole. Perhaps (and, again, as discussed below), the monopoly is not perfect and thus the power is not perfect either, but the power nonetheless exists.

As also discussed in chapter 21, the persons who exercise this de facto power are, in the first place, the House of Delegates of the ABA, and in the second place, state and local bar associations.

### "Effective"

Section 1.2 of the constitution of the ABA describes the association's purposes as follows:

> [T]o uphold and defend the Constitution of the United States and maintain representative government; to advance the science of jurisprudence; to promote throughout the nation the administration of justice and the uniformity of legislation and of judicial decisions; to uphold the honor of the profession of law; to apply the knowledge and experience of the profession to the promotion of the public good; to encourage cordial intercourse among the members of the American bar; and to correlate and promote the activities of the bar organizations in the nation within these purposes and in the interests of the profession and of the public.[14]

The ABA is surely effective in serving some, and perhaps even many of these purposes. But nowhere is a purpose relating to access to justice listed, much less the purpose "ensure equal access to justice for all" or the purpose "develop effective, accountable and transparent institutions at all levels."

Whether or not ensuring access to justice figures among the purposes of the ABA, and whether or not it should figure as one of its purposes, are debatable issues. Regardless of the outcome of those debates, however, given the severity of the unmet need for legal services in the United States, it is clear that no institution in the United States, including the ABA, has been effective in serving this purpose.

## "Accountable"

The ABA is a private, voluntary, nongovernmental organization that counts nearly 400,000[15] of the country's 1.2 million lawyers as its members. Section 6.1 of the ABA's constitution states that its House of Delegates is the "legislative body of the Association," and that it "shall formulate policy for the Association."[16] Section 6.2 continues that the House of Delegates "is designed to be representative of the legal profession of the United States."[17] The approximately 560 members of this body are not elected by the public at large. They are not elected by the members of the legal profession at large. Most are not even elected by the members of the ABA. More specifically, of the 560 delegates:[18]

- 231 are "State Bar Association Delegates" appointed (or, in some cases, elected) by state bar associations,[19]
- 74 are "Local Bar Association Delegates" appointed (or, in some cases, elected) by local bar associations,[20]
- 52 are "State Delegates" elected by state, by the members of the ABA, based upon the state to which the member is "accredited,"
- 18 are "Delegates-at-Large" elected by the members of the ABA at large,
- 75 are "Present and Former Officers and Board Members,"
- 73 are "Section, Division and Conference Delegates," appointed or elected by the relevant ABA Section Division or Conference,
- 2 are "Ex Officio Members" (officers of the ABA),
- 28 are "Affiliated Organization Delegates" appointed or elected by "affiliate organizations such as the American Immigration Lawyers Association, the American Judicature Society, the American Law Institute, the Association of American Law Schools, the Association of Life Insurance Counsel and the Conference of Chief Justices,[21]
- 4 are delegates representing: Virgin Islands Bar Association, American Samoa, Guam, and Commonwealth of Northern Mariana Island, and
- 3 are "Members-at-Large."

Members of the public cannot submit policy proposals to the House of Delegates, nor can attorneys who are not members of the ABA. Members of the ABA can submit them but, as the chair of the House has explained, most are submitted by state and local bar associations and by the sections and committees of the ABA.[22] The meetings of the House of Delegates are open to the members of the ABA as well as to the media, but they are not open to the public at large, and the House can vote to exclude from its meetings anyone who is not a member of the House.[23]

It would be wrong to say that the House of Delegates is not accountable. It surely is, most especially to state and local bar associations. But it would be equally wrong to say that the House of Delegates is accountable to the public. It would be wrong to say that the House of Delegates is accountable to any publicly elected or other body, governmental or otherwise, that has public accountability. It would be wrong to say that the House of Delegates is accountable to actual or potential users of legal services. It would be wrong to say that the House of Delegates is accountable to the legal profession as a whole.

Given that the members of the ABA elect only 70 out of the 560 members of the House of Delegates, the accountability of the House of Delegates to even the members of the ABA is tenuous at best. Some have argued that "the leadership of the bar associations . . . comes from the most prestigious law firms,"[24] and that the persons who make decisions for the ABA make them not in the interests of the legal profession as a whole, or in the interests of the membership of the association, but in the interests of the corporations who are the clients of their law firms.[25]

## "Transparent"

The United Nations 2030 Agenda for Sustainable Development is not the first document to call for transparency in regulation. To the contrary, transparency and accountability, together, are often cited as essential elements of "good governance,"[26] necessary to ensure "economic growth and development"[27] as well as "responsive[ness] to the present and future needs of society."[28] Transparency in regulation has been defined in different ways—a common definition is:

> Transparency means that decisions taken and their enforcement are done in a manner that follows rules and regulations. It also means that information is freely available and directly accessible to those who will be affected by such decisions and their enforcement. It also means that enough information is provided and that it is provided in easily understandable forms and media.[29]

Information about the identity of the members of the House of Delegates of the ABA and how to contact them is not freely available to the public.[30] It is not even freely available to members of the legal profession who are not members of the ABA. Without knowing who the relevant persons are, it is not possible to ascertain any conflicts of interest they may have in the exercise of their de facto regulatory role, nor is it possible to communicate directly with them, as de facto regulators, for lobbying purposes. Further, when regulatory power—such as that of the ABA House of Delegates and other bar associations—is exercised in a de facto manner rather than in the de jure manner provided by law, the power is not being exercised in a manner that follows the rules.

With respect to the very topic of alternative structures, the ABA has been criticized for its lack of transparency. Kenneth Grady, CEO of SeyfarthLean Consulting, describes the processes of the ABA in this manner:

> I have trouble concluding the ABA is following [a transparent, fact-based and unbiased] process. The materials I have read do not include standards for analyzing the issue, data about the performance of schemes with or without ABS, or descriptions of the data needed to decide the issue. Nevertheless, the position of the ABA is that "the case for making changes has not been made . . . "[31] Put simply, the public cannot understand what would permit the ABA to permit ABS arrangements. This opaque process makes it difficult to build public trust and supports the perception that a decision on the issue will be made behind closed doors to a politics and emotion process.[32]

In sum, the ABA's de facto regulatory power cannot be described as transparent.[33]

It is on this world stage—and in the context of these international obligations—that the legal profession in the United States enjoys a monopoly on the provision of legal services in the United States.

## NOTES

1. *International Covenant on Civil and Political Rights*, December 16, 1966, Art. 2(3)(a), http://www.ohchr.org/en/professionalinterest/pages/ccpr.aspx. See also *The Universal Declaration of Human Rights*, Art. 8, http://www.un.org/en/documents/udhr/.
2. *International Convention on the Elimination of All Forms of Racial Discrimination*, December 21, 1965, Art. 5(a), http://www.ohchr.org/EN/ProfessionalInterest/Pages/CERD.aspx.
3. *International Convention on the Elimination of All Forms of Racial Discrimination*, Art. 6. See also *The Universal Declaration of Human Rights*, Art. 7.
4. *International Covenant on Civil and Political Rights*, December 16, 1966, Art. 2(2), http://www.ohchr.org/en/professionalinterest/pages/ccpr.aspx.
5. "UN Adopts New Global Goals, Charting Sustainable Development for People and Planet by 2030," United Nations News Centre, September 25, 2015, http://www.un.org/apps/news/story.asp?NewsID=51968#.Vgo773qqqko.
6. United Nations Summit for the Adoption of the Post-2015 Development Agenda, "Transforming Our World: The 2030 Agenda for Sustainable Development," October 21, 2015, 24–25, http://www.un.org/ga/search/view_doc.asp?symbol=A/RES/70/1&Lang=E (hereinafter "Agenda for Sustainable Development").
7. Ibid., 9.
8. Ibid.
9. Hadfield, "The Cost of Law," 45.
10. Ibid.
11. Hadfield, "Innovating to Improve Access," 5.
12. Ibid.

13. Agenda for Sustainable Development, 9.

14. American Bar Association, "Constitution and Bylaws Rules of Procedure House of Delegates," 2014–2015, 1, http://www.americanbar.org/content/dam/aba/administrative/house_of_delegates/aba_constitution_and_bylaws_2014.authcheckdam.pdf (hereinafter "ABA Constitution").

15. "About the ABA," American Bar Association, accessed May 29, 2016, http://www.americanbar.org/about_the_aba.html.

16. ABA Constitution, 4.

17. Ibid.

18. "House of Delegates—General Information," American Bar Association, accessed August 25, 2015, http://www.americanbar.org/groups/leadership/delegates.html.

19. Eighteen states of the United States have voluntary bar associations—that is, the lawyers of those states are not obliged to join the state's bar association.

20. Membership in a local bar association is voluntary, not obligatory.

21. ABA Constitution, 10 (Section 6.8).

22. Patricia Lee Refo, "ABA House of Delegate Chair: How an Idea Becomes ABA Policy," March 25, 2015, 00:28, http://www.americanbar.org/news/abanews/aba-news-archives/2015/03/aba_house_of_delegat.html.

23. ABA Constitution, 47 (Section 42.1).

24. John C. Payne, "The Weakness of Bar Associations," *Journal of the Legal Profession* 2 (1977): 55–76, 69, http://www.law.ua.edu/pubs/jlp_files/issues_files/vol02/vol02art06.pdf.

25. Ibid., 69–71.

26. "Transparency and Accountability," International Institute for Sustainable Development, accessed August 25, 2015, https://www.iisd.org/trade/policy/transparency.asp.

27. Ved P. Nanda, "The 'Good Governance' Concept Revisited," *Annals of the American Academy of Political and Social Science* 603 (January 2006): 269–83, 274.

28. Friedl Weiss and Silke Steiner, "Transparency as an Element of Good Governance in the Practice of the EU and the WTO: Overview and Comparison," *Fordham International Law Journal* 30 (2006): 1545–86, 1549, http://ir.lawnet.fordham.edu/cgi/viewcontent.cgi?article=2076&context=ilj.

29. United Nations Economic and Social Commission for Asia and the Pacific, "What is Good Governance?," 2009, http://www.unescap.org/sites/default/files/good-governance.pdf.

30. The website of the ABA includes a page entitled "Welcome to the House of Delegates Directory," but sign-in is required and the page states that "membership is required to access this exclusive member content." See http://www.americanbar.org/directories/people_directories/hod_people_directory_members/people_directory_members.html (accessed September 9, 2015).

31. Kenneth Grady, Video Testimony to the ABA Commission on the Future of Legal Services, 1:15 to 1:54, February, 2015, http://bcove.me/x9hwfqsq.

32. Ibid., 3:22 to 3:38.

33. An additional example of lack of transparency: The author requested from the ABA minutes of the meetings of Commission on Ethics 20/20 held on April 12–13, June 1, August 4–5 and October 25–26, 2012. She did not receive a response regarding the April, June, or October minutes. As regards the August 2012 minutes, the response stated, "The August meeting also consisted of preparing to present the Resolutions to the House and negotiating proposed friendly amendments or other issues and doing what was needed to visit ABA HOD delegations. So there are no minutes from that meeting." The author was particularly interested in the minutes of the April 12–13 meeting because according to the statement issued by the commission on April 16, 2012, it was at the April 12–13 meeting that the commission decided not to propose changes to the ABA policy to prohibit nonlawyer ownership of law firms. The only explanation for this decision provided in the one-page April 16 announcement was that "[t]he Commission considered the pros and cons . . . and concluded that the case had not been made." Presumably the minutes of the April 12–13 meeting contain more information about the commission's decision-making process. See http://www.americanbar.org/content/dam/aba/administrative/ethics_2020/20120416_news_release_re_nonlawyer_ownership_law_firms.authcheckdam.pdf.

The author also requested from the ABA minutes of the meetings of Commission on the Future of Legal Services. The response stated that the minutes are not available online, nor are they otherwise available to the public.

*Chapter Twenty-Three*

# Endless Objections and Calls for Evidence and the Lawyer Monopoly on Legal Services (Or, Having Your Cake and Eating It, Too)

Alternative structures are controversial, if not highly controversial. Much has been said and written about them and, no doubt, much more will be. Many objections have been raised and many calls for evidence have been made. With each response, a new objection is raised or a new call for evidence is made. Part I of this book addresses the more commonly raised objections and calls for evidence, but there are a great many more. Here are some of the additional objections:

- "It is not clear how the implementation of ABS, by themselves, would contribute to enhancements in technology."[1]
- "Systems for checking conflicts would necessarily have to become much more complex."[2]
- "Different providers of professional services (which presumably, under an ABS model, could provide services under the same roof) will have different professional codes of conduct, and these may be in conflict with one another—including provisions in different professional codes relating to privilege."[3]
- "[I]magine someone who has diverted a lot of cash from his business and is looking for a quick way to clear it up. Buy a law firm and run it through the trust account. Works like a charm, and who thinks . . . regulators will catch it."[4]

- "[ABS does not] result in a better quality of service. . . . In the UK, professionalism of the bar has remained steady since 2011. In contrast, in Illinois disciplinary charges are decreasing and formal disciplinary complaints are at an all-time low."[5]
- "The nonlawyer investment ownership and management reforms adopted by our common law cousins were put into place many years ago. Given the quick pace of technological change those reforms . . . may simply no longer be applicable or appropriate for the current American experience."[6]
- "ABS structures could erode reputational incentives that exist today to encourage lawyers to perform their best work."[7]
- "[L]awyers [would become] salaried employees of legal services corporations, lawyers would become mere revenue producing units for outside business owners. On balance, we believe fewer lawyers would prefer that system over the current system."[8]
- "ABS could result in a widening gap in income among top tier lawyers and the rest of the profession . . . the lawyer "middle class" would shrink."[9]
- "Nonlawyer ownership would have allowed Enron."[10]
- "Maurice Blackburn, [one of] Australia's three largest personal injury firms . . . has not gone public. Because Maurice Blackburn has been able to scale and grow the firm without going public, a comparison of this firm to [Slater and Gordon and Shine] may cast doubt on whether outside ownership is necessary to achieve economies of scale."[11]
- "Investment by nonlawyers may allow firms to scale and grow their brand and increase advertising funding, to better allow customers to comfortably rely on brands when trying to seek a legal service provider. . . . However, in reality, the attachment of a brand name to a product is a tenuous guarantee of its quality."[12]
- "Well-known companies which own legal service providers may be less likely to offer legal services to publicly unpopular clients out of fear of harming their brand."[13]
- "[There has been] a dramatic increase in marketing by personal injury lawyers . . . For the most part, this advertising in in very poor taste. In an ABS world, the amount of advertising by personal injury firms would likely increase. . . . Skillful marketing by financial backers of unskilled lawyers will result in uninformed consumers not getting proper representation."[14]
- "[We] are concerned about the disappearance of lawyers who provide complex, noncommoditizable services like criminal and family law with no solution for replacing access to justice in these areas, especially for low to middle income clients."[15]
- "[A]ny growth of unregulated legal services does not necessarily imply that existing regulatory restrictions are unduly constraining innovation,

but could indicate instead that the public is being sold services with little or no value albeit at low costs."[16]
- "ABS advances in technology are overstated."[17]
- "Many [bar] associations depend on revenue from [continuing legal education ("CLE")] programs to ensure their financial existence. With firms like Slater and Gordon offering internal [CLE] courses to their staff, without charge, there is no reason for their staff to register and pay for outside [CLE] programs and courses, thus significantly reducing the overall revenue to local [bar] associations."[18]
- "ABS entities . . . may include disbarred lawyers, licensees who have had their licenses revoked or even candidates who petitioned for a license and were refused due to bad character or other issues."[19]
- "[T]here is an inherent risk that by introducing non licensed shareholders into the equation, women paralegals will continue to endure more systemic barriers as there is no guarantee that ABS entities will view diversity and equity on the boards as a must."[20]
- "[T]here may be other regulated possibilities worth exploring."[21]
- "ABS would . . . take so much money out of the public that the public would have that much less to devote to charitable endeavours."[22]
- "[S]everal of the large ABS entities in England have suffered badly and have lost millions and millions of pounds."[23]
- "ABS is mostly a smoke-screen to avoid doing anything about the time and cost of litigation."[24]
- "Would anyone like our most prestigious firms, or the bulk of our mid to small firms . . . to be owned by Arthur Andersen, AIG, Enron, WorldCom, Societe Generale, Royal Bank of Scotland, Lehman Brothers, Bear Stearns, Volkswagen, Barker Trust, Barlow Clowes, Phar-Mor, Bernie Madoff, Allan Stanford, Tyco International, Health South, Swissair, Baninter, HIH Insurance, Polly Peck, Barings Bank, Bank of Credit and Commerce, Nordbanken, Carrian Group, Bre-X, Equitable Life Assurance, Pacific Gas and Electric, One.Tel, Adelphia, Parmalat, Nortel, Dynergy, Banco Espirito, Union Carbide, and future versions of Medici Bank and the South Sea Company? . . . What about being owned by divisions of arms manufacturers, drug cartels looking to launder money, immigration fraud companies? Russian carpetbaggers with close ties to global destabilization efforts? Companies ostensibly independent but really controlled by foreign communist or totalitarian regimes looking for an in? . . . How would you like to be a lawyer on the payroll of those entities and then try to get a job when they are exposed for what they are? How do you wash that taint off?"[25]
- "We are so proud that the American legal system, while flawed, is the best in the world. . . . We are DIFFERENT for a reason that we should be proud of and embrace. Our system should not look backwards to what

other, more flawed, legal systems have had to become. They should be more like us and not us like them."[26]

And here are some of the additional calls for evidence:

- "[C]omparisons [to the use of ABS in foreign countries] are of extremely limited utility, in the absence of comprehensive data concerning how the legal systems of those countries operate . . . in countries such as the UK and Australia, the distinction between barristers and solicitors is still maintained. . . . European countries employ a civil law system, dramatically different from the common law heritage of the United States. The point is that what works well and is beneficial in the context of one society may not be productive at all in the context of another. Further study, or at least further explanation, is needed before attempting to justify an ABS on the basis of its existence in other countries."[27]
- "ABS proponents also need to show that ABS structures can work in the regulatory regime we have, not just in the very different regulatory regimes of other common law jurisdictions (if indeed ABS works even in those jurisdictions—a question it is too early to answer)."[28]
- "There is currently little evidence supporting the conclusion that ABSs are having a transformative effect on the delivery of legal services in the United Kingdom."[29]
- "[T]here has been no showing that firms cannot achieve their goals of providing seamless law-related services to clients (if that is what they want to do) by forming ancillary entities as is presently permitted."[30]
- "[T]here is not enough empirical evidence available from the jurisdictions in which ABS is permitted (namely Australia and UK), to endorse permitting ABS. . . . Until empirical evidence on the benefits of ABS to access to justice and the market as a whole is available and has been fully and critically reviewed . . . the introduction of ABS on any level would be premature and, therefore, ill-advised."[31]
- "[M]ore discussion is needed about the true impact for the unemployed licensee before preference is given to nonlicensees."[32]
- "[T]he deliberations need to remain focused on who will stand to lose the most as opposed to who will gain from ABS."[33]
- "[The] impact ABS will have on access to justice in both rural communities and urban communities [should be examined] before concluding that alternative business structures are appropriate."[34]
- "What evidence is there to show that ABS has had no negative impact—professional or business on the bar and, in particular, on soles and smalls in Australia and England? . . . [We] should be cautious and only proceed once a strong empirical case can be made and only once the practicing bar

fully appreciates the impacts to the profession and their business model."[35]

- "[C]hanges to the regulation of the legal profession made primarily for the purpose of enhancing access to justice should only be made on the basis of unequivocal evidence of successes from other jurisdictions, and not on theoretical arguments or assertions that ABS will enhance access to justice. . . . [There should be] unequivocal empirical evidence compiled over a significant period of time of substantial net benefit to the public."[36]
- "[T]here is a lack of data on the impact of [ABS] on equity and diversity in the legal profession and on access to justice."[37]
- "To the extent that proponents of ABS predict benefits from economies of scale in the delivery of service, it is important to determine whether, and to what extent, these require changes to the regulatory framework."[38]
- "The decision we face in regards to nonlawyer ownership of law firms will have far reaching consequences that will affect/effect the rule of law, and the very foundation of our government; therefore this issue should be reviewed and discussed exhaustively. . . . There must be a philosophic line of inquiry to accompany the soft science research. . . . To discuss this matter philosophically will help us identify where we want to go as a profession and, ultimately, as a country. . . . We should commission an in-depth study by comparative law scholars and attorneys who practice internationally in order to compare the legal culture, legal structures, and constitutional structures of [the jurisdictions outside the United States] to our own."[39]
- "There is an absence of empirical data showing savings to consumers of legal services. . . . [T]here are segments in the legal system that have particular access concerns, especially in the family law context [yet] no evidence has been brought forward to show how these access concerns will be effectively addressed and reduced through ABS."[40]
- "Proponents of ABS who argue that it offers technological benefits that are unavailable to traditional law firms have thus far fallen woefully short in producing any evidence in support of such claims."[41]
- "There is, quite simply, a lack of any empirical evidence that shows:

    1. Why ABS was introduced in the UK and Australia;
    2. Whether the problems sought to be solved in other jurisdictions correlate in any way to the legal landscape in Ontario;
    3. Whether the introduction of ABS has in fact solved the problems it presumably sought to resolve in the UK and Australia;
    4. Whether there has been significantly improved access to justice (particularly in areas of practice where access to justice is a concern);

5. Whether core values such as avoiding conflicts of interest and the independence of counsel have been compromised to any extent with the introduction of ABS;
6. Whether the regulatory bodies in the UK and Australia have been effective in dealing with ABS-related issues as they arise (which includes an examination of the structure of the regulatory bodies and complaints reporting systems); and
7. What the overall impact has been for the profession and the public interest since the introduction of ABS in jurisdictions where it has been adopted."[42]

These examples show that there are a great many objections that can be raised and calls for evidence that can be made in relation to alternative structures. They are infinite in number and limited only by imagination.

Under the rules of 50 states, only licensed lawyers may provide legal services. As a result of this restriction, licensed lawyers, and the traditional law firm structures in which they practice, hold a monopoly on the provision of legal services. No other person, and no other type of structure—and notably not a multidisciplinary practice or a structure owned in whole or in part by a nonlawyer—may offer legal services without the risk of running afoul of unauthorized practice of law (UPL) and fee sharing rules.[43] (There are two exceptions: Since 1990 Washington, DC, has permitted a limited form of nonlawyer ownership, and in 2015 Washington State began licensing "Limited License Legal Technicians." These are individuals—not organizations—who are licensed to provide legal advice and assistance in specified areas of the law without the supervision of a lawyer.)

Certainly, the full scope of the monopoly is difficult to describe.[44] Further, nonlawyers and nontraditional structures have attempted to chip away at the monopoly, such that some have described the role of the legal profession as having become "a subset of a larger industry that is increasingly populated by nonlawyers, technologists and entrepreneurs."[45] Others make what is essentially the same observation but from a different perspective—they say, for example, that "legal services to big companies are . . . already de facto deregulated."[46]

To be sure, UPL rules have not succeeded in keeping all nonlawyers and all nontraditional structures out of the market—companies like RocketLawyer, LegalZoom, Axiom, Shake, and Modria are proof of that. But UPL and fee sharing rules have succeeded in keeping a great many out. As Gillian Hadfield observed: "There are many things that U.S. companies cannot do, and the fact that there is a little going on at the margins does not come close to what could be done if the restrictions were not there."[47]

Much has been written and said, on the one hand to defend UPL rules (lawyers, by reason of their legal education and training, are more effective and more ethical than nonlawyers) and on the other hand to oppose them (in certain if not many situations, nonlawyers and/or nontraditional structures can provide services of adequate quality and entirely ethically, and thus make legal services available to a greater number of people who otherwise would be forced to go without them altogether).[48]

Without minimizing the importance of that debate, UPL restrictions raise a second and equally important issue: The laws in place in the United States today allocate the entire legal services market to the legal profession—to the legal profession only—and those laws (more or less successfully) support bar associations and other groups of lawyers when they attempt to keep nonlawyers and nontraditional structures out of the market.

Yet, those same laws do not require the legal profession to meet the needs of the entire market. Indeed, when in 2013 the New York Court of Appeals adopted a rule requiring New York attorneys not to provide any minimum amount of pro bono service, but simply to report the number of hours they do spend on pro bono work (as well as any financial contributions they make to organizations that provide legal services to the poor and underserved), the New York State Bar Association (NYSBA) strongly objected. In a letter to the chief judge of the State of New York, David Schraver, the president of the NYSBA and a partner at Nixon Peabody in Rochester, wrote that "the provision of legal services to the poor is a public responsibility" and that the reporting requirement was "an invasion of privacy."[49] In 2015 the rule was scaled back to require only anonymous reporting.[50]

If Schraver is correct in saying that "the provision of legal services to the poor is a public responsibility," then isn't the effect of the monopoly to severely limit the public's room for maneuver in meeting its responsibility? Doesn't the monopoly essentially mean that the only way "the public" can meet its responsibility is to provide money to pay lawyers to provide legal services to the poor? That the public will not be permitted any other means to meet its responsibility?

Further, if "the provision of legal services to the poor is a public responsibility," why isn't the provision of legal services to the middle class and to the rich also a public responsibility? If Schraver is drawing a line in order to allocate what is the responsibility of the legal profession as opposed to what is the responsibility of the "public," why does he draw the line at "legal services to the poor"?

If the laws of the United States accord to the legal profession the *exclusive privilege* to serve the entire market, shouldn't the counterpart to that exclusive privilege be the corresponding *obligation* to serve the entire market? If it is the legal profession—and the legal profession only—that has the right, by law, to serve the legal services market, then shouldn't the legal profession have the obligation, by law, to develop and implement solutions that do effectively serve the entire market? Beverley McLachlin, the chief justice of the Supreme Court of Canada, has stated it in this manner: "If you're the only one who can provide a fundamental social need from which you benefit, I think it follows that you have to provide it."[51]

If the United States is not willing to change its laws, either at the federal or state level, in order to oblige the legal profession to serve the needs of the legal services market in its entirety, then doesn't the United States have the obligation to change its laws in order to open the market to others—including nonlawyers and alternative structures? As discussed in part III, one of the many objections made to alternative structures is that there is no proof they will increase access to justice. But why should such proof be required? If the provision of legal services to the poor is a public responsibility, shouldn't members of the public be allowed to try to provide them, even if they may fail? Isn't this all the more true in light of the examples of Australia and England and Wales—which demonstrate, each with its own example, how nonlawyers and nontraditional structures can play a greater role in the delivery of legal services safely—without the dire consequences to ethical standards that so many have predicted?

Viewed from this context, all of the arguments made in opposition to alternative structures and all of the calls for greater evidence lose their relevance. The bottom line is that there is a massive unmet need for legal services in the United States—a need that some consider a human rights crisis. By law, the members of the legal profession are the only persons who are allowed to meet this need. Yet, the legal profession does not have the means to meet it, and, speaking through its bar associations, it rejects that it has the obligation to do so. At the same time, the government of the United States is obliged under international treaties "to provide effective remedies to rights violations," "to guarantee equal treatment before the tribunals and other organs administering justice," and "to protect against discrimination and provide equal protection under the law." And under the Agenda for Sustainable Development, the United States has committed to "ensur[ing] equal access to justice for all," as well as to "develop[ing] effective, accountable and transparent institutions at all levels" that are needed for that purpose.

In this context, what continues to justify the lawyer monopoly on legal services in the United States? Ending the lawyer monopoly on legal services will not, by itself, solve the access to justice problem in its entirety, but it is an important and necessary element. And it will certainly be cheaper than spending an additional $46.3 billion per year on legal aid, not to mention more realistic than expecting (let alone requiring) the 1.2 million lawyers of the United States to increase their average number of pro bono hours to 900 per year.

# NOTES

1. The Advocates' Society, Letter to the Law Society of Upper Canada's Working Group on Alternative Business Structures, December 19, 2014, 2, http://www.lsuc.on.ca/uploaded Files/The%20Advocates'%20Society.pdf.
2. Ibid.
3. Ibid., 3.
4. Nicholas E. Gehl, Letter to the Law Society of Upper Canada's Working Group on Alternative Business Structures, December 9, 2014, 2, http://www.lsuc.on.ca/uploadedFiles/ GEHL,%20Nicholas.pdf.
5. Illinois State Bar Association, "Issues Paper Regarding Alternative Business Structures: Request for Comments," 3.
6. Ibid., 4.
7. International Association of Defense Counsel, "ABA Commission on the Future of Legal Services—Alternative Business Structures," 1.
8. Ibid., 2.
9. Ross, Letter to Katy Englehart, 2.
10. Richard M. Leslie, "Nonlawyer Ownership of Law Firms," May 1, 2016, http:// www.americanbar.org/content/dam/aba/images/office_president/richard_m_leslie_abs.pdf.
11. McLeish Orlando, "Submissions Regarding the Implementation of Alternative Business Structures in Ontario," December 17, 2014, 4, http://www.lsuc.on.ca/uploadedFiles/McLe ish%20Orlando.pdf.
12. Ibid., 5–6.
13. Ibid., 14.
14. Ibid., 15–16.
15. Ontario Bar Association, "Alternative Business Structures," 8.
16. Ibid.
17. Ontario Trial Lawyers Association, "Submission on Alternative Business Structures," 1.
18. Ibid., 19.
19. Women's Paralegal Association of Ontario, Letter to the Law Society of Upper Canada's Working Group on Alternative Business Structures, January 30, 2015, 2–3, http:// www.lsuc.on.ca/uploadedFiles/Womens%20Paralegal%20Association%20of%20Ontario.pdf.
20. Ibid., 3.
21. Ibid.
22. Bradley Wright, December 30, 2014 (6:28 pm), comment on Mitch Kowalski, "Anti-ABS Arguments Continue to Be Based on Emotion."
23. Ibid.
24. Bradley Wright, January 2nd, 2015 (4:45 pm), comment on Mitch Kowalski, "Anti-ABS Arguments Continue to Be Based on Emotion."
25. Bradley Wright, January 20, 2016 (8:00 pm), comment on Karen Dyck, "Innovating Regulation on the Prairies," *Slaw*, January 20, 2016, http://www.slaw.ca/2016/01/20/innovat ing-regulation-on-the-prairies/.
26. Laura Bellegie Sharp, "Comments Regarding the Alternative Business Solutions Issues Paper," April 28, 2016, 2, http://www.americanbar.org/content/dam/aba/images/office _president/laura_sharp_abs.pdf.
27. J. Richard Caldwell, Jr., "Report on 'Alternative Business Structures,'" April 29, 2016, http://www.americanbar.org/content/dam/aba/images/office_president/j_richard_caldwell _jr_abs.pdf.
28. New York State Bar Association, "New York State Bar Association's Comments," 7.
29. Perlman, "Towards the Law," 85.
30. Richmond, "Discussion Paper on Alternative Law Practice Structures," 3.
31. Ontario Trial Lawyers Association, "Submission on Alternative Business Structures," 1–2.
32. Lorne Berndt et al., 2.
33. Ibid., 3.

34. ABA Standing Committee on Legal Aid and Indigent Defendants, "Comments on Issues Paper on Alternative Business Structures," May 5, 2016, http://www.americanbar.org/content/dam/aba/images/office_president/legal_aid_and_indigent_defendants.pdf.

35. The County & District Law Presidents' Association, "CDLPA's Response to the Discussion Paper on Alternative Business Structures: The Voice of the Practising Lawyer in Ontario," n.d., 14, http://www.lsuc.on.ca/uploadedFiles/The%20County%20District%20Lawyers%20Presidents'%20Association%20(CDLPA).pdf.

36. Thunder Bay Law Association, "Submission to the Law Society of Upper Canada's Working Group on Alternative Business Structures," February 18, 2015, 1, http://www.lsuc.on.ca/uploadedFiles/thunder-bay-law-association.pdf.

37. Equity Advisory Group Working Group on Alternative Business Structures, Memo to the Law Society of Upper Canada's Working Group on Alternative Business Structures, January 21, 2015, 2, http://www.lsuc.on.ca/uploadedFiles/Equity%20Advisory%20Group%20Working%20Group%20on%20ABS.pdf.

38. Ontario Bar Association, "Alternative Business Structures," 8.

39. William M. Leech, "Comment: Issues Paper Regarding Alternative Business Structures April 8, 2016," May 2, 2016, http://www.americanbar.org/content/dam/aba/images/office_president/william_m_leech_abs.pdf.

40. Ontario Trial Lawyers Association, "Submission on Alternative Business Structures," 1, 9.

41. Ibid., 17.

42. Ibid., 35.

43. See, generally, Derek A. Denckla, "Nonlawyers and the Unauthorized Practice of Law: An Overview of the Legal and Ethical Parameters," *Fordham Law Review* 67 (1999): 2581–99, http://ir.lawnet.fordham.edu/cgi/viewcontent.cgi?article=3572andcontext=flr. See also Hadfield, "Innovating to Improve Access," 3–4.

44. Laurel S. Terry, "Putting the Legal Profession's Monopoly on the Practice of Law in a Global Context," *Fordham Law Review* 82 (2014): 2907, http://fordhamlawreview.org/assets/pdfs/Vol_82/No_6/Terry_May.pdf.

45. William D. Henderson, "A Blueprint for Change," *Pepperdine Law Review* 40 (2013): 461–507, 462, http://ssrn.com/abstract=2202823.

46. Michael Mills, "The Future of Legal Services: The American Bar Association Commission," *Neota Logic Blog*, April 13, 2015, http://www.neotalogic.com/news/the-future-of-legal-services.

47. Laura Snyder, "Does the UK Know Something We Don't About Alternative Business Structures?," *ABA Journal*, January 1, 2015, http://www.abajournal.com/magazine/article/does_the_uk_know_something_we_dont_about_alternative_business_structures.

48. See, for example, W. Bradley Wendel, "The Profession's Monopoly and Its Core Values," Forward to "Colloquium: The Legal Profession's Monopoly on the Practice of Law," *Fordham Law Review* 82 (2014): 2563–85, http://fordhamlawreview.org/assets/pdfs/Vol_82/No_6/Wendel_May.pdf; Deborah L. Rhode and Lucy Buford Ricca, "Protecting the Profession or the Public? Rethinking Unauthorized-Practice Enforcement," *Fordham Law Review* 82 (2014): 2587–610, http://fordhamlawreview.org/assets/pdfs/Vol_82/No_6/RhodeRicca_May.pdf; Laurel A. Rigertas, "The Legal Profession's Monopoly: Failing to Protect Consumers," *Fordham Law Review* 82 (2014): 2683–703, http://fordhamlawreview.org/assets/pdfs/Vol_82/No_6/Rigertas_May.pdf.

49. David M. Schraver, "Mandatory Reporting of Pro Bono Service and Contributions," 1.

50. "Pro Bono Reporting Requirements—Attorney Registration," New York State Unified Court System, last modified May 4, 2015, https://www.nycourts.gov/attorneys/probono/reportingreqs-intro.shtml#a.

51. Kirk Makin, "Access to Justice Becoming a Privilege of the Rich, Judge Warns," *The Globe and Mail*, February 10, 2011, http://www.theglobeandmail.com/news/national/access-to-justice-becoming-a-privilege-of-the-rich-judge-warns/article565873/.

## *Chapter Twenty-Four*

# Good Governance Requires . . . Actual Governance

Presumably all governments aspire to good governance. Going further, presumably the government of the United States—as well as the governments of each of the 50 states—do not just aspire to good governance, but take the concept very seriously. If this is the case, it is worth asking: What is good governance and why does it matter?

The United Nations Office of the High Commissioner for Human Rights explains the key attributes and the importance of good governance in this manner: The key attributes of good governance [are]:

- transparency
- responsibility
- accountability
- participation
- responsiveness (to the needs of the people)

> Good governance and human rights are mutually reinforcing. Human rights principles provide a set of values to guide the work of governments and other political and social actors. They also provide a set of performance standards against which these actors can be held accountable. Moreover, human rights principles inform the content of good governance efforts: they may inform the development of legislative frameworks, policies, programmes, budgetary allocations and other measures.
>
> On the other hand, without good governance, human rights cannot be respected and protected in a sustainable manner. The implementation of human rights relies on a conducive and enabling environment. This includes appropriate legal frameworks and institutions as well as political, managerial and administrative processes responsible for responding to the rights and needs of the population.[1]

Under the Agenda for Sustainable Development, the United States has committed—on the world stage—to "ensure equal access to justice for all" for its own citizens. Given the huge extent of unmet need for legal services in the country today—considered by some a human rights crisis—this is no small undertaking.

But that is not all. Also under the Agenda for Sustainable Development, the United States has recognized the importance of the institutions that are needed to fulfill the commitment of ensuring equal access to justice for all. That is why the United States has also committed to "develop effective, accountable and transparent institutions at all levels." In other words, the United States has committed to develop the governance that is needed in order for the country to be in a position to "ensure equal access to justice for all." In the United States today, the problem is not that there is bad governance of legal services—the problem is that there is little governance of legal services to speak of.

Laurel Terry has recommended that when the ABA wears its "quasi-regulator hat" that the ABA should "try to stand in the shoes of the regulators and develop well-balanced rules that properly take into account all of the competing interests."[2] However, the ABA is a professional association. The ABA is not a governing body, and it has neither the vocation (to serve the public interest in priority over the interests of its members) nor the resources (funding or expertise) to act as one. Any expectation—from inside or outside the association—that it fill the shoes of a governing body that "properly take into account all of the competing interests," let alone that it provide "good governance" in the meaning of the High Commissioner, is nonsensical. This is not a criticism of the ABA, of its actual vocation, or of its access to resources. This is simple reality. It simply cannot be done by a professional or trade association of any kind, and any attempt to do so is doomed to failure. In this case, the failure is evidenced by the 80 percent of low-income persons as well as many of moderate incomes who are unable to access the legal services that they need, and by the World Justice Project Rule of Law Index's ranking of the United States as 65th out of 102 countries as regards the question of affordable and accessible civil justice (again, a rank that places the United States behind Russia, Ukraine, and Kyrgyzstan).

While this is not a criticism of the ABA, it is a criticism of the competent governing bodies. To the extent there is an expectation that the ABA attempt to fill the shoes of one or more governing bodies, it is because those bodies have left those shoes unfilled—that is, they have abdicated—they have defaulted on their obligations not just to provide good governance, but to provide any governance at all.[3] If the United States is to have any chance to come close to meeting its commitment to "ensure equal access to justice for all," this abdication must end.

The United States needs a new regulatory framework for legal services. Mere tweaks to the existing framework will not suffice—an entirely new framework is needed. The new framework must go far beyond the simple regulation of lawyers as individuals—it must regulate legal services as a whole, by anyone that may provide them—lawyers, yes, but also nonlawyers, be they organizations or individuals. This is a massive undertaking, at the beginning in order to develop and implement the new framework, and then on an ongoing basis in order to ensure regulatory oversight.

The ABA—let alone state and local bar associations or other groups of practicing lawyers—are not and never will be positioned to do this, whether acting individually or collectively. A de facto (or quasi) regulator whose primary mandate is to act in the interests of certain members of a professional association cannot do this job—it must be done by a de jure (a true) governing body whose primary mandate is to act in the public interest. A professional association with a limited treasury and access only to legal expertise cannot do this job—it must be done by a true governing body that can marshal a far larger budget as well as a far larger range of expertise (economic policy, human rights, competition, consumer affairs). Who is the right governing body? It isn't clear.

The Agenda for Sustainable Development might suggest an answer. Neither the ABA nor any state or local bar association makes any commitments under this document. No state supreme court makes any commitments under this document. No state executive or legislative branch makes any commitments under this document. The commitments under this document are made by the "Heads of State and Government," including that of the United States. That is who has promised, by 2030, both to "ensure equal access to justice for all" and to "develop effective, accountable and transparent institutions at all levels" for that purpose. Is that where the responsibility for a new regulatory framework lies? And is the responsibility far greater than simply appropriating more or less money for legal aid?[4]

## NOTES

1. "Good Governance and Human Rights," Office of the High Commissioner for Human Rights, accessed August 25, 2015, http://www.ohchr.org/EN/Issues/Development/GoodGovernance/Pages/GoodGovernanceIndex.aspx.

2. Laurel S. Terry, "Globalization and the ABA Commission on Ethics 20/20," 118.

3. Again, Benjamin Barton provides a detailed and interesting analysis of the extent to which state supreme courts abdicate their regulatory power and the multiple motivations they have to do so: Barton, "An Institutional Analysis," 1167–250.

4. Hadfield and Rhode argue in favor of a single, national licensing authority for entities combined with state-based regulatory powers, notably with respect to lawyers as individuals. Hadfield and Rhode, "How to Regulate Legal Services," 40–48.

*Part V*

# Stories

Most discussions of alternative structures, including the one in the first four parts of this book, could be described as theoretical, general, or academic. The purpose of part V is to bring alternative structures into the realm of the concrete, the specific, and the entirely real. Over the course of 2014 through mid-2016, I conducted interviews with over 60 people, including persons who have created, are managing, are employees of, and/or have invested in alternative or nontraditional legal service providers in England and Wales, Australia, and the District of Columbia and Canada, as well as the people who regulate them. In addition, I interviewed a person who has closely studied alternative structures that existed in the United States a century ago, as well as an advisor to plaintiff law firms in the United States today.

Taken as a whole, these interviews—the stories they tell—provide insight into the breadth and depth of alternative and nontraditional structures that exist outside the 50 states, how and why those structures were created, the services they provide, the challenges they face, what it is like to work for them, and what it is like to regulate them. In essence, the interviews bring alternative structures alive.

The interviews are grouped into categories, but given their breadth and depth, this was difficult to do—many could fall into several categories, whereas others are in a category of their own. For each category, one interview, in excerpt form, was selected to appear in this book. Full redacted versions of all the interviews are available online at www.notjustforlawyers.com.

For more information about the stories, please see “The Story Behind the Stories” at the end of the this chapter. The appendix to this book contains a full listing of all the stories that are available online.

## *Chapter Twenty-Five*

# Letting the Old Lady Scream

USING BUSINESS AND IT PROCESSES TO INCREASE EFFICIENCY AND REDUCE COSTS

Many alternative structures have developed and implemented business and IT processes to increase efficiency and reduce costs. The alternative structures of this category have done this in order to serve a large number of individual clients, in most cases also by deepening their areas of specialization and offering the services at affordable, often fixed prices.

### Tom Curran, CEO, Kings Court Trust

UK-based Kings Court Trust (KCT) is a probate service assisting families through the probate process upon the death of a loved one. It operates on a volume model supported by online platforms. KCT is owned, in part, by private equity firm Smedvig Capital. In the excerpt below, Curran, who is not a lawyer, briefly describes the company's founding, its case management system, and its lawyers' role in that system:

> KCT was founded in 2002 by a very farsighted lawyer and accountant who knew that the changes to the UK regulations to permit non-lawyer ownership of law firms were coming. They asked themselves, if they were going to set up a probate and estate administration business on a blank sheet of paper, how would they do it? The answer was using fixed fees and transparent service delivery, two of the foundations upon which KCT is built. KCT eventually became an ABS in 2012, when the regulatory changes finally came into effect.
>
> KCT is a business that uses the expertise of lawyers. We are not legal experts who are trying to run a business.
>
> This is how we work: we assign a case manager to each case. This person is not a lawyer, this person is essentially a project manager. They have two

jobs—to make sure that each case is handled effectively and efficiently, and to handle communications with the client. Lawyers are our technical experts—our case managers seek the advice of the lawyers on their cases.

As a result of this model, our lawyers see a huge number of probate cases. The experience that our lawyers get here, in terms of variation, volume, breadth, and complexity sets them apart from general practitioners, who, because they do a little bit of everything, can't necessarily develop the same level of expertise in any one kind of matter.

To be clear, we do not expect our lawyers to bring in business—they are not evaluated, promoted or compensated in any way on that basis. That is not their job—we have sales and marketing people whose job it is to bring in business. Our legal positions are easy to fill as there is an awareness that the market is moving in this direction, and there is a lot of openness towards businesses like ours.

## BUSINESS OUTSOURCING

Like the alternative structures featured above, the alternative structures of this category have also developed and implemented business and IT processes to increase efficiency and reduce costs. However, they have done so in order to offer a greater variety of services to corporate rather than to individual clients.

### Alexander Hamilton, CEO, Radiant Law

UK-based ABS Radiant Law combines legal service outsourcing with contract negotiation and dispute resolution for larger commercial contracts. It uses bespoke technology and processes to improve contracting processes and shorten sales cycles for companies with large volumes of commercial contracts. Radiant's non-executive chair (and a minority shareholder) is Greg Tufnell, who is not a lawyer. In the excerpt below, Hamilton explains the reasons for the creation of Radiant Law, how it differs from traditional commercial law firms, and why it became an ABS:

I was partner at Latham and increasingly frustrated by the gap that I perceived between what clients needed from us and what I was actually able to do in that environment. I ended up writing a memo for the executive committee of Latham and Watkins.[1] In the memo, I gave my analysis of the market and what changes were coming, and described the things that I thought Latham and Watkins could benefit from doing. That memo did not go anywhere, and I look back at my hopes for engagement as wonderfully naive!

I had never really thought of starting a law firm, but I ended up in a conversation with a friend of mine in New York about setting up their London branch. While that did not work out, it planted the idea in my head that you could actually set up a law firm. As I looked around the market and talked to people, I realized that the issues I raised in the memo were not Latham and Watkins issues; they were market-wide issues.

So there we were: five transactional, outsourcing tech lawyers. Our basic premise at the beginning was that clients want the judgment calls and the experience, so we would just be senior lawyers. We sent our junior work to an LPO [legal process outsourcer]. We progressively used technology, not just off-the-shelf systems, but also those we developed for ourselves.

We got rid of timesheets and billable hours, not just because clients were asking for fixed pricing, but also to allow us to completely re-engineer how we did things. It allowed us to focus on what clients need rather than our need to churn out hours.

All this set us on a journey that we are still on. We restructured ourselves as a real company with a CEO and executive positions, moved to salaries and bonuses instead of the traditional model of pulling money out at the end of the year. And we clarified our vision and strategy, with an absolute focus on creating business value by helping companies create great relationships through their commercial contracts. That simplification and clarification—of structure, of roles, of mission—became liberating, because it became obvious what we needed to do next.

We became an ABS in May, 2014. This permitted us to bring in Greg Tufnell as our non-executive Chairman. Greg used to run retail fashion companies. He brings with him an approach that you don't see in law. In the fashion world, you are massively exposed to reality in a way that lawyers generally try to avoid. He has brought us rigor, business acumen, financial know-how, and overall knowledge on how to run a company and the discipline to do it.

Our clients are multinational companies. We have a lot of work outside the UK, including with many US-based clients. We as a firm only practice English law, but around the world, a contract is a contract. Our clients' in-house counsel will take a view as to whether local legal advice is required. Fundamentally, what we do can be boiled down to rules, and those rules can be reviewed by local lawyers.

What makes us competitive is our combination of legal judgment calls with technology, design and better processes. We are open to external ideas, wherever they may come from, notably outside the legal profession. The fact that we are outside the traditional partnership model is an advantage—we don't have to worry about bringing people along, slow decision making, or technology laggards. We have freedom to experiment and we don't have management that operates in fear of big rainmakers. We have an open culture where everyone gets to improve the way of doing things, but we do have a way of doing things—the Radiant Way. That is unusual in a law firm, where trainee lawyers have to learn to be actors, and do things differently for each partner.

Clients need help in ways that have not been available before. Law firms have left a huge space in managed legal services, so we expect to grow a lot. The growth will come by producing more products, tools and approaches, we'll open in other countries, and we'll grow in size. And we will at some point look for outside investment in order to really fuel growth.

## ADOPTING A CORPORATE STRUCTURE TO FOSTER GROWTH

Some law firms have adopted a corporate structure and became an ABS (England and Wales) or ILP (Australia) in order to foster the growth of the firm, notably by introducing professional management and raising and retaining capital for investment.

### John Kain, Managing Director, Kain C+C

Based in Adelaide, Australia, Kain Corporate + Commercial Lawyers (Kain C+C) is a legal consulting company that specializes in complex transactions, disputes, and advice. Kain C+C has adopted a corporate structure; two of its three board members are not lawyers. In the excerpt below, Kain explains the reasons the firm adopted a corporate structure and what the structure has meant for the firm:

> I started Kain C+C about ten years ago. The firm is an incorporated legal practice. From the beginning it has been run under a corporate, rather than a partnership, model. The company has four shareholders, each holding different shareholding proportions. We are currently exploring a broader employee share plan.
>
> We have a clear distinction between the shareholders, the Board and the management, and their respective roles. Our shareholders' agreement mandates that our Board must have an independent Chair and at least half of our Board as independent Directors. Independent means no financial interest in the business and not an employee of the business.
>
> We have a Board of three, plus me as MD. The Chair used to be the CEO of another law firm; today he is the Executive Director of an accounting and commercial advisory practice. The second Board member is the Executive Director of a large advertising firm, and the third Board member is an internal appointment.
>
> Our commitment to a corporate model allows us to ensure (i) that decisions are made in the best interests of the business, and not the interests of the individual owners, and (ii) that the right people are appointed into the right positions. Both of these outcomes are difficult to achieve in the partnership model, where too often decisions are weighted toward the interests of the individual partners rather than the interests of the business, and where standards gravitate to the lowest common denominator.
>
> In my view, a true legal services company (as distinct from a firm) has three key elements: (i) it is an incorporated company, (ii) it has a corporate governance structure, and (iii) it has a corporate management structure. There are countless incorporated legal practices in Australia—but they are not true legal services companies because the governance and management structures are still partnerships in nature. Some have an external Chair, but the decision making still fundamentally resides with the partners. That is not the case with Kain C+C. Outside of the few powers reserved for the shareholders, all decision making rests with an independent Board appointed on merit, not because

they are owners—that is a corporate governance model. Our Board has the power to hire and fire and set remuneration, even for shareholders—and has exercised that power—that is a corporate management model. You will see these three elements in the listed legal companies in Australia, but to our knowledge, our structure is unique among unlisted Australian law firms.

I think this has placed us in good stead. We can objectively look at business and the world around us. On the whole, we have got the big decisions right and we have executed them reasonably well. I put much of that down to the objectivity that comes from having an independent Board, and to the ability to appoint the right people with the rights skills, to every position in the business. All appointments are made on merit which helps us, indirectly, to better serve our clients.

Our structure allows our lawyers to do what they are good at, without requiring them to do things they are not good at. A common weakness of legal businesses is that responsibility for key management decisions is divvied up amongst the lawyers. For example a lawyer is put in charge of IT because they are interested in IT, even though they might be shockingly bad at implementing it. Because we have disassociated management from the technical legal services, lawyers can focus on providing legal services and not need to worry about the other things.

We believe that our structure offers us a competitive advantage. For example, a number of our team were equity partners in traditional law firms who were motivated to join us because of the failings they saw in the partnership structure, and we were one of the very few places that offered them a different structure. Being clear on how we operate and what we stand for is vital. This becomes self-selecting—people with a similar view of the world are attracted to us; those who don't select themselves out.

At the end of the day, it does not matter who owns a legal business. A legal business does not need to be owned by a specific kind of person in order for the ethical behavior of that firm to be regulated. It is entirely possible to regulate ethics and standards without regulating ownership.

## HOLISTIC SERVICES

Legal issues rarely exist in a vacuum, separate from other, nonlegal issues. For this reason, a number of alternative structures seek to assist clients with the totality of a given situation, not just its legal aspects.

### Christopher Mills, Partner and COO, Schillings

Before acquiring ABS status in 2013, Schillings operated as a traditional law firm, specializing in privacy and defamation and family law. Upon acquiring ABS status, Schillings integrated a cyber-security business and recruited risk management professionals from the management consulting world, transforming itself into a reputation and privacy multidisciplinary practice combining legal services with intelligence gathering, risk consulting, and cyber security. In the excerpt below, Mills, who is not a lawyer, explains the importance of the ABS structure for the firm's transformation and growth:

> 2007 was a great year for Schillings. But by 2008, everything had changed. Before, there were a small number of players, everything was in print, and issues rarely expanded outside the borders of the UK. Today, the market is diluted with many new entrants, everything moves very quickly and nothing stays within borders.
>
> We could have stayed a traditional law firm, but opportunities for growth were limited. We could have diversified into other legal sectors, but we did not see a future with that either, because the market is saturated. In the end, the best option we saw was to stick with our core competency of reputation, privacy and family law, but to add non-legal, or what we call "extra-legal" services. So, knowing that the new rules would soon come into effect, we bought a cyber-security business, and, as soon as we could, we combined it with our legal practice into one entity.
>
> As an ABS, we have transformed our business. Today we are international consultants specialising in defending reputation and protecting privacy, as well as international family law. Our professional staff includes lawyers as well as intelligence analysts, risk consultants and cyber security specialists. We are the only business in the world to complement a reputation, privacy and family legal offering with intelligence gathering, risk consulting and cyber security. No other single provider groups these legal and non-legal services together the way we do—typically clients need to work with three or four other organizations to get the same services. Compared to that, we are able to provide both a higher quality as well as seamless service to our clients.
>
> Our status as an ABS allows us to do much more than we could if we were not an ABS. It allows us to help our clients in the ways that they really need help. Although we are more than law, law is still important to who we are, in fact it's our USP because we bring legal rigour and legal privilege that other non-legal providers can't.
>
> Our clients are international businesses and high net-worth individuals. What defines them is that they are global citizens. They have activities and assets in a number of countries, which may or may not include the UK. Our non-legal services are not bound by jurisdiction.
>
> More specifically regarding our individual clients—their main country of residence could be anywhere in the world, and at any given moment, they could be anywhere else in the world: Americas, Far East, Middle East. They are some of the world's most successful individuals, and our work is geared around their private lives.
>
> Currently, I am one of two non-lawyer partners in the firm. The second person is Major General Tim Robinson, who served in the British Army. He brings a highly strategic approach to crisis management and prevention. We are planning that by the end of 2016, we will have a total of seven partners who are lawyers and four partners who are not lawyers (their backgrounds will be in intelligence, risk consulting and/or cyber security). This reflects the diversity of our business. It also reflects where our business is going—the revenue generated by our non-legal staff is growing very quickly, and we

expect that soon it will equally match the revenue generated by our legal staff. Our partners are our principal client-facing people. They do not all need to be lawyers. They do all need to be problem-solvers.

In the old days, the partners did client work, business development, supervision, and firm management. Today, many firms have woken up to the fact that you need to bring in experienced, qualified professionals to run areas like finance, marketing, operations—if you want to run a professional organization, those are not just things that you do after-hours or on the weekend. In a corporation, the question would not even be asked—you would naturally have qualified persons with business skills and experience who know how to run a business. The ability to offer partnership to non-lawyers is important in recruiting and retaining the best people. You have to be able to motivate them and reward them. If you want to grow the business, it is important to give them skin in the game.

Since we became an ABS, our revenue has doubled, and we project that over the next few years our revenue will double again. Our explanation for this is that our ABS allows us to think differently and to offer more services. Our ABS also allows us to be what our clients want us to be—able to provide intelligence, cyber, advisory and legal services seamlessly and without being limited by jurisdiction.

## DISPERSED LAW FIRMS

In England and Wales and Australia, alternative structures have been used to create "dispersed" law firms to serve corporate clients. For lawyers, these models offer flexibility with respect to workload, type of work, type of client, and place of work. For corporate clients, these models offer flexibility with respect to headcount, access to specific areas of subject matter expertise, and pricing.

### Ken Jagger, CEO, AdventBalance

Australia-based ILP AdventBalance provides "insourced" lawyers to corporate clients on a fixed-fee basis. In the excerpt below, Jagger explains the advantages of AventBalance's "insourced" model for clients as well as lawyers, and how a corporate structure facilitates it:

My background is as a partner with one of the larger firms in Australia, Freehills, which is now Herbert Smith Freehills. When I was with Freehills, it occurred to me that there are many lawyers who enjoyed working more flexibly. Also, we sent a lot of lawyers on secondment—where our lawyers went to work in the premises of our clients' business. Our lawyers learned a lot and the clients loved it as they got switched on people who really understood their business. The only people who didn't enjoy it were us, the partners of the law firm. We felt we were losing money as we couldn't charge as much for the seconded lawyers and there was a significant risk that the lawyers that we had trained would take up permanent employment with our clients.

I realized that there was a business opportunity with this type of arrangement, but that it needed to be done from a different structure. It couldn't be done from a traditional partnership structure where it was all about the hourly rates. This could succeed only if it were done in a totally different way.

This is what makes our regulations in Australia important. It allows us to set up a corporate structure and not a partnership, and to run it on corporate principles.

What is great about what we do is that it allows the new generation of lawyers to work differently. They no longer are obliged to go to a law firm, where they work for many years 10, 12, 14 hours a day, seven days a week, with the holy grail of partnership at the end of it. We allow lawyers to work in a different way, and also give clients what they want.

There are a variety of reasons why our clients can need a lawyer on a temporary basis—to fill a gap when a member of the legal department needs to focus on a specific project or is on leave of absence, to meet an increase in workload due to specific projects, to provide special expertise for a specific project, or when a company simply needs a more flexible labor force and isn't ready to hire a lawyer for a permanent position.

The reason it works is because we keep our overheads very low. In our offices, we have just a small number of management and administrative staff. Our lawyers work at our clients' premises. By keeping our overheads low, we are able to pay our lawyers what they would have earned if they had stayed with a traditional law firm.

We have a Board of six people, including the Chair. We run Advent Balance as a company, not as a partnership.

We have 13 shareholders—just five are involved in the operation of the business. All of our shareholders are individuals. Some of them are lawyers, but many of them are not. Those that are not have some connection to law, for example they studied law but now work in other fields. The fact that they have a connection of some kind to law has helped them to understand the business, and to be comfortable as in investor in it. They have also been encouraged by the success of other legal companies, like Slater and Gordon, and Axiom in the US, and they've seen a lot of potential for investment in the legal sector.

We have about 140 lawyers. Being an AdventBalance lawyer isn't for everyone though—our lawyers are put into new situations every three, six, nine months—it's like starting a new job each time, and there is uncertainty. Some people like moving around and having new challenges like that, but some do not.

What our lawyers like is the flexibility. They can work on a project for those three, six, nine months, and then take time off without being afraid of losing their jobs or being set back in their careers. They also like the variety—for example, on one project they will work in a bank and then on the next one they will work in an oil and gas company.

While we have lawyers of all ages and lengths of experience, our typical lawyer is in their 30s and early 40s, with about 12 to 15 years' experience. They will have worked at top tier law firms. They are at that stage of life where they want or need to work flexibly, and they do not want to work all hours of the day and night.

We give our clients a fixed price per day. But the day is not from 7 am to 10 pm—it is a sensible length—that is the deal we make with the client. Our lawyers can maintain a work life balance. That is what attracts lawyers in their 30s and 40s to us.

Companies today are so conscious of their law firms' costs that they give them very small pieces of information, and ask them to work on very discreet tasks. In contrast, our lawyers are able to get to know the client and understand its objectives in a way that an external lawyer never could.

To get the lawyers we want, we have to pay market salary. Lawyers want the flexibility, but they are not willing to sacrifice salary for it. By stripping out the overhead, we are able to charge the client less than what they would have paid to a traditional firm. But even more important for the client is the price certainty. Clients like that we charge them a fixed price, and that, unlike with hourly billing, there are no surprises when they receive our invoices.

Since we do not bill by the hour, we do not evaluate our lawyers based on the number of hours they bill. We evaluate our lawyers entirely based on the feedback we get from the client, and how happy the client was with the lawyer's service. Our lawyers like this a lot—no timesheets, no worries about billing 2000 hours a year.

## TURNING EMPLOYEES INTO OWNERS

Certain ABSs in England and Wales have made a point of either creating an employee share scheme or offering partnership to nonlawyers, with the expectation that such schemes and partnership will work to inspire and motivate their employees in ways that the mere payment of salary cannot.

### David Simon, Chair, Triton Global

Triton Global integrates insurance claims administration, legal defense and representation, and claim investigation and adjusting for professional indemnity insurers and policyholders. As an ABS, Triton Global was the first legal services provider to offer employee share ownership, and to become a member of the UK Employee Ownership Association. In the excerpt below, Simon explains how since becoming an ABS the company and its clients have benefited from the company's employee share scheme:

> In the UK, we offer to our insurer clients a "one-stop-shop" for handling their claims work: legal, claims management and loss adjustment. We have also been able to create a team to provide world-wide audit and inspection services for our insurance client base. Before the Legal Services Act, those services had to be offered separately, through different entities. Now we have lawyers, loss adjusters and insurance professionals all working together to produce a single integrated product

We thought that it's nonsense for insurers to buy three lots of services. Why can't they, if they want to, get all their claims management services from one place? Our clients love it—they like the fact that they can come to the same place for their claims defense work, and that they can negotiate to have it all handled for one, predictable fixed price over a long term basis. With us, insurers no longer feel like they are writing blank checks to have their claims management work done. Insurers no longer have to hope that the cost of defending claims will not exceed the amount of the premiums they collect.

In creating the ABS, we have become something very different than we were before. We pooled the three existing businesses, including the law firm, into one company, and eliminated the partnership structure in favor of a corporate structure, with a Chief Executive. I was nervous about it—I'd been self-employed for over 40 years and then I became an employee. For our lawyers, we decided to keep the title of Partner because that is what the market, and notably the law firms we service as policyholders, recognizes as what the most important lawyers are called.

What we are most excited about with the ABS structure is the possibility to offer to our staff a stake in the business. Before ABSs, only lawyers could have ownership of a law firm. With an ABS, we can offer share ownership to all of our staff, not just the lawyers. We believe that this is a very important way to inspire and motivate our employees, and research shows that it results in significant improvement in employee productivity and retention. We've even become a member of the Employee Ownership Association. Another reason to be happy about this is—what do you do when you retire? Law firm partners don't have anything to sell when they retire—with an ABS, you have something you can sell.

Another benefit of becoming an ABS is that it permits us to demonstrate to clients that we are a well-managed, stable business, that we can make decisions faster than a traditional law firm, and that we are not held hostage to a handful of prima donnas. Our clients have responded very favorably to this—some have asked us why we did not do it sooner.

For the future, we see the form of ABS as a growth mechanism for us. It will permit us to bring in external investors (if we wish to), to expand our overseas operations, and to attract like-minded, progressive thinking lawyers and insurance professionals.

The legal profession, not just in the UK but everywhere, is facing problems that are two faces of the same coin: declining profitability and a large number of law graduates who cannot find jobs. The ABS model offers a way to address those problems. And the days of amateur management are over.

## OPPOSITES ATTRACT? LAW, CHARITY, AND FREE LEGAL SERVICES

For many, free legal services is an oxymoron, and law and charity are not an obvious pairing. Looking deeper, it becomes evident that they can be, in a variety of contexts, and not only in the present day, but also in the past.

## Luke Geary, Managing Partner, Salvos Legal and Salvos Legal Humanitarian

Salvos Legal is a not-for-profit law firm that provides commercial and property services to corporations, government agencies, and not-for-profits. The fees collected by Salvos Legal, less expenses, are used to fund Salvos Legal Humanitarian.

Salvos Legal Humanitarian is a full-service law firm that provides services to the "disadvantaged and marginalized" in family law, housing, social security, migration and refugee matters, debt, criminal law, and other areas. The services of Salvos Legal Humanitarian are offered free of charge; the firm has a staff of lawyers whose salaries are paid from the funding of Salvos Legal. In the excerpt below, Geary explains the firms' relationship to the Salvation Army and the challenges the firms faced to establish themselves:

> Both Salvos Legal and Salvos Legal Humanitarian are wholly owned by The Salvation Army and the two companies have the same Board of Directors. I am one of the six Directors on each Board, and the only lawyer—four Directors are trustees of The Salvation Army, and the sixth is a retired Salvation Army Officer.
>
> Both Salvos Legal and Salvos Legal Humanitarian are not-for-profit law firms. The reason for their existence is to serve people in need. They are an expression of the social work of The Salvation Army, in a justice sense.
>
> Our nonlawyer Directors have fiduciary obligations to the companies and to The Salvation Army itself. They have no motivation to cause either company to act in an unethical manner. At any rate, the nonlawyer Directors defer to me on legal issues.
>
> That being said, there are many aspects of running a law firm that lawyers are not necessarily gifted in, or are not exclusively gifted in. The Directors of the two companies are senior executives running a major public organization, and Salvos Legal and Salvos Legal Humanitarian are businesses. In addition, The Salvation Army requires them to conform to a code of conduct.
>
> Salvos Legal Humanitarian, to date, has provided free legal assistance on 16,000 matters, at no cost either to the government or to The Salvation Army. That's 16,000 cases of access to justice that otherwise would not exist. And that number goes up with each passing day.
>
> I think that there are lawyers in other countries who would like to do what we are doing at Salvos Legal, and there will probably also be those who would see Salvos lawyers as second class lawyers. They might think that if you are worth a million dollars, then you go and get a million dollars—you do not sell yourself short for a community service.
>
> When Salvos Legal first pitched for commercial work, we faced questions about whether or not we were serious. And our lawyers faced similar questions—whether they had what it takes to work in a "real" law firm environment.
>
> We overcame the preconceptions against us by attracting "one big fish," which was one of the largest banks in Australia. Once we had one big client

who recognized that this was something they wanted to do with their legal work that meant that the next big client would not be so nervous. Since they knew that the Commonwealth Bank of Australia had taken that leap, they felt that they could as well. And the third client was even easier, and so on. And now that conception of us no longer exists.

At Salvos Legal, we are showing that it is possible to create opportunities to provide community service, but still maintain your professionalism and the quality of your work. We are not a $2 law firm out in the suburbs.

There is a significant problem with access to justice. An important reason for this is that the legal profession has typically not been open to doing things differently, has not been open to creativity. If you want change, then you have to be creative. Or, at a minimum, don't stop those who are.

## LAW SCHOOL: ALTERNATIVE STRUCTURE AS AN EDUCATIONAL PROGRAM AND CENTER FOR RESEARCH AND EXPERIMENTATION

Like the structures profiled immediately above, the structure profiled below also combines legal services with a charitable mission. But it does so in a different environment: a law school.

### Jenny Holloway, Associate Dean, Nottingham Law School and Nick Johnson, Pro Bono Director, Nottingham Law School Legal Advice Centre

Nottingham Law School Legal Advice Centre is a program of the Nottingham Law School. It offers free legal advice and assistance in the areas of employment, business law, housing, property and environmental law, debt and welfare rights, and tribunal and court representation. The services are offered through students of the law school, who work under the supervision of qualified solicitors. The Centre received an ABS license in October 2015. In the excerpt below, Holloway and Johnson explain why the Centre sought an ABS license and the benefits the license provides:

> The Legal Advice Centre was founded in 2006. Our new status as an ABS has permitted us to establish a legal status separate from the university.
>
> The Centre serves both individuals and businesses. About 50 percent of the work we do is in employment. We also do a lot of work in housing, as well as property and environmental law. The other areas we cover are welfare, debt, contracts, and some intellectual property. All of these services are provided pro bono (free of charge).
>
> Our principal purpose is to provide experience for our students. Of course an additional purpose is to help the community.
>
> Before we obtained ABS status, we could not perform or charge for any of the six reserved activities, which meant that our services with respect to litiga-

tion were limited to employment and social security tribunals. With our newly acquired ABS status, we can do more types of litigation.

In the past year, we've handled about 170 cases. Most of those are cases that can be resolved relatively quickly—on a student schedule—but some, such as miscarriage of justice cases, take a few years to resolve.

Our clients come from a variety of sources—from our website, from referrals from local volunteer agencies. Some of our clients are students and members of the university staff. Most of our clients are local to Nottinghamshire County, but some come from other places in the country. We find that the unmet need for legal services is so high we do not have to do much for clients to find us.

We offer an outreach service at community centres, where people can come in to talk to us about their cases. We try to provide some preliminary advice on the spot and then follow up with them later by phone or in-person appointments.

[The] ABS structure offer[s] us a number of additional advantages:

To begin, [it] permit[s] us to offer a wider range of services, and be able to charge for some of them.

The Centre is an expensive facility for the law school to run. Much of the work that we do now will continue to be pro bono. But, as an ABS, we can also offer additional services, such as to entrepreneurs, start-ups and small businesses, for a fee but at below market rates. These types of clients don't have the funds to pay full market rates for legal services, but they are able to pay something. We see a huge unmet need in this area—we want to fill the gap. In addition, many of our students are studying and intend to practice commercial law—this will give them practical experience in that area, and with that an advantage over other students.

In this manner, the fee-paying work subsidizes the pro bono work.

[As] an ABS, we believe we'll have more flexibility in how we work with third parties, and notably with external legal providers. It will be easier for work to be referred to us and that will lead to an expansion in the services we offer. Also, universities are large organizations and negotiating deals can be a slow process—as a smaller organization we'll be more nimble—we'll be able to act more quickly.

As a university, we have had subsidiaries before, for example a cancer research center, and a conference center, each of which are separate entities. When a university wants to do something that is different from the usual activities of a university, it is better to set up a separate structure rather than trying to muddle through with the university's larger structure, trying to do things that a university doesn't do. It delineates the activities and gives them commercial freedom—both are very useful. In this context, the ABS structure fits us very well.

The Centre is all about access to justice. The legal profession resists changes that offer the possibility to improve access to justice. It resists the unbundling of legal services. It resists outside investment that might reduce the cost of providing legal services. We need more entrepreneurial models in legal services—entrepreneurial models that take advantage of the huge opportunities that technology offers.

The Centre is small. As we mentioned, last year we handled about 170 cases. Some legal aid centers handle several thousand cases in a year—it will take us a long time to get up to that number. We can't be a substitute for a comprehensive publicly funded legal service—which we no longer have in this country anyway. The Centre cannot singlehandedly make a significant improvement in the access to justice problem in the UK—we cannot plug the hole. On the other hand, we can reduce the flow—that is, we can reduce the problem.

Another thing that we do is give our students an education in access to justice—we help them to understand the difficulties in providing access to justice, and how lawyers fit into that picture. The Centre provides access to justice through student training, through looking at the culture of legal services and how doing good fits into it.

There is one way in which, with an ABS structure, we may be able to significantly alter the legal landscape: We can become a research establishment, experimenting with different ways of providing legal services. Like other university departments that research developments in science, we can research and develop new methods of delivering legal services and access to justice that could be exploited commercially later on. Universities do that—they develop things, and the good ideas are used by the rest of society, and help people in that way. For example, what about a short module on how to conduct your own litigation, that is available to people for a fee, like car mechanics classes? Why not experiment with ideas like that?

## IN-HOUSE LEGAL AS SOURCE OF REVENUE

In-house legal departments in both the private and the public sector can develop knowledge and expertise that are difficult for external law firms to match. Some of those in-house legal departments are capitalizing on that knowledge and expertise by creating alternative structures and using those structures to expand their client base. In doing so, they are able to serve clients that, in some cases, are poorly served by traditional law firms. In all cases, the in-house legal department is no longer perceived merely as a source of expenditure, but as a source of revenue.

### Archana Makol, Director, BT Law Ltd.

BT Law Ltd. is a wholly owned BT group company. Acquiring ABS status in March 2013, BT Law draws upon the expertise and resources of its in-house legal department to provide legal and claims handling services to external corporate clients, in the areas of motor claims, public liability, employers' liability, and employment law. In the excerpt below, Makol, who is both director of BT Law and chief counsel at BT, explains why BT Law sought an ABS license and how BT Law works within the larger BT organization:

Just under 20 years ago BT began collecting all its volume claims handling work into one location. There was no need for that location to be in a high-cost hub like London, so Sheffield, a town in northern England was chosen. Initially the focus was on handling BT's own property damage claim work: how can we develop a process and technology for it? How can we be sure that we claim the monies owed to us rather than let it leak through poor processes? Over a period of 10 years, we enlarged the scope of that work to include third party claims to the business, employee injury claims, and eventually motor vehicle claims. BT was not completely happy with the service it was receiving from external service providers, and so it brought all of that work in-house. At the same time, our employment law team was developing its practice based in the Midlands and London.

When an in-house department builds this kind of service, it does not do it with profit in mind. It builds it on the basis that everyone wants more for less, so you must be efficient, you must have well-managed work flows and you must understand the data and trends.

The brand of our business is critical. Regardless of whether a claim is big or small, the people handling the claim are the face of the business, and they need to take care. This does not mean an open checkbook—to the contrary. It means handling each claim with the bigger picture in mind. It means being firm, but also decent and polite, it means taking a customer service approach, it means keeping a lookout for fraudulent claims. Those are not things that our external service providers—including some external lawyers—necessarily did, or did well.

Even though the Legal Services Act was not adopted until 2007, we had known for some time that changes were afoot. Indeed, we, as an in-house team, had been approached a few times and asked to act for other companies. At the end of a case, some opponents had come to us and asked, "Would you do that for us next time?" I believe they saw that we handled claims in a clean and fair manner, and that we did what we said we would do, when we said we would do it. It was flattering to be asked but of course we couldn't represent them. As in-house counsel, we could only act on behalf of our employer.

But it got us thinking. We started to improve our processes even further, with the possibility of one day offering it to external clients. There are ways you can work in-house that need to be refined for external clients. For example, we reviewed how we managed money, our business continuity plans, and our IT. It was quite a wait from 2007 when the Legal Services Act was passed until 2012 when the first ABSs were authorized. That gave us time to get our act together.

What has been key for us has been the ability to offer a genuine cradle to grave service to all of our clients, in-house and external. We aim to have the same person handle a claim from the time the incident occurs right up to the Court of Appeal if necessary. This is more efficient than having a claim change hands at several points as it progresses, and it gives our team the ability to track trends. In order to be able to offer this to others as a legal service including litigation, we needed an ABS license.

BT Law is operated under a secondment model. BT Law does not have any of its own employees—all its work is carried out by BT Legal (BT plc) employees and using the resources of BT Legal. It is a complex model, but it provides us with a lot of flexibility. It allows us to take a more credible and cautious approach.

We want to work for businesses who share our values. Notably, we want to work for businesses who understand the importance of brand and the wider ramifications of their claims handling practice, and who also need to bring their costs down. When a client comes to us, they get the benefits of an in-house team without having to build an in-house team. We have a real understanding of brand and of business process. Because of that understanding, we handle cases differently than many other practices would.

We ring fence the work we do for non-BT clients, to ensure we comply with our regulation and keep their information confidential. Client money is handled separately in accordance with the rules. At times a lawyer wears the hat of a BT Legal lawyer and at other times the hat of a BT Law lawyer. At first I thought it would be a nightmare to organize, but in fact it has been quite easy and seamless. We think it has worked so well because BT has always been highly regulated, so adding an additional level of regulation was not a big leap.

It is still early days for us. We are no longer seen as just a cost center for BT. At the moment, we seek to offer cost neutrality, and we are moving towards becoming a profit center.

The shift that BT Law took is not a big shift. We went from offering certain services to our internal client to offering the same services to other, external clients. It is not the same thing as a brand new structure offering a brand new service.

## IS IT OR ISN'T IT AN ALTERNATIVE STRUCTURE?

One Australian ILP combines elements of a partnership with elements of a company, with the result that it is not clear which one it actually is.

### Greg Tucker, CEO, Maurice Blackburn

ILP Maurice Blackburn is a plaintiff law firm with 30 permanent locations in Australia. It has approximately 1,000 employees, of which 300 are lawyers. The firm's shares are privately held by approximately 25 of the firm's lawyers, called principals. In the excerpt below, Tucker explains the firm's hesitant journey from partnership to corporation and the firm's place in a consolidating market:

We are a very large firm. We have over 15,000 cases open at any time, most of them personal injury matters, run on a "no win no fee" basis. These cases mean that we have a strong and steady cash flow. In addition, unlike commercial law firms, we retain a portion of our earnings in order to invest in our future.

Maurice Blackburn became an Incorporated Legal Practice in 2003, before I joined the firm. The reasons why the firm decided to become an ILP are difficult to understand, but I believe it was for a combination of these reasons:

- There was a question of succession planning—with partners coming and going, an ILP was seen as a means to assure an enduring structure.
- The firm contemplated providing multidisciplinary services (but it ultimately decided not to do so).
- For a variety of reasons, at that moment in time, the value of the firm was estimated to be quite low. This meant that the tax consequences to make the change were low, meaning that if the change was to be made, that was the right time to do it.

On one level I do not think it was a good idea for the firm to become an ILP. I think that if a firm will in fact be run like a company, then becoming an ILP makes sense. But if the firm will psychologically and culturally continue to be a partnership instead of a company, and if it will continue to be run like a partnership, then becoming an ILP does not make sense. If you will continue to act like partners and not shareholders, then trying to run the structure as a company is at odds with that. The shift from one to the other is difficult and painstaking.

For example, Maurice Blackburn has a Board—it has taken years to establish the pre-eminence of the Board. This is because everyone still regarded themselves as a partner with the right to have a hand in the decision making. This is no longer the case today, but it took the firm over five years to adjust to that change. Again, this was painstaking, requiring a significant cultural shift.

To be clear, while I think that the ILP structure is awkward for Maurice Blackburn, I think that the ILP structure itself offers benefits, and it can be the right structure for firms that truly do operate as companies. It's too bad that there is no hybrid structure between a company and a partnership, as it could have served Maurice Blackburn well during the psychological transition. A clear advantage of this structure has been the ability to compare ourselves with the two listed companies.

We have considered bringing in a passive investor, but we've decided not to. This is because we see the key ingredient of Maurice Blackburn is discretionary effort. Usually a passive investor will want their pound of flesh. That is, they will want to drive ongoing exceptional returns / dividends as well as having an exit strategy for their shareholding, which usually takes the form of a significant payment or public listing. We don't believe that we need the capital or having someone outside of the firm having some influence over it. This focus is prone to damage our culture.

Normally in a professional services environment, profits, in full, are distributed quarterly or at least half-yearly. That is not our model. As a plaintiff law firm, we have to retain earnings. Under our "no win, no fee" arrangements, we pay the client's expenses along the way. At any moment we have tens of millions of dollars which we've paid for clients. In addition, many of our class actions we fund ourselves—that requires a reservoir of capital. Finally, we get involved in litigation funding—funding other law firm's litigation—

to do this we use partly our share capital and partly debt. So, in sum, we need to retain earnings as part of our business model.

Another thing that we do differently from some other law firms is that we have many offices—30 at the moment. We have to go where injured people are—they don't come to capital cities just because you are a good law firm. Having so many offices requires us to have effective internal communications as well as external. So we spend a lot on IT, to be sure that our communication networks work, to communicate with each other and with our clients. That being said, many of our clients prefer personal contact to contact over the phone, SMS and Skype—at least at this stage.

We are also investing in IT to review processes to become more efficient and automated where appropriate: standardization of documentation and online processing of documents, for example.

In personal injuries litigation, we have one of the largest market shares in Australia. That being said, we do not see ourselves as a consolidator of the market because we think it is best to grow organically. We have acquired some firms, but nowhere near the number our competitors have. Organic growth permits us to protect and enhance our culture.

Even if we are not a consolidator, we are in a consolidating market, and because our brand is so strong, we do attract a large share of the market.

I have heard the fear expressed that in a consolidating market, the consolidating firms will cherry pick the most profitable work and neglect the least profitable. I don't think that this would be a wise strategy to adopt, for two reasons. The first is that there is a legislative risk—if you pick a narrow range of services, you could lose your entire livelihood because of a legislative change (for example if a no-fault scheme is adopted). A second reason is that some work is part of our DNA. It's work that clients expect us to do, and if we didn't do it, it's unlikely we would get the referrals we need for the more profitable work.

## WHAT IS IT LIKE FOR A LAWYER TO BE EMPLOYED BY AN ALTERNATIVE STRUCTURE?

The stories above are all with persons who have founded and/or are managing alternative structures (ABSs or ILPs). In contrast, the stories of this category are with persons—lawyers—who are employed by alternative structures. These stories demonstrate that while the experiences of these employees are all different, they share an essential commonality: In each case, the alternative structure provides an environment for lawyers to flourish.

### Dina Tutungi, General Manager—Personal Injury Victoria, Slater and Gordon Lawyers

Slater and Gordon Lawyers is a consumer law firm with 70 locations in Australia and 25 locations in the United Kingdom. Slater and Gordon is a publicly held company with shares listed on the Australian Securities Exchange. The Slater and Gordon Group also owns Slater Gordon Solutions in the UK, which provides claims, motor, and health services. In the excerpt below, Tutungi describes her career with Slater and Gordon, including her experiences after each of her two maternity leaves:

> Slater and Gordon is a very dynamic and flexible place to work. Much of what we do is different and innovative. We are always busy. In general, this is a very positive place to work.
>
> Slater and Gordon is structured in a way that it can recognize people's strengths and skills, and provide opportunities that suit those strengths and skills. Slater and Gordon is also a place that can provide a lot of different and empowering opportunities for lawyers at all levels.
>
> For example, when I was a fifth year lawyer, I put a proposal to our Managing Director (Andrew Grech) and the Executive team, to open a new suburban office, Ringwood. They supported this proposal. The sentiment was to "go for it." I was well supported but also provided ample autonomy such that the lease on the premises was executed based on my recommendation and review of premises. I ran that office, as a junior to mid-level lawyer, for five years.
>
> When I first joined Slater and Gordon, I worked in class actions, and I had the opportunity to work on large scale projects. That was a great opportunity for me, especially since I got to work directly with three senior partners. But after a while I wanted to have a different experience, I wanted to get the experience of working for individuals in a traditional setting, with a traditional file load. An opportunity arose in motor vehicle accidents in Head Office, and I did that for a year or two, then I opened the regional Ringwood office, and I did that for five years.
>
> Part way through that, I was asked if I wanted to run the national superannuation [national disability and disability insurance scheme] practice. I saw that practice as having great potential, so I accepted that request while continuing to run the Ringwood office. . . . Later the opportunities of further career progression have come and I have accepted those roles, including my current position as General Manager for Personal Injury in Victoria, [a role into which I was promoted while I was out on parental leave with my second child].
>
> I am up for a challenge and I like change. I have enjoyed taking something that has potential and turning it around so it meets its potential—in understanding what systems and processes need to be improved, and then developing those systems and processes. Slater and Gordon has given me the opportunity to do that. I think I would be quite bored if I were working in a well-established practice that simply needed to be maintained.
>
> I had my first child a couple of years ago. At that time, I was appreciative that when you have a child and you come back to work, you can select a flexible working arrangement that suits you. Flexible work arrangements are part and parcel of being a working parent at Slater and Gordon. Many staff members are on flexible working arrangements involving a mish-mash of hours and days, including my own supervisor who is the head of our Australian personal injuries practice. That has certainly been my experience. When I

returned from parental leave to my usual role, my request to work three days a week, leaving at 4:30 pm was accepted.

I have attended a couple leadership forums for women, and in each the messaging has been that this is a time for your career to take a back seat, that you cannot have both, that women in the law will generally go back to roles that are not the same as before, that their jobs will change. That's not been my experience or those of the talented woman I work with. That's not to say that juggling both a progressing career and family with small children is easy. But with the right support and workplace attitudes, it is achievable.

This says a lot about being at Slater and Gordon, where many women have continued to progress their careers during the time they have small children and are working part-time. The flexibility that Slater and Gordon shows for working parents is important. There are many part-time working parents at Slater and Gordon—if I am not mistaken, more than 30 percent of Slater and Gordon's work force is on a flexible working arrangement, including part-time work, compressed working weeks, job share arrangements and working from home. When someone wants to come back part-time after they have a baby, we always attempt to accommodate their request.

When I am interviewing a lawyer new to Slater and Gordon, I tell them that the opportunities here are varied. I advise them that their first priority needs to become an excellent lawyer and specialist. It takes about five years for a junior lawyer to really nail that, but once it becomes second nature, the opportunities at Slater and Gordon are endless. We have 70 offices across the country and also offices in the UK, there are opportunities to be involved in localities, in a region, to become a practice group leader, a subject-matter expert and train junior lawyers. There are also purely operational jobs in management services and business development. There are lawyers (like myself) who are very focused on business development and client service. And there are lawyers who do research, who publish articles and books. Slater and Gordon probably isn't for everyone, but I think that it offers many more opportunities to lawyers than a traditional law firm, where your options are usually limited to either becoming partner or not.

## PERSPECTIVE OF AN INVESTOR

External investors in alternative structures have a unique perspective on the legal services market, as evidenced in the interview below.

### Jordan Mayo, Managing Director, Smedvig Capital

Smedvig Capital is a private equity firm that invests in fast-growing businesses. In the excerpt below, Mayo explains Smedvig's reasons for investing in legal services and its experiences as an investor:

> We have invested in two legal service providers: Kings Court Trust (KCT) and myhomemove (MHM). We got involved in legal investing back in 2005, so well before the UK Legal Services Act came into effect. This happened be-

cause the Council for Licensed Conveyancers permitted ABS-type structures for conveyancing that far back. At that time, we were not specifically looking to enter legal services—we simply liked MHM—the dynamics of its market, the management team, their use of technology in a disruptive way to take out cost and increase customer service, and they were doing that in a very scaleable way. Those are the same things we look for in all our investments, regardless of the sector.

MHM has been a success in the ten plus years we've been an investor. We plan to remain an investor for some time yet—it's very profitable, it's the market leader in the UK, it's much larger than the number two, and it is growing very quickly. But its market share is still relatively low, since it remains a very fragmented market, spread among High Street law firms who have no technology and who have high prices.

Since we had a good experience with MHM, when ABSs for other types of legal services finally happened, we started to proactively think about in what other segments in legal services you could apply the same sort of business model and have the same sort of value creation: by bringing in external capital, by using technology to automate, by increasing the speed of the processes, and by offering legal services over the internet in a way that people can help themselves. We also looked for segments that would benefit from greater expertise with sales and marketing, in order to promote rapid growth by approaching different distribution channels. It was with this sector by sector analysis that we identified probate.

Probate is a very large but also very fragmented market. Generally the service is very poor, the prices are very high, and those in the market are not technology specialists at all. That is exactly what we like as it gives us the opportunity to become the service leader and the market leader.

We have been able to help MHM and KCT in two ways. Of course, our capital has allowed them to do things they otherwise could not have done, and notably further develop their technology and offshore support, their sales and marketing infrastructure and their people. We've also provided guidance and expertise, to fill in the non-legal gaps in the management team, and to share our experiences and learning from our other investments in fast-growing business sectors.

In investing in these businesses, it is important to take a long-term approach, as these things take time. If a law firm has a partnership structure, it can't do this—all the money is taken out at the end of each year, and any investments are seen as coming out of today's salaries. That is a real barrier.

Between 2010 to 2013, we met with at least 150 law firms seeking investment, but in the end, we invested in only one more, KCT, bringing our total investment in the legal sector to just two. The reason we did not invest in those other businesses is because they could not explain what they would do with the money. They said they were seeking investment because it sounded like something they should do, or because they liked the idea of having some capital. But any business we get involved with needs to have a clear plan for how they will use the money, and their plans need to be distinctive and scaleable. In contrast to those other firms, MHM and KCT had clear plans, they were distinctive and they were scaleable.

Today we see in some sectors of legal services dynamics that you don't see anywhere else. Take MHM, for example. Today it has about 3 percent market share, and that's three times the size of the number two. It is the cost and quality leader, and it has the ability to grow into a 15 or 20 percent market share position over the next few years. This is a fantastic opportunity. Probate offers the same opportunities. The opportunities lie especially in the sectors like these that are fragmented—where there are thousands of firms in the space, but most of them are small and practically none of them are specialists—they do a little bit of everything. It is because those firms are not differentiated that it will be so hard for them to continue to compete with specialists who are investing properly in the technology and the service delivery.

We think there remain many opportunities in legal services. We feel we are just getting started in what we can do and the sort of businesses we can invest in and help grow. Our challenge is to find the right team, the right approach and the right strategy for the business.

We were surprised by how poorly the competition was prepared for someone like MHM to enter the market. There seemed to be an attitude of "this will never happen, or, if it does, it will be ok" rather than proactively thinking it through. Because of MHM, conveyancing customers now expect to be able to follow their case and manage all their documents online if they want to, and they expect to have things turned around overnight. This type of change in the market can happen very quickly, and if you are law firm who never really thought about technology or customer service, there is a risk the market will pass you by very quickly. As soon as experienced managers with the right skill sets are able to come in and create efficient, customer service businesses, the entire market will change. It's a huge opportunity. We are only at the beginning of a very long period of investment, of innovation and of change.

## ALTERNATIVE VOICES: FOR CONSUMERS, FOR CITIZENS, AN INDUSTRY OBSERVER

In England and Wales, the Legal Services Act created a Legal Services Consumer Panel and in doing so ensured a voice for consumers in the regulation of legal services. While neither the United States nor Australia has a direct counterpart, they do have persons like John Ray and Paddy Oliver.

### Elisabeth Davies, Chair, Legal Services Consumer Panel

The Legal Services Consumer Panel was created by the Legal Services Act 2007 and began operating in late 2009. The panel is an independent arm of the Legal Services Board and is made up of eight lay (nonlawyer) members whose appointments are approved by the Lord Chancellor. The panel provides advice to the LSB, in order to help it make decisions that are shaped around the needs of users. The panel has a remit to represent the interests of the many different consumers of legal services, including small businesses and charities, and with a priority for vulnerable groups of consumers. The panel has legal powers to publish its advice, and the LSB has a legal duty to explain its reasons when it disagrees with the advice that the panel publishes. In the excerpt below, Davies describes how the panel measures the impact of the Legal Services Act on consumers and on access to justice:

> Two of the most important things that we do are a Tracker Survey and a Consumer Impact Report. The Tracker Survey we commission ourselves. This is our annual survey of 3000 members of the general public and consumers of legal services. Each year, we ask the same questions, in order to determine what is and is not changing for them.
>
> The Consumer Impact Report we issue every other year. This combines evidence from our Tracker Survey with information from other parts of the sector, in order to shed even more light on what is and is not changing for consumers, where there have been improvements and where more improvement is needed.
>
> The reforms of the 2007 Legal Services Act were necessary. There is no question that we needed to move away from the centuries of self-regulation that we had before. And the reforms have resulted in positive changes for consumers. But the reforms were only a first step—more change is needed.
>
> As regards ABSs, it is still too early to judge the full impact of the reforms. They've only been in existence for a few years, and we are still in early days. The question of ABSs reminds me of the Bill Gates quote—that people tend to overestimate the change that will occur in two years but underestimate the change that will occur in ten. I think that some people overestimated the pace of change that would occur as regards ABSs. On the other hand, our most recent Consumer Impact Report demonstrates that there has been a large amount of activity as regards new business models and investment in the market. But it will take time to feed through to what ordinary people experience on the ground.
>
> That being said, our Tracker Survey demonstrates that consumers are becoming more empowered: people are shopping around more, and there is an increased use of fixed fees, which is something that people have been asking for. Take family law for example—you can see some real changes there, and notably as regards fixed fees, as in 2012 these were used only 10 percent of the time, whereas in 2014 they were used nearly half the time. The entry of a very high profile competitor, The Cooperative Legal Services, made a considerable impact on the family law market.
>
> Showing cause and effect is tricky, but if you look at the Tracker Survey, you can map out the tangible changes that have taken place in the market as regards consumer satisfaction, use of quality marks, use of comparison websites, use of unbundling . . . .
>
> There are those in the UK who still think that access to justice just means access to a lawyer. At the Panel, we think that access to justice means something much larger—putting the consumer at the heart, access to justice means access to legal services, access to the support that a consumer needs. That support may be provided by a lawyer, by it may also be provided by an unregulated provider or by the voluntary sector. People are going to a myriad of providers, and it is important that they have that choice. We look carefully

at changes that increase the number of entrants into the legal services ecosystem in its entirety, and we think that the regulatory reforms in the UK were needed in order to create choice and diversity that did not exist before.

When ABSs were first introduced in the UK, there were fears that they would "cherry pick" the most profitable work and squeeze out law firms that subsidize less profitable work with more profitable work. But the data today does not support those fears. If you look at the SRA's data in particular, you'll see that ABSs have captured a significant portion of the market in the areas of mental health and social welfare. ABSs have gone for the areas of law where there is significant unmet need. They have provided access to services that previously people didn't have access to at all.

The legal services market [in England and Wales] is no longer limited to [lawyers]. The legal services market is a much larger ecosystem. Access to justice is a nuanced and complicated problem that requires nuanced responses and solutions.

## EXPERIENCE FROM WASHINGTON, DC

Washington, DC, is the only jurisdiction in the United States that allows for nonlawyer ownership of law firms, albeit in a limited manner. There are no statistics revealing the number of Washington, DC, firms that have nonlawyer owners. They are believed to be small in number, but there are a few.

### Michael McDevitt, Co-Founder and Chief Executive Officer, Tandem Legal Group

Tandem Legal Group is a corporate and commercial law firm serving young and fast-growing companies. McDevitt is not a lawyer. In the excerpt below, he explains his reasons for cofounding Tandem Legal and his experiences as a nonlawyer at the head of a law firm:

Randy Price and I founded Tandem Legal Group in 2012. Our objective was to create a law firm that had a better understanding of and alignment with its client base than most other firms have today.

In [my previous] positions I worked extensively with lawyers. But I struggled to communicate with them—they never seemed to understand the core purpose for which I was hiring them and this led to a lot of frustration for me. I tried many attorneys at many firms, trying to find the right person. My experience was that the good attorneys who also understood my business were no longer practicing law—they felt that they had to choose between law and business, and they chose business.

At Tandem Legal, my role as CEO is not to get involved in the legal matters of the clients. My role is to represent the clients to the lawyers—to help the lawyers at Tandem understand the clients and their perspective—to be a communications bridge between our lawyers and the clients. My entire reason for being at Tandem is because I have this kind of business capability and understanding.

Our clients are fast growing companies, and when they need something, they need it fast. We offer clients access to a trusted circle of the different resources and expertise that they need (operations, marketing, finance and fund raising, . . .)—a circle of people that can communicate very quickly and very effectively. This helps companies get through challenging times much better than a bunch of one-off, isolated relationships with no communication amongst them.

I like to tell the story of how Randy Price proposed that I join him to co-found Tandem Legal. When he learned that the DC rules permit a limited form of nonlawyer ownership of law firms, he called me and said "Hey Mike, you know how you can't stand working with attorneys?" and I responded "yes I am very much aware of how much I can't stand working with attorneys."

He told me that he had found a way for me to fix it—I could stop complaining about attorneys and instead do something to make a difference. "With your experience as a CEO, you can help us to understand what the CEOs of our clients want from us."

It is extremely challenging to be the only nonlawyer in the room. Luckily, with my experience, I can offer Tandem lawyers something that they want to learn. My challenge with the Tandem lawyers is to break down the mindset that they gained after so many years in a big law firm. Their instinct is to see how risky something is and to see all the reasons why something won't work. I help them to see past that, to see opportunities and why something can work.

It is a popular thing nowadays for law firms to bring a nonlawyer into a law firm on a salaried basis to take on a role of CEO, or COO. This is very different than what we are at Tandem. In fact, what they are doing is a very tricky thing. I think that such a person would struggle to gain the authority and respect they would need to be effective in their roles amongst the attorneys. They would probably be little more than figureheads trying to bring best practices into the firm, with little or no accountability. Also, in essence, they cannot be paid based on their success, as they would have to be on a salary, and not rewarded for profitability or revenue growth. That is only for attorneys to gain from. In my case, coming in both with my level of experience and as an owner instead of as a salaried employee makes a big difference.

## CANADA'S ALMOST ALTERNATIVE STRUCTURES

As discussed earlier in this book, some companies have shown that it is possible to develop new models for the delivery of legal services while remaining within the limitations of the existing, restrictive rules. US-based examples include LegalZoom, Axiom, RocketLawyer, Shake, and Modria. In Canada, the same has occurred: That is, there are a certain number of companies that have also developed new models within the confines of comparably restrictive rules. Even so, because of the restrictive rules, their ability to further develop their models and to grow is limited.

## Monica Goyal, Founder and Principal, Aluvion Law

Aluvion Law is a Canada-based law firm that uses automated processes to reduce the cost of legal services for small businesses. In the excerpt below, Goyal explains the experiences that led her to create Aluvion, how Aluvion uses technology to reduce cost and time, and how Canada's restrictive regulatory environment limits Aluvion's ability to grow:

> I have a background in technology and electrical engineering. I worked in Silicon Valley, and completed a master's degree in electrical engineering at Stanford. I did those things before I went to law school, at the University of Toronto.
>
> After I finished law school, I worked for a large firm in Toronto. When I was there, I was struck by the access to justice problems in the law. Having worked in technology, I understood what was possible; I understood the innovations in processes that technology offered. But there seemed to be such a big gap between that and how I saw things get done at the law firm.
>
> It was 2008, and I saw companies like LegalZoom and RocketLawyer in the US taking off, which told me that there are people who are happy to obtain legal services online.
>
> So, I created My Legal Briefcase, which offers a streamlined solution to the legal process for small businesses. The site automatically generates documents, based upon the responses that the user provides to certain questions.
>
> But my experience with My Legal Briefcase has shown me that in Canada people are not ready to access legal services online. They are willing to go online to look for general information to self-diagnose their legal issue, but they remain reluctant to access a legal service online.
>
> What I realized was that the people who were visiting the My Legal Briefcase site had specific questions that they needed a lawyer for, and they were looking for help in getting connected to a lawyer.
>
> So I started referring these people to other lawyers. But when I followed up after these referrals, I discovered that the conversion rate was very low. That is, very few people actually engaged the lawyer that I referred them to.
>
> I wanted to understand why that was. After all, I am a lawyer, why can't I help these people? I thought to turn the model around—instead of the client using the tools, I will use the tools in order to service the clients.
>
> People seemed to like what we were offering, and we had a lot of customers. What I realized is that most of the people who were using the service were small business owners. So, focusing on small businesses, we took a good look at everything we did and asked what could be automated even further—to bring the costs down and to bring the time to do the work down.
>
> For our clients, we are a law firm. We serve corporate commercial needs. But we do it at a very cost effective rate. The reason we can do that is because of our internal use of automatic processes. As a result, certain services, like incorporation, we can do at approximately half the price of a traditional law or accountancy firm.
>
> I incorporated My Legal Briefcase with the intention of receiving outside investment. But it turned out that that model was not the right one for the

Canadian market at that time. Of course, now with Aluvion's model we cannot, under the current rules in Canada, obtain outside funding. This limits us in significant ways. It means that we have to be entirely self-funding. We could grow much faster if we had access to external funding.

To me, innovation is technology. Of course you can have innovation without technology—Conduit and Cognition are examples of that. But for me, who has a background in technology, innovation is technology, and technology is capital intensive. The common model for technology innovation companies is equity financing. There are people, in the US and in other places, who are creating innovations in legal services using equity financing—they are thumbing their noses at the regulators—they are claiming a grey space between what is and is not allowed. But they have to—they do not have a choice because of the regulations. So, yes, the rules today do inhibit the development of technology for use in legal services.

## VOICES OF MODERN REGULATION

The regulatory changes in England and Wales and in Australia to allow for ABSs and ILPs did not occur in isolation. To the contrary, they occurred in a larger context of the modernization of their rules governing legal services. Today comparable processes are occurring in a number of Canadian provinces, and perhaps also in Colorado and Illinois. The stories of this category provide insight into the approaches of some of these modern regulators.

### David Clementi

Sir David Clementi is a former governor of the Bank of England and is the author of the December 2004 "Review of the Regulatory Framework for Legal Services in England and Wales—Final Report," otherwise known as "The Clementi Report." This report, prepared at the request of the Blair government, served as the basis for the subsequent reforms of the regulatory framework for legal services in England and Wales. In the excerpt below, Clementi explains why he, a nonlawyer, was selected to perform the review, and the problems he perceived with self-regulation:

> In 2003, Lord Chancellor Falconer had on his desk a paper prepared by his staff which concluded that the regulatory system for lawyers was confusing, that the complaint system needed overhaul, and that the legal profession was full of restrictive practices that worked against the consumer and in favor of the profession.
>
> He asked me to prepare a report. I believe he selected me for two reasons: The first reason was that I had experience of regulatory practices in other professions. I had been a regulator of the accountancy profession, I had sat on the board of the financial regulator for five years, and I had worked with the Bank of England on regulatory systems for many years.

The second reason was that I was not a lawyer. Falconer told me that the profession had little objectivity: There was a tendency to think that the profession is "very well run, because it is run by people like ourselves."

If you review the history of English and Welsh law, about every 20 to 30 years there has been a major review of the regulatory system. But almost all of these reviews in the past had been done by lawyers; and these reviews tended to conclude that everything was basically fine, but we'll have this little tweak and that little tweak.

Prior to the Clementi Report, the Law Society and the Bar Council carried out both representative and regulatory functions. But in other industries in the UK it was felt that, whilst providers could represent themselves, they were not good at regulating themselves: that banks couldn't regulate banks, that brokers couldn't represent brokers—that self-regulation, in financial services as well as other services, did not work well and that the days of self-regulation were over. Lawyers seemed to agree with that, for all areas except their own.

I argued that regulation is a public service. It should be carried out in the interest of the public, and be independent of representation of the profession. When lawyers are self-regulating, their focus is rarely on access to justice or other consumer outcomes. Their focus is on whether services are being provided at a high enough standard. Lawyers did not like it when I recommended the end to self-regulation, but today they have more or less accepted it.

## THE STORY BEHIND THE STORIES

The 58 stories referenced in this book and posted online at www.notjustforlawyers.com are the work-product of oral interviews I conducted between March 2014 and June 2016. The principal way that I identified candidates to tell their stories was to scour the website Legal Futures.[2] This website is a treasure trove of information especially (but by no means only) with respect to alternative structures in England and Wales. In particular, this is the go-to website for information about newly licensed ABSs—in searching the archives as well as the current pages of this site, it was possible for me to identify not only the ABSs that merited attention, but also the best person with those ABSs for me to contact for an interview. Once I identified a candidate, my next step was to search for that person's contact information. In most cases a simple and quick Google search sufficed to produce an email address, but in a few cases lengthier and more in-depth Google sleuthing was required.

The other way I was able to identify as well as access candidates was through personal introductions. In this context, I am indebted to a number of persons for making those introductions, and most notably to Neil Rose (the editor of *Legal Futures*), John Chisholm, Mitch Kowalski, Colin Lachance, Lisa Webley, and Paddy Oliver.

I wasn't sure what kind of reaction I would get when I reached out to request an interview. Would they agree to speak with me? Would they even respond to me? How long would it take to receive a response? At the beginning, some (but not many) of the people I contacted did not respond to me. In retrospect, I think this was because they were not the people I needed, and they recognized that faster than I did. In time I got better at identifying the people I needed, and as I did, nearly everyone I contacted not only responded to me, but also responded relatively quickly and expressed little hesitation in agreeing to speak with me.

I conducted the interviews either by phone or Skype, with one exception (Sir David Clementi, with whom I met in person). Most interviews lasted about one hour. A small number were shorter—about 30 minutes—and some were much longer—up to two hours, with some of those taking place over more than one call. When I conducted the first interviews in early 2014, I had no idea what I was doing: I wasn't sure what questions to ask, I wasn't sure in what order to ask them, and I wasn't adept at formulating follow-up questions. After the first few interviews, I got the hang of it. The interviews became semi-structured, with the support of a topic guide.

More specifically, I developed a core set of questions. Before each interview, I studied the publicly available information about the organization and the interviewee, and tailored the core set of questions to reflect the specificities of both. As I listened to each interviewee, I got into the habit of noting follow-up questions and I got better at identifying the right moments to ask them. Because I was never sure that I asked all the right questions, my last question became "What should I have asked, but didn't?" Often it was this question that elicited the most interesting comments.

In most instances, the interviews were recorded with the permission of the interviewee, and I also took handwritten notes as needed. After each interview, I prepared a write-up. I quickly recognized that a simple transcript of the interview wouldn't work: Hearing the spoken word is one thing—reading the spoken word is something entirely different. Run-on sentences, sentence fragments, and the repetition of words and ideas are tolerated and even expected in speech, but not in writing. So, what I did was take the words and ideas that the interviewee expressed orally and organized them on paper (or, more precisely, on a screen) in a way that they could be easily accessed by a reader rather than a listener. Because I wanted the focus of the reader to be on the interviewee and not on the interviewer (me), I excluded from the write-up the questions that I posed and any other limited commentary I occasionally made during the interviews. An unfortunate by-product of this is that sometimes in reading the stories, the transitions can be abrupt.

I sent each write-up back to the interviewee. In doing so, I invited him/her to make comments and corrections. At first, I wasn't sure how "warmly" I should extend this invitation. Naturally I wanted any factual errors to be corrected. More than that, I wanted the interviewee to be comfortable with the write-up. At the same time, however, I didn't want the write-up to be transformed into something that no longer reflected the interview, and I especially didn't want changes that would transform the write-up from an interview to advertising. In progressing with the first few write-ups, I discovered that those fears were mostly unfounded—most interviewees made very few if any substantive changes. And when substantive changes were made, in most cases I felt that they improved the write-up. So, after those first few write-ups, I became comfortable extending what I intended to be a warm invitation to make comments and corrections, saying "please don't feel wedded to what I have typed" and "it is important that you are comfortable." And when I received a write-up back, usually in the form of a mark-up, I did not question or quibble with the changes—instead, in nearly all cases I accepted all of them, and then went back through the revised document simply to correct any spelling or grammatical errors.

As noted above, the interviews were conducted between March 2014 and June 2016. In August 2015 I contacted everyone I had interviewed up to that time, and I invited them to work with me to update their write-ups—most of them did so, if not immediately, then over the course of the following months.

Finally, because of spacing concerns, it was impossible to include all of the interviews in this book. The interviews that are included are excerpts. As noted above, full versions of all the interviews can be accessed at www.notjustforlawyers.com.

## NOTES

1. This memo can be accessed at http://alexhamiltonrad.tumblr.com/post/78751332144/innovation-opportunities.
2. http://www.legalfutures.co.uk/.

# Appendix

On the following pages is a list of all the stories, the full versions of which are available at www.notjustforlawyers.com.

| *Category* | *Name* | *Title* | *Affiliation* |
|---|---|---|---|
| Using business and IT processes to increase efficiency and reduce costs | Tom Curran | CEO | Kings Court Trust |
| | Oliver Jackson | Director of Strategy and Growth | Roberts Jackson |
| | Andrew Grech | Group Managing Director | Slater and Gordon Lawyers |
| Business outsourcing | Alexander Hamilton | CEO | Radiant Law |
| | Karl Chapman | Chief Executive | Riverview Law |
| | Ursula Hogben | Practice Leader and General Counsel | LegalVision |
| Adopting a corporate structure to foster growth | John Kain | Managing Director | Kain C+C |
| | Rod Cunich | National Practice Group Leader | Slater and Gordon Lawyers |
| | David Beech | CEO | Knights Solicitors LLP |
| Holistic services | Christopher Mills | Partner and COO | Schillings |
| | Julia Hulme | Managing Director | Omnia Strategy LLP |
| | Jeff Winn | Managing Director | Winn Solicitors |
| | Adrian Powell and Richard Stephens | Partners | Proelium Law |
| | Keith Arrowsmith | Partner | Counterculture Partnership LLP |
| Dispersed law firms | Ken Jagger | CEO | AdventBalance |
| | William Robins | Operations Director | Keystone Law |
| | Warren Kalinko | CEO | Keypoint Law |
| Turning employees into owners | David Simon | Chair | Triton Global |

| | | | |
|---|---|---|---|
| | Jenny Beck | Partner | Stephensons Solicitors LLP |
| | Robert Camp | Managing Partner | Stephens Scown LLP |
| | Martin Powell | Director | OmniaLegal Limited |
| Opposites attract? Law, charity, and free legal services | Luke Geary | Managing Partner | Salvos Legal and Salvos Legal Humanitarian |
| | Chris Byron | Managing Director | Aspire Law |
| | Glenda Terry | Practice Manager | Castle Park Solicitors |
| | Martin Langan | Founder | Road Traffic Representation |
| | Felice Batlan | Professor of Law | IIT Chicago-Kent College of Law |
| Law school: alternative structure as an educational program and center for research and experimentation | Jenny Holloway | Associate Dean | Nottingham Law School |
| | Nick Johnson | Pro Bono Director | Nottingham Law School Legal Advice Centre |
| In-house legal as source of revenue | Archana Makol | Director | BT Law Ltd. |
| | Anne Copley | Head of Legal | BPIF Legal |
| | Viv Du-Feu | Director of Legal Services | BMA Law |
| | Yuliya Andresyuk | Founding Partner | Oracle Family Office |
| | Geoff Wild | Director | Kent Legal Services |
| Is it or isn't it an alternative structure? | Greg Tucker | CEO | Maurice Blackburn |
| What is it like to be employed by an alternative structure? | Dina Tutungi | General Manager—Personal Injury Victoria | Slater and Gordon Lawyers |

| | | | |
|---|---|---|---|
| | Sue Bence | Head of M&A Operations and Integration—UK | Slater and Gordon Lawyers |
| | Andrea Pierce | Legal Services Director | Kings Court Trust |
| | Nadia Haque | Associate | Radiant Law |
| | Tamyn Hearne | Associate | Radiant Law |
| Perspective of an investor | Jordan Mayo | Managing Director | Smedvig Capital |
| Alternative voices: for consumers, for citizens, for industry observers | Elisabeth Davies | Chair | Legal Services Consumer Panel |
| | John Ray | Senior Consultant | Law Firm Consulting Group |
| | Paddy Oliver | Managing Director and Founder | Lexcel Consulting |
| Experience from Washington, DC | Michael McDevitt | Cofounder and CEO | Tandem Legal Group |
| | Randy Price | Cofounder and Managing Partner | Tandem Legal Group |
| Canada's almost alternative structures | Monica Goyal | Founder and Principal | Aluvion Law |
| | Mark Morris and Lena Koke | Founders | Axess Law |
| | Peter Carayiannis | Founder and President | Conduit Law |
| | Rubsun Ho and Joe Milstone | Founding Partners | Cognition LLP |
| Voices of modern regulation | David Clementi | Author | The Clementi Report |
| | Robert Cross | Project Manager (Research) | Legal Services Board |
| | John Briton | Former Legal Services Commissioner | Queensland Legal Services Commission |
| | Darrel Pink | Executive Director | Nova Scotia Barristers' Society |

| | | | |
|---|---|---|---|
| | Kristin Dangerfield | CEO | The Law Society of Manitoba |
| | Ross Earnshaw | Chair, Task Force on Compliance-Based Entity Regulation | Law Society of Upper Canada |
| | Margaret Drent | Policy Counsel | Law Society of Upper Canada |
| | Herman Van Ommen | Chair, Law Firm Regulation Task Force | Law Society of British Columbia |
| | James Coyle | Attorney Regulation Counsel | Colorado Supreme Court |
| | James J. Grogan | Deputy Administrator and Chief Counsel | Illinois ARDC |
| The Story Behind the Stories | | | |

# Bibliography

An online version of the bibliography, including hyperlinks, is available at www.notjustforlawyers.com.

ABA Commission on Ethics 20/20. "ABA Commission on Ethics 20/20 Will Not Propose Changes to ABA Policy Prohibiting Nonlawyer Ownership of Law Firms." April 16, 2012. http://www.americanbar.org/content/dam/aba/administrative/ethics_2020/20120416_news_release_re_nonlawyer_ownership_law_firms.authcheckdam.pdf.

ABA Commission on the Evaluation of the Rules of Professional Conduct ('Ethics 2000'). "Chair's Introduction." August 2002. http://www.americanbar.org/content/dam/aba/administrative/professional_responsibility/e2k_chair_intro.authcheckdam.pdf.

ABA Commission on Lawyer Assistance Programs. "Proposed Resolution Regarding Model Regulatory Objectives." October 28, 2015. http://www.americanbar.org/content/dam/aba/images/office_president/lawyer_assistance_programs.pdf.

ABA Commission on the Future of Legal Services. "For Comment: Issues Paper Concerning Unregulated LSP Entities." March 31, 2016. http://www.americanbar.org/content/dam/aba/images/office_president/final_unregulated_lsp_entities_issues_paper.pdf.

———. "For Comment: Issues Paper Regarding Alternative Business Structures." April 8, 2016. http://www.americanbar.org/content/dam/aba/images/office_president/alternative_business_issues_paper.pdf.

———. "Issues Paper Concerning New Categories of Legal Services Providers." October 16, 2015. http://www.americanbar.org/content/dam/aba/images/office_president/delivery_of_legal_services_completed_evaluation.pdf.

ABA Commission on the Future of Legal Services, Standing Committee on Professional Discipline Criminal Justice Section, Law Practice Division, Standing Committee on Legal Aid And Indigent Defendants, Standing Committee on Client Protection. "Report to the House of Delegates." November, 2015. http://www.americanbar.org/content/dam/aba/images/office_president/final_regulatory_objectives_resolution_november_2015.pdf.

ABA Resource Center for Access to Justice Initiatives. "Supreme Court Leadership on State Legislative Funding for Civil Legal Aid." July 15, 2015. http://www.americanbar.org/content/dam/aba/images/legal_aid_indigent_defendants/ls_SC%20Best%20Practices.pdf.

ABA Standing Committee on the Delivery of Legal Services. "Issues on the Future of Legal Services." December 2, 2014. http://www.americanbar.org/content/dam/aba/images/office_president/delivery_of_legal_services.pdf.

ABA Standing Committee on Legal Aid and Indigent Defendants. "Comments on Issues Paper on Alternative Business Structures." May 5, 2016. http://www.americanbar.org/content/dam/aba/images/office_president/legal_aid_and_indigent_defendants.pdf.

ABA Standing Committee on Professionalism. "Standing Committee on Professionalism Comment on Issues Paper Regarding Alternative Business Structures." May 5, 2016. http://www.americanbar.org/content/dam/aba/images/office_president/professionalism_abs.pdf.

The Advocates' Society. Letter to the Law Society of Upper Canada's Working Group on Alternative Business Structures. December 19, 2014. http://www.lsuc.on.ca/uploadedFiles/The%20Advocates'%20Society.pdf.

American Bar Association. "ABA Mission and Goals." Accessed February 11, 2016. http://www.americanbar.org/about_the_aba/aba-mission-goals.html.

———. "Constitution and Bylaws Rules of Procedure House of Delegates," 2014–2015. http://www.americanbar.org/content/dam/aba/administrative/house_of_delegates/aba_constitution_and_bylaws_2014.authcheckdam.pdf.

———. "House of Delegates — General Information." Accessed August 25, 2015. http://www.americanbar.org/groups/leadership/delegates.html.

———. "Model Rules of Professional Conduct: Preface." Accessed August 27, 2015. http://www.americanbar.org/groups/professional_responsibility/publications/model_rules_of_professional_conduct/model_rules_of_professional_conduct_preface.html.

———. "Resolution 105." February, 2016. http://www.americanbar.org/content/dam/aba/images/abanews/2016mymres/105.pdf.

Adams, Edward S. and John H. Matheson. "Law Firms on the Big Board?: A Proposal for Nonlawyer Investment in Law Firms." *California Law Review* 86 (1998): 1–40. http://scholarship.law.umn.edu/cgi/viewcontent.cgi?article=1100&context=faculty_articles.

Ambrogi, Robert. "Washington State Moves Around UPL, Using Legal Technicians to Help Close the Justice Gap." *ABA Journal*, January 1, 2015. http://www.abajournal.com/magazine/article/washington_state_moves_around_upl_using_legal_technicians_to_help_close_the/.

Antonelli, Mark R. "For Comment: Issues Paper Regarding Alternative Business Structures." April 27, 2016. http://www.americanbar.org/content/dam/aba/images/office_president/mark_r_antonelli_abs.pdf.

"ArchCity Defenders Municipal Courts White Paper." 2014. http://s3.documentcloud.org/documents/1279541/archcity-defenders-report-on-st-louis-county.pdf.

Arentz, Oliver, Hans Manner, Leonard Münstermann, Clemens Recker, and Steffen J. Roth. "Services Liberalisation in Germany Overview and the Potential of Deregulation: A Study by the Institute for Economic Policy at the University of Cologne." Otto-Wolff-Institut Discussion Paper 1b/2015, March 2015. https://iwp.uni-koeln.de/fileadmin/contents/dateiliste_iwp-website/publikationen/DP/dp01b_2015.pdf.

Arnold, Jens M., Beata S. Javorcik, and Aaditya Mattoo. "Does Services Liberalization Benefit Manufacturing Firms? Evidence from the Czech Republic." *Journal of International Economics* 85 (2011): 136–46. http://www.sciencedirect.com/science/article/pii/S0022199611000523.

Associated Press. "Iowa Discipline Board Reprimands Attorney." *KCRG.com*, August 31, 2014. http://www.kcrg.com/subject/news/iowa-discipline-board-reprimands-attorney-20140831.

Attorney Registration & Disciplinary Commission. "Annual Report of 2015." April 27, 2016. https://www.iardc.org/AnnualReport2015.pdf.

Ayotte, Mike. "How Fixed Fees Are Going to Change BigLaw Forever." *The Last Honest Lawyer*. August 28, 2013. http://lasthonestlawyer.org/2013/08/28/how-fixed-fees-are-going-to-change-biglaw-forever/.

Balko, Radley. "How Municipalities in St. Louis County, Mo., Profit From Poverty." *Washington Post*, September 3, 2014. https://www.washingtonpost.com/news/the-watch/wp/2014/09/03/how-st-louis-county-missouri-profits-from-poverty/.

Barone, Guglielmo and Federico Cingano. "Service Regulation and Growth: Evidence from OECD Countries." *The Economic Journal* 121 (2011): 931–37. http://dx.doi.org/10.1111/j.1468-0297.2011.02433.x.

Barton, Benjamin H. "An Institutional Analysis of Lawyer Regulation: Who Should Control Lawyer Regulation—Courts, Legislatures, or the Market?" *Georgia Law Review* 37 (2003): 1167–250.

———. "Do Judges Systematically Favor the Interests of the Legal Profession?" University of Tennessee Legal Studies Research Paper No. 1, 2007. http://ssrn.com/abstract=976478.

———. "Economists on Deregulation of the American Legal Profession: Praise and Critique." *Michigan State Law Review* 2011 (2011): 11-13. http://ssrn.com/abstract=2008942.

———. "The Lawyer's Monopoly—What Goes and What Stays." *Fordham Law Review* 82 (2014): 3067–90. http://ir.lawnet.fordham.edu/cgi/viewcontent.cgi?article=5008&context=flr.

Bass, Julia H., W. A. Bogart, and Frederick H. Zemans. *Access to Justice for a New Century: The Way Forward*. Toronto, Ontario, Canada: Law Society of Upper Canada, 2005.

Batlan, Felice. *Women and Justice for the Poor: A History of Legal Aid, 1863-1945*. New York: Cambridge University Press, 2015.

Beal Law Firm. "Comment in Opposition to Alternative Business Structures." April 28, 2016. http://www.americanbar.org/content/dam/aba/images/office_president/beal_law_firm_abs.pdf.

Beck, Susan. "Divided ABA Adopts Resolution on Nonlawyer Legal Services." *The American Lawyer*, February 8, 2016. http://www.americanlawyer.com/id=1202749202171/Divided-ABA-Adopts-Resolution-on-Nonlawyer-Legal-Services?mcode=0&curindex=0&curpage=ALL.

Beisner, John. "Comments of the US Chamber Institute for Legal Reform on the Issues Paper Concerning Alternative Business Structures." June 1, 2011. http://www.americanbar.org/content/dam/aba/administrative/ethics_2020/ethics_20_20_comments/uschamberinstitute-forlegalreform_issuespaperconcerningalternativebusinessstructures.authcheckdam.pdf.

Benathen, Steve. "Non-Lawyers Owning Law Firms." *Illinois Business Law Journal*, October 21, 2012. http://www.law.illinois.edu/bljournal/post/2012/10/21/Non-Lawyers-Owning-Law-Firms.

Bennett, Daniel and Wesley Yin. "The Market for High-Quality Medicine: Retail Chain Entry and Drug Quality in India." NBER Working Paper No. 20091, November 17, 2014. http://home.uchicago.edu/~dmbennett/chainentry.pdf.

Bennet, Paul. "Comment on Alternative Business Structures." April 25, 2016. http://www.americanbar.org/content/dam/aba/images/office_president/paul_w_bennett_abs.pdf.

Berndt, Lorne, Alycia Middleton, Christal Côté, Cheryl Sheffer, Tania Castonguay, Paula Callaghan, Denis Sabourin, Linda Schmidt, and Kayla Minor. "Alternative Business Structure Call For Input." December 20, 2014. https://www.lsuc.on.ca/uploadedFiles/BRENDT,%20Lorne%20and%20group.pdf.

Betke, Christopher G. "Proposal for ABS." April 27, 2016. http://www.americanbar.org/content/dam/aba/images/office_president/christopher_g_betke_abs.pdf.

Bindman, Dan. "ABSs Frustrated by Acquisition Targets That Are Either Not Ready or 'Financial Basket Cases.'" *Legal Futures*, November 12, 2013. http://www.legalfutures.co.uk/latest-news/abss-frustrated-acquisition-targets-not-ready-financial-basket-cases.

———. "Not-for-Profit's Groundbreaking ABS Eyes Expansion." *Legal Futures*, June 4, 2014. http://www.legalfutures.co.uk/latest-news/abs-lives-not-profits-groundbreaking-abs-eyes-expansion.

Blakely, Susan Smith. "Why Do Women Lawyers Leave?" *Ms. JD*, April 24, 2014. http://ms-jd.org/blog/article/why-do-women-lawyers-leave.

Blasi, Joseph R., Richard B. Freeman, and Douglas Kruse, *The Citizen's Share: Putting Ownership Back into Democracy*. New Haven: Yale University Press, 2013.

Bonn, Kristian. "The Future Law Firm: Lawyers in the Minority." Bonn Law, December 3, 2014. http://bonnlaw.ca/2014/12/03/lawyers-minority-access-to-justice/.

Bourlès, Renaud, Gilbert Cette, Jimmy Lopez, Jacques Mairesse, and Giuseppe Nicoletti. "Do Product Market Regulations in Upstream Sectors Curb Productivity Growth? Panel Data Evidence for OECD Countries." *The Review of Economics and Statistics* 95 (2013): 1750–68.

Bourlès, Renaud, Gilbert Cette, Jimmy Lopez, Jacques Mairesse, and Giuseppe Nicoletti. "Do Product Market Regulations in Upstream Sectors Curb Productivity Growth? Panel Data Evidence For OECD Countries: Supplementary Web Appendix," 2013. http://www.mitpressjournals.org/doi/suppl/10.1162/REST_a_00338/suppl_file/REST_a_00338_esupp.pdf.

*Brittany L. McConniel v. State of Indiana, In the Court of Appeals of Indiana*, Opinion for Publication. September 11, 2012. http://www.in.gov/judiciary/opinions/pdf/09111201ebb.pdf.

Bronner, Ethan. "Right to Lawyer Can Be Empty Promise for Poor." *New York Times*, March 15, 2013. http://www.nytimes.com/2013/03/16/us/16gideon.html?pagewanted=all&_r=1.

Brown, Chrissy. "How to Go From Citizen to Criminal in Under 10 Minutes." *Thoughts On Liberty*, July 23, 2013. http://thoughtsonliberty.com/how-to-go-from-citizen-to-criminal-in-under-10-minutes.

Brown, Toby. "The Legal Profession is Doomed." *3 Geeks and a Law Blog*. February 10, 2015. http://www.geeklawblog.com/2015/02/the-profession-is-doomed.html?utm_content=buffera11a0&utm_medium=social&utm_source=twitter.com&utm_campaign=buffer.

Caldwell, J. Richard, Jr. "Report on 'Alternative Business Structures.'" April 29, 2016. http://www.americanbar.org/content/dam/aba/images/office_president/j_richard_caldwell_jr_abs.pdf.

Campbell, Ray Worthy. "Rethinking Regulation and Innovation in the US Legal Services Market." *New York University Journal of Law & Business* 9 (2012): 1–70. http://www.nyujlb.org/wp-content/uploads/nyb_9-1-1_scissored.7-76.pdf.

Campos, Paul. "The Collapsing Economics of Solo Legal Practice." *Lawyers, Guns & Money*. May 25, 2015. http://www.lawyersgunsmoneyblog.com/2015/05/the-collapsing-economics-of-solo-legal-practice.

Canton, Erik, Daria Ciriaci, and Irune Solera. "The Economic Impact of Professional Services Liberalisation." European Commission Economic Papers 533, September 2014. http://ec.europa.eu/economy_finance/publications/economic_paper/2014/pdf/ecp533_en.pdf.

Carter, Terry. "Judges Say Litigants Are Increasingly Going Pro Se—At Their Own Peril." *ABA Journal*, July 12, 2010. http://www.abajournal.com/news/article/judges_say_litigants_increasingly_going_pro_se--at_their_own_/.

Catholic Charities Archdiocese of Washington. "Catholic Charities Legal Network Annual Report 2015." https://www.catholiccharitiesdc.org/file/Legal_Network_Annual_Report FY2015.pdf.

———. "Immigration Legal Services." Accessed April 25, 2016. https://www.catholiccharitiesdc.org/ILS.

CBA Legal Futures Initiative. "Futures: Transforming the Delivery of Legal Services in Canada." August, 2014. http://www.cba.org/CBAMediaLibrary/cba_na/PDFs/CBA%20Legal%20 Futures%20PDFS/Futures-Final-eng.pdf.

Centre for Innovative Justice. "Affordable Justice — A Pragmatic Path to Greater Flexibility and Access in the Private Legal Services Market." October 2013. http://mams.rmit.edu.au/qr7u4uejwols1.pdf.

Cette, Gilbert, Jimmy Lopez, and Jacques Mairesse. "Product and Labour Market Regulations: Production Prices, Wages and Productivity." NBER Working Paper No. w20563, 2014. http://ssrn.com/abstract=2505868.

Chadderton, Sam. "Crash Course to Success." *The Lawyer*, February 4, 2013. http://www.thelawyer.com/analysis/market-analysis/crash-course-to-success/3000339.article.

Chambliss, Elizabeth and David B. Wilkins. "A New Framework for Law Firm Discipline." *Georgetown Journal of Legal Ethics* 16 (2002): 335–51. http://heinonline.org/HOL/LandingPage?handle=hein.journals/geojlege16&div=18&id=&page=.

Chandler, Mark, Charles J. Kalil, Thomas L. Sager, Brackett B. Denniston III, Robert C. Weber, A. Douglas Melamed, Glenn E. Bost II, Randal S. Milch, and Frank R. Jimenez. "Comments of Nine General Counsel on the ABA Commission on Ethics 20/20's Discussion Paper on Alternative Law Practice Structures." February 29, 2012. http://www.americanbar.org/content/dam/aba/administrative/ethics_2020/ethics_20_20

_comments/ninegeneralcounselcomments_alpschoiceoflawinitialdraftproposal.auth checkdam.pdf.

Chanen, Jill Schachner. "Early Exits." *ABA Journal*, August 6, 2006, http://www.abajournal.com/magazine/article/early_exits.

Chaserant, Camille and Sophie Harnay. "The Regulation of Quality in the Market for Legal Services: Taking the Heterogeneity of Legal Services Seriously." *The European Journal of Comparative Economics* 10 (2013) 267–91. http://eaces.liuc.it/18242979201302/182429792013100208.pdf.

Cheng, David. "Why So Many Lawyers Are Unhappy with Their Jobs." *Business Insider*, August 29, 2013. http://www.businessinsider.com/why-lawyers-are-unhappy-at-work-2013-8#ixzz3jieKXqLN.

Christensen, Clayton and Mark Johnson. "What Are Business Models, and How Are They Built?" 2010. http://www.thefgi.net/wp-content/uploads/2010/09/What-is-a-Business-Model.pdf.

Clarke, Brian S. "Law Professors, Law Students and Depression . . . A Story of Coming Out." *Journal of Law* 4 (2014): 219–34. http://journaloflaw.us/5%20The%20Post/4-2/JoL4-2,%20TP4-2,%20Clarke.pdf.

Clearwater, Karen. "President's Report: The Map Followed..." *The Law Society of Manitoba Communiqué 2.0*. May, 2015, 1. http://www.lawsociety.mb.ca/publications/communique/May%202015.pdf.

Clementi, Sir David. "Report of the Review of the Regulatory Framework for Legal Services in England and Wales." December, 2004. Accessed August 20, 2015. http://webarchive.nationalarchives.gov.uk/+/http://www.legal-services-review.org.uk/content/report/index.htm.

Clifton, William W., Jr. "ABA Commission on the Fuiture [sic] of Legal Services Report." April 28, 2016. http://www.americanbar.org/content/dam/aba/images/office_president/william_w_clifton_jr_abs.pdf.

Columbia Law School Human Rights Institute and Northeastern University School of Law Program on Human Rights and the Global Economy. "Equal Access to Justice: Ensuring Meaningful Access to Counsel in Civil Cases, Including Immigration Proceedings — Response to the Seventh and Ninth Periodic Reports of the United States to the Committee on the Elimination of All Forms of Racial Discrimination." July, 2014. http://web.law.columbia.edu/sites/default/files/microsites/human-rights-institute/files/equal_access_to_justice_-_cerd_shadow_report.pdf.

Commission d'Etude des Effets de la Loi Pour la Croissance et l'Activité. "Réformes des Professions Réglementées du Droit." January, 2015. http://www.strategie.gouv.fr/sites/strategie.gouv.fr/files/atoms/files/fiche-professions_0.pdf.

Commission on Legal Empowerment of the Poor. *Making the Law Work for Everyone, Volume I: Report of the Commission on Legal Empowerment of the Poor*. New Jersey: Toppan Printing Company America, 2008.

———. *Making the Law Work for Everyone, Volume II: Working Group Reports*. New Jersey: Toppan Printing Company America, 2008.

"Complaint for Declaratory and Injunctive Relief." *Jacoby & Meyers Law Offices LLP v. the Justices of the Supreme Court of New Jersey*, May 18, 2011. http://pdfserver.amlaw.com/nj/Jacoby_%20Meyers_complaint.pdf.

"Complaint." *Michele Burke Craddock v. LeClairRyan*. In the United States District Court for the Eastern District of Virginia, January 6, 2016. http://amlawdaily.typepad.com/Craddock-Complaint.pdf.

Conference of Chief Justices and Conference of State Court Administrators. "The Importance of Funding for the Legal Services Corporation from the Perspective of the Conference of Chief Justices and the Conference of State Court Administrators." 2012. http://www.ncsc.org/~/media/Files/PDF/Services%20and%20Experts/Government%20Relations/Final%20CCJCOSCA%20white%20paperonLSCFunding33012CleanVersion1%20w%20resolution.

———. "Resolution 1: In Support of Continued Federal Funding for the Legal Services Corporation." February 1, 2012. http://ccj.ncsc.org/~/media/Microsites/Files/CCJ/Resolutions/

02012012-In-Support-of-Continued-Federal-Funding-for-the-Legal-Services-Corporation.ashx.

———. "Resolution 1: In Support of Continued Federal Funding for the Legal Services Corporation." July 25, 2012. http://ccj.ncsc.org/~/media/Microsites/Files/CCJ/Resolutions/07252012-In-Support-of-Continued-Federal-Funding-for-the-Legal-Services-Corporation.ashx.

———. "Resolution 11: In Support of Increased Federal Funding For the Legal Services Corporation." August, 2009. http://ccj.ncsc.org/~/media/Microsites/Files/CCJ/Resolutions/08012009-In-Support-of-Increased-Federal-Funding-For-the-Legal-Services-Corporation.ashx.

———. "Resolution 4: In Support of the Statement of Best Practices for State Funding of Civil Legal Aid Prepared by the ABA Resource Center for Access to Justice Initiatives." 2015. http://ccj.ncsc.org/~/media/Microsites/Files/CCJ/Resolutions/07252015-Support-Statement-Best-Practices-State-Funding-Civil-Legal-Aid.ashx.

———. "Resolution 7: In Support of State Supreme Court Leadership in Increasing Funding for Civil Legal Assistance." July 28, 2010. http://ccj.ncsc.org/~/media/Microsites/Files/CCJ/Resolutions/07282010-In-Support-of-State-Supreme-Court-Leadership-in-Increasing-Funding-for-Civil-Legal.ashx.

———. "Resolution 7: Reaffirming the Critical Importance of Adequate Funding of the Legal Services Corporation." 2015. http://ccj.ncsc.org/~/media/Microsites/Files/CCJ/Resolutions/07252015-Reaffirming-Critical-Importance-Adequate-Funding-Legal-Services-Corporation.ashx.

———. "Resolution 9: In Support of Continued Funding for the Legal Services Corporation Commensurate with Its Vital Role in the Administration of Justice." January 24, 2002. http://ccj.ncsc.org/~/media/Microsites/Files/CCJ/Resolutions/01242002-Support-Continued-Funding-Legal-Services-Corporation-Administration-Justice.ashx.

———. "Resolution 9: In Support of the Federal Funding Legal Services Corporation." August 3, 2011. http://ccj.ncsc.org/~/media/Microsites/Files/CCJ/Resolutions/08032011-In-Support-of-the-Federal-Funding-Legal-Services-Corporation.ashx.

———. "Resolution 9: Recommending Consideration of ABA Model Regulatory Objectives for the Provision of Legal Services." February 3, 2016. https://richardzorza.files.wordpress.com/2016/02/ccj-2016-res-9.pdf.

Corsmeier, Joseph A. "Ethics Alert — Iowa Supreme Court Reprimands Lawyer who Billed Corporate Client for Costs of Sanctions Which 'Resulted From His Own Lack of Diligence and Communication.'" *Lawyer Ethics Alert Blogs*, September 5, 2014. https://jcorsmeier.wordpress.com/tag/lawyer-failure-to-communicate/.

Corugedo, Emilio Fernández and Esther Pérez Ruiz. "The EU Services Directive: Gains from Further Liberalization." IMF Working Paper No. 14/113. July 2014. http://ssrn.com/abstract=2475012.

The County & District Law Presidents' Association. "CDLPA's Response to the Discussion Paper on Alternative Business Structures: The Voice of the Practising Lawyer in Ontario." n.d. http://www.lsuc.on.ca/uploadedFiles/The%20County%20District%20Lawyers%20Presidents'%20Association%20(CDLPA).pdf.

Council for Licensed Conveyancers. "ABSs Leading the Way on Information Technology." *CLC Blog*. April 13, 2016. http://www.conveyancer.org.uk/CLC-Blog/April-2016/ABSs-Leading-the-Way-on-Information-Technology.aspx.

Coyle, Jim. "A New Model of Attorney Regulation?" Colorado Supreme Court. Fall, 2015. http://www.coloradosupremecourt.us/newsletters/fall2015/a%20new%20model%20of%20regulation.htm.

Creamer, Robert A. "Get Ready for Illinois' New Rules of Professional Conduct." *Illinois Bar Journal* 97 (October 2009): 500. http://www.isba.org/ibj/2009/10/getreadyforillinoisnewrulesofprofes.

Cross, Robert. "Balancing Regulatory Risk." Presentation at UCL International Access to Justice Conference, London, England, June 20, 2014. https://research.legalservicesboard.org.uk/wp-content/media/UCL-AtoJ-Conference-presentation-20-June-2014.pdf.

Daicoff, Susan Swaim. *Lawyer, Know Thyself.* Washington, DC: American Psychological Association, 2004.

Dempster, Michael. "The Hurting Profession." *National*, April–May 2012, 12–20, http://cbanational.rogers.dgtlpub.com/2012/2012-05-31/pdf/Lawyers_in_crisis.pdf.

Denckla, Derek A. "Nonlawyers and the Unauthorized Practice of Law: An Overview of the Legal and Ethical Parameters." *Fordham Law Review* 67 (1999): 2581–99. http://ir.lawnet.fordham.edu/cgi/viewcontent.cgi?article=3572&context=flr.

Devlin, Edward. "Hacking Ashton Partners Set for Shortfall." *Insider Media*, December 9, 2013. http://www.insidermedia.com/insider/midlands/104420-hacking-ashton-partners-set-shortfall/.

Devlin, Richard and Ora Morison. "Access to Justice and the Ethics and Politics of Alternative Business Structures." *Canadian Bar Review* 91 (2012): 483–553. http://ssrn.com/abstract=2437035.

Dewan, Shaila. "A Surreptitious Courtroom Video Prompts Changes in a Georgia Town." *New York Times*, September 4, 2015. http://www.nytimes.com/2015/09/05/us/a-surreptitious-courtroom-video-prompts-changes-in-a-georgia-town.html?_r=0.

Dinovitzer, Ronit. "Law and Beyond: A National Study of Canadian Law Graduates," May 27, 2015. http://dx.doi.org/10.2139/ssrn.2615062.

Dodek, Adam M. "Regulating Law Firms in Canada." *Canadian Bar Review* 90 (2012): 383–440. http://dx.doi.org/10.2139/ssrn.1984635.

Domberger, Simon and Avrom Sherr. "The Impact of Competition on Pricing and Quality of Legal Services." *International Review of Law and Economics* 9 (1989): 41–56.

"[Draft] Regulatory Objectives of the Supreme Court of Colorado." November 12, 2015. http://www.americanbar.org/content/dam/aba/images/office_president/supreme_court_of_colorado.pdf.

DRI—The Voice of the Defense Bar. "Issues Paper Regarding Alternative Business Structures." May 4, 2016. http://www.americanbar.org/content/dam/aba/images/office_president/dri_the_voice_of_the_defense_bar_abs.pdf.

Duesterberg, Thomas J. and Donald A. Norman. "Why Is Capital Investment Consistently Weak in the 21st Century Economy?" April, 2015. https://www.mapi.net/system/files/attachments/files/Capital_Investment_4_0.pdf.

Duroni, Lance. "US Law Firms Still Flirting with Going Public." *Law 360*, July 15, 2015. http://www.law360.com/articles/671281/us-law-firms-still-flirting-with-going-public.

Dyck, Karen. "Innovating Regulation on the Prairies." *Slaw*, January 20, 2016. http://www.slaw.ca/2016/01/20/innovating-regulation-on-the-prairies/.

Dzienkowski, John S. and Robert J. Peroni. "Multidisciplinary Practice and the American Legal Profession: A Market Approach to Regulating the Delivery of Legal Services in the Twenty-First Century." *Fordham Law Review* 69 (2000): 83–207. http://ssrn.com/abstract=2277718.

Eliades, Paris P. "Testimony to the ABA Commission on the Future of Legal Services." February 7, 2015. http://www.americanbar.org/content/dam/aba/images/office_president/paris_eliades.pdf.

Ellis, Christian. "Comment on Future of Legal Services." April 28, 2016. http://www.americanbar.org/content/dam/aba/images/office_president/christian_ellis_abs.pdf.

EPP Group in the European Parliament. "EPP Group Policy Paper: Five Building Blocks for Growth and Jobs." February 23, 2015. http://www.eppgroup.eu/system/files_force/publications/2015/02/EPP_Policy%20Paper_Growth_148x210_EN_LR.rev_.11.02.105.pdf.

Equity Advisory Group Working Group on Alternative Business Structures. Memo to the Law Society of Upper Canada's Working Group on Alternative Business Structures. January 21, 2015. http://www.lsuc.on.ca/uploadedFiles/Equity%20Advisory%20Group%20Working%20Group%20on%20ABS.pdf.

Evans, Dale B. "Why Lawyers Can't Manage." *Law Practice Management* 19 (October, 1993): 26. http://evans-legal.com/dan/manage.html.

Ezell, Stephen J. and Robert D. Atkinson. "Fifty Ways to Leave Your Competitiveness Woes Behind: A National Traded Sector Competitiveness Strategy." September, 2012. http://www2.itif.org/2012-fifty-ways-competitiveness-woes-behind.pdf.

Facebook, Inc. "Remembering Lauren McConniel, 10/3/2004 - 03/09/2010." Accessed May 21, 2016. https://www.facebook.com/pages/Remembering-Lauren-McConniel-1032004-03092010/128472153894713?sk=info&tab=page_info.

Falker, Greg B. and Charles Weiss, Jr. "An Analytic Framework for Measuring Technological Development." In *The Emerging Technological Trajectory of the Pacific Rim*, edited by Denis Fred Simon, 385–400. New York: M.E. Sharpe, 1995.

Forlani, Emanuele. "Competition in the Service Sector and the Performances of Manufacturing Firms: Does Liberalization Matter?" CESifo Working Paper Series No. 2942, February, 2010. http://ssrn.com/abstract=1553654.

Fortney, Susan Saab. "Promoting Public Protection through an 'Attorney Integrity' System: Lessons from the Australian Experience with Proactive Regulation of Lawyers." *The Professional Lawyer* 23 (2015): 1-12. http://www.americanbar.org/content/dam/aba/publications/professional_lawyer/volume_23_number_1/ABA_PLN_v023n01_001_promoting_public_protection_through_an_attorney_integrity_system_lessons_from_the_australian_experience_with_proactive_regulation_of_lawyers.authcheckdam.pdf;

———. "The Role of Ethics Audits in Improving Management Systems and Practices: An Empirical Examination of Management-Based Regulation of Law Firms." *St. Mary's Journal on Legal Malpractice and Ethics* 4 (2015): 112–49. http://ssrn.com/abstract=2660358.

Forum on the Entertainment and Sports Law Industries. "ABA Commission on the Future of Legal Services—Issues Paper on Alternative Business Structures/Comments Requested." May 3, 2016. http://www.americanbar.org/content/dam/aba/images/office_president/entertainment_and_sports_abs.pdf.

Fouzder, Monidipa. "SRA Says 'Sorry' Over ABS Application Delays." *The Law Society Gazette*, April 21, 2015. http://www.lawgazette.co.uk/practice/sra-says-sorry-over-abs-application-delays/5048340.fullarticle.

Fox, Lawrence J. "What Would Bob MacCrate Think?" 2016. http://www.americanbar.org/content/dam/aba/images/office_president/lawrence_j_fox_abs.pdf.

"Framework Document: Agreement between the Ministry of Justice and the Legal Services Board." June 2011. http://www.legalservicesboard.org.uk/about_us/lsb_framework_document/pdf/moj_framework_agreement_june_2011.pdf.

Freeman, Steven F. "Effects of ESOP Adoption and Employee Ownership: Thirty Years of Research and Experience." Organizational Dynamics Programs Working Paper #07-01. January 4, 2007. http://repository.upenn.edu/cgi/viewcontent.cgi?article=1001&context=od_working_papers.

Friedman, Ken. "Could Dental-Board Decision Unlock Lawyer Control of State Bar Regulations?" *Forbes*, March 4, 2015. http://www.forbes.com/sites/danielfisher/2015/03/04/dental-board-decision-could-unlock-lawyer-control/#75de2e7b68cf.

Gallivan, Henry Mills. "ABA Proposal on Alternative Business Structures." April 28, 2016. http://www.americanbar.org/content/dam/aba/images/office_president/henry_mills_gallivan_abs.pdf.

"Gateley Set to Raise £30m from AIM Listing, as Slater and Gordon's Acquisition of Quindell Completes." *Legal Futures*, May 29, 2015. http://www.legalfutures.co.uk/latest-news/gateley-set-to-raise-30m-from-aim-listing-as-slater-gordons-acquisition-of-quindell-completes.

Gehl, Nicholas E. Letter to the Law Society of Upper Canada's Working Group on Alternative Business Structures. December 9, 2014. http://www.lsuc.on.ca/uploadedFiles/GEHL,%20Nicholas.pdf.

Gibeaut, John. "'It's a Done Deal': House of Delegates Vote Crushes Chances for MDP." *ABA Journal* 9 (2000): 92–93. http://www.jstor.org/stable/27841689.

Gluckman, Neil. "Complaint Alleges Gender Discrimination at LeClairRyan." *The American Lawyer*, January 7, 2016. http://www.americanlawyer.com/id=1202746570645/Complaint-Alleges-Gender-Discrimination-at-LeClairRyan?mcode=0&curindex=0&curpage=ALL.

Goldfinger Personal Injury Law. "Alternative Business Structures and the Legal Profession in Ontario." *Toronto Injury Lawyer Blog*, April 16, 2015. http://www.torontoinjurylawyerblog.com/2015/04/alternative-business-structures-and-the-legal-profession-in-ontario.html.

Gordon, Tahlia and Steve Mark. "Access to Justice: Can You Invest in It?" April, 2015. http://legal.opaxweb.biz/wp-content/uploads/2015/05/Access-to-Justice-ABS-GordonMark-Final.pdf.

Gordon, Thomas M. "Comments on: Alternative Law Practice Structures." January 30, 2012. http://www.americanbar.org/content/dam/aba/administrative/ethics_2020/ethics_20_20_comments/responsivelaw_alpsdiscussiondraft.authcheckdam.pdf.

———. "Comments on: Civil Justice Strategies Task Force 'New Group' Draft Recommendations." May 11, 2015. http://www.responsivelaw.org/images/testimony/Civil_Justice_Strategies_Task_Force_Comments.pdf.

———. "Comments on: Issues Paper on the Future of Legal Services." December 10, 2014. http://www.americanbar.org/content/dam/aba/images/office_president/responsive_law.pdf.

———. "Comments On: Issues Paper Regarding Alternative Business Structures." May 2, 2016. http://www.americanbar.org/content/dam/aba/images/office_president/responsive_law_abs.pdf.

———. "Testimony On: Allowing Innovation to Meet Unmet Legal Needs." September 27, 2013. http://www.responsivelaw.org/files/Responsive_Law_-_NY_Task_Force_2013.pdf.

———. "Comments on: Alternative Business Structures." May 31, 2011. http://www.americanbar.org/content/dam/aba/administrative/ethics_2020/ethics_20_20_comments/responsivelaw_issuespaperconcerningalternativebusinessstructures.authcheckdam.pdf.

Gotham City Research, LLC. "Quindell PLC: A Country Club Built on Quicksand." April, 2014. https://www.scribd.com/fullscreen/219517633?access_key=key-11nxwoeikqzat6ii6acl&allow_share=true&escape=false&view_mode=scroll.

Grady, Kenneth. Video Testimony to the ABA Commission on the Future of Legal Services. February, 2015. http://bcove.me/x9hwfqsq.

Granat, Richard. "Is Axiom Law a Law Firm?" *eLawyering Blog*, April 8, 2013. http://www.elawyeringredux.com/2013/04/articles/outsourcing/is-axiom-law-a-law-firm/.

Greacen, John M. "Services for Self-Represented Litigants in Arkansas: A Report to the Arkansas Access to Justice Commission." July 26, 2013. http://www.arkansasjustice.org/sites/default/files/file%20attachments/Arkansas%20Final%20Report%207-26-13.pdf.

Grech, Andrew and Kristen Morrison. "Slater and Gordon: The Listing Experience." *Georgetown Journal of Legal Ethics* 22 (2009): 535–40.

Grech, Andrew and Tahlia Gordon. "Modern Law Firm Management: Should Non-Lawyer Ownership Be Endorsed and Encouraged?" Working Paper, April 2015. http://www.law.georgetown.edu/academics/centers-institutes/legal-profession/upload/Grech-Gordon-Non-Lawyer-Ownership-Paper-Final.pdf.

Grossman, Leonard R. "Alternative Business Structure Proposal of the ABA." May 2, 2016. http://www.americanbar.org/content/dam/aba/images/office_president/leonard_r_grossman_abs.pdf.

Haddad, Sam. "Shine Corporation (SHJ): Significant Growth for Well into the Future." *Bell Potter Analyst Report*, March 16, 2015. https://www.bellpotter.com.au/media/148570/shj_20150316.pdf.

Hadfield, Gillian and Larry Fox, "Regulating the Future Delivery of Legal Services." Webinar, 39:45. http://bcove.me/la7z1w1b.

Hadfield, Gillian K. and Jamie Heine. "Life in the Law-Thick World: The Legal Resource Landscape for Ordinary Americans." USC CLASS Research Papers Series No. CLASS15-2; USC Law Legal Studies Paper No. 15-2. January 9, 2015. http://dx.doi.org/10.2139/ssrn.2547664.

Hadfield, Gillian K., and Deborah L. Rhode. "How to Regulate Legal Services to Promote Access, Innovation, and the Quality of Lawyering." *Hastings Law Journal*, forthcoming; USC CLASS Research Papers Series No. CLASS16-6; USC Law Legal Studies Paper No. 16-7 (2016). http://ssrn.com/abstract=2733382.

Hadfield, Gillian. "Innovating to Improve Access: Changing the Way Courts Regulate Legal Markets." *Daedalus* 143 (2014): 83–95. http://ssrn.com/abstract=2419308.

———. "Legal Barriers to Innovation: The Growing Economic Cost of Professional Control Over Corporate Legal Markets." *Stanford Law Review* 60 (2008): 101–46. http://ssrn.com/abstract=1104902.

———. "Legal Infrastructure and the New Economy." *I/S: A Journal of Law and Policy for the Information Society* 8 (2012): 1-59. http://ssrn.com/abstract=1567712.

———. "The Cost of Law: Promoting Access to Justice through the (Un)Corporate Practice of Law." *International Review of Law and Economics* 38 (2014): 43–63. http://ssrn.com/ab stract=2333990.

Hasselback, Drew. "Why That Proposal to Let Non-Lawyers Own Canadian Law Firms Is Probably Toast." *Financial Post*, August 12, 2015. http://business.financialpost.com/legal-post/drew-hasselback-that-proposal-to-open-canadian-law-firm-ownership-to-non-lawyers-is-probably-toast.

Hellier, David. "Slater & Gordon Targeted by Aggrieved Investors for Potential Class Action." *The Guardian*, February 29, 2016. http://www.theguardian.com/business/2016/feb/29/slat er-and-gordon-law-firm-targeted-investors-potential-class-action.

Henderson, William D. "A Blueprint for Change." *Pepperdine Law Review* 40 (2013): 461-507. http://ssrn.com/abstract=2202823.

Herman, Dan and Anthony D. Williams. "Driving Canadian Growth and Innovation: Five Challenges Holding Back Small and Medium-Sized Enterprises in Canada." May, 2013. http://deepcentre.com/wordpress/wp-content/uploads/2013/03/DEEP-Centre-May-2013-Driving-Canadian-Growth-and-Innovation.pdf.

Hilborne, Nick. "Gove Poised to Back Call for Less Overbearing Regulatory Regime for ABSs." *Legal Futures*, November 19, 2015. http://www.legalfutures.co.uk/latest-news/gove-poised-to-back-call-for-less-overbearing-regulatory-regime-for-abss.

———. "My 'Bog Standard Law Firm' Has Become a 'Roll-Out Specialist', Says High Street ABS Chief." *Legal Futures*, November 20, 2015. http://www.legalfutures.co.uk/latest-news/my-bog-standard-law-firm-has-become-a-roll-out-specialist-says-high-street-abs-chief.

———. "Slater and Gordon Tight-Lipped as Australian Law Firms Recruit Shareholders for Group Actions." *Legal Futures*, December 24, 2015. http://www.legalfutures.co.uk/latest-news/slater-gordon-tight-lipped-as-australian-law-firms-recruit-shareholders-for-group-actions.

———. "COLPs Failing to Report Problems to SRA, Groundbreaking Study Finds." *Legal Futures*. March 3, 2016. http://www.legalfutures.co.uk/latest-news/colps-failing-to-report-problems-to-sra-groundbreaking-study-finds.

———. "Separation Would be Better for Both of Us, SRA Leaders Tell Law Society." *Legal Futures*, December 3, 2015. http://www.legalfutures.co.uk/latest-news/separation-would-be-better-for-both-of-us-sra-leaders-tell-law-society.

Hill, Benjamin H., III. "Non-Lawyer Ownership of Law Firms." April 25, 2016. http://www.americanbar.org/content/dam/aba/images/office_president/benjamin_j_hill_abs.pdf.

Hodges, Silvia. "I Didn't Go to Law School to Become a Salesperson — The Development of Marketing in Law Firms." *Georgetown Journal of Legal Ethics*, 26 (2013): 225–60. http://ssrn.com/abstract=2343341.

Hoffman, David A. and Richard N. Wolman. Multidisciplinary Practice: Three-Dimensional Client Service." *Massachusetts Psychological Association Quarterly*. Summer 2004. http://www.bostonlawcollaborative.com/blc/60-BLC/version/default/part/AttachmentData/data/2005-07-mass-psych-multi-practice.pdf?branch=main&language=default.

Holderman, Paula Hudson. "Commentary on the Report from the ABA's Commission on the Future of Legal Services." April 27, 2016. http://www.americanbar.org/content/dam/aba/images/office_president/paula_hudson_holderman_abs.pdf.

Hubbard, William C. "Remarks of William C. Hubbard, President of the American Bar Association." Presentation to Meeting of American College of Trial Lawyers, Miami, Florida, February 28, 2015. http://www.americanbar.org/groups/leadership/office_of_the_president/selected-speeches-of-aba-president-william-c--hubbard/american-college-of-trial-lawyers--february-2015-.html.

Hurst, James Willard. *The Growth of American Law: The Law Makers*. Boston: Little, Brown and Company, 1950.

Iacobucci, Edward M. and Michael J. Trebilcock. "An Economic Analysis of Alternative Business Structures for the Practice of Law." Paper presented at the Law Society of Upper Canada's symposium for the Alternative Business Structures, October 4, 2013. http://www.lsuc.on.ca/uploadedFiles/ABS-report-Iacobucci-Trebilcock-september-2014.pdf.

"ILH Group Ltd Says Sale of Eaton Capital Partners." *Reuters*, August 15, 2014. http://www.reuters.com/finance/stocks/ILH.AX/key-developments/article/3050863.

Illinois State Bar Association. "Issues Paper Regarding Alternative Business Structures: Request for Comments." 2016. http://www.americanbar.org/content/dam/aba/images/office_president/illinois_state_bar_association_abs.pdf.

Illinois Supreme Court. "Supreme Court Adopts New Rules of Professional Conduct for Lawyers." July 1, 2009. http://www.illinoiscourts.gov/media/pressrel/2009/070109.pdf.

"Innovating Regulation: A Collaboration of the Prairie Law Societies." November, 2015. http://www.lawsociety.sk.ca/media/127107/INNOVATINGREGULATION.pdf.

*In re Co-operative Law Co.* 198 NY 479 (CA NY 1910). https://casetext.com/case/matter-of-co-operative-law-co.

International Association of Defense Counsel. "ABA Commission on the Future of Legal Services – Alternative Business Structures." May 3, 2016. http://www.americanbar.org/content/dam/aba/images/office_president/international_association_of_defense_counsel_abs.pdf.

*Iowa Supreme Court Attorney Disciplinary Board v. Cameron A. Davdison*. Order of Public Reprimand no. 14-0878. August 18, 2014. http://www.abajournal.com/images/main_images/Davidson.pdf.

ISBA/CBA Joint Committee on Ethics 2000. "Revised Final Report." January 8, 2004 (Corrected April 1, 2004). http://www.illinoiscourts.gov/supremecourt/public_hearings/rules/2007/isbacbafinalreport.pdf.

Jackson, Liane. "Minority Women are Disappearing from BigLaw—and Here's Why." *ABA Journal*, March 1, 2016. http://www.abajournal.com/magazine/article/minority_women_are_disappearing_from_biglaw_and_heres_why.

Jogal, Anastasia. "Less Than Half of All Law Grads Find Work After Call: Survey." *Canadian Lawyer Magazine*, January 11, 2016. http://www.canadianlawyermag.com/5885/Less-than-half-of-law-grads-find-work-after-call-survey.html.

Johnson, Carrie. "Rights Advocates See 'Access to Justice' Gap in U.S." NPR, March 10, 2014. http://www.npr.org/sections/thetwo-way/2014/03/10/288225649/rights-advocates-see-access-to-justice-gap-in-u-s.

Johnson, Gene. "Washington Experiments with More Affordable Legal Advice." *Seattle Times*, September 27, 2015. http://www.seattletimes.com/seattle-news/washington-experiments-with-more-affordable-legal-advice/.

Jones, Ashby. "In Down Times, Depression Taking Hold Among More Lawyers." *Wall Street Journal*, May 5, 2009. http://blogs.wsj.com/law/2009/05/05/in-down-times-depression-taking-hold-among-more-lawyers/.

Juetten, Mary. "Technology and the Unauthorized Practice of Law." *Law Technology Today*. June 12, 2015. http://www.lawtechnologytoday.org/2015/06/technology-and-the-unauthorized-practice-of-law/.

Jüriloo, Kristel. "Free Legal Aid — A Human Right." *Nordic Journal of Human Rights* 33 (2015): 203–19. http://dx.doi.org/10.1080/18918131.2015.1066143.

Kalajdzic, Jasminka. "Memo to Linda Langston of the Ontario Trial Lawyers Association." December 1, 2014. https://www.otla.com/index.cfm?pg=NonLawyerOwnership.

Katz, Dan.Video "Innovation in the Legal Services Industry — The Future is Already Here, It is Just *Not* Evenly Distributed." Posted October 2, 2013. http://computationallegalstudies.com/2013/10/innovation-in-the-legal-services-industry-the-future-is-already-here-it-is-just-not-evenly-distributed-via-reinvent-law-channel/.

Kay, Fiona M., Stacey Alarie, and Jones Adjei. "Leaving Law and Barriers to Re-entry: A Study of Departures from and Re-entries to Private Practice." A Report to the Law Society of Upper Canada. April 2013. http://www.lsuc.on.ca/WorkArea/DownloadAsset.aspx?id=2147494539.

Kelly, Michael. "Ethical Issues Associated with Multidisciplinary Practices in Texas." *Saint Mary's Law Journal* 41 (2010): 733–77. http://www.stmaryslawjournal.org/pdfs/kelly.pdf.

Kidd, Kenneth. "Woman's Fight Opens Legal Titans' Secret Files." *The Star*, September 3, 2009. http://www.thestar.com/news/gta/2009/09/03/womans_fight_opens_legal_titans_secret_files.html.

Kim, E. Han and Paige Ouimet. "Broad-Based Employee Stock Ownership: Motives and Outcomes." *The Journal of Finance* 69 (2014): 1273–319. doi:10.1111/jofi.12150.

King, Ann. "North Staffordshire Law Firm Hacking Ashton Closes Down." *The Sentinel*, October 2, 2013. http://www.stokesentinel.co.uk/North-Staffordshire-law-firm-Hacking-Ashton/story-19872528-detail/story.html#ixzz3jjNbftYm.

Knake, Renee Newman. "Democratizing the Delivery of Legal Services," *Ohio State Law Journal* 73 (2012): 1–46. http://dx.doi.org/10.2139/ssrn.1800258.

Koba, Mark. "No New Lawyers! Economy Can't Handle Them." *The Fiscal Times*, March 21, 2013. http://www.thefiscaltimes.com/Articles/2013/03/21/No-New-Lawyers-Economy-Cant-Handle-Them.

Koppel, Nathan. "More Strapped Litigants Skip Lawyers in Court." *Wall Street Journal*, July 22, 2010. http://www.wsj.com/news/articles/SB10001424052748704229004575371341507943822?mg=reno64-wsj&url=http%3A%2F%2Fonline.wsj.com%2Farticle%2FSB10001424052748704229004575371341507943822.html.

Koske, Isabell, Isabelle Wanner, Rosamaria Bitetti, and Omar Barbiero. "The 2013 Update of the OECD's Database on Product Market Regulation: Policy Insights For OECD and Non-OECD Countries." OECD Economics Department Working Papers No. 1200, March 31, 2015. http://dx.doi.org/10.1787/5js3f5d3n2vl-en.

Kowalski, Mitch. "Anti-ABS Arguments Continue to Be Based on Emotion — Not Fact." *Slaw*, December 30, 2014. http://www.slaw.ca/2014/12/30/anti-abs-arguments-continue-to-be-based-on-emotion-not-fact/.

———. "Entity Regulation Comes to Canada." *Financial Post*, February 23, 2016. http://business.financialpost.com/legal-post/mitch-kowalski-entity-regulation-comes-to-canada.

———. "Why One Scandal Shouldn't Doom a New Twist on Law Firm Ownership." *Financial Post*, August 17, 2015. http://business.financialpost.com/legal-post/why-one-scandal-shouldnt-doom-a-new-twist-on-law-firm-ownership.

Krill, Patrick R., Ryan Johnson, and Linda Albert. "The Prevalence of Substance Use and Other Mental Health Concerns Among American Attorneys." *Journal of Addictive Medicine* 10 (2016): 46–52. doi: 10.1097/ADM.0000000000000182.

Krill, Patrick. "Why Lawyers are Prone to Suicide." *CNN*, January 21, 2014. http://edition.cnn.com/2014/01/20/opinion/krill-lawyers-suicide/.

Krischer Goodman, Cindy. "Why Aren't Women Lawyers Reaching the Top of Their Firms in Pay and Respect?" *Miami Herald*, April 12, 2012. http://miamiherald.typepad.com/worklifebalancingact/2012/12/do-law-firms-discriminate-against-women.html.

Lachance, Colin. "ABS D.O.A? Idk." *Slaw*, February 6, 2015. http://www.slaw.ca/2015/02/06/abs-d-o-a-idk/.

Lampel, Joseph and Ajay Bhalla, "How Employee-Owned Businesses Deliver Sustainable Performance in the UK?" January 28, 2015. http://www.boeckler.de/pdf/v_2015_01_28_29_lampel_bhalla.pdf.

Lampel, Joseph, Ajay Bhalla, Mridula Chordia, and Pushkar P. Jha. "Does Employee Ownership Confer Long-Term Resilience? A Follow-Up Study to 'Model Growth: Do Employee Owned Businesses Provide Sustainable Advantage?'" January 14, 2014. http://www.cassknowledge.com/sites/default/files/article-attachments/Employee-Ownership-Report-January-14-2014.pdf.

Langan, Martin. Video "Martin Langan—AI Law." Reinvent Law Channel. n.d. https://vimeo.com/72383554.

Law Firm Regulation Task Force. "Law Firm Regulation Consultation Brief." October 26, 2015. https://www.lawsociety.bc.ca/docs/newsroom/highlights/FirmRegulation-brief.pdf.

The Law Societies of Alberta, Manitoba and Saskatchewan. "Alternative Business Structures." Accessed May 16, 2016. http://www.lawsocietylistens.ca/abs-discussion-forum/forum_topics/alternative-business-structures1.

———. "Innovating Regulation." Accessed May 16, 2016. http://www.lawsocietylistens.ca/.

The Law Society of British Columbia. "Law Firm Regulation – Consultation." Accessed March 4, 2016. https://www.lawsociety.bc.ca/page.cfm?cid=4195&t=Law-firm-regulation.

———. "Law Firm Regulation Consultation: FAQs." n.d. https://www.lawsociety.bc.ca/docs/newsroom/highlights/FirmRegulation-FAQ.pdf.

———. "Law Firm Regulation Consultation, Phase Two." January 28, 2016. https://www.lawsociety.bc.ca/newsroom/highlights.cfm#c4191.

The Law Society of Manitoba. "Innovating Regulation: Collaboration on the Prairies." Accessed February 1, 2016. http://www.lawsociety.mb.ca/news/innovating-regulation-collabo ration-on-the-prairies.

The Law Society of Upper Canada Compliance-Based Entity Regulation Task Force. "Call for Input Consultation Paper: 'Promoting Better Legal Practices.'" January 2016. https://www.lsuc.on.ca/uploadedFiles/compliance-based-entity-regulation-consultation-paper.pdf.

———. "Report to Convocation." December 4, 2015. https://www.lsuc.on.ca/uploadedFiles/For_the_Public/About_the_Law_Society/Convocation_Decisions/2015/convocation%20 december%202015%20compliance.pdf.

The Law Society of Upper Canada Professional Regulation Committee. "Report to Convocation." September 24, 2015. http://www.lsuc.on.ca/uploadedFiles/For_the_Public/About _the_Law_Society/Convocation_Decisions/2015/convocation-september-2015-prc.pdf.

The Law Society of Upper Canada. "Compliance-Based Entity Regulation." Accessed February 2, 2016. https://www.lsuc.on.ca/better-practices/.

Lawyers' Assistance Program. "The Happy Lawyer: The Path from Stress to Well-Being." Presentation for Continuing Legal Education Credit, April 13, 2015. On file with author.

Lee, Keith. "What's Worse than Billing a Client for Bottled Water? Billing Them for Sanctions." *Above the Law*, September 5, 2014. http://abovethelaw.com/2014/09/whats-worse-than-billing-a-client-for-bottled-water-billing-them-for-sanctions/.

Leech, William M. "Comment: Issues Paper Regarding Alternative Business Structures April 8, 2016." May 2, 2016. http://www.americanbar.org/content/dam/aba/images/office _president/william_m_leech_abs.pdf.

Legal Action Group. "Legal Aid's 2015 Roll Call of Honour." June, 2015. http://www.lag.org.uk/magazine/2015/06/legal-aid%E2%80%99s-2015-roll-call-of-honour.aspx.

Legal Ombudsman. "Annual Report and Accounts for the Year Ending 31 March 2015." January 28, 2016. http://www.legalombudsman.org.uk/wp-content/uploads/2014/09/Annu al-Report-2014-15.pdf.

Legal Services Board. "Evaluation: Changes in Competition in Different Legal Markets—An Empirical Analysis." October, 2013. https://research.legalservicesboard.org.uk/wp-content/media/Changes-in-competition-in-market-segments-REPORT.pdf.

———. "Evaluation: How Can We Measure Access to Justice for Individual Consumers? A Discussion Paper." September 2012. https://research.legalservicesboard.org.uk/wp-content/media/Evaluation-measuring-A2J-11-09-12-Discussion-paper-FINAL-FORMATED.pdf.

———. "LSB Framework Document. Accessed August 22, 2015. http://www.legal servicesboard.org.uk/about_us/lsb_framework_document/index.htm.

Legal Services Consumer Panel. "Consumer Impact Report 2014." December 5, 2014. http://www.legalservicesconsumerpanel.org.uk/publications/research_and_reports/documents/Consumer%20Impact%20Report%203.pdf.

Legal Services Corporation. "Documenting the Justice Gap in America—The Current Unmet Civil Legal Needs of Low-Income Americans: An Updated Report of the Legal Services Corporation." September, 2009. http://www.lsc.gov/sites/default/files/LSC/pdfs/document ing_the_justice_gap_in_america_2009.pdf.

Leslie, Richard M. "Nonlawyer Ownership of Law Firms." May 1, 2016. http://www.americanbar.org/content/dam/aba/images/office_president/richard_m_leslie_abs.pdf.

Li, Victor. "Board Members Quit, Blast Washington State Bar in Fight over UPL, Legal Technicians." *ABA Journal*, November 9, 2015. http://www.abajournal.com/news/article/Board_members_quit_blast_Washington_State_Bar_in_fight_over_UPL.

Makin, Kirk. "Access to Justice Becoming a Privilege of the Rich, Judge Warns." *The Globe and Mail*, February 10, 2011. http://www.theglobeandmail.com/news/national/access-to-justice-becoming-a-privilege-of-the-rich-judge-warns/article565873/.

Mann, Bruce A. "Comments on Proposed Amendments of Rules 1.5 and 5.4," February 24, 2012. http://www.americanbar.org/content/dam/aba/administrative/ethics_2020/ethics_20_20_comments/mann_alpschoiceoflawinitialdraftproposal.authcheckdam.pdf.

Mann, Harriet. "What Was the Cause of Quindell's Share-Price Slump?" *Interactive Investor*, April 23, 2014. http://www.iii.co.uk/articles/161814/what-was-cause-quindells-share-price-slump.

"Mark I. Levy." *Wikipedia*, last modified September 22, 2014. https://en.wikipedia.org/wiki/Mark_I._Levy.

Mark, Steve. "The Future Is Here: Globalisation and the Regulation of the Legal Profession — Views from an Australian Regulator." May 27, 2009. http://www.americanbar.org/content/dam/aba/migrated/cpr/regulation/steve_paper.authcheckdam.pdf.

Maute, Judith L. "Global Continental Shifts in a New Governance Paradigm in Lawyer Regulation and Consumer Protection: Riding the Wave." In *Alternative Perspectives on Lawyers and Legal Ethics: Reimagining the Profession*, edited by Francesca Bartlett, Reid Mortensen, and Kieran Tranter, 11–55. London: Routledge, 2011.

McKinley, Sands. "The Access to Justice Myth." Sands McKinley On the Future of Law, March 6, 2015. http://www.sandsmckinley.com/access-justice-myth/.

McLeish, Orlando. "Submissions Regarding the Implementation of Alternative Business Structures in Ontario." December 17, 2014. http://www.lsuc.on.ca/uploadedFiles/McLeish%20Orlando.pdf.

McQueen, MP. "The Legal Profession's Drinking Problem Is Worse Than We Thought." *The American Lawyer*, February 4, 2016. http://www.americanlawyer.com/id=1202748847326/The-Legal-Professions-Drinking-Problem-Is-Worse-Than-We-Thought#ixzz41lu34mta.

Medows, Deborah Beth. "Justice as a Luxury?: The Inefficacy of Middle Class Pro Se Litigation and Exploring Unbundling as a Partial Solution." October 28, 2013. http://dx.doi.org/10.2139/ssrn.2346267.

"Memorandum Opinion," *United States District Court, Southern District of New York, Jacoby & Meyers, LLP and Jacoby & Meyers USA II, PLLC v. the Presiding Justices of the First, Second, Third and Fourth Departments, Appellate Division of the Supreme Court, et al.*, July 15, 2015. http://iln.isba.org/sites/default/files/blog/2015/07/judge-rejects-challenge-non-lawyer-ownership-law-firms/jacoby%20%26%20meyers.pdf.

Meehle, Suzanne. "10 Things I Hate About Being A Solo Practitioner (and Why I'm Still Happy Being Solo!)." *Solo Practice University Blog,* March 24, 2011. http://solopracticeuniversity.com/2011/03/24/10-things-i-hate-about-being-a-solo-practitioner-and-why-im-still-happy-being-solo/.

Melnitzer, Julius. "ABS Firm's Expansion Offers New Fodder for Ontario Debate." *Law Times*, April 20, 2015. http://www.lawtimesnews.com/201504204617/headline-news/abs-firm-s-expansion-offers-new-fodder-for-ontario-debate.

Mercer, Malcolm. "So Many Lawyers, So Many Unmet Legal Needs." *Law Practice Magazine*, July/August 2015, 44–47. http://www.lawpracticemagazine.com/lawpracticemagazine/july_august_2015#pg46.

———. "Utopia, Dystopia and Alternative Business Structures." *Slaw,* November 11, 2013. http://www.slaw.ca/2013/11/11/utopia-dystopia-and-alternative-business-structures/.

———. "Yet Again the Question Is 'Where Were the Lawyers?'" *Slaw*. May 5, 2016. http://www.slaw.ca/2016/05/05/yet-again-the-question-is-where-were-the-lawyers/.

Merritt, Chris. Integrated Legal Holdings Calls for Reprieve on $12.6m Loan Repayments." *The Australian*, September 12, 2014. http://www.theaustralian.com.au/business/legal-affairs/integrated-legal-holdings-calls-for-reprieve-on-126m-loan-repayments/story-e6frg97x-1227055657940.

Mezrani, Leanne. "Legal Stars Shine Light on What Is Possible." *Lawyers Weekly*, August 12, 2014. http://www.lawyersweekly.com.au/news/15615-legal-stars-shine-light-on-what-is-possible.

Middlesex County Bar Association. "Issues Paper Regarding Alternative Business Structures." May 6, 2016. http://www.americanbar.org/content/dam/aba/images/office_president/middlesex_county_bar_association_abs.pdf.

Mills, Michael. "The Future of Legal Services: The American Bar Association Commission." *Neota Logic Blog*, April 13, 2015. http://www.neotalogic.com/news/the-future-of-legal-services.

Mocci, Cristina, Stefania Pozzuoli, Francesca Romagnoli, and Cristina Tinti. "Deregulation and Growth in Italy." Government of the Italian Republic (Italy), Ministry of Economy and Finance, Department of the Treasury Working Paper No. 3, May, 2014. http://ssrn.com/abstract=2445863.

Mogill, Kenneth M. "Trying an Attorney Discipline Case." *Michigan Bar Journal*. March 2014, 44-45. http://www.michbar.org/file/journal/pdf/pdf4article2351.pdf.

Moliterno, James E. *The American Legal Profession in Crisis: Resistance and Responses to Change*. New York: Oxford University Press, 2013.

Moorhead, Richard Lewis and Avrom Sherr. "An Anatomy of Access: Evaluating Entry, Initial Advice and Signposting Using Model Clients." December 4, 2002. http://orca.cf.ac.uk/44851/1/modelclientpaper.pdf.

"More People Acting as Their Own Lawyers: Courts Clog Up as Americans Represent Themselves, Even in Complex Cases." *NBC News*, November 24, 2008. http://www.nbcnews.com/id/27894755/ns/us_news-crime_and_courts/t/more-people-acting-their-own-lawyers/#.VdijULKqqkp.

Morgan, Thomas D. "Comments of Professor Thomas D. Morgan on the Discussion Paper on Alternative Law Practice Structures." January 30, 2012. http://www.americanbar.org/content/dam/aba/administrative/ethics_2020/ethics_20_20_comments/morgan_alpsdiscussiondraft.authcheckdam.pdf.

———. "The Rise of Institutional Law Practice." *Hofstra Law Review* 40 (2012): 1005–26. http://scholarlycommons.law.hofstra.edu/cgi/viewcontent.cgi?article=2682&context=hlr.

———. "The Shift to Institutional Law Practice." In *The Relevant Lawyer: Reimagining the Future of the Legal Profession*, edited by Paul A. Haskins, 143–55. Chicago: ABA Publishing, 2015.

Murphy, James T. "Comment: Issues Paper Regarding Alternative Business Stuctures [sic]." April 26, 2016. http://www.americanbar.org/content/dam/aba/images/office_president/james_t_murphy_abs.pdf.

Murrell, Larry D. "Ethics 20/20 Non-lawyer Ownership of Law Firms." March 2, 2012. http://www.americanbar.org/content/dam/aba/administrative/ethics_2020/ethics_20_20_comments/murrell_alpsdiscussiondraft.authcheckdam.pdf.

Nanda, Ved P. "The 'Good Governance' Concept Revisited." *Annals of the American Academy of Political and Social Science* 603 (January 2006): 269–83.

National Association of Women Lawyers. "Report of the Ninth Annual NAWL National Survey on Retention and Promotion of Women in Law Firms." October 27, 2015. http://www.nawl.org/p/cm/ld/fid=82#reports.

National Center for Employee Ownership. "A Conceptual Guide to Employee Ownership for Very Small Businesses." Accessed May 4, 2016. http://www.nceo.org/articles/employee-ownership-very-small-businesses.

———. "Key Studies on Employee Ownership and Corporate Performance." Accessed May 4, 2016. http://www.nceo.org/articles/studies-employee-ownership-corporate-performance.

———. "Research on Employee Ownership, Corporate Performance, and Employee Compensation." Accessed May 4, 2016. http://www.nceo.org/articles/research-employee-ownership-corporate-performance.

National Organization of Bar Counsel. "Comments to 'Issues Paper Concerning New Categories of Legal Services Providers.'" December 21, 2015. http://www.americanbar.org/content/dam/aba/images/office_president/lspcomments_national_organization_of_bar_counsel.pdf.

———. "Entity Regulation: Frequently Asked Questions." July 14, 2015. http://www.nobc.org/docs/Global%20Resources/Entity%20Regulation/Entity.Regulation.Committee.FAQs.FINAL.07142015.(00000003).pdf.

Nelson, Felicity. "Australian Law Awards Winners Revealed." *Lawyers Weekly*, September 18, 2015. http://www.lawyersweekly.com.au/news/17171-australian-law-awards-winners-announced.
New Jersey State Bar Association. "Comment Submitted to ABA Commission on Ethics 20/20." January 31, 2012. http://www.americanbar.org/content/dam/aba/administrative/ethics_2020/ethics_20_20_comments/njstatebarassociation_alpsdiscussiondraft.authcheckdam.pdf.
New York State Bar Association. "New York State Bar Association's Comments on the ABA Commission on the Future of Legal Services' Issues Papers on Legal Checkups, Unregulated LSP Entities and Alternative Business Structures." April 28, 2016. http://www.americanbar.org/content/dam/aba/images/office_president/new_york_state_bar_association_abs.pdf.
New York State Unified Court System. "Pro Bono Reporting Requirements—Attorney Registration. Last modified May 4, 2015. https://www.nycourts.gov/attorneys/probono/reportingreqs-intro.shtml#a.
Newman, Ryan. "Why the Slater & Gordon Limited Share Price was Slammed Another 33% Today." *The Motley Fool*, March 1, 2016. http://www.fool.com.au/2016/03/01/why-the-slater-gordon-limited-share-price-was-slammed-another-33-today/.
Norman, Forrest A. "Alternative Business Structures – Comment." April 26, 2016. http://www.americanbar.org/content/dam/aba/images/office_president/forrest_a_norman_abs.pdf.
*North Carolina State Board of Dental Examiners v. Federal Trade Commission*. February 15, 2015. http://www.supremecourt.gov/opinions/14pdf/13-534_19m2.pdf.
Nova Scotia Barristers' Society. "A Management System for Ethical Legal Practice (March 2016)." Accessed May 16, 2016. http://nsbs.org/sites/default/files/cms/page/2016-03-29_revisedmselpselfassessment.pdf.
———. "Legal Services Regulation." Accessed May 16, 2016. http://nsbs.org/legal-services-regulation.
———. "Legal Services Regulation: The Policy Framework." May 21, 2016. http://nsbs.org/legal-services-regulation-policy-framework.
———. "Regulation Reform: A Cross-Canada Checkup." Accessed May 20, 2016. http://nsbs.org/regulation-reform-cross-canada-checkup.
———. "Transforming Regulation: Will You Volunteer for Pilot Project?" Accessed May 16, 2016. http://nsbs.org/news/2016/04/transforming-regulation-will-you-volunteer-pilot-project.
Office of the High Commissioner for Human Rights. "Good Governance and Human Rights. Accessed August 25, 2015. http://www.ohchr.org/EN/Issues/Development/GoodGovernance/Pages/GoodGover
nanceIndex.aspx.
Olmstead, John W. "Best Practice: The Equity Partner Problem." *Illinois Lawyer Now*, January 6, 2016. http://iln.isba.org/blog/2016/01/06/best-practice-equity-partner-problem.
Olson, Elizabeth. "A Call for Law Firms to Go Public." *New York Times*, February 18, 2015. http://dealbook.nytimes.com/2015/02/18/a-call-for-law-firms-to-go-public/?_r=1.
Ontario Bar Association. "Alternative Business Structures and the Legal Profession in Ontario." n.d. https://www.lsuc.on.ca/uploadedFiles/Ontario%20Bar%20Association.pdf.
Ontario Trial Lawyers Association. "Submission on Alternative Business Structures." December 15, 2014. http://www.lsuc.on.ca/uploadedFiles/Ontario%20Trial%20Lawyers%20Association.pdf.
Organisation for Economic Co-operation and Development. "Protecting and Promoting Competition in Response to 'Disruptive' Innovations in Legal Services: Issues Paper by the Secretariat." March 9, 2016. http://www.oecd.org/officialdocuments/publicdisplaydocumentpdf/?cote=DAF/COMP/WP2(2016)1&docLanguage=En.
Park, Rhokeun, Douglas Kruse, and James Sesil. "Does Employee Ownership Enhance Firm Survival?" In *Employee Participation, Firm Performance and Survival*, edited by Virginie Perotin and Andrew Robinson (*Advances in the Economic Analysis of Participatory and Labor-Managed Firms*, v.8), 3–33. Bingley, Washington: Emerald Group Publishing Limited, 2004.

Parker, Christine, Tahlia Ruth Gordon, and Steve A. Mark. "Regulating Law Firm Ethics Management: An Empirical Assessment of the Regulation of Incorporated Legal Practices in NSW." *Journal of Law and Society* 37 (2010): 466–500. http://dx.doi.org/10.2139/ssrn.1527315.

Parsons, Farina. "The Consolidation of the Legal Services Profession is a Growth Opportunity for Slater and Gordon." *Morning Star Analysis Report*, July 10, 2015. http://analysisreport.morningstar.com/stock/research?t=SGH&culture=en-US&region=aus&cur=AUD&productcode=MLE.

Paton, Paul D. "Multidisciplinary Practice Redux: Globalization, Core Values, and Reviving the MDP Debate in America." *Fordham Law Review* 78 (2010): 2193-2244. http://ir.lawnet.fordham.edu/cgi/viewcontent.cgi?article=4527&context=flr

Payne, John C. "The Weakness of Bar Associations." *Journal of the Legal Profession* 2 (1977): 55–76. http://www.law.ua.edu/pubs/jlp_files/issues_files/vol02/vol02art06.pdf.

Perlman, Andrew M. "Towards the Law of Legal Services." *Cardozo Law Review* 37 (2015): 49–112. http://ssrn.com/abstract=2561014.

Pierce, Jon L. and Candace A. Furo. "Employee Ownership: Implications for Management." *Organizational Dynamics* 18 (1990): 32–43.

Pro Bono Australia Impact 25. "Luke Geary." Accessed May 5, 2016. http://www.pbaimpact.com/#!luke-geary-/oinwt.

Queensland Legal Services Commission. "Incorporated Legal Practices Self-Assessment Audit." Accessed December 31, 2015. https://www.lsc.qld.gov.au/__data/assets/pdf_file/0005/97781/ILP-Self-Assessment-Audit-Form-Version-4.pdf.

———. "Obligations of LPDs." Last modified November 11, 2013. https://www.lsc.qld.gov.au/compliance/incorporated-legal-practices/obligations-of-legal-practitioner-directors.

———. "Self-Assessment Audits." Last modified November 11, 2013. https://www.lsc.qld.gov.au/compliance/compliance-audits/self-assessment-audits.

Rabinowitz, Marco. "Legal Profession in Crisis? Law School Bubble, Weak Job Market Signal Precarious Changes." *Benzinga*, May 2, 2012. http://www.benzinga.com/trading-ideas/short-ideas/12/05/2553116/legal-profession-in-crisis-law-school-bubble-weak-job-market#ixzz3jfT9aBq4.

Ramirez, Florencio. "The Debate Continues." *GPSolo*, Vol. 18 No.1, January/February 2001. http://www.americanbar.org/content/newsletter/publications/gp_solo_magazine_home/gp_solo_magazine_index/2001_jan_feb_ramirez.html.

Rappleye, Hannah and Lisa Riordan Seville. "The Town That Turned Poverty Into a Prison Sentence." *The Nation*, March 14, 2014. http://www.thenation.com/article/town-turned-poverty-prison-sentence/.

Rayne, Renee. "Do U.S. Firms Need External Equity Investments to Remain Competitive?" *Texas International Law Journal* 49 (2014): 559–81. http://www.tilj.org/content/journal/49/num3/Rayne559.pdf.

Reardon, Jayne. "Where Is Our Legal Profession Heading? (Part Two)." 2Civility, April 21, 2016. http://www.2civility.org/where-is-our-legal-profession-heading-part-two/.

Redmond, Richard A. Letter to John Nicoara, Chair, Supreme Court Rules Committee. February 20, 2007. http://www.illinoiscourts.gov/SupremeCourt/Public_Hearings/Rules/2007/ProfRespReport.pdf.

Rees, Victoria. "Transforming Regulation and Governance in the Public Interest." Paper prepared for Council of the Nova Scotia Barristers' Society. October 15, 2013. https://nsbs.org/sites/default/files/cms/news/2013-10-30transformingregulation.pdf.

Refo, Patricia Lee. "ABA House of Delegate Chair: How an Idea Becomes ABA Policy." March 25, 2015. http://www.americanbar.org/news/abanews/aba-news-archives/2015/03/aba_house_of_delegat.html.

Responsive Law. "Mission Statement." Accessed May 4, 2016. http://www.responsivelaw.org/index.php/about-us.

Rhode, Deborah L. "Whatever Happened to Access to Justice." *Loyola of Los Angeles Law Review* 42 (2009): 869–911. http://digitalcommons.lmu.edu/cgi/viewcontent.cgi?article=2670&context=llr.

Rhode, Deborah L., and Lucy Buford Ricca. "Protecting the Profession or the Public? Rethinking Unauthorized-Practice Enforcement." *Fordham Law Review* 82 (2014): 2587-2610. http://fordhamlawreview.org/assets/pdfs/Vol_82/No_6/RhodeRicca_May.pdf.

Richmond, Douglas R. "Discussion Paper on Alternative Law Practice Structures." January 6, 2012. http://www.americanbar.org/content/dam/aba/administrative/ethics_2020/ethics_20_20_comments/richmond_alpsdiscussiondraft.authcheckdam.pdf.

Rickman, Jess C. "ABS Survey—Rejection of the Proposal." April 27, 2016. http://www.americanbar.org/content/dam/aba/images/office_president/jess_c_rickman_abs.pdf.

Riddell, Kelly. "Catholic Church Collects $1.6 Billion in U.S. Contracts, Grants Since 2012." *The Washington Times*, September 24, 2015. http://www.washingtontimes.com/news/2015/sep/24/catholic-church-collects-16-billion-in-us-contract/?page=all.

Rigertas, Laurel A. "The Legal Profession's Monopoly: Failing to Protect Consumers." *Fordham Law Review* 82 (2014): 2683–703. http://fordhamlawreview.org/assets/pdfs/Vol_82/No_6/Rigertas_May.pdf.

Ripperger, Jerry L. "How Employee Ownership Benefits Executives, Companies, and Employees." July 21, 2014. http://www.amanet.org/training/articles/How-Employee-Ownership-Benefits-Executives-Companies-and-Employees.aspx.

Robinson, Nick. "When Lawyers Don't Get All the Profits: Non-Lawyer Ownership of Legal Services, Access, and Professionalism." *Georgetown Journal of Legal Ethics* 29 (2016): 1–62, HLS Program on the Legal Profession Research Paper No. 2014-20. http://ssrn.com/abstract=2487878.

Roddan, Michael. "Slater & Gordon Shares Suspended." *The Australian*, February 24, 2016. http://www.theaustralian.com.au/business/legal-affairs/slater--gordon-shares-suspended/news-story/936f361f1dbbcce7ed048b7ebbbf503c.

Rogers, Joan C. "ABA Commission Suggests Overall Regulatory Objectives." *BNA News*, October 21, 2015. http://www.bna.com/aba-commission-suggests-n57982062517/.

Rose, Neil. "ABSs to the Fore as Quindell Claims 15% of PI Market and Countrywide Sees Profits Rise." *Legal Futures*, February 22, 2013. http://www.legalfutures.co.uk/latest-news/abss-fore-quindell-claims-15-pi-market-countrywide-sees-profits-rise/.

———. "Complaints About Lawyers Fall to Lowest Level Yet." *Legal Futures*, January 29, 2016. http://www.legalfutures.co.uk/latest-news/complaints-about-lawyers-fall-to-lowest-level-yet.

———. "Exclusive: Quindell Legal Services Chief Departs." *Legal Futures*, January 6, 2015. http://www.legalfutures.co.uk/latest-news/exclusive-quindell-legal-services-chief-departs.

———. "Ex-Halliwells Partners Win Immunity from Liquidator Claims." *Legal Futures*, October 29, 2014. http://www.legalfutures.co.uk/latest-news/ex-halliwells-partners-win-immunity-liquidator-claims.

———. "Legal Regulators Urge Government to Ease Burdens on ABSs." *Legal Futures*, July 21, 2015. http://www.legalfutures.co.uk/latest-news/legal-regulators-urge-government-to-ease-burdens-on-abss.

———. "Looking to Play the Markets? Then Invest in Law plc." *Legal Futures*, January 7, 2016. http://www.legalfutures.co.uk/latest-news/looking-to-play-the-markets-then-invest-in-law-plc.

———. "Private Equity Pair Take Majority Stake in Leading PI Firm." *Legal Futures*, September 3, 2013. http://www.legalfutures.co.uk/latest-news/private-equity-pair-take-majority-stake-leading-pi-firm.

———. "Slater and Gordon's Share Price Collapses in Response to Autumn Statement." *Legal Futures*, November 26, 2015. http://www.legalfutures.co.uk/latest-news/slater-gordons-share-price-collapses-in-response-to-autumn-statement.

———. "Terry Quits as Chairman of Ailing Quindell." *Legal Futures*, November 18, 2014. http://www.legalfutures.co.uk/latest-news/terry-quits-chairman-ailing-quindell.

———. "The Sorry Tale of a Fallen Giant," *Legal Futures*, March 2, 2016, http://www.legalfutures.co.uk/blog/the-sorry-tale-of-a-fallen-giant.

———. "UK Litigation Funder to Back Shareholder Class Action Against Slater & Gordon." *Legal Futures*, March 2, 2016. http://www.legalfutures.co.uk/latest-news/uk-litigation-funder-to-back-shareholder-class-action-against-slater-gordon.

———. "Why the Fuss Over Quindell and Slater and Gordon?" *Legal Futures*, August 14, 2015. http://www.legalfutures.co.uk/blog/why-the-fuss-over-quindell-and-slater-gordon.

Ross, Brett A. Letter to Katy Englehart. April 28, 2016. http://www.americanbar.org/content/dam/aba/images/office_president/brett_a_ross_abs.pdf.

Ruffin, Charles. Comment Submitted to ABA Commission on Ethics 20/20, February 10, 2012. http://www.americanbar.org/content/dam/aba/administrative/ethics_2020/ethics_20_20_comments/ruffin_alpsdiscussiondraft.authcheckdam.pdf.

Salvos Legal. "The 2010-2014 Media Collection." Accessed August 21, 2015. https://fliphtml5.com/qokx/mguh.

Salyzyn, Amy. "What If We Didn't Wait?: Canadian Law Societies and the Promotion of Effective Ethical Infrastructure in Law Practices." *Canadian Bar Review* forthcoming, Ottawa Faculty of Law Working Paper No. 2015-15, March, 2015. http://ssrn.com/abstract=2533229.

Sandefur, Rebecca. "Accessing Justice in the Contemporary USA: Findings from the Community Needs and Services Study." August 8, 2014. http://ssrn.com/abstract=2478040.

Schepard, Andrew I. *Children, Courts and Custody: Interdisciplinary Models for Divorcing Families*. Cambridge, UK: Cambridge University Press, 2004.

Schetzer, Louis, Joanna Mullins, and Roberto Buonamano. "Access to Justice & Legal Needs: A Project to Identify Legal Needs, Pathways and Barriers for Disadvantaged People in NSW, Background Paper." Law & Justice Foundation of New South Wales. August 2001. http://www.lawfoundation.net.au/ljf/site/articleIDs/012E910236879BAECA257060007D13E0/$file/bkgr1.pdf.

Schmitt, Richard B. "A Death in the Office." *ABA Journal*, November 2, 2009. http://www.abajournal.com/magazine/article/a_death_in_the_office/.

Schneyer, Ted. "Professional Discipline for Law Firms." *Cornell Law Review* 77 (1991): 1–46. http://scholarship.law.cornell.edu/cgi/viewcontent.cgi?article=3509&context=cr.

———. "The Case for Proactive Management-Based Self-Regulation to Improve Professional Self-Regulation for US Lawyers." *Hofstra Law Review* 42 (2013): 233–65. http://www.hofstralawreview.org/wp-content/uploads/2014/02/BB.7.Schneyer.final2_.pdf.

———. "A Tale of Four Systems: Reflections on How Law Influences the 'Ethical Infrastructure' of Law Firms," *South Texas Law Review* 39 (1998): 245–77.

Schpak, Andrew. Video Testimony to the ABA Commission on the Future of Legal Services. February, 2015. http://bcove.me/ntiu0oxy.

Schraver, David M. "Mandatory Reporting of Pro Bono Service and Contributions." June 26, 2013. http://nylawyer.nylj.com/adgifs/decisions/062813letter.pdf.

Scott, Lindsay. "Young Lawyers, Read This LSUC Report." *Canadian Lawyer*, May 20, 2013. http://www.canadianlawyermag.com/4660/Young-lawyers-read-this-LSUC-report.html.

Seiler, Thomas W. "Non Lawyer Ownership of Law Firms." April 29, 2016. http://www.americanbar.org/content/dam/aba/images/office_president/thomas_w_seiler_abs.pdf.

Seligman, Martin E. P. "Why Are Lawyers So Unhappy?" *Lawyers with Depression*, November 16, 2012. http://www.lawyerswithdepression.com/articles/why-are-lawyers-so-unhappy.

Semple, Noel. *Legal Services Regulation at the Crossroads: Justitia's Legions*. Cheltenham, UK: Edward Elgar Publishing, 2015.

Seto, Megan. "Killing Ourselves: Depression as an Institutional, Workplace and Professionalism Problem." *Western Journal of Legal Studies* 2 (2012). http://ir.lib.uwo.ca/cgi/viewcontent.cgi?article=1053&context=uwojls.

Shanker, Deena. "Why are Lawyers Such Terrible Managers?" *Fortune*, January 11, 2013. http://fortune.com/2013/01/11/why-are-lawyers-such-terrible-managers/.

Shapiro, Jonathan. "Slater & Gordon Shares Suspended Ahead of Earnings." *The Sydney Morning Herald*, February 24, 2016. http://www.smh.com.au/business/markets/slater--gordon-shares-suspended-ahead-of-earnings-20160223-gn1yy5.html.

Sharp, Laura Bellegie. "Comments Regarding the Alternative Business Solutions Issues Paper." April 28, 2016. http://www.americanbar.org/content/dam/aba/images/office_president/laura_sharp_abs.pdf.

Slater and Gordon. "Prospectus: An Underwritten Offer of 35 Million Shares at an Offer Price of $1.00 per Share, Payable in Full on Application." April 13, 2007. https://media

.slatergordon.com.au/prospectus.pdf.
Smith, Casey and Carey A. Spinwall. "Increasing Number Going to Jail for Not Paying Fines: Inability to Pay Costs Plenty for All." *Tulsa World*, November 13, 2013. http://www.tulsaworld.com/news/local/increasing-number-going-to-jail-for-not-paying-fines/article_8b8d2229-c7ad-5e7f-aea2-baeb13390880.html.
Smith, Reginald Heber. *Justice and the Poor*. New York: Carnegie Foundation, 1919.
Smith, Scott A., Juan Pablo Paredes, Rebecca M. Baker, and Mark Han-Ku Kim. Letter to Washington Supreme Court Justices. November 9, 2015. http://www.abajournal.com/files/Letter_to_Supreme_Court_Explaining_Resignations.pdf.
Smith, Sean. "Administrators Called in to ILH." *West Australian*, December 18, 2014. https://au.news.yahoo.com/thewest/a/25810173/administrators-called-in-to-ilh/.
Snyder, Laura. "Does the UK Know Something We Don't About Alternative Business Structures?" *ABA Journal*, January 1, 2015. http://www.abajournal.com/magazine/article/does_the_uk_know_something_we_dont_about_alternative_business_structures.
Solicitors Regulation Authority. "Magnetic Forces: Consolidation in the Legal Services Market." March, 2014. http://www.sra.org.uk/risk/resources/magnetic-forces.page.
———. "Research on Alternative Business Structures (ABSs): Findings from Surveys with ABSs and Applicants that Withdrew from the Licensing Process." May 2014. http://www.sra.org.uk/sra/how-we-work/reports/research-abs-executive-report.page.
"Solos' Incomes Take a Deep Dive." *Illinois Bar Journal* 103 (August 2015): 49.
Somin, Ilya. "Challenging the Conventional Wisdom About the Job Market for Lawyers." The Volokh Conspiracy, October 17, 2011. http://volokh.com/2011/10/17/challenging-the-conventional-wisdom-about-the-job-market-for-lawyers/.
State Bar of Texas. Letter to Katy Englehart. May 5, 2016. http://www.americanbar.org/content/dam/aba/images/office_president/state_bar_of_texas_abs.pdf.
Steare, Roger, Pavlos Stampoulidis, Peter Neville Lewis, and Patrick Woodman. "The MoralDNA of Employee-Owned Companies: Ownership, Ethics and Performance." September 2015. https://www.managers.org.uk/~/media/Files/MoralDNA/The_MoralDNA_of_Employee-Owned_Companies.pdf.
Stephen, Frank H. *Lawyers, Markets and Regulation*. Cheltenham, UK: Edward Elgar, 2013.
Stephen, Frank H., James H. Love, and Alan A. Paterson. "Deregulation of Conveyancing Markets in England and Wales." *Fiscal Studies* 15 (1994): 102–18.
Sterling, John. "Non-Lawyers: A Critical Success Factor for the Law Firm of the Future." Sterling Strategies, December 5, 2013. http://sterlingstrat.com/non-lawyers-a-critical-success-factor-for-the-law-firm-of-the-future.html.
Stewart, James B. "The Collapse: How a Top Legal Firm Destroyed Itself." *The New Yorker*, October 14, 2013. http://www.newyorker.com/magazine/2013/10/14/the-collapse-2.
Sweeney, Marlisse Silver. "The Female Lawyer Exodus." *Daily Beast*, July 31, 2013. http://www.thedailybeast.com/witw/articles/2013/07/31/the-exodus-of-female-lawyers.html.
Tabo, Tamara. "What Lawyers Must Learn From Dentists About The Unauthorized Practice Of Law." *Above the Law*, March 2, 2015. http://abovethelaw.com/2015/03/what-lawyers-must-learn-from-dentists-about-the-unauthorized-practice-of-law/?rf=1.
Task Force to Expand Access to Civil Legal Services in New York. "Report to the Chief Judge of the State of New York." November 2010. https://www.nycourts.gov/accesstojusticecommission/PDF/CLS%20TaskForce%20Report%202014.pdf.
———. "Report to the Chief Judge of the State of New York." November, 2011. https://www.nycourts.gov/accesstojusticecommission/PDF/CLS-2011TaskForceREPORT_web.pdf.
———. "Report to the Chief Judge of the State of New York." November, 2012. https://www.nycourts.gov/accesstojusticecommission/PDF/CLS-TaskForceREPORT_Nov-2012.pdf.
———. "Report to the Chief Judge of the State of New York." November, 2013. https://www.nycourts.gov/accesstojusticecommission/PDF/CLS-TaskForceReport_2013.pdf.
———. "Report to the Chief Judge of the State of New York." November, 2014. https://www.nycourts.gov/accesstojusticecommission/PDF/CLS%20TaskForce%20Report%20

2014.pdf.

Tawfik, Myra and James Hinton. Letter to the Law Society of Upper Canada's Working Group on Alternative Business Structures. December 23, 2014. http://www.lsuc.on.ca/uploadedFiles/Centre%20for%20International%20Governance%20Innovation%20(CIGI).pdf.

Teitel, Murray. "A Dumb Idea Threatens Both Lawyers, Clients." *Lawyers Weekly*, September 26, 2014. http://www.lawyersweekly-digital.com/lawyersweekly/3419?pg=4#pg4.

Terry, Laurel S. "Globalization and the ABA Commission on Ethics 20/20: Reflections on Missed Opportunities and the Road Not Taken." *Hofstra Law Review* 43 (2014): 95–137. http://www.hofstralawreview.org/wp-content/uploads/2015/01/BB.3.Terry_.final2_.pdf.

———. "Putting the Legal Profession's Monopoly on the Practice of Law in a Global Context." *Fordham Law Review* 82 (2014): 2903–37. http://fordhamlawreview.org/assets/pdfs/Vol_82/No_6/Terry_May.pdf.

Terry, Laurel S., Steve Mark, and Tahlia Gordon. "Adopting Regulatory Objectives for the Legal Profession." *Fordham Law Review* 80 (2012): 2685–760. http://ssrn.com/abstract=2085003.

Texas Association of Defense Counsel, Texas Trial Lawyers Association, and Texas Chapters of the American Board of Trial Advocates. "Comment and Opposition by Texas Association of Defense Counsel, Texas Trial Lawyers Association, and Texas Chapters of the American Board of Trial Advocates on Alternate Business Structures." May 4, 2016. http://www.americanbar.org/content/dam/aba/images/office_president/texas_association_of_defense_counsel_abs.pdf

Thies, John E. "President's Page: The Battle against Non-Lawyer Involvement in Legal Practice." *Illinois Bar Journal* 101 (2013): 8. http://www.isba.org/ibj/2013/01/thebattleagainstnonlawyerinvolvemen.

Thies, Richard L. Letter to the ABA Commission on Ethics 20/20. February 23, 2012. http://www.americanbar.org/content/dam/aba/administrative/ethics_2020/ethics_20_20_comments/thies_alpsdiscussiondraft.authcheckdam.pdf.

Thunder Bay Law Association. "Submission to the Law Society of Upper Canada's Working Group on Alternative Business Structures." February 18, 2015. http://www.lsuc.on.ca/uploadedFiles/thunder-bay-law-association.pdf.

"Top Media Firm and Regional Practice Seeking External Cash Help Take ABS Total to Over 100." *Legal Futures*, March 5, 2013. http://www.legalfutures.co.uk/latest-news/top-media-firm-regional-practice-seeking-external-cash-help-take-abs-total-100.

Tort Trial & Insurance Practice Section. "ABA Commission on the Future of Legal Services / Issue Paper Regarding Alternative Business Structures." May 6, 2016. http://www.americanbar.org/content/dam/aba/images/office_president/tips_abs.pdf.

Truitt, Jack E. "ABA's Commission on the Future of Legal Services — Alternate Business Structures for Law Firms." April 25, 2016. http://www.americanbar.org/content/dam/aba/images/office_president/jack_e_truitt_abs.pdf.

Turley, Jonathan."D.C. Lawyer Mark Levy Reportedly Dead by Suicide at His Kilpatrick Stockton Office." *Jonathan Turley Blog*, April 30, 2009. http://jonathanturley.org/2009/04/30/dc-lawyer-mark-levy-reportedly-killed-himself-at-his-kilpatrick-stockton-office/.

Turner, Channing. "Tribe: Gap in Justice a 'Dramatically Understated' Crisis." *Main Justice*, June 18, 2010. http://www.mainjustice.com/2010/06/18/tribe-gap-in-justice-a-%E2%80%98dramatically-understated%E2%80%99-crisis-2/.

Turner, James C. and Suzanne M. Mishkin. "Time for a Whupping: Across the Country, Attorney Discipline Systems Disgrace the Profession." *Legal Times*, August 18, 2003. http://www.turnerhome.org/jct/Clips/turner-legal-times-08-18-03.pdf.

"UN Adopts New Global Goals, Charting Sustainable Development for People and Planet by 2030." United Nations News Centre, September 25, 2015. http://www.un.org/apps/news/story.asp?NewsID=51968#.Vgo773qqqko.

United Nations Department of Economic and Social Affairs. "Detailed Structure and Explanatory Notes - ISIC Rev.3 Code 74." Accessed December 26, 2015. http://unstats.un.org/unsd/cr/registry/regcs.asp?Cl=2&Lg=1&Co=74.

United Nations Economic and Social Commission for Asia and the Pacific. "What is Good Governance?" 2009. http://www.unescap.org/sites/default/files/good-governance.pdf.

United Nations Summit for the Adoption of the Post-2015 Development Agenda. "Transforming Our World: The 2030 Agenda for Sustainable Development." October 21, 2015. http://www.un.org/ga/search/view_doc.asp?symbol=A/RES/70/1&Lang=E.

United States of America. "Periodic Report of the United States of America to the United Nations Committee on the Elimination of Racial Discrimination Concerning the International Convention of the Elimination of All Forms of Racial Discrimination." June 12, 2013. http://www.state.gov/documents/organization/210817.pdf.

Wagner, Bill. "For Comment: Issues Paper Regarding Alternative Business Structures (ABS)." April 27, 2016. http://www.americanbar.org/content/dam/aba/images/office_president/bill_wagner_abs.pdf.

Walko, Matthew. "Comment on ABA's Issues Paper Regarding Alternative Business Structures dated April 8, 2016." April 25, 2016. http://www.americanbar.org/content/dam/aba/images/office_president/matthew_walko_abs.pdf.

Ward, Stephanie Francis. "Pulse of the Legal Profession." *ABA Journal*, October 1, 2007. http://www.abajournal.com/magazine/article/pulse_of_the_legal_profession.

Weiss, Debra Cassens. "$200M Class Action Claims 'Boys Club' at Greenberg Traurig Hogs Work and Origination Credit." *ABA Journal*, December 3, 2012. http://www.abajournal.com/news/article/class_action_claims_boys_club_at_greenberg_traurig_hogs_work_and_originatio/.

———. "Lawyer Who Billed Corporate Client for His Sanctions is Reprimanded." *ABA Journal*, September 2, 2014. http://www.abajournal.com/news/article/lawyer_who_billed_corporate_client_for_his_sanctions_is_reprimanded_partly.

———. "Why More than 75% of Minority Female Lawyers Leave Law Firms Within 5 Years." *ABA Journal*, July 22, 2009. http://www.abajournal.com/news/article/why_more_than_75_of_minority_female_lawyers_leave_law_firms_within_5_years/.

Weiss, Friedl, and Silke Steiner. "Transparency as an Element of Good Governance in the Practice of the EU and the WTO: Overview and Comparison." *Fordham International Law Journal*, 30 (2006): 1545–86. http://ir.lawnet.fordham.edu/cgi/viewcontent.cgi?article=2076&context=ilj.

Wellner, Brian. "Q-C Attorney Reprimanded for Mishandling Deere Case." *Quad-City Times*, August 29, 2014. http://qctimes.com/news/local/crime-and-courts/q-c-attorney-reprimanded-for-mishandling-deere-case/article_c6f6f209-93df-59dd-896b-40a4765efb57.html.

Wendel, W. Bradley. "The Profession's Monopoly and Its Core Values." Forward to "Colloquium: The Legal Profession's Monopoly on the Practice of Law." *Fordham Law Review* 82 (2014): 2563–85. http://fordhamlawreview.org/assets/pdfs/Vol_82/No_6/Wendel_May.pdf.

Weston, J. Michael. "ABA Commission on the Future of Legal Services – Alternative Business Structures." April 27, 2016. http://www.americanbar.org/content/dam/aba/images/office_president/lederer_weston_craig_abs.pdf.

Whealing, Justin. "ILH's Future under a Cloud." *Lawyers Weekly*, December 19, 2014. http://www.lawyersweekly.com.au/news/15962-ILH-s-future-under-a-cloud.

"When Workers are Owners: The Received Wisdom that Employee Ownership Is a Good Thing Comes with Caveats." *The Economist*, August 22, 2015. http://www.economist.com/news/business/21661657-received-wisdom-employee-ownership-good-thing-comes-caveats-when-workers-are.

Wilder, Gita Z. "Are Minority Women Lawyers Leaving Their Jobs? Findings from the First Wave of the After the JD Study." The NALP Foundation for Law Career Research and Education and the National Association for Law Placement, Inc., 2008. http://www.nalp.org/assets/1280_ajdminoritywomenmonograph.pdf.

Winston, Clifford, Robert W. Crandall, and Vikram Maheshri. *First Thing We Do, Let's Deregulate All the Lawyers*. Washington D.C: R.R. Donnelley, 2011.

Wiseman, David. "Alternative Business Structures and Access to Justice . . . for Whom?" *Slaw*, August 28, 2014. http://www.slaw.ca/2014/08/28/alternative-business-structures-and-access-to-justice-for-whom/.

"Without Funds to Pay Fines, Minor Incidents Can Mean Jail Time." *PBS Newshour*, April 12, 2014. http://www.pbs.org/newshour/bb/without-funds-pay-fines-minor-incidents-can-mean-jail-time/.

Women's Paralegal Association of Ontario. Letter to the Law Society of Upper Canada's Working Group on Alternative Business Structures. January 30, 2015. http://www.lsuc.on.ca/uploadedFiles/Womens%20Paralegal%20Association%20of%20Ontario.pdf.

Woodhill, Samantha. "Australasian Law Awards Winners Announced." *Australasian Lawyer*, May 22, 2015. http://www.australasianlawyer.com.au/news/australasian-law-awards-winners-announced-200668.aspx.

The World Justice Project, *Rule of Law Index 2014*, 2014. http://worldjusticeproject.org/sites/default/files/files/wjp_rule_of_law_index_2014_report.pdf.

The World Justice Project, *Rule of Law Index 2015*, 2015. http://worldjusticeproject.org/sites/default/files/roli_2015_0.pdf.

Zacharias, Fred C. "The Myth of Self-Regulation." *Minnesota Law Review* 93 (2009): 1147–90. http://www.minnesotalawreview.org/wp-content/uploads/2012/01/Zacharias_MLR.pdf.

Zarnow, Zachary H. "Obligation Ignored: Why International Law Requires the United States to Provide Adequate Civil Legal Aid, What the United States is Doing Instead, and How Legal Empowerment Can Help." *Journal of Gender, Social Policy & the Law* 20 (2011): 273–309. http://ssrn.com/abstract=2090054.

Zorza, Richard. "Good News from the ABA — Regulatory Objectives Adopted." *Richard Zorza's Access to Justice Blog*, February 9, 2016. http://accesstojustice.net/.

# Index


ABA. *See* American Bar Association
ABA Journal, x–xi, xxvi, 131
ABS. *See* England and Wales
access to justice, xvi, xviii, 103, 157n35, 167, 209, 218; Australia, 169–170, 172–174, 175; complexity of, 169, 171, 175; and corporate practice of law, 38–39; definition, 169, 170–171, 173, 175; empirical evidence (demand for), 89, 170, 177, 220, 221; England and Wales, 7, 169–170, 174–175, 255–256; examples, 173–174, 178–183; measurement, 171–172, 183, 255–256; and purposes of ABA, 211–212. *See also* human rights; monopoly, lawyer (on legal services); Task Force to Expand Access to Civil Legal Services in New York; unauthorized practice of law (UPL); United Nations 2030 Agenda for Sustainable Development
Adams, John, 52
Adelphia, 219
administrative tasks (burden of), 128, 129, 132, 134, 173
AdventBalance, 134, 239–241
The Advocates' Society, 159n68
AIG, 219
AIM. *See* Alternative Investment Market
Akazaki, Lee, 160n70
Alberta, xxiv, 14–15, 146–147, 153, 155. *See also* entity regulation; proactive management based regulation (PMBR)
Albright, Madeleine, 102
alcoholism, drug abuse, depression, and suicide, 127, 131–132
alternative business structures. *See* England and Wales
Alternative Investment Market (AIM), 162
Aluvion Law, 44, 46, 258–259
Amazon.com, 53
American Bar Association (ABA), xxi, xxv; Commission on Ethics 20/20, xxiii, xxvii, 21–23, 38, 215n33; Commission on the Future of Legal Services, xxiii, 23–25, 38, 205, 207n34, 215n33; Commission on Lawyer Assistance Programs, 127; "competing interests" and failure to consult nonlawyer experts, xxiii, 22, 23, 32n17, 33n29, 201, 203, 228, 229; composition and governance, xxii, 20–21, 212–213; Ethics 2000 Commission, 199, 200, 202; and funding for legal aid, 98–99, 104; history of resistance to change, xxv, xxviiin11–xxixn12, 23, 26–27; House of Delegates, xxii–xxiii, 20–21, 23, 24, 25, 26, 32n8, 33n29, 34n40, 199–200, 207n34, 211, 212–214; mission, 21, 24–25, 206; opposition to legislative role in regulation of legal profession, 206n18; political accountability (lack of), 20, 26,

212–213; purposes, 211–212; role as regulator (quasi- or de facto), 21–26, 30, 33n29, 199–203, 205–206, 211, 214, 228, 229; role as representative of legal profession (advocacy), 21, 24, 25; transparency, lack of, 213–214, 215n30, 215n33. *See also* good governance; Model Rule 5.4; Model Rules of Professional Conduct; regulatory objectives; self-regulation
American Lawyer, 3
American Management Association, 49–50
Andresyuk, Yuliya, 142
Apple, 53
ARDC. *See* Illinois Attorney Registration and Disciplinary Commission
Arentz, Oliver, 120–121
Arkansas, 34n52, 187–188, 191–192
Arnold, Jens M., 120
Arrowsmith, Keith, 181
Arthur Andersen, 219
Aspen Institute, 64
Aspire Law, 78–79, 82, 182, 183
attorney-client privilege, 3, 40, 217, 238
Audet, Julie, 159n69
Australia, x, xxiv, 5–7, 11, 16, 19, 31, 60, 90, 118, 143, 152, 161, 169, 218, 220, 221, 222, 224, 231; incorporated legal practices (ILPs), xxiv, xxvi–xxvii, 5–6, 7, 60, 87, 144–145, 150, 151, 236, 249; multi-disciplinary partnerships (MDPs), xxvii; unincorporated legal practices (ULPs), xxvii. *See also* access to justice; consolidation, market; entity regulation; Legal Practitioner Director (LPD); New South Wales; personal injury; proactive management based regulation (PMBR); Queensland; Victoria
Australian Securities Exchange, xxiv, 162, 250
Austria, 118
Axelworthy, Lloyd, 102
Axess Law, 44
Axiom Law, 40, 44, 222, 240, 257

Ball, James, 160n70
Baker, Ron, x
Banco Espirito, 219
Baniter, 219
Bank of Credit and Commerce, 219
Bank of England, xxiv, 259
bar associations, 20, 29–30, 92, 213, 223, 224, 229; alleged bullying of those who hold different opinions, 204; and continuing legal education, 219; state bar associations, xxi–xxii, 1, 20, 21, 26, 27, 28, 32n8, 199, 200–203, 211, 212; unified bar associations, 28, 29; voluntary bar associations, 28. *See also* American Bar Association (ABA); discipline, attorney; self-regulation
Barings Bank, 219
Barlow Clowes, 219
Barone, Guglielmo, 113–115, 119, 121, 124n55
Barrie Real Estate Lawyers, 159n68
Bar Standards Board, 156n3
Barton, Benjamin, 123n25
Batlan, Felice, 80–82, 101, 103, 104
Bear Sterns, 219
Beck, Jenny, 55, 178
Belgium, 118
Benathen, Steven, 39
Bence, Sue, 135
billing, hourly, xvi–xvii, 75–76, 86, 128, 129, 130, 132, 134, 185, 235, 240, 241. *See also* fixed pricing
Blair, Tony, xxii, 259
Blasi, Joseph R., 52–55
Bloomberg, 53
BMA. See British Medical Association; BMA Law
BMA Law, 140, 142, 182, 183
Boston, Massachusetts, 80
Botsford, Blair, 159n68
Bourlès, Renaud, 115–119, 121
BPIF. *See* British Printing Industries Federation; BPIF Legal
BPIF Legal, 140, 142, 182, 183
branding of legal services, xx, 4, 68, 128, 132–133, 180, 183, 218, 250, 255
Brendt, Lorne, 159n68
Bre-X, 219
British Columbia, xxiv, 15, 147. *See also* entity regulation; Law Society of British Columbia; proactive management based regulation (PMBR)

British Medical Association (BMA), 140, 182
British Printing Industries Federation (BPIF), 140
British Telecom, 139–140, 246–247, 248
Briton, John, 8, 17, 31, 72, 155
Brown, Toby, 27
BT. *See* British Telecom; BT Law Ltd.
BT Law Ltd., 139–140, 141, 246–248
Bulgaria, xviii, 187
burden of proof, 89–90, 92, 167, 220–222
businesses (access to legal services), 78, 170, 245, 254; difficulties in accessing legal services, xvi, xviii, 75–76, 85–86, 108–109, 185
business models, 162, 164, 249–250; "new" or alternative business models, 122, 135, 174, 183, 255; scalability (importance of), xvii–xviii, xx, xxi, 46, 60, 61, 67–68, 76, 85, 86–87, 100, 218, 252–254; "traditional" business model, 34n46, 67, 128, 130–131, 132, 133, 220. *See also* solution shop model
business processes, xvii, xx, 4, 60, 61, 68, 69, 71, 86, 87, 122, 133, 173, 178–180, 183, 233–235, 247, 250, 251, 253, 258. *See also* solution shop model
Byron, Chris, 82, 182

California, 28, 38; failure to adopt ABA Model Rules of Professional Conduct, xxii, 21, 199
Campbell, Ray, xxviiin7, 67
Camp, Robert, 55
Cargill, 53
Carrian Group, 219
Canada, xxiv, 6, 12–15, 63, 64–65, 78, 102, 107, 143, 145, 163–164, 223, 257–259; job satisfaction of lawyers, 136n11. *See also* Alberta; British Columbia; entity regulation, Manitoba; Nova Scotia; Ontario; proactive management based regulation (PMBR); Saskatchewan
Canadian Bar Association (CBA): Legal Futures Initiative, xxiv
Canadian Defense Lawyers, 160n70
Canton, Eric, 113, 115
capitalization of law firms, xvi, xix, xx–xxi, xxviiin11, 8, 38, 63, 69, 89, 93, 110, 249–250, 259; bank loans, 65; consequences of lack of access to capital, xx–xxi, 8, 38, 39–40, 46–47, 64–65, 68, 258–259; investors, 60, 61, 252–254. *See also* employee share ownership; law firms, publicly owned
Carayiannis, Peter, 46
Cardoso, Fernando Henrique, 102
Castle Park Solicitors, 79, 82
Catholic Charities, 77
CBA. *See* Canadian Bar Association; Chicago Bar Association
CCJ. *See* Conference of Chief Justices
Centre for Digital Entrepreneurship and Economic Performance, 64–65
Centre for Innovative Justice (RMIT University, Australia), 70, 172–174, 175
Centre for International Governance Innovation (Waterloo, Ontario), 78, 159n69
Cette, Gilbert, 120
Chapman, Karl, 122, 180
Chartered Management Institute, 51
Chasse, Ken, 159n68
Chevron, 53
Chicago Bar Association (CBA), 200, 201, 202–203
child abuse. *See* unmet need for legal services (civil)
Chisholm, John, x, 260
Cingano, Federico, 113–115
Ciriaci, Daria, 113
Cisco Systems, 108
Clarke, Brian, 127–128
CLC. *See* Council for Licensed Conveyancers
Clementi Report, xxiv, 25, 169, 259–260
Clementi, Sir David, xxiv, 25, 31, 169, 259–260, 261
CLEP. *See* Commission on Legal Empowerment of the Poor
COFA. *See* Compliance Officer for Finance and Administration
Cognition LLP, 47, 159n69, 259
Colemans-ctts, 60–61

Colorado, 34n52, 259; and regulatory objectives, 205. *See also* entity regulation; Office of Attorney Regulation Counsel; proactive management based regulation (PMBR)
Colorado Supreme Court, 15, 152
COLP. *See* Compliance Officer for Legal Practice
Commission on Legal Empowerment of the Poor (CLEP), 102–104; and community-based organizations and advocacy groups, 103; and unauthorized practice of law, 102–103
competition, 169, 170; anticompetitive behavior by incumbents (legal professional organizations), 34n46, 35n55, 39, 92; difficulty for professional bodies to take into account questions of, 22, 25, 26, 33n29, 34n46, 92, 201, 203, 229; insulation from competition in legal services market, effects of, xvii, 108–109, 254; to justify federal regulation of legal services, xxv–xxvi, 29, 35n55. *See also* access to justice; consolidation, market; unmet need for legal services (civil)
complaints, lawyer, 150, 163–164, 169, 218, 222, 259; and proactive management based regulation, 7, 10n23, 14, 16, 148–149, 151, 152, 155, 158n52
compliance based regulation. *See* proactive management based regulation (PMBR)
Compliance Officer for Finance and Administration (COFA), ix, 6, 7, 12, 143
Compliance Officer for Legal Practice (COLP), ix, 6, 7, 12, 87, 143, 151
concentrations, corporate. *See* consolidation, market
Conduit Law, 44, 46, 159n69, 259
Conference of Chief Justices (CCJ), xxv, 205, 212; and funding for legal aid, 97, 99, 104; membership and governance, 97; and regulation of legal services, 20, 21, 205, 228. *See also* judicial regulation; state supreme courts
Conference of State Court Administrators (COSCA), 97, 99
conflicts of interest: between lawyers and clients, 4, 6, 11, 14–15, 217, 222; raised by self-regulation, 25, 31, 213
Congress, US. *See* federal government
consolidation, market, 61; Australia, 68–69, 69, 70, 72, 250; and choice in marketplace, 63, 66, 67, 70, 174, 256; and competition, 63; and competitiveness, 63, 64, 65; crisis or opportunity, 71; desirability (in legal services market), 66–69, 71, 72; and economic growth, 63–64, 65–66; effect on prices for legal services, 63; England and Wales, 68–71; fragmentation of market for legal services, 66–67, 68, 71, 253, 254; importance of access to capital by small businesses, 65; and independence (lawyer), 63; and investment (under or lack of), 64–65; (ir)reversibility, 63, 90; potential to broaden access to legal services, 71; and productivity, 64, 65–66; and service quality, 67–68; small companies (limitations of), 64–65; and standard of living/prosperity, 64, 65; undesired, 66
consumer affairs: failure to take into account, 22, 33n29, 175n2, 201, 203; to justify regulation of legal services by legislative and/or executive branches, 29, 34n46, 108–109, 229. *See also* Legal Services Consumer Panel
Co-operative Law Co., In re, 91–92
Copley, Anne, 142, 182
Corugedo, Emilio Fernandez, 120
COSCA. *See* Conference of State Court Administrators
Council for Licensed Conveyancers (CLC), xxxn35, 44, 156n3, 252–253
Counterculture Partnership LLP, 181, 183
County of Carleton Law Association, 159n68
County District Lawyers Presidents' Association, 159n68
Coyle, James, 156
Crandall, Robert W., 107, 109–110, 123n25
Criger, Janis, 159n68
Criminal Lawyers Association, 159n68
Cross, Robert, 175

Cunich, Rod, 88, 134
Curran, Tom, 71, 233–234
Czech Republic: study on relationship of reforms in services sector on productivity of local producers, 120

Dangerfield, Kristin, 8, 17, 93, 155, 175
Davidson, Cameron A., 149–150, 151
Davies, Elisabeth, 122, 175, 254–256
Davis, Steven, 59
Deere and Co., 149
depression. *See* alcoholism, drug abuse, depression and suicide
Devlin, Richard, xxxn24, 32n18, 203
Dewey and LeBoeuf, 59, 163
discipline, attorney, 5; disciplinary authority, 20; disciplinary procedures, 145, 148, 149–150
discrimination, xviii, 186–187, 209, 224. *See also* women, minorities
District of Columbia, xxi, xxii, 21, 28, 29, 34n51, 131, 177, 181, 222, 256
diversity, xxiii, 13, 16, 219, 221
divorce law. *See* family law
Dodek, Adam, 148–149
Domberger, Simon, 111–112
De Soto, Hernando, 102
Drent, Margaret, 155
drug abuse/addicition. *See* alcoholism, drug abuse, depression, and suicide
Du-Feu, Viv, 142, 182
Dzienkovski, John S., 39

eaga Trust, 51
earnings premium (or rent), 109–110, 118
Earnshaw, Ross, 155
Eaton Capital Partners, 162
economic effects (on downstream markets of anticompetitive regulations in services markets, including legal services), 108–109, 110–122; business dynamics (entry and exit of firms due to reallocation of capital and labor), 113; developed countries and global competition, 117, 119; form of business as anti-competitive restriction, 124n55; effect on growth in downstream markets, 114, 118–119, 120; effect on prices in downstream markets, 114; effect on productivity in downstream markets, 120; effect on value added in downstream markets, 114, 120; effect on a country's international comparative advantage and specialization, 114–115; importance of efficiency in services markets for international competitiveness of downstream markets, 114, 117, 119; importance of services to the gross value added process in manufacturing (waste of resources and unexploited innovation potential), 120–121; liberalization of conveyancing in England and Wales in 1980s, 111–112; stronger effects for countries close to technological frontier, 116, 119, 121, 122; stronger effects for large countries (due to larger downstream industries), 115, 121–122
economic policy: economic costs of current regulatory framework, 107–108; ethics and consumer protection vs. economic policy, 108–109; legal work as economic activity, 107–108; and legal services regulation, xxvi, 22, 29, 33n29, 38, 92, 107–108, 201, 203, 229. *See also* competition; consolidation, market; earnings premium (or rent)
employee share ownership, xix–xx; alignment of stakeholders, 55; arguments against, 49; combined with other forms of participatory compensation, 53–54; and company culture, 50, 51, 52, 54; and company ethics, 51; and company performance/ profitability/value, 46, 49, 50, 51, 53, 55; and company's ability to withstand recession, 50; and customer service, 55, 56, 256–257; and employee commitment, 51, 54, 55; and employee motivation, 55, 239, 242; and employee recruitment and retention, 46–47, 49–51, 52, 54, 242; failures of, 53; and higher employment levels, 50–51; historical roots (US), 52–53; and innovation, 54, 55, 56; and insurers, 55; and job satisfaction, 50, 51, 54; and

long term results, 55; and productivity, 49, 50, 242; and quality of company leadership, 51, 257; and succession planning/exit strategies, 50, 242
England and Wales, xxiv, 5, 152; alternative business structures (ABSs), xxiv, xxvii, 60–61, 87, 143–144, 161, 162–164, 171–172, 174, 175, 175n3, 255; innovation in legal services, 44, 59–60; legal disciplinary practices (LDPs), 7; Legal Services Act, xxiv, 172, 235, 247, 254–255; liberalization of conveyancing in 1980s, 111–112; licensed bodies, xxvi–xxvii; and self-regulation, 19, 30–31, 259–260; value of investments, 60–61. *See also* access to justice; consolidation (market); entity regulation; Legal Services Board; Legal Services Consumer Panel; proactive management based regulation (PMBR); Solicitors Regulation Authority (SRA)
Enron, 53, 218, 219
entity regulation, xvi, xix, xxiii, xxviiin11, 11–12, 28, 33n34, 34n54, 147, 148–149, 150, 151, 229n4; adoption in absence of alternative structures, 12, 13, 15, 146, 152–153; Alberta, xxiv, 14–15, 146; Australia, xxiv, 5–6, 12, 17, 143, 144; British Columbia, xxiv, 15, 147, 155; Colorado, 152; England and Wales, xxiv, 5, 6, 7–8, 12, 143; Illinois, 152, 218; Manitoba, xxiv, 8, 13–15, 17, 146, 155; National Organization of Bar Counsel, 148, 151, 205–206; New Jersey, 147–148; New York, 147–148; Nova Scotia, xxiv, 8, 12, 13, 17, 145–146, 155; Ontario, xxiv, 15, 147, 154–155; and Panama Papers, 158n52; Saskatchewan, xxiv, 14–15, 146. *See also* proactive management based regulation (PMBR)
Equity Advisory Working Group on ABS, 160n70
Essex Law Association, 159n68
European Union Directive on the Recognition of Professional Qualifications, 113
European Union Directive on Services in the Internal Market, 113
Exxon, 53

failures: examples of, 161–163; implications for liberalization of regulatory framework, 61
Fairpoint Group, 60
Falconer, Charles, 259–260
family law, 38, 70, 76, 80, 82, 100, 104, 173, 178, 186, 191, 192, 218, 221, 237, 238, 243, 255
federal government, 227, 228, 229; executive branch, xxv, 29, 187, 210, 229; legislative branch, xxv, 20, 29, 210, 229
Federal Trade Commission (FTC), 20, 29, 35n55. *See also* North Carolina Board of Dental Examiners v. FTC
Federation of Asian Canadian Lawyers, 160n70
Fidelity Investments, 53
Fieldfisher, 51
financing. *See* capitalization of law firms
Fitzgerald, Thomas R., 201
fixed pricing, xvii, xx, 70, 79, 82, 132, 170, 173, 178, 183, 233, 235, 241, 242, 255
Flood, John, ix
Ford, Henry, 37
Forlani, Emanuele, 120
Fortney, Susan Saab, 16, 152
France, ix; Commission d'Etude des Effets de la Loi Pour la Croissance et l'Activité, 112, 123n38; study on effect of competition in service sectors on productivity of downstream manufacturing firms, 120
Freeman, Richard B., 52–55
Founding Fathers, 52
FTC. *See* Federal Trade Commission

Gately, 60–61
Geary, Luke, 77, 100, 104, 243–244. *See also* Salvos Legal and Salvos Legal Humanitarian
Gehl, Nicholas, 159n68
Germany: study regarding the effect of the regulation of the services sector on the manufacturing sector and the economy as whole, 120–121
Goldman Sachs, 53

good governance, 227–229; key attributes of, 227; lack of (for legal services in US), 228–229; necessary for the protection of human rights, 227. *See also* United Nations 2030 Agenda for Sustainable Development
Google, 53, 108
Gordon, Tahlia, 173
Gotham City Research, 162
Goyal, Monica, 46, 258–259
Grady, Kenneth, 214
Granton, Joseph, 159n69
Graybar Electric, 53
Great Depression, 92
Grech, Andrew, 55, 71–72, 251
Greenberg Traurig, 130, 137n28
Grogan, James J., 16, 156, 203
Grow, Galusha, 52–53

Hacking Ashton, 161, 164
Hadfield, Gillian K., 34n54, 38, 45–46, 77, 100, 107–109, 110, 185–186, 210, 222
Halliwells, 163
Hamilton, Alexander (1755–1804), 52
Hamilton, Alexander (CEO of Radiant Law), 122, 234–235
Haque, Nadia, 88, 134
Harris, Gordon, 159n68
Hawaii, x
Hazelton Betty Ford Foundation, 132
HealthSouth, 219
Hearne, Tamyn, 135, 179
Heine, Jamie, 45–46
Herbert Smith Freehills, 239
Hickey, Jim, 161
Hinton, James, 78
Hodgkinson, Phil, 163
Hogben, Ursula, 56, 122, 181
holistic services. *See* multidisciplinary practices
Holland and Knight, 200–201
Hollander, John, 160n70
Holloway, Jenny, 83, 182–183, 244–246
Homestead Act, 52
Ho, Rubsun, 47
Huggins, Amber, 187–189, 190, 191, 192–193
Hulme, Julia, 180
human rights, xxvi, 227; unmet need for legal services as human rights crisis, xviii, 45–46, 185–194, 210, 224; US treaty obligations (and breach of), 186–187, 197, 209, 210, 224. *See also* good governance; United Nations 2030 Agenda for Sustainable Development; unmet need for legal services (civil); World Justice Project Rule of Law Index
Hurst, James Willard, 92

Iacobucci, Edward, 107, 108–110
IBM, 53
ICAEW. *See* Institute of Chartered Accountants in England and Wales
ILH Group Ltd., 162, 164
Illinois, 16, 152–153, 259. *See also* entity regulation; proactive management based regulation (PMBR)
Illinois Attorney Registration and Disciplinary Commission, 16, 149, 156, 200, 201, 203
Illinois State Bar Association (ISBA), 200, 201–203
Illinois Supreme Court, 200–202
ILPs. *See* Australia
incorporated legal practices (ILPs). *See* Australia
in-house lawyers. *See* legal departments, in-house
Indiana, 187, 188–190, 192
individuals (access to legal services), xvi–xvii, 45, 67, 68, 70, 100–101, 169, 172–174, 185–186, 187, 190, 210; high income, 170, 187, 223; low income, xviii, 45–46, 75–82, 170, 185, 186, 187, 223; middle income, xviii, 46, 75–76, 170, 185, 186, 187, 223; minorities, 170, 186, 187; vulnerable persons, 78, 79–80, 190, 192–193; women, 170, 186. *See also* businesses (access to legal services); litigants, pro se (unrepresented)
Information Technology and Innovation Foundation, 64
Institute of Chartered Accountants in England and Wales (ICAEW), xxxn35, 156n3

insurance, professional liability, ix, 55, 161
integrated bar. *See* bar associations
Intellectual Property Regulation Board (IPReg), xxxn35–xxxin36, 156n3
interest on lawyer trust accounts (IOLTA), xx, 99–100
investment. *See* capitalization of law firms
IOLTA. *See* interest on lawyer trust accounts
Iowa Supreme Court Attorney Discipline Board, 149
IPReg. *See* Intellectual Property Regulation Board
ISBA. *See* Illinois State Bar Association
Irwin Mitchell, 182

Jackson, Oliver, 55, 71
Jacoby and Meyers, 39–40, 44
Jagger, Ken, 134, 239–241
Javorcik, Beata S., 120
Jefferson, Thomas, 52
Johnson, Nick, 83, 182–183, 244–246
judicial regulation: passive nature (abdication of regulatory power), xxii, xxv, 20, 21, 26, 28, 28–29, 200–205, 228. *See also* Conference of Chief Justices (CCJ); state supreme courts
JZ International, 61, 69

Kain, John, 236–237
Kain C+C, 236–237
Kalajdzic, Jasminka, 177, 183
Kalinko, Warren, 134
Kennedy, Anthony, 102, 103–104
Kent County, 141
Kent Legal Services, 141, 142
Keypoint Law, 134
Keystone Law, 134
Kilpatrick Stockton, 131, 133
Kings Court Trust, 71, 134, 178, 183, 233–234, 252, 253
Knake, Renee Newman, 38–39
Kowalski, Mitch, 153–154, 159n69, 260
Krill, Patrick, 132
Kruse, Douglas K., 52–55
Kyrgyzstan, xviii, 187, 228

LaBuik, Devon, 159n69
Lachance, Colin, 260
Lane and Waterman, 149–150, 151
Langan, Martin, 80, 82, 104, 180–181
Latham and Watkins, 234
Law Firm Consulting Group, 8, 31, 93
law firm regulation. *See* entity regulation
law firms, xv–xvi, xvii; barriers to promotion, 128; corporate structure, xix, xxi, 132–133, 134, 235, 236–237, 240, 242, 248–249; management of, 8, 59, 60; readiness for external investment, 59, 60. *See also* capitalization of law firms; law firms, publicly owned; partnerships, law firms; self-regulation; sole practitioners
law firms, publicly owned, xxiv, 39, 60–61, 68–69, 163–164; subject to greater public scrutiny, 4–5, 8, 163–164; vulnerability to short sellers, 4–5, 162, 164
LawPRO, 160n70
law schools, 34n40–34n41, 78, 83, 109, 182–183, 202, 212, 244–246
Law Society of British Columbia, 15, 147, 155
Law Society of Manitoba (LSM), 8, 13–15, 17, 93, 146–147, 153, 155, 175
Law Society of Upper Canada, 15, 147, 155, 158n52; Alternative Business Structures Working Group, 153–155
Law Students' Society of Ontario, 160n70
lawyers: employment of/unemployment, 85–86, 127, 128; investment in legal education, 85, 87; job satisfaction, 127–128, 129, 132, 134; law school graduates, 39, 85–86, 127, 128; and solution shop model, 86; "surplus", 86–87. *See also* alcoholism, drug abuse, depression, and suicide; earnings premium (or rent); legal profession; minorities; self-regulation; sole practitioners; women
lay lawyers, 80, 81, 92, 101, 103
LeclairRyan, 130, 137n28
Ledgerwood, Liam, 159n69
Lee, Robert, 188, 189–190, 192
legal aid, xx, xxi, 75, 76–77, 185–186, 187–188, 190; funding of, 76–78, 97–101; sustainability, xxi, 76, 78. *See also* American Bar Association (ABA);

Batlan, Felice; Castle Park Solicitors; Conference of Chief Justices (CCJ); human rights; Legal Services Corporation; Road Traffic Representation (RTR); Salvos Legal and Salvos Legal Humanitarian
legal departments, in-house, 108, 139–142, 182
Legal Futures, 60, 260
Legalmatters Ltd., 79, 180–181, 194
Legal Ombudsman, 7–8, 10n23
Legal Practitioner Director (LPD), 6, 87, 144, 145, 151
legal profession: independence of, 3, 4, 22, 30–31, 49, 63, 89, 222; profession or business, 3, 22. *See also* law firms; partnerships, law firm; self-regulation
legal services: evolution of, xv–xviii, xx–xxi, 44; how regulated today, xxi–xxiv, xxv, 12, 21, 28–30; purpose of, 71, 87, 220
Legal Services Board, 19, 30–31, 44, 156n3, 171–172, 174, 175, 254–255
Legal Services Consumer Panel, 7, 70, 122, 174–175, 254–256
Legal Services Corporation, 97–98, 100, 210. *See also* legal aid
legal technology, xx
LegalVision, 56, 122, 181
LegalZoom, 40–41, 44, 222, 257, 258
Lehman Brothers, 53, 219
Levy, Mark, 131, 133
Lexcel Consulting, 8
licensed bodies. *See* England and Wales
Limited License Legal Technicians (LLLTs), 27, 204–205, 222
Lipinski, Baruch, 159n69
Lippman, Jonathan, 77, 190
litigants, pro se (unrepresented), 186, 187–188, 190–192, 193–194
LLLTs. *See* Limited License Legal Technicians
LPD. *See* Legal Practitioner Director
Lopez, Jimmy, 120
Louisiana Purchase, 52
LSM. *See* Law Society of Manitoba

MacCrate, Robert, 24, 33n34
Macron, Emmanuel, 123n38
Madison, James, 52
Madoff, Bernie, 219
Maheshri, Vikram, 107, 109–110, 123n25
Mairesse, Jacques, 120
Makol, Archana, 141, 246–248
Mars, 53
management based regulation. *See* proactive management based regulation (PMBR)
management expertise, xxi, 39, 233, 235, 237, 239, 253, 254, 256, 257
Manitoba, xxiv, 13–15, 146, 155. *See also* entity regulation; Law Society of Manitoba (LSM); proactive management based regulation (PMBR)
Mark, Steve, 7, 9n19, 173
Mattoo, Aaditya, 120
Maurice Blackburn, 69, 70, 163, 218, 248–250
Mayo, Jordan, 61, 252–254
May, Rollo, 132
McCarthy Tetrault, 136n11
McConniel, Brittany, 188–190, 192
McConniel, Lauren, 187–190, 191, 192–193
McConniel, Ryan, 187–190, 192
McDermott, Will and Emery, 200
McDevitt, Michael, 256–257
McLachlin, Beverly, 223
McLeish Orlando, 159n68
Medici Bank, 219
mental health disorders. *See* alcoholism, drug abuse, depression, and suicide
Mercer, Malcolm, 158n52
Mexico, xxv, 187
Microsoft, 53
Mills, Christopher, 237–239
Milstone, Joe, 47
minorities: barriers to promotion, 128; discrimination, 130; opportunities (limited), 127, 130–131. *See also* human rights, US treaty obligations (and breach of); individuals (access to legal services); unmet need for legal services (civil), connection to spiral of poverty and incarceration
Mocci, Cristina, 119–120
Model Rule 5.1, 147–148, 149–150
Model Rule 5.3, 147–148, 149–150

Model Rule 5.4, xxii–xxiii, xxv, 11, 21, 31, 40, 41, 61n7, 89, 131, 132, 139, 152
Model Rules of Professional Conduct, xxii–xxiii, xxv, 20, 21–22, 23, 25, 28, 33n29, 49, 147, 150, 199–200, 201, 202–204. *See also* Model Rule 5.1; Model Rule 5.3; Model Rule 5.4
Modria, 44, 222, 257
Moliterno, James E., xxviiin11–xxixn12, 26–27, 206n18–207n19
Mongolia, 187
monopoly, lawyer (on legal services), xvi, 103, 109, 197, 214, 222–224. *See also* unauthorized practice of law (UPL)
Moore Blatch, 78
Moorhead, Richard, 67
Morgan, Thomas D., xxviin1
Morison, Ora, xxxn24, 32n18, 203
MPRE. *See* Multistate Professional Responsibility Examination
multidisciplinary practice, xvi, xx, xxi, xxiv, 3, 38, 39, 80, 180, 181, 237–239, 241–242; objections to, 217
Multistate Professional Responsibility Examination (MPRE), 202
Myhomemove, 252–254

National Association of Women Lawyers (NAWL), 130
National Conference of Bar Presidents, 27
National Organization of Bar Counsel (NOBC), 147–148, 151, 205–206
NAWL. *See* National Association of Women Lawyers
New Jersey, 39, 44, 147–148
New Jersey State Bar Association (NJSBA), 22
NewLaw Solicitors, 60
New South Wales, xxiv, 5, 7, 16, 151
New York (state), xxviiin11, 39, 44, 45–46, 77, 91, 99, 147–148, 190, 223, 234. *See also* New York State Bar Association; Task Force to Expand Access to Civil Legal Services in New York
New York State Bar Association, xxii, 77, 223
Nicoara, John, 200, 201
Nicoara and Steagall, 201
Nixon Peabody, 223
NJSBA. *See* New Jersey State Bar Association
NOBC. *See* National Organization of Bar Counsel
nonlawyers, xxviiin11; fee sharing with, 11, 13, 14, 38, 146, 222; influence on lawyers, 4, 8; lawyers' need to work with, xv–xvi, xix–xx, xxi; problems with (limitations of), 11. *See also* lay lawyers
Nordbanken, 219
Nortel, 219
North Carolina Board of Dental Examiners v. FTC, 29
Northern Ireland, xxiv
Northwest Ordinance of 1787, 52
Nottingham Law School, 83, 182–183, 244–246
Nova Scotia, xxiv, 155. *See also* entity regulation; Nova Scotia Barristers' Society; proactive management based regulation (PMBR)
Nova Scotia Barristers' Society, 8, 12, 13, 17, 31, 145–146, 152–153, 155, 158n52; Management System for Ethical Legal Practice Self-Assessment Tool, 146; Policy Framework, 12–13, 145–146. *See also* entity regulation; Nova Scotia; proactive management based regulation (PMBR)

OECD. *See* Organisation for Economic Co-operation and Development
Office of Attorney Regulation Counsel (Colorado), 15–16, 156. *See also* Coyle, James
Oliver, Paddy, 8, 254, 260
OmniaLegal Ltd., 56
Omnia Strategy LLP, 180, 183
One.Tel, 219
Ontario, xxiv, 15, 147, 153–155. *See also* entity regulation; Law Society of Upper Canada; proactive management based regulation (PMBR)
Ontario Bar Association, 159n68
Ontario College of Social Workers and Social Service Workers, 160n70

Ontario Trial Lawyers Association, 159n68, 177
Oracle Capital Group, 140
Oracle Family Office, 140, 142
Organisation for Economic Co-operation and Development (OECD): regulatory indicators, 113, 114, 115, 119, 121; statement regarding regulatory frameworks and barriers to innovation, xxviiin3, 34n46, 35n55
outcomes focused regulation. *See* proactive management based regulation (PMBR)

Pacific Gas and Electric, 219
Panama Papers, 158n52
Parker, Christine, 151
Parmalat, 219
partnerships, law firm, xvii; billable hours, importance of, 128, 130; leveraged pyramid, 128; limitations, xix, 39, 59, 129, 236, 240, 253; rainmaking, importance of, 128, 129, 131, 234
Perlman, Andrew, xxviiin11, 23, 32n8, 33n29, 61n7, 175n3
Permanent Commission on Access to Justice. *See* Task Force to Expand Access to Civil Legal Services in New York
Peroni, Robert J., 39
personal injury: adverstising, 218; law firms (plaintiffs'), 78, 140, 173, 179, 182, 218, 248–252; market, 68–69, 70, 72, 163. *See also* Aspire Law; Maurice Blackburn; Moore Blatch; Shine; Slater and Gordon
Pflaum, Steven, 200
Phar-Mor, 219
Picard, Nathalie, 159n69
Pierce, Andrea, 134, 178
Pink, Darrel, 8, 17, 31, 155, 158n52
PMBR. *See* proactive management based regulation
POLB. *See* Practice of Law Board
Powell, Adrian, 55, 134
Powell, Martin, 56
Practice of Law Board (POLB), 204
Prairie provinces. *See* Alberta; Manitoba; Saskatchewan
Price, Randy, 181
primogeniture, ban on, 52
proactive management based regulation (PMBR), xxviiin11, 9n14, 11–12, 13, 150, 151–153; adoption in absence of alternative structures, 12, 13, 15, 146, 152–153; Alberta, 14–15, 146–147; Australia, 6, 7, 17, 143, 144–145, 150, 155; British Columbia, 15, 147, 155; Canada, 6, 12, 143, 147; Colorado, 15–16, 25, 152–153, 156; England and Wales, 6–7, 143, 143–144; Illinois, 16–17, 152, 156; Manitoba, 14–15, 146–147; National Organization of Bar Counsel, 151; New Jersey, 147–148; New York, 147–148; Nova Scotia, 13, 17, 145, 146; Ontario, 15, 147, 154–155; and Panama Papers, 158n52; Saskatchewan, 14–15, 146–147. *See also* complaints, lawyer; entity regulation; self-assessment
pro bono legal services, xxi, 77, 185–186, 210, 223, 224. *See also* legal aid
Proctor and Gamble, 53
Proelium Law, 55, 134
professional consultancy model. *See* solution shop model
professionalism, 3–5, 8, 218, 244
property ownership (real property), 52
proscriptive rules-based regulation, 5, 12, 150–151, 158n52
pro se representation. *See* litigants, pro se (unrepresented)
Protective Agency for Women and Children, 80
publicly owned law firms. *See* law firms, publicly owned
public sector, 139, 141, 142, 170
Publix, 53
Pusey, Allen, x

Queensland, 6, 8, 12, 17, 144
Queensland Legal Services Commission, 8, 17, 31, 72, 144–145, 155
Quindell Legal Services, 162–163, 164

Radiant Law, 88, 122, 134–135, 179, 183, 234–235
Ray, John, 8, 31, 93, 254
Redde plc, 60

Redmond, Richard A., 200–201
regulation: of lawyers as individuals, xvi, xix, xxviiin11, 12, 147–148; resources required and adequacy of, 11, 12; risk-based, 8, 12, 13, 71, 145. *See also* entity regulation; proactive management based regulation (PMBR); proscriptive rules-based regulation; regulatory framework
regulatory framework, xvi, xix, xxv–xxvi, 5, 12, 20, 229; as barrier to competition, xxviiin3; as barrier to innovation, 107
regulatory objectives, xxiii, 13, 169, 205
Reinvent Law, x
Responsive Law, 32n17, 38
Review of the Regulatory Framework for Legal Services in England and Wales. *See* Clementi Report
Rice, Kathleen, 190
Riverview Law, 122, 180, 183
Rhode, Deborah, 34n54, 170–171, 229n4
Road Traffic Representation (RTR), 79–80, 82, 101, 103, 104, 180–181, 183, 194
Roberts Jackson, 55, 71
Robinson, Mary, 102
Robins, William, 134
RocketLawyer, 44, 222, 257, 258
Romania, xviii
Rose, Neil, 260
Royal Bank of Scotland, 219
RTR. *See* Road Traffic Representation
Ruiz, Esther Pérez, 120
rule of law, 13, 45, 98, 109, 123n25, 187, 209, 211, 221. *See also* United Nations 2030 Agenda for Sustainable Development
Russia, xviii, 187, 228

Salvation Army, 76, 77, 82, 100–101, 104, 243
Salvos Legal and Salvos Legal Humanitarian, 76–78, 100–101, 103, 104, 174, 192, 243–244; online counter of number of matters for which free legal assistance has been provided, 83n7, 105n13
Saskatchewan, xxiv, 14–15, 146–147, 153, 155. *See also* entity regulation; proactive management based regulation (PMBR)
Schepard, Andrew, 191
Schillings, 237–239
Schneyer, Ted, xxviiin1, 9n14, 9n19, 32n12
Schraver, David, 77, 223
S.C. Johnson & Sons, 53
Scotland, xxiv
self-assessment, 13, 16, 144–145, 146, 151, 152, 156
self-regulation, 19–31, 199–200, 211; disagreement over extent of self-regulation in US, 19–20; and independence of the legal profession, 30–31, 31, 260; role of American Bar Association, 20–30, 199, 201–203, 205–206, 228, 229; role of individual law firms, 20, 199, 200–201, 229; role of individual practicing lawyers, 20, 200–201, 229; role of state and local bar associations, 20, 21, 23, 28, 32n8, 200–203, 211, 212, 213, 229. *See also* England and Wales, and self-regulation; judicial regulation
Semple, Noel, 157n35, 175n2
SeyfarthLean Consulting, 214
Shake, 44, 222, 257
Sharp, Laura Bellegie, 34n40
Sherr, Avrom, 111–112
Shine, 69, 70, 173, 218
Simon, David, 55, 241–242
Simpson Millar, 60
Slater and Gordon, 55, 68–69, 70, 71–72, 88, 134, 135, 162, 163–164, 179, 182, 183, 218, 219, 250–252
Slaw, 153–154
Smedvig Capital, 61, 233, 252–254
Smith, Reginald Heber, 81
social work/social services, law and, 80–82, 101, 103, 104, 173, 192
Société Générale, 219
sole practitioners, 16, 22, 38, 60, 70, 71, 128–129, 131, 143, 147, 156. *See also* law firms
Solera, Irune, 113
Solicitors Regulation Authority (SRA), xxxn35, 6, 30, 35n61, 71, 143–144, 156n3, 256; ABS application process (conservative approach), 143, 171–172,

174
solution shop model, xvii, 67–68, 86; compared to value chain model, 67. *See also* business processes
Souter Investments, 61, 69
South Sea Company, 219
Southwest Airlines, 53
Southwest Region Women's Law Association, 159n68
specialization (vs. generalization), 68, 71, 72, 178, 183, 233, 234, 252, 254
SRA. *See* Solicitors Regulation Authority
standardization, 67, 68, 183, 250
Stanford, Allen, 219
state legislatures, xxi, xxv, xxxin44, 19, 26, 29, 99, 203, 206n18–207n19
state supreme courts, xxi, xxii, xxv, 19–20, 21, 28–29, 30, 191, 199, 205, 228, 229; and funding for legal aid, 98–99, 210. *See also* Conference of Chief Justices (CCJ); judicial regulation; United States Supreme Court
Stephen, Frank H., 67–68
Stephens, Richard, 55
Stephensons Solicitors LLP, 55, 178, 183
Stephens Scown LLP, 55
Stewart Title, 159n68
Summers, Lawrence, 102
Supreme Court. *See* state supreme courts; United States Supreme Court
sustainable development. *See* United Nations 2030 Agenda for Sustainable Development
Swissair, 219

Tandem Legal Group, 181, 183, 256–257
Task Force to Expand Access to Civil Legal Services in New York, 38, 45–46, 99, 190
Tawfik, Myra, 78
Teitel, Murray, 159n68
Tennessee, 187–188, 190, 192
Terry, Glenda, 82
Terry, Laurel S., 21–22, 23, 33n29, 228
Texas, 98–99
Thunder Bay Law Association, 159n68
Trebilcock, Michael J., 107, 110–108
Tribe, Laurence, 186
Triton Global, 55, 241–242
Tucker, Greg, 248–250
Tufnell, Greg, 234, 235
Tutungi, Dina, 88, 135, 179, 250–252
Twain, Mark, xxvi
Tyco International, 219

Ukraine, xviii, 187, 228
unauthorized practice of law (UPL), xxv, 102–103, 222; across state borders, xvi; by nonlawyers, xvi, xx, 222–223; and Great Depression, 92. *See also* monopoly, lawyer (on legal services)
unbundled (or modular or limited-scope) legal services, 178, 183, 191–192, 255
unethical conduct, 3, 4–5, 7–8
Union Carbide, 219
United Airlines, 53
United Nations: Committee on the Elimination of Racial Discrimination, 186, 187; Development Programme, 102; Office of the High Commissioner for Human Rights, 227, 228. *See also* United Nations 2030 Agenda for Sustainable Development
United Nations 2030 Agenda for Sustainable Development, 209–210, 211, 213, 224, 228, 229; accountable institutions and ABA, 212–213; effective institutions and ABA, 211–212; ensure equal access to justice for all, 210, 211; Goal 16, 209; transparent institutions and ABA, 213–214
United States Supreme Court, 20, 29–30, 102, 103, 131
unmet need for legal services (civil), xviii, 38, 45–46, 77, 99, 100, 175, 177, 210, 211–212, 224, 228, 245, 256; connection to child abuse, 187–192; connection to spiral of poverty and incarceration, 193–194; and insulation from competition, 108–109. *See also* access to justice; human rights, unmet need for legal services as human rights crisis; monopoly, lawyer (on legal services)
UPL. *See* unauthorized practice of law

Valls, Manuel, 123n38

Van Ommen, Herman, 147, 155
Verasage Institute, x
Victoria, 5, 144
Virgin Islands, xxii
Volkswagen, 219

Wales. *See* England and Wales
Walmart, 4
Washington, DC. *See* District of Columbia
Washington, George, 52
Washington (state), xxviiin11, 204–205, 222. *See also* Limited License Legal Technicians (LLTs); Practice of Law Board (PLB); Washington State Bar Association (WSBA)
Washington State Bar Association (WSBA), 204–205
Waterloo Region Law Association, 159n68
Webley, Lisa, ix, 260
Westminster, University of, ix
Wild, Geoff, 141, 142
Winn, Jeff, 61, 180
Winn Solicitors, 61, 69, 180, 183
Winston, Clifford, 107, 109–110, 123n25
Wiseman, David, 160n70
Women: barriers to promotion, 128, 219; discrimination, 130, 137n28; opportunities (or lack of), 127, 130–131, 251–252; partnerships as story of institutional failure, 130. *See also* Batlan, Felice; individuals (access to legal services); lay lawyers; social work/social services, law and
*Women and Justice and the Poor* (book), 81–82, 101
Women's Educational and Industrial Union, 80
Women's Paralegal Association of Ontario, 159n68
WorldCom, 53, 219
World Justice Project Rule of Law Index, xviii, 187, 228
WSBA. *See* Washington State Bar Association
Wyoming, 99

Younger, Stephen, xxii

# About the Author

During the more than 20 years since she graduated from law school, **Laura Snyder** has had the opportunity to experience legal services from multiple perspectives: as a law firm associate, as in-house counsel, and as a consumer for herself and on behalf of family members. She has also had the opportunity to experience legal services on an international basis: in the United States, the United Kingdom, and France, as well as in a host of other countries in Europe, the Middle East, Central Asia, and Africa. These experiences taught her both that the regulation and the delivery of legal services are universal concepts and that neither their limitations nor their potential are constrained by borders.

Born and raised in the United States, Snyder holds a JD from the University of Illinois College of Law, a DEA in *droit privé* from the University of Paris I (Panthéon-Sorbonne), and she completed the TRIUM Executive MBA program (an alliance of the London School of Economics, New York University Stern School of Business, and HEC School of Management). Snyder is a member of the bars of Illinois, New York, and Paris. She is based in France.

Lightning Source UK Ltd.
Milton Keynes UK
UKOW04n0657161217
314508UK00013B/1105/P

9 781498 529792